1990

LEADERSHIP SKILLS

LEADERSHIP SKILLS

Standout Performance
for Human Resources Managers

William R. Tracey

amacom

AMERICAN MANAGEMENT ASSOCIATION

This publication is designed to provide accurate and authoritative
information in regard to the subject matter covered. It is sold with the
understanding that the publisher is not engaged in rendering legal,
accounting, or other professional service. If legal advice or other
expert assistance is required, the services of a competent professional
person should be sought.

Library of Congress Cataloging-in-Publication Data

Tracey, William R.
    Leadership skills : standout performance for human resources
managers / William R. Tracey.
      p.   cm.
    ISBN 0-8144-5960-9
    1. Personnel management.   I. Title.
HF5549.T7125   1990   89-46213
    658.3—dc20   CIP

Printing number

10   9   8   7   6   5   4   3   2   1

For my wife, Kathleen,

my children,
William Jr., Kevin, Brian,
Kathleen, Maura, and Sean,
and
my grandchildren,
Tamra, Jacqueline, Sean, and Michele
Laine, William III, Kristina, and Timothy

with
high hopes
great pride
much love
and
many prayers

Contents

Preface

Human resources management is becoming more and more demanding. Today, it is not enough to stay on top of developments within a rapidly changing discipline. What is required is mastery of a broader set of important skills—skills that will enable HR managers to manage well and to give executives, line managers, and staff officers the critical guidance and assistance they need to deal with key problems and issues.

Managing the HR function has always been one of the toughest positions in any organization. Now, and in the immediate future, it is arguably the most complex and demanding of *all* managerial jobs. Part of the reason is the knotty problem of measuring the contributions of the HR element to the profitability of an organization using the normal standard—dollars. But, more important, there are a lot of other things that HR managers can do that will profoundly affect people, and, in turn, the viability of their organizations. It is undoubtedly far easier for HR managers to make big mistakes than it is to take actions that will have an immediate and positive effect on company operations.

So, as we enter the 1990s, a new set of challenges tests the mettle and talents of HR managers. Unless they develop the skills and attitudes they need to cope with these challenges, many will not measure up and will become casualties of their own deficiencies. What are some of these challenges?

- Planning for downsizing, streamlining, and restructuring
- Dealing with mergers and takeovers
- Linking HR goals, objectives, plans, and programs to the company's strategic plans
- Getting the management group to realize that human resources are as critical to the success of the organization as financial resources
- Helping the organization to become or remain competitive on a worldwide basis

- Attracting, motivating, and retaining a qualified and competent work force
- Improving the productivity of people and the quality of products and services
- Reeducating, retraining, and redeploying people
- Dealing sensitively, compassionately, and successfully with employee performance problems
- Cultivating ethical behavior, trust, and teamwork

A large part of the solution to these problems rests in the HR manager's skills—in technology and marketing sensitivity, in finding fresh and innovative approaches, in moving from a research–technology–product orientation to a marketing and customer-oriented stance, in providing top-notch leadership.

This book is a companion volume to *Critical Skills: The Guide to Top Performance for Human Resources Managers*. The earlier book focused on communication skills: this one concentrates on the skills that mark the difference between a competent manager and a competent leader—a person with the know-how and maturity to win the confidence and respect of employees, the board of control, and the general public, a person with balanced concern for people, productivity, quality, and profit.

This book focuses on four areas crucial to effective HR management:

1. *The business component*—forecasting, strategic planning, budgeting, and marketing
2. *The people component*—resolving conflict, disciplining, rewarding, and leading
3. *The technical component*—innovating, improving productivity, managing change, and managing costs
4. *The personal component*—managing time, managing ethics, and developing oneself

The book aims to develop understanding by HR managers of their role and the managerial behaviors that lead to the highest levels of commitment and productivity in their organizations. It attempts to provide them with increased understanding of their potential strengths and weakness and the impact they produce. It focuses on increasing effectiveness by improving their confidence and skills and their ability to choose the most effective managerial behavior in different situations. And it is hoped that mastery of the skills described here will also increase the commitment and performance of groups—work teams, task forces, and committees—by developing a greater understanding of group processes and the role of the leader. The book contains models for increasing productivity through commitment rather than exclusively by control, for making discipline more rational and effective, for increasing interpersonal awareness, and for improving interpersonal relations and performance.

This book attempts to build or hone a repertoire of managerial skills not typically covered during the professional or technical training and education of HR managers—the very skills that are crucial to both the organization and the HR managers. It is not overstating the matter to say that the effective use of these skills will determine the viability and permanence of the organization in the marketplace, and also the role, influence, and respect accorded HR managers.

In fact, it might well be said that the book describes the skills of the new HR managers, the "redesigned" managers that are required by the organization of today and tomorrow. Managers who understand the whole organization and the environment in which it operates—and not just their area of specialization; managers who welcome change—accept it, master it, use it, and deliberately cause it; managers who are proactive rather than reactive, innovators rather than imitators; managers who confront all constraints rather than simply accept them and the limitations on action that they impose when accepted; managers who take risks rather than avoid them; managers who continue to develop themselves professionally, technically, and personally.

I thank Adrienne Hickey, AMACOM senior acquisitions and planning editor, Barbara Horowitz, AMACOM associate editor, and Marty Stuckey, editor, for their guidance and assistance during the two years it took to produce this book.

W. R. T.

LEADERSHIP SKILLS

1
Forecasting
Prelude to Planning

Forecasting the future is certainly not new. Seers and prophets, using crystal balls, tea leaves, and playing cards, have been around for ages. Today's futurists, of which there are thousands, use state-of-the-art computers and sophisticated trend-analysis technologies—although they are not necessarily more accurate.

Forecasting, sometimes called futuring, has been defined as projecting trends and visualizing possible and probable futures and their implications. It involves a period of five to ten years, and its primary purpose is to provide information that will enable planners and managers to make better decisions.

Sometimes the terms "projection," "forecast," and "prediction" are used interchangeably. However, some experts make important distinctions.[1]

> A *projection* is simply an extrapolation into the future. Sometimes the projection is done by an automatic extrapolation of past data; hence, the so-called *straight-line projection*, sometimes intuition, judgment, and speculation are also used. In either case there is no necessary assertion of validity.
>
> In a forecast the analyst tries to establish which events are possible and then to assign at least rough probabilities to the various contentions, as for example, first finding out what horses are running in a race and then assigning odds to each of them.
>
> A prediction is based on establishing high, perhaps overwhelming, probabilities in favor of a specific event, as for example the probability that a tossed coin will turn up heads at least once in five tosses.

This chapter describes the role of HR managers in the forecasting process. It focuses on their responsibilities for developing the HR forecast, which will be used as input to the overall corporate

---

[1]Herman Kahn and B. Bruce-Briggs, *Things to Come: Thinking About the Seventies and Eighties* (New York: The Macmillan Company, 1972), p. 40.

1

forecast and as the basis for designing HR plans, programs, and services. The end product of the forecasting process is a description of trends and developments, probable future conditions and events, and the impact of those conditions on the HR department and the organization and its people. That output is then used as the basis for developing HR strategic and operational plans, policies, budgets, systems and programs, and services.

Why Bother With Forecasts?

Forecasts are projections—a look into the future. This means they are subject to error. But they are indispensable tools that the HR manager can use to plan for the future. Good forecasting—and that means a combination of qualitative and quantitative methods—will allow you to get reliable answers to questions such as these: What will our future work-force requirements be? For executives? Managers? Scientists? Supervisors? Technicians? Other employees? What products and services should be marketed? What skills will be required to produce them? What jobs are likely to become obsolete? Will we have the human resources to meet the demand? Will we be able to get the kinds and numbers of employees we will need?

Stated another way, a careful, systematic forecast can provide these benefits:

- *Reduced risk.* Business has become much too complex to rely on hunches and rules of thumb. Correct forecasts help top management avoid the financial loss that comes with bad decisions.
- *Basis for planning.* By defining the most probable future business conditions, forecasting enables organizations to develop sound plans for producing quality products and services and maximizing profits.
- *Awareness of key factors.* The process of developing a forecast involves identifying the technological, economic, social, and environmental conditions that will change the way people work in the coming decade.
- *Better budgets.* With a good forecast, the task of preparing a realistic and rational budget—one that is adequate to meet requirements for people, space, facilities, and equipment—is greatly simplified.
- *Better control and accountability.* The process of building the forecast is likely to bring to light any weaknesses in control information.

Forecasting and Human Resources

The Critical Role of the HR Manager

Human resources forecasting demands time and work and, for good results, economic and analytical skills of a high order. One might assume the best approach would be to use forecasting specialists, but it isn't. HR forecasting is far too important to be left to professional forecasters alone. HR managers must reach their own conclusions about the "people" outlook of their companies. Even if their organizations have staff forecasters and economists or hire outside consultants, the responsibility for making final judgments about the business outlook should remain with top executives, and final judgments about the human resources required to support business plans should remain with the HR manager. Thus, HR managers must improve their competence as forecasters and strategic planners.

In terms of the corporate forecast, HR managers are responsible for:

- Helping corporate officers recognize the implications of futurist HR data for themselves and the organization
- Assisting corporate executives, functional managers, and staff officers develop and implement policies and practices that impinge on human resources
- Helping other managers and staffers collect future data relating to HR functions and activities, organize it, analyze and synthesize it, absorb it, and use it
- Helping others identify trends and developments, probable futures, and their impacts

Factors Shaping the HR Function

Several factors shape the HR function in all types of organizations, and the HR forecast must take them into account.

Socioeconomic, political, and technological factors. This is undoubtedly the broadest, most complex, and most difficult constellation of factors to observe, analyze, and understand. It includes the economy, both foreign and domestic, with its many components— the value of the dollar, the money supply, the balance of trade, interest rates, inflation rates, competition for markets, and the like. It also includes the political environment, with its effect on tax policies, regulation, deregulation, laws, and court decisions.

The work force. Then there is the composition of the work force, its size and diversity in terms of age, sex, marital and parental status, national origin, language, educational level, literacy, skills, physical, mental, and emotional condition, attitudes, values, expectations, priorities, lifestyles, and loyalty. And, as a separate but related element, the values, perceptions, attitudes, and skills of executives, managers, and supervisors must be analyzed.

Technology. Next is technology and its current or potential impact on corporate products and services, facilities, operations, productivity, profitability, and efficiency—and of course on worker skills, job satisfaction, and quality of work life. We have seen many advances in both the hard technologies (computers, robotics, new communication and learning systems, and the like) and the soft technologies (computer and robotics programming, artificial intelligence, organization and individual development strategies, and dynamic programming). And we are likely to see many more.

Organization structure. The way the organization is structured has always been an important factor in HR forecasting and planning activities. In earlier years, the concern was centered on the form of the organization structure—line, line and staff, staff, or matrix. But recently, much more dramatic changes in structure have had a tremendous impact on the work of the HR department: downsizing, restructuring, and delayering, mergers, acquisitions, and takeovers, decentralization, centralization, and diversification. And those changes and developments are quite likely to continue, even accelerate.

What Makes a Good HR Forecast?

HR forecasts should look five or more years into the future. They should examine projected turnover (from resignations, retirements, or terminations), the number, quality, and types of employees that will be needed in the future (based on changes in decisions to compete in new markets, or programs to improve productivity), and the financial and other resources likely to be available to the department.

To be effective and usable, HR forecasts must meet certain minimum requirements. They must make use of local and national research data on social, demographic, economic, and technological trends. They must take into account company history and experience, and must be based on the organization's long-range plans and

■ ■

CHARACTERISTICS OF HR FORECASTS

A Good Forecast	*A Bad Forecast*
• Looks five or more years into the future	• Projects less than five or more than ten years ahead
• Considers both national and regional demographic trends	• Fails to take local and regional demographic trends into account
• Uses corporate forecasts, long-range plans, and personnel projections	• Is prepared independently and without regard to corporate forecasts and related futures data
• Addresses the needs of all categories of employees	• Focuses on the needs of one or two groups of employees
• Takes into account organizational history and experience	• Disregards organizational history and experience
• Considers planned or projected organizational changes	• Ignores planned organizational changes
• Is timely and comprehensive in scope	• Provides too little information too late
• Is objective and realistic	• Is highly subjective
• Is logical and credible	• Is farfetched
• Is usable	• Is nonfunctional
• Is cost-effective	• Provides an inadequate return on investment

■ ■

forecasts of many factors: the general economy, industry, personnel, labor, product, services, equipment, and processes. They must also consider company plans for expansion or consolidation, downsizing and restructuring, mergers and acquisitions, and other changes in structure.

Content Guidelines

The HR forecast should address how the following areas affect the organization and its way of doing business:

- *Demographics*—population growth and distribution, and work force changes in terms of sex, age, marital status, handicapping conditions, and educational and literacy levels
- *Economics*—productivity indexes, rate of inflation, marketing opportunities, growth industries, employment statistics, do-

mestic and foreign competition, balance of payments, the value of the dollar, changes in gross national product
- *Government policies*—developments in equal employment opportunity and affirmative action, compensation and benefits, taxes, consumer protection, energy conservation, health and safety regulations, environmental controls, and mandated training and development
- *Technology*—advances in physical and social engineering, in knowledge of organizational and individual development and adult learning, and in new strategies and delivery systems for improving communication, motivation, job performance, job satisfaction, and learning

To be most useful, the HR forecast should address both needs and capabilities, current and projected. Needs in these ten areas should be analyzed:

1. Recruitment, selection, orientation, and assignment of new employees
2. Trade, semiskills, sales, safety, dealer, and technical training
3. Executive succession and managerial development
4. Presupervisory training and development
5. Scientist and engineer training and development
6. Organization development
7. Team building
8. Compensation, benefits, and incentives
9. Job enrichment, career development, and promotion
10. Reassignment, termination, outplacement, and retirement

The forecast should also include a current and a projected assessment of the capabilities of the HR department to provide the required programs and services in these six areas:

1. The number, quality, and skills of personnel in all functions and at all levels
2. The amount, kind, and availability of organizational and employee programs and services
3. The amount and kind of space, facilities, and equipment
4. The type, quality, and availability of materials
5. The funds required and available
6. The cost benefits to be derived

Training and Development Forecasts

An integral part of the HR forecasting process is the forecast of the future needs for, and capabilities in, training and development. This training and development forecast may be either a part of the overall HR forecast, if the training and development function is contained with the HR department, or a separate document if it is a department on its own.

Training and development problems are constantly growing in number and complexity, as a direct result of rapid and substantive changes in society, business organizations, and technology. Unfortunately, solutions to those problems are not keeping pace. In too many organizations, the machinery for keeping up with changing training and development requirements is simply unable to meet the demands being placed on it. The problem is mainly one of inadequate identification of training needs. Admittedly, the process is not simple, and the HR manager can spend resources ineffectively unless a systematic, well-conceived plan for needs assessment is followed.

Approaches to needs assessment. Several different but complementary approaches may be used to survey training needs: interviews, observation, tests, and analysis of records and reports. Specific methods include use of advisory committees, analysis of plans and forecasts, assessment centers, attitude, climate, and critical incident surveys, group discussions, employee and exit interviews, analysis of job descriptions and applicant specifications, management requests, needs inventories, nominal group technique, observation of behavior, outside surveys, performance appraisals, performance documents and records, product evaluation, questionnaires, and skills tests.

Personnel covered. All levels of employees, from the CEO to hourly workers, are included in needs assessment surveys; all have input of value. Skills of current employees should be compared with those specified in job descriptions to identify shortfalls. Employee performance ratings can be analyzed to determine whether training programs can raise performance. Personnel and production records can be studied to identify problems that training could help solve.

Contributions of operating elements. Operating elements of the organization also must provide input to the training and development forecast. Training activities must serve the needs of the organization. Of course, a line manager or staff officer with a problem that he or she thinks can be solved by training is not necessarily right, but the HR manager has an obligation to analyze the problem and either provide the training or convince the manager that the problem can be solved by other means.

In any case, operating and staff personnel should survey their training and development needs at least annually. To do the job properly, they need guidance—and that is the job of the HR manager and staff. One of the simplest ways to get the needed information in readily usable form is to use a questionnaire that covers the following items:

1. What jobs, processes, or skills are now completely new in your operation?
2. What jobs, processes, or skills are likely to change in the future? In what way? When?
3. What jobs, processes, or skills require additional training because of technological advances? Now? In the future?
4. What jobs, processes, or skills require additional training to bring employees up to the required level of performance? Now? In the future?

The HR Forecasting Process

Step 1. Get total involvement. Forecasting is a cooperative enterprise. It requires the participation of the key people in the organization: board of control, executives, managers at all levels, supervisors, staff personnel, scientists, engineers, and technicians. Top executives must provide two essentials: support in the form of resources needed for the forecasting process, and input. They should be systematically questioned about the organization, the industry, and competitors to gather whatever information they can add about the past, the present, and their future intentions. The same can be said of the other categories of personnel. Getting them directly involved at the outset will pay dividends later on when the forecast is staffed.

To achieve this kind of support throughout the organization, forecasters need to become sensitive to some common obstacles that can interfere with total involvement, and learn to defuse them. One such problem is misunderstanding. Unfortunately, the forecasting process is neither widely nor thoroughly understood. Managers too often look for total accuracy, failing to understand that *all* forecasts include the element of guesswork. The objective in forecasting is to reduce the outside limits of error to a minimum.

There are psychological barriers, the very human tendency to be more concerned about the present—which is real—than the future—which is uncertain. Forecasting usually results in the identification of changes that executives and managers would rather ignore, hoping they will go away. Then, too, many managers, even those employed by large organizations where forecasting is a large and sophisticated staff function, tend to be skeptical about formal forecasting. They either oppose it as psychic nonsense, or reject it because they previously had a disappointing experience.

Another problem area is time span. The longer the span, the less accurate forecasts are likely to be. So the more distant is the future time that managers are considering, the more clouded is their view of what is likely to happen. Finally, there is the issue of cost. Forecasting requires money as well as the time of key people. It always represents overhead costs: the salaries of those who do the forecasting, the costs of getting and analyzing the information required, and the costs of false starts and detours that often occur.

Step 2. Establish objectives. One of the most important steps in initiating an HR forecast is to determine the purposes and objectives the forecast will serve. Because the ultimate purpose of all forecasts is to improve decision making, the identification of objectives must begin there—with an analysis of the decision-making process of the organization and the HR department, to determine what information in what form would be most useful to managers in that process.

When you have clearly identified how decisions are made and what information is needed to reach a timely decision, you establish your long-term goals—what you want to accomplish and where you want your department to be in five or more years. These goals should provide guidelines for your forecasting effort by ensuring that your attention and resources are focused on important ends. Here are two examples of goals:

- To identify technical trends and developments, probable futures, and their effects on the organization
- To assist functional departments and staff elements of the organization in collecting, organizing, analyzing, synthesizing, and using future data related to human resources requirements

You are then ready to set your objectives for the forecasting effort. Here you get more specific. You identify precisely what is to be accomplished by the forecast, by whom and by when. Here are two sample objectives:

- Using the corporate forecast and strategic plan, progression and personnel inventory charts, and input from functional

managers, to collect data pertaining to the organization's
need during 1991–1996 for managers of functional departments in terms of numbers, capabilities, and experience and
to identify potential sources of those managers. Action: HR
manager. Target date for completion: April 1, 1990.

- Using the corporate forecast (technological advances, and
changes in products, services, equipment, materials, and
processes) and strategic plan, to collect data pertaining to the
need for retraining the incumbents of technical operational
positions during 1991–1996 in terms of specific skills requirements, numbers, and time phasing. Action: HR staff. Target
date: June 1, 1990.

Step 3. Select the forecasting methods. Many forecasting
methods are in use; they cluster into four general categories, each
based on different assumptions and principles, and each involving a
somewhat different approach. Detailed, "how-to" explanations of
the many types of forecasts are beyond the scope of this book; to
learn more, refer to the sources listed at the end of the chapter,
particularly Vanston, "Technology Forecasting." Briefly, the four
types are:

1. *Surveillance*—based on observing the situation. It requires a
large data base and computer support. It is easy to set up, can be
tailored to fit the organization, is compatible with other activities,
and is easily integrated with other forecasting techniques. Three
common surveillance techniques differ primarily in their focus and
intensity: *scanning* takes a very broad stroke, *monitoring* is more
focused, and *tracking* more focused still.

2. *Projective*—based on the assumption that the future will be
like the past, unless the fundamental forces that shaped the past
should change significantly. Common projective techniques are:

- Trend extrapolation: if past trends can be established, they
can be extended into the future by extrapolating.
- Trailblazer: certain key developments lead the way for other
predictable changes in the same area.
- Substitution analysis: notes the degree to which new technology has replaced old, and thus quantifies the amount of
change that has occurred.
- Delphi technique: using multiple rounds of contacts, collects
and consolidates opinions about trends from a range of
experts.

- Structured interview: collects the best judgment of key leaders through individual personal interviews.
- Nominal group technique: collects the best judgment of five to seven key leaders through a structured group meeting.

3. *Normative* (goal-oriented)—based on the premise that future developments will be caused by future needs. If future needs can be projected, the means of meeting them can also be forecast. Two common techniques are:

- Morphological analysis: the current characteristics of an issue, and possible alternatives, are listed on two axes of a grid, and unusual combinations are explored.
- Relevance trees: various elements of a decision are divided into smaller components (drawn in a "tree" structure) and assigned a priority ranking against which proposed solutions are rated.

4. *Integrative*—permits decisions makers to consider an integrated picture, taking multiple forces into account. Four techniques are:

- Cross-impact analysis: a small group of experts explicitly investigates the interaction of specific internal and external forces, one at a time, using a matrix format to compare how possible developments would affect the area under investigation.
- Scenarios: key individuals develop stories about the future, based on an agreed theme, and the stories are consolidated into one unified narrative.
- Mathematical models: models that simulate future situations are constructed on a computer, permitting easy comparison of "what-if" variables.
- Iterative approach: a group of people, working as individuals, answers a set of questions in writing. Their responses are summarized and circulated to the others, who add their comments, eventually resulting in a written statement that represents consensus.

The task in Step 3 is to select the most appropriate forecasting methods. Note the plural—more than one method should be used, as an internal check of the reliability of the end product, and at least one method should be integrative. What is the best way to choose the methods you will use? Follow these guidelines:

- The methods chosen will result in the collection of critically important and usable data.
- The methods are appropriate for collecting the kinds of information needed; they are neither too sophisticated nor too simplistic.
- Data are either readily available or can be obtained with relative ease and reasonable cost.
- The required data-gathering and analytical skills are available in-house or can be obtained at a reasonable cost.
- The methods are acceptable to both top management and participants in the forecasting effort.
- The net results of using the methods are worth the costs incurred.

Step 4. Develop baseline data. Here the task is one of building a structure on which estimates of future conditions can be based. It is done by conducting an orderly investigation of internal and external factors that affect the organization in general and HR aspects in particular. It begins with a look at the company, its history, its products and services, and its current status.

Most larger organizations will have produced corporate forecasts and long-range plans, in the process accumulating much research data that is useful to HR managers. If this is the case in your organization, start with these corporate documents, and use them as the basis for developing the detailed HR forecast. If not, you will have to start back at the beginning, by doing your own research.

Here are some of the questions you will want to answer: How and when did the company start? What was the original mission? Has the mission changed over time? How and how much? What significant trends have emerged over the history of the firm? Are these trends characteristic of the industry? Has the company been gaining or losing ground in the industry? Is productivity all that it should be? Product quality? Customer service?

How was the company organized originally? How has the organization changed? Has it been restructured? Downsized? Has the trend been toward centralization or decentralization? Have there been takeovers? If so, were they hostile or friendly? What has happened with respect to unionization and collective bargaining? Compensation and benefits? Executive succession? Training and development? Employee services? Turnover? Quality of work life? Employee attitudes, skills, productivity, loyalty? Have personnel resources been adequate in kinds, numbers, and skills to support company growth?

Your first step is your own department: the "people" data in personnel records can help you identify changes in personnel requirements down the road, particularly if it is readily accessible and easily usable, which generally means computerized. Then, check in with the following departments for relevant information:

- Accounting—marketing data, budgets, resource allocations, and capital expenditures.
- Data processing—automated data to meet your needs can be retrieved on demand.
- Sales—information from the sales force usually has a near-term orientation but it is extremely useful to track these data over time.
- Marketing—particularly the data generated by the marketing research unit.

In addition, there is a small mountain of research material available from external sources; the challenge for the HR manager is to identify and sort out the useful and relevant data.

- Annual reports of your own company and competitors, plus companies in other industries that affect yours
- Competitor literature—catalogs, new-product announcements, and other promotional pieces distributed by firms of all types
- Government reports, especially from the Securities and Exchange Commission, Bureau of the Census, and Departments of Commerce, Labor, Energy, and Health and Human Services
- Research organizations—in universities, federal and state government agencies, and private "think tanks"—that specialize in personnel research data
- Newspapers and magazines, both specific industry journals and the general business press
- Industry and professional associations, especially their periodicals and research reports
- Networks of all kinds—person-to-person, company-to-company, and computer-to-computer

Step 5. Analyze and evaluate internal and external factors. At this point, a great amount of information about the business environment, the industry, competitors, and the company has been collected, cataloged, and tabulated. Now the job is to find out what the various bits and pieces of information mean—the discovery of relationships and the identification of trends. The objective is to show how the operations of the company as a whole and the HR department in particular have varied throughout the period under study. That requires comprehensive analysis: studying trends, analyzing relationships, performing correlation analysis, and building models.

The first task is to develop company and industry trends from the historical data already assembled. Trends that involve figures, such as the number of employees in each category at the end of each of the last five years, the number of personnel trained in each category, annual sales of training videotapes, expenditures for tuition aid, number of programs, and so on, can be plotted on cross-ruled charts or graph paper. Of course, software is now available to automate trend-line production simply by inputting the raw data into a computer.

Next, identify and analyze relationships between trends wherever possible. Usually, these relationships are described by ratios or percentages; for example, the ratio between sales volume and the number of employees required to generate the sales. Examples in the human resources arena could include the percentage of employees in each category of personnel that have historically elected a particular set of options from the menu of available benefits, the ratio between the number of products or services produced and the number of employees of each category required to produce that volume of output, and the percentage of employees in specific occupational categories electing retirement at specific ages.

Correlation analysis is a mathematical process used to determine the statistical relationship between two variables. For example, to forecast personnel requirements by correlation analysis would involve determining whether two factors, such as some measure of departmental activity and staffing levels, are related. If they are and if you can forecast the level of departmental activity, you can then forecast personnel requirements much more accurately than by either trend or ratio analysis. Correlations can be computed manually or by computer program.

Finally, an automated data system can be used to develop mathematical, statistical, and descriptive models, equations that represent relationships and simulate reality, into which different figures can be plugged. A model can test "what-if" conditions, manipulate variables, identify interrelationships and dependencies, and accumulate new data for use in developing the final forecast.

Step 6. Prepare the forecast. At this point all key functionaries are again brought into the forecasting process. The knowledge and experience of key executives and managers are particularly valuable since the task here is to determine the probable future of the company in its industry and the human resources needed in that future. But it is equally important for them to participate at this point because responsibility for the forecast should be shared. No one manager should become the target for criticism if the forecast proves to be inaccurate.

To prevent detours and miscalculations, it is important to make very clear to participants the purposes, objectives, and procedures to be used in developing the forecast and their individual responsibilities. They should be described in writing, and the instructions covering the mechanics of the process must be provided to each participant (see Figure 1-1). Essentially, what is needed is the key managers' and executives' best judgment on what the key trends and relationships mean for the future of the company.

Next, the opinions of these key people should be solicited. There are six key questions to address:

1. What is the future of the business or industry as a whole during the next ten years, based on extensions of past trend lines and either upward or downward adjustments based on the executive's judgment of anticipated business conditions?
2. What is the future of the company or department and its products, services, or programs?
3. What are the most likely threats, challenges, and opportunities that the company and the department must face in the next ten years?
4. How many people with what knowledge, skills, and experience will we need in each employee category (primarily executive, managerial, professional, and technical)?
5. To what extent can personnel requirements be met in-house through career planning, training, and development?
6. How many outside candidates will we need to fill the gap between demand and availability?

After collecting these opinions, a group meeting is held with all participants. The objective is to share opinions, discuss them, and reach consensus. Strong leadership is required during this phase because differences of opinion will need to be ironed out. There are certain to be overly optimistic and overly pessimistic opinions to be reconciled so that a clear, realistic, and hardheaded view of the department's future can be developed. It is important that the company's own plans and what is known about competitors' plans

Figure 1-1.   A sample set of instructions for the forecasting team.

Forecasting Policy and Procedures

Purpose

The purpose of this document is to describe purposes, objectives, responsibilities, and procedures of the HR forecasting program.

Objectives

Forecasting is the process of identifying probable future conditions that will constitute the business environment of XYZ Corporation and are most likely to affect the human resources component of company operations in the next five to ten years. The forecasting effort will be targeted on the human resources needs of the organization. Analysis of the implications of the findings and conclusions of the forecast will provide the basis for developing and updating strategic and operational plans in the HR department.

Responsibilities

1. The board of directors establishes overall policies for the collection, analysis, and synthesis of baseline data and approves major findings and conclusions used as a basis for developing forecasts and formulating strategic plans.
2. The CEO establishes objectives, delegates authority, and approves procedures for the preparation of forecasts and provides the leadership and support required to ensure the success of the effort.
3. The planning and forecasting office establishes a schedule and procedures for the collection, analysis, and use of forecasting data, oversees the collection effort, prepares and staffs the draft forecast, reviews, audits, and evaluates the forecast on a continuing basis, and provides functional managers with an updated corporate forecast annually. (Note: If there is no planning and forecasting office, the HR manager, with the prior approval of the CEO, should assume this responsibility.)
4. Functional managers and staff officers develop baseline data for their areas of responsibility in accordance with the methods and techniques prescribed by the planning and forecasting office, provide input to the HR forecast, and review and comment on the draft forecast to assure its internal consistency, reliability, and credibility.

Procedures

The following procedures should be followed by functional managers in developing their input to the HR forecast:

1. Review the latest version of the HR forecast in total to identify areas that require investigation, data collection, and analysis.
2. Carefully consider the implications of key trends, findings, and conclusions on their functional areas.
3. Network with professionals in their primary areas of responsibility to share ideas on trends and developments.
4. Establish a small (two or three people), informal, part-time forecasting group.
5. Investigate areas of concern, collect the required data by the most appropriate means, tabulate and analyze the data, and draw their own conclusions.
6. For each major finding or conclusion, develop a list of possible impacts, and then select the most probable.
7. Staff their preliminary findings within their own elements.
8. Coordinate preliminary findings with other elements that will be affected by their decisions and actions.
9. Submit their findings and conclusions to the planning and forecasting office (or, in the absence of such an office, to the HR manager) in a report using the following format:
   • Office
   • Key trends and developments
   • Probable future conditions impacting your area of responsibility
   • Implications of each condition for your area [identify alternative actions required]

are taken into account as well as participants' knowledge of any unusual limiting or enhancing internal conditions.

The next step is to translate the consensus of executives and managers into a formal report showing the anticipated trends of the industry, the company, the department, and individual company products, services, and programs throughout the forecast period and the number of people from inside and outside needed to meet requirements. The consensus should be written up in a brief statement that, when staffed and approved, becomes the official department forecast.

Step 7. Audit and adjust the forecast. Once the forecast is written, don't file it away and forget about it. To get a return on the investment of time and talent in preparing the forecast, results must be compared with predictions during the entire forecast period. Don't be concerned about minor variations, but major variations—or repeated minor deviations—should be examined closely. When the causes of deviations have been isolated, take direct and speedy action to correct the situation. One of those actions may well be adjusting the forecast.

Realize, too, that no forecast is static and unchanging. Change in the business environment must always be considered a given. If the forecast is to reflect all influences accurately, it must be reviewed periodically and adjusted. That review should involve a fresh look at key factors and another group meeting of executives and managers to reach consensus on adjustments to the forecast.

Step 8. Use the forecast. The official department forecast must now be applied operationally: Identify specific targets in the form of goals and objectives, translate them into plans, and establish programs in such areas as HR budgeting, purchasing, capital investment, marketing, and production. Remember the ultimate purpose of forecasts: to serve as the starting point for HR planning of all varieties: long-term, strategic, and operational. And that is the subject of Chapter 2.

The Future of the Human Resources Field—A Sample Forecast

To provide an illustration of a forecast—what it looks like, what it covers, how it is presented—I have developed this description of the future of the field of human resources. It is my hope that, in addition to serving as an example of the end product, it will also provide you with some information about your profession.

What follows is a set of incomplete predictions about the future five to ten years down the road. It represents a collage of items in categories that HR experts generally agree affect human resources—and are affected by it—in one way or another. They come from books, professional, technical, and popular magazines, research reports, brochures, and the like. They are incomplete in two senses. First, they do not cover everything; second, they deal mainly with the *nature* of the changes and developments and do not fully address their *implications* for the HR field. Some of those effects are left to the reader to forecast.

Some of the predictions may never happen. Essentially this is a forecast of *some* of the changes that *could* occur in the future. Taking a look at the future and trying to understand it, HR managers may be able to influence the direction it takes, rather than simply observing change and reacting to it. As some very wise manager once said, "The best way to predict the future is to invent it."

Government and politics. Although the 1980s have seen a somewhat less intrusive federal government in some areas, notably in the area of regulations for American business, that is not likely to prevail much longer. Both the federal government and the states are likely to take more activist roles, particularly with respect to enforcement, in such areas as equal employment opportunity, affirmative action, environmental protection, employee health and safety, drug sales, distribution, and testing, substance abuse, consumer protection, and comparable worth.

Congress and state legislatures are likely to become more involved in programs and policies relating to employment, pay and benefits, particularly health insurance and portable pensions, training and development, worker relocations and dislocations, mergers and acquisitions, downsizing and plant closings, and adjustments to worker unemployment, safety, disability, and welfare programs.

There will also be increased interest and action on such items as employer and employee tax credits and other incentives for child care, elder care, training, and education. And there will increased attention to "workfare," "earn while you learn," and job partnership training programs to help the unemployed and underemployed prepare themselves for good jobs and require able-bodied persons on welfare to receive training to become self-supporting—and at the same time fill job vacancies, reduce welfare expenditures and entitlement payments, and improve the quality of life of the disadvantaged.

There will be greater involvement of corporations in public policy matters and programs aimed at improving the education and training of young people—cooperative efforts of public and private colleges and technical schools to provide reading, math, language, and specific job skills to prepare young people for jobs. And company-sponsored or cooperative programs with local and state public and private agencies will be established to reduce teenage pregnancy, school dropout rates, teenage street crime, and drug and alcohol abuse.

Here are some specific projections of the impact on human resources of these government actions:

- More government intervention in the area of private-sector job training to reduce unemployment
- Special tax incentives for employers who provide training for

older workers, minorities, and for difficult-to-fill jobs in industries with severe labor shortages
- More government-mandated training
- Expansion of the Job Partnership Training Act

The economy. The name of the game over the next decade is change: a shorter development cycle and a precarious future for businesses, products, jobs, and careers. There will be increased competitive and economic pressures on American business—public and private, for-profit and not-for-profit—to reduce or contain expenditures.

Major changes will take place in the economic base of the United States. Instead of industrial manufacturing, the greatest sources of economic wealth, and our primary exports, will be information and services. Both domestic and foreign competition for markets will become even more intense as the European Community (formerly the European Common Market) expands in numbers of members and in competitive position and strength.[2] As a consequence of this economic rivalry, there will be high demand for more efficient U.S. workers with different and better skills.

Shifts in the economy are certain to cause more job dislocations, and financial problems for government (in terms of welfare assistance), for business and industry (in terms of retraining programs), and individual wage earners (in terms of loss of income and its impact on the family and the need for relocation or retraining). Close cooperation and collaboration among federal, state, and local government agencies, unions, and corporate management will be needed to provide the assistance and solutions required.

Business will become globalized and there will be a sharp increase in the number of multinational companies. U.S. production operations will continue to relocate to foreign countries, and the number of joint manufacturing ventures in those countries and in the United States will also grow in numbers and diversity.

What are some of the implications for the HR function?

- Development and implementation of programs to improve the quality of company products and services
- Establishment of productivity improvement strategies and programs

---

[2]Original members of the European Community were France, West Germany, Belgium, the Netherlands, Italy, and Luxembourg. Added in the intervening years: Great Britain, Ireland, Denmark, Greece, Spain, and Portugal. By 1992, a gross domestic product of $325 billion is predicted.

• Greater attention to the cost effectiveness and cost benefits of all HR programs and services

Corporate culture. Corporate culture will change dramatically because of changing work-force demographics as the numbers of women, older workers, and members of minority groups increase. The diversity of backgrounds, heritage, culture, and values will be striking. Although some companies may try to stick with a standard company style, most will be forced to accept, even encourage, diversity. The challenges to corporate leadership will be unparalleled, and many managers will not meet the test.

The way organizations will work in the future will also change dramatically as a result of decentralization or centralization, downsizing, restructuring, streamlining, and delayering, and mergers, acquisitions, and diversification. The middle-management layer is likely to be replaced by work teams and task forces.

The change from a production-centered to service-centered economy will require organizations to be more customer-oriented. Top-quality service, as well as products, will be demanded by consumers. Line managers and staffers will be brought into the strategic planning, marketing and sales, and customer relations aspects of the business.

Personnel policies will change to match changes in demographics, the value systems of society, and two-earner households—flexible work hours, more part-time work, evening work, parental leave, tuition assistance, health insurance, and the like. Women and minority groups will continue to force changes in corporate attitudes and bring legal pressure to bear on corporate employers for meaningful work. The result will be further improvements in working conditions, more nearly equitable salaries, and progress on the principle of comparable worth. On-site, near-site, and company-sponsored child daycare and elder care facilities will be more common, as will company payments for such care off premises.

Another effect of the demographic changes will be greater emphasis on strategic human resource planning and the allocation of a larger share of the corporate budget to the recruitment, selection, training, motivation, and development of people.

The compensation, benefits, and job security of employees at all levels will be tied to corporate performance—profitability and return on investment in the case of for-profit companies and efficiency and effectiveness in the case of not-for-profit organizations.

In an era of mergers and takeovers, more consideration will be given to the compatibility of the human resources policies and practices of the prospective partners and making sure that their culture and management systems mesh properly prior to the merger. The HR staff will become members of all merger, acquisition, downsizing, streamlining, and restructuring teams to ensure that human resource implications of the change are taken into account.

The role of business in society will be transformed. Corporations will give greater attention to such issues as fairness, equity, and ethics, including the appearance of ethical behavior in all their relationships.

Here are some sample effects of corporate cultural change on HR:

- Development and implementation of more organizational diagnosis, planning, and design of training
- Refocusing and realignment of management and executive development programs
- More and better team training
- Greater and more effective use of organization development strategies and interventions
- New approaches to employee performance appraisal

Unions. While collective bargaining is certainly here to stay, the future of unions over the next decade is unclear. On the one hand, they could grow dramatically in size and influence if the large, currently nonunion populations of white-collar technicians, data entry, administrative and secretarial workers, salespersons, and low-skill service workers become unionized. Professional, technical, and employee associations also may well become targets for union recruitment.

On the other hand, the disastrous effects of prolonged strikes in recent years on the financial well-being of large blocks of Americans in diverse occupations, to say nothing of the negative public reactions, have had an adverse impact on the popularity of unions. An additional impediment to the growth of unions has been the positive actions taken by corporate America to institute policies and practices to improve the lot of their employees—better pay and benefits, career counseling, more accessible training and development, formal grievance and appeal procedures, participation of employees in policy and decision making, improved working conditions, and, in general, a better quality of work life.

Here are some of the most likely effects on human resources:

- The development of more nonunion operations training programs

- A push for improved labor relations and negotiations training for managers and supervisors
- More and better team-building programs and quality of work life training programs for supervisors and other groups of employees
- Broader training for HR managers in administering compensation and benefits
- Greater involvement of unions in planning and implementing training and development programs

Workforce. The pool of workers will be smaller, with a considerably higher percentage of women, middle-aged and older persons, and larger numbers of immigrants and minorities, particularly Hispanics and Asians, the handicapped, and the disadvantaged. They will be less well prepared in terms of language skills and basic workplace abilities, and there will be a high percentage of functional illiterates.

The shift from manufacturing to services and information will create a demand for workers with different and more highly developed job skills and abilities. The emphasis will be on creativity and analytical skills, problem solving, critical thinking, and interpretive and innovative skills rather than manipulative skills.

Another shift in the work force: fewer and fewer workers will be engaged in agribusiness. The shift in the location of the nation's farms from the South to the Midwest will continue, and there will be fewer farms and farmers, more city-dwelling service workers.

The aging of the work force will cause serious problems for corporations because of the serious need for career counseling and training for older workers whose career advancement will be stalled by job changes and new requirements. Older workers will perform more poorly, productivity and customer satisfaction will suffer, and profitability will decline. The impact will extend beyond these plateaued workers—the sight of stalled careers will demoralize younger workers who will be upset by the vision of what the future holds for them.

The percentage of college graduates will continue to grow, perhaps exceeding the number of jobs that require a college degree. Accepting positions outside one's field of preparation or overqualification for the job is certain to cause a great deal of dissatisfaction. On the other side of the coin we shall see the results of the failure of the American public education system to provide literate, trainable people. The number of high school dropouts, functional illiterates, and marginally literate people (including high school graduates) will continue to grow.

To overcome the shortage of people for low-level jobs, the number of visiting or itinerant workers (foreign nationals with green cards) will increase dramatically—and will lead to serious communication and training problems caused by cultural differences and language difficulties.

Employees will feel that their status, jobs, compensation, and benefits are less secure because management will be forced by economic conditions and competition to tie pay, benefits, and job security to corporate performance.

The values of the work force will continue to change dramatically. Employees will expect the job to be tailored to their needs, priorities, and lifestyles. More and more workers will be willing to work half time, contract for temporary work, share jobs with others, or hold multiple jobs. Many will take long leaves of absence to explore other geographical areas, lifestyles, and kinds of work, or to become home-based workers or homemakers. The availability of company-sponsored career planning and education, training, and development will become major factors in an organization's ability to attract and retain workers.

Here are some of the specific measures that will be employed by the HR function to meet the challenge of demographic change:

- More and better-designed retraining programs for older workers with obsolescent skills
- Improved programs to train women for employment in what have traditionally been male jobs
- More sophisticated and more effective management succession programs
- Increased emphasis on upward mobility programs for minorities
- More advanced alternative training (lateral development) programs
- Better career counseling and more career-change training
- Refocused executive, management, and supervisory development programs
- More extensive use of organization development strategies and interventions

Society. Lifestyles are certain to continue to change. Whereas the 1980s centered attention on health and fitness with diet and exercise as the primary focal points, the 1990s are likely to turn attention to easier, less taxing, and more satisfying lifestyles. But toleration of so-called recreational drugs and excessive use of alcohol will lose support.

Full partnership of women as breadwinners will be the norm; so will smaller families. There will be more single-parent households as well as large numbers of employees who have been reared in one-parent homes—with the dilemmas that will pose for managers who may not be able to relate to the problems associated with a single income and child care requirements.

The "saving" tendencies of the adults of the 1970s and 1980s are likely to be replaced by the "spending" propensities of the baby boomers—the thirty-five to fifty-five-year-olds who spend freely now and will continue to do so.

Despite continuing technological advances, the decline in the prestige of some of the hard sciences, such as physics and mathematics, and the professions associated with them (physical sciences and engineering), will continue; the life sciences, psychology, and sociology will flourish.

What will the effects be on HR? Here are a few predictions.

- More extensive employee assistance programs (EAPs) covering such areas as career counseling, drug, alcohol, child, and spouse abuse, financial and family planning, retirement planning, and outplacement programs
- More child-care and elder-care services, supported at least in part by the organization
- Refocused management development programs

Technology. Technology has always had an important impact—in the way HR products and services are developed and delivered, such as in training, but even more in the scope of activities of the HR department and the number and kinds of people in all categories it recruits, selects, trains, assigns, develops, promotes, motivates, terminates, and retires. Technology will continue to have a great impact, with the automation of many functions of the corporation and the HR department and more extensive use of telecommunications, computers, robotics, videotapes and videodiscs, and the like.

Rapid and pervasive technological change will be characteristic of the next decade. Technology will continue to change the content of jobs—the knowledge and skills required for optimal performance. There will be less dependence on manipulative jobs and a growing need for managers and supervisors skilled in working with people in teams and with people–computer teams.

The problems of integrating university-based, independent, and in-house technological developments will become even more difficult and pressing than they are now.

Here are some of the probable effects of advancing technology on HR.

- Greater emphasis on strategies to anticipate the probable direction and impact of technological change on the organization, jobs, people, and training and development programs
- Development of strategies to exploit the potential of new production tools and at the same time minimize the negative effects on employees
- Retraining programs for all groups of workers affected by technological changes
- Development of ergonomics (people–machine interface) training programs

Human resources. Human resources will be the most critical resource for private and public enterprise in the 1990s. The reasons for this pivotal position are changing demographics, the change in the composition and size of the work force, increasing occupational obsolescence, and increasing recognition of the HR function as the key element in meeting corporate and public goals and objectives. The predominant role played by HR managers in human resources recruitment, selection, training, and development will give them greater responsibilities in all types of organizations for maximizing the use of available human resources.

It appears very likely that in the 1990s the principal shapers of the work force will be:

- The changing size and nature of the population
- The changing profile of the entry-level worker
- Mismatches between supply and demand for specific job skills
- Increased generational, gender, ethnic, and cultural conflict and confrontation
- Less acceptance of the traditional work ethic
- Changing lifestyles, value systems, and expectations
- Increased competition for domestic and foreign markets
- Rapid growth of technology, especially in the areas of information, communication, and automation
- The change from a production- to a service-centered economy
- Mergers, acquisitions, downsizing, delayering, and restructuring
- Increased participation of employees in managing organizations
- Uncertainty about the role of unions

These items have important implications for every area of thought and activity. These shapers of the work force will create more requirements for employee services, modifications to compensation and benefits programs, career planning, individual employee training and retraining, organization development and team building, and individualized handling and treatment of employees, to name but a few.

Here are some of the most profound changes projected for the human resources function.

There will be general acceptance of the fact that everything that happens in any organization is in some way influenced by its human resources and that human resources go far beyond the traditional personnel functions; that in fact they are central to the operation of an organization, and thus human resources must be integrated with overall corporate planning, both strategic and tactical.

The HR function will become even more visible and will be more widely recognized as a key factor in corporate viability and profitability. As a consequence, more resources will be invested in human capital improvements than in plant and equipment.

More and more HR departments will become profit centers, selling their products and services both inside and outside the company. The HR manager will become an intrapreneur, running the HR business as a company within a company.

Human resources pratitioners will become more professional and more competent—and will be recognized and compensated for their professionalism. They will be faced with the challenge of meeting corporate strategic goals and objectives, translating higher worker expectations into productive, pleasant, safe, and cost-effective environments, and providing integrated employee services in a timely, coordinated, cost-effective manner based on a thorough knowledge of corporate culture, politics, and financial resources and employee needs, wants, and levels of expectation.

Because of the changes in the business environment, the size, composition, and lack of skills of the work force, compounded by technical change, job obsolescence, mergers, acquisitions, downsizing, and a host of other factors, HR planning will occupy a larger share of corporate budgets so that organizations can attract, train, and retain a quality work force, adequate in size and competencies.

Much more will be expected of HR managers and practitioners. They will be expected to be action-oriented—"move it, fix it, try it." To study it enough, but not study it to death. They must:

- Focus on managing *results*—bottom-line outcomes
- Practice *managerial* skills and behavior

- Participate as full partners in corporate strategic planning
- Implement programs, services, and activities that are effective in changing attitudes, behavior, and performance in desirable ways
- Objectively determine accomplishments and results
- Communicate accomplishments to the total enterprise—up, down, and laterally
- Identify and communicate significant problems and barriers to accomplishment
- Demonstrate and promote innovation and creativity
- Build an atmosphere of openness, trust, and respect
- Perform as leaders

There will be increased emphasis on the development and application of measures of HR contributions and effectiveness in supporting organizational growth, development, and accountability.

Because of the dwindling pool of highly qualified people, medium-size to large organizations will concentrate on developing their own supervisors, managers, and executives. Small organizations will compete intensively to attract and retain highly qualified executives, managers, scientists, engineers, and technicians. They will pool their resources and collaborate with public and private colleges and technical schools to meet their training and development needs.

Company training programs will be more difficult to conduct because of the high rate of illiteracy and the growing numbers of people who are marginally literate. More organizations will provide on-site basic skills programs. Similarly, organizations will become more deeply involved in community and in-house programs aimed at reducing school drop-out rates, street crime, and drug and alcohol abuse.

The concept of lifelong learning will continue to grow and prosper. There will be increased emphasis on self-directed learning and learner-centered training and education. The projected shortage of opportunities for advancement will create a need for realistic career expectations and increased emphasis on the potential rewards of lateral transfers and the enrichment of current jobs.

Variable, cafeteria-style compensation and benefits packages will become more common: schedules of bonuses, incentives, pension and savings plans to allow individuals to choose the combination that best suits their needs.

There is likely to be a dramatic increase in the number of firms offering benefits to meet the demands of working women for safe, high-quality, accessible, and affordable child care. Similarly, parental and family-leave policies and programs, designed to enable parents to care for newly arrived and sick or disabled children, will increase in numbers and extent of coverage. The underlying reasons: the high percentage of women in the work force, including those in managerial positions, intense competition for the recruitment and retention of high-potential and high-performance employees, comparatively lower costs for such programs than for hiring replacements, and increased federal and state legislation supporting such programs.

Mental health and substance-abuse costs will continue to soar and will prompt significant reforms to bring costs under control over the next several years. Those reforms will take several forms: reducing coverage, changing the benefits structure, modifying the way care is provided, implementing preauthorization, concurrent review, and alternative programs, and subjecting provider payments to utilization review.

Across-the-board pay raises and automatic increases in benefits will become a thing of the past; they will be replaced by a system that rewards exceptional performance or shortage-area value-based skills. More incentives will be offered to gain company loyalty and long-term commitment.

The growth of technology, particularly in the areas of computers, robotics, and telecommunications, will increase the demand for more broadly and better-trained workers and supervisors—people who are able to deal with such subjects as electronics, computer programming, hydraulics, and mechanics. Supervisors will have to learn to use computers, data bases, and spreadsheets and solve other problems by expert systems and computers.

Health care costs for employees and retirees will continue to rise, due to cost-shifting by the government and insurance carriers and the high incidence rate and expense of AIDS, substance abuse, and mental illness. The number of workers with AIDS or ARC will continue to increase. That will require not only the expenditure of large sums of money for treatment but also positive steps to minimize the impact of the disease on the work force, productivity, and profitability. Clear and firm policies, with respect to testing, treatment, nondiscrimination, and provisions for education of employees and supervisors will be essential.

The continued growth in the number of drug and alcohol users and abusers in the work force will raise problems relating to policies about drug testing, treatment, and the establishment or expansion of EAPs, and provisions for the education and training of employees and supervisors.

Franchises will continue to grow in numbers and in types—in

food service, auto and equipment repair, convenience stores, hotels and motels, and so on. They will create a need for training programs.

There will be more emphasis on the holistic concept—dealing with the whole person, physically, mentally, emotionally, and spiritually.

The way organizations are structured will have an even greater impact on training and development than it has in the past. Decentralized organizations will require long-range training—often in the form of self-instructional programs on videodisc or computers, teleconferencing, or corporate satellite television. Centralized organizations will require corporate training centers and an emphasis on team building.

There will be an increased need for language, intercultural and cross-cultural training for professionals of every stripe, as well as for managers, scientists, engineers, and technicians, so that they can develop cultural knowledge and empathy. They will have to learn the dos and don'ts of behavior while doing business in foreign cultures both within and outside the United States.

Other areas of emphasis in training programs are certain to include the use of high-tech tools (computers and robots), effective listening, speaking and writing, time and stress management, thinking and acting innovatively and creatively, and managing others engaged in innovative and creative activities.

To save instructor cost, program development time, and trainee expenses, a large percentage of in-house training and development programs in decentralized organizations will be conducted via satellite corporate television networks. There will be much less "stand-up" training and more use of hardware and software. More outside consultants will be employed to meet the increased need for highly specialized expertise.

Training will be customized to meet the specific needs of the group. It will focus on specific results, in terms of knowledge and skills, and on measurable objectives that relate to improved efficiency and productivity.

Training and development followup strategies will receive the attention and effort so long denied to them. The focus of this effort will be on the degree to which behavior, performance, and work attitudes have been changed by the programs offered.

There will be a greater need for accelerated learning strategies—shorter knowledge and skill modules making use of advances in learning technologies. Focal points will be such objectives as learning how to learn, problem sensing and problem solving, and working as a member of a team.

Quality of work life issues will assume an even greater amount of the time and attention of managers and HR practitioners because of workers' expectation, if not demand, for more options, flexibility, opportunities, and challenge in their jobs.

Summary

Forecasting is an essential preliminary activity to planning in all its forms: long-range, strategic, and operational. Essentially, HR forecasting is the process of deliberately and systematically collecting, analyzing, synthesizing, and drawing implications from study of probable changes that are most likely to affect the organization in general and the HR function in particular over a period of five to ten years.

Several external and internal key factors shape the HR function in all types of enterprise and have significant effects on operations. They span social, economic, political, and technological developments and many types of changes in the size and composition of the work force.

Other key factors include the profiles of the organization itself and its managers—the organizational culture, structure, goals, management style, priorities, policies, products, services, and a host of other characteristics that make it unique.

Hundreds of forecasts and reports are published every year by federal and state government agencies, professional, technical, and trade associations, private research organizations, foundations, universities, and individuals. Information of value in developing forecasts can also be found in company annual reports, the brochures, catalogs, and advertisements of competitors, and the popular, professional, and technical press. Within most companies, the accounting or financial, marketing, and data processing departments, the sales force, consultants, and clients can provide useful information. Review of company documents, such as plans, personnel and production records, and in-house research reports and studies, will provide additional valuable data.

Several complementary forecasting methods can be used to collect and analyze information for use in preparing a forecast: surveillance, projective, normative, and integrative. Regardless of the approach used, a good forecast is reasonable, objective, realistic, accurate, internally consistent, logical, usable, credible, and cost effective.

The forecasting process involves the following sequence of steps:

1. Get total involvement.
2. Establish objectives.
3. Select the forecasting methods.
4. Develop baseline data of external and internal factors.
5. Analyze and evaluate data through trend, relationship, and correlation analyses.
6. Prepare and write the forecast.
7. Audit and adjust the forecast.
8. Use the forecast.

The use of systematically developed forecasts will do more to improve the completeness, relevance, and overall quality of strategic and operational plans than any other single action. Forecasts, therefore, are indispensable tools for HR managers.

For Further Reading, Viewing, and Listening

Cook, Mary F. "What's Ahead in Human Resources?" *Management Review*, April 1988, pp. 41–44.

Dalton, Gene W., and Paul H. Thompson. *Novations: Strategies for Career Management*. Glenview, Ill.: Scott, Foresman & Company, 1986.

Dickson, Paul. *The Future File*. Austin, Tex.: Learning Concepts, 1977.

Drucker, Peter F. *Managing in Turbulent Times*. New York: Harper & Row, 1980.

Gentilman, Ruth, and Barbara Nelson. "Futuring: The Process and Implications for Training and Development Practitioners." *Training and Development Journal*, June 1983, pp. 30–38.

Hatakeyama, Yoshio. *Manager Revolution: A Guide to Survival in Today's Changing Workplace*. Cambridge, Mass.: Productivity Press, 1985.

Houze, William C. *Career Veer*. New York: McGraw-Hill Book Company, 1985.

An Introduction to Forecasting (individualized computer-based lesson). LEARNCOM, 215 First St., Cambridge, MA 02142, 1987.

Jones, Robert T. "Looking Ahead: Trends in the Workforce and Job Training." *Management Review*, May 1988, pp. 46–48.

Kahn, Herman, and B. Bruce-Briggs. *Things to Come: Thinking About the 70's and 80's*. New York: Macmillan Company, 1972.

Key Demographic Trends for the 1990's and Beyond: Past + Present = Future. Or Does It? (60-minute videocassette). Produced by Video Education Network, 1986. Distributed by Dartnell, 4660 Ravenswood Ave., Chicago, IL 60640.

London, Manuel. "Human Resources Forecasting and Planning." Chapter 8 in *Change Agents: New Roles and Innovation Strategies for Human Resource Professionals.* San Francisco: Jossey-Bass, 1988.

Mahoney, F.X. "The Future and Human Resources Management." Chapter 3 in *Human Resources Management and Development Handbook,* edited by William R. Tracey. New York: AMACOM, 1985.

Making Short-Term Projections (individualized, computer-based lesson). LEARNCOM, 215 First St., Cambridge, MA 02142, 1987.

Makridakis, Spyros and Steven C. Cartwright, eds. *The Handbook of Forecasting: A Manager's Guide.* 2nd ed. New York: John Wiley & Sons, 1987.

Manzini, Andrew O. "Human Resources Planning and Forecasting." Chapter 35 in *Human Resources Management and Development Handbook,* edited by William R. Tracey. New York: AMACOM, 1985.

Merriam, John E. and Joel Makower. *Trend Watching: How the Media Create Trends . . . and How to Be the First to Uncover Them.* New York: AMACOM, 1988.

Moffitt, Donald, ed. *The Wall Street Journal Views America Tomorrow.* New York: Dow Jones & Company, 1977.

Morgan, Brian S., and William A. Schiemann. *Supervision in the '80s: Trends in Corporate America.* Princeton, N.J.: Opinion Research Corp., 1984.

Naisbitt, John. *Megatrends.* New York: Warner Books, 1982.

———. *The Year Ahead: These Ten Trends Will Shape the Way You Live, Work and Make Money in 1985.* Washington, D.C.: The Naisbitt Group, 1985.

Piercy, Nigel, ed. *The Management Implications of the New Information Technology.* Beckenham Kent, England: Croom Helm, 1984.

"Predictions: Looking Ahead." *Training,* July 1988, pp. 79–84.

Projecting Long-Term Trends (individualized, computer-based lesson). LEARNCOM, 215 First St., Cambridge, MA 02142, 1987.

Rogers, F. G. "Buck." *Riding the Winds of Change* (audiotape). Work Dynamics, 715 Sandor Court, Paramus, N.J. 07652.

Rukeyser, Louis. *What's Ahead for the Economy?* New York: Simon and Schuster, 1983.

Toffler, Alvin. *The Adaptive Corporation.* New York: McGraw-Hill Book Company, 1985.

———. *The Third Wave.* New York: William Morrow and Company, 1980.

Vanston, John H., Jr. "Technology Forecasting." Chapter 6 in *Human*

Resources Management and Development Handbook, edited by William R. Tracey. New York: AMACOM, 1985.

Yankelovich, Daniel. *New Rules: Searching for Self-fulfillment in a World Turned Upside Down.* New York: Random House, 1981.

Zemke, Ron. "Training in the 90's." *Training,* January 1987, pp. 40–53.

2
Strategic Planning
Matching Resources and Conditions

One of the most dramatic changes now taking place in the business world is the movement away from almost total reliance on numerical analysis toward a balanced mixture of quantitative approaches and strategic planning. The new concept, which uses empirical observation and business sense as the basis for planning, is beginning to replace more traditional planning models. The success or failure of any business today is not decided solely by its resources or by the conditions under which it operates, but rather by the ability of its managers to match the two. And that is what strategic planning is all about.

Strategic planning represents a commitment to the future of the organization rather than just letting things happen. And it is no longer the exclusive province of large companies, but is now practiced by a growing number of small and medium-sized firms. (In fact, planning is *more* important in a small business.)

Strategic planning is one phase of an overall, wide-angle approach to leading an organization to success (however that be defined by the company). In very broad terms, this is the flow: A mission statement is articulated, capturing in words the essence of the organization's reason for being. Goals are set that make the mission tangible. The best minds go to work forecasting the probable future environment the company will be operating in (see Chapter 1). And then strategic plans are worked out—an orderly set of corporate strategies that define how the goals will be achieved, considered in the light of that forecast.

Strategic planning is not the same as long-range planning. Long-range planning is concerned with a forecast of where a company's sales and profits *might* be in ten or twenty years. Strategic planning is concerned with identifying the *most likely* issues, opportunities, challenges, and options over a shorter period, usually either five or ten years. It focuses on such basic questions as these: What business should the company be in? What programs, products, and services should be marketed, and how will they generate enough profit (or other corporate benefits) to justify the investment of resources? What changes in the environment constitute threats or risks? For example, the globalization of business and the relocation of U.S. production operations overseas have created a demand for language-qualified, cross-culturally competent technicians and managers that far exceeds the supply.

Essentially, then, strategic planning involves taking a searching look into the future as a means of avoiding disasters and crises. Although that objective is shared by the forecasting process, in strategic planning the focus is sharpened by identifying specific strategies that will avoid potential debacles. The "look" includes the effects of potential changes in government policies, demographic and social changes, economic trends and technological advances, and a host of others. In addition, the strategic plan contains goals and objectives, financial data, and breakeven analysis—a sales objective expressed in either the number of dollars or units of production at which the business will be breaking even (that is, revenues from sales and costs of producing the product or service will be equal).

In sum, a strategic plan is a means of matching the resources of an organization with the internal and external conditions within which it must operate to attain its mission and achieve its goals and objectives. It improves the operations of the company's various functions: marketing and sales, research and development, human resources, and so on. It prepares an organization to deal with change. It provides a basis for developing alternative actions based on different scenarios, and so gives the company the flexibility it needs to adjust to unanticipated changes. It provides a means of building a competitive edge. In short, it is an essential tool for giving a company the firm direction it needs to survive and prosper in an uncertain future. Companies without strategic plans are certain to be surprised; they may even fail.

Goal Setting and Planning: The Big Picture

Introducing TEA, Inc.

At this point, we introduce a hypothetical business called TEA, Inc. To illustrate the many steps and nuances in strategic planning, we will follow this company throughout the chapter.

TEA, Inc., a small, private manufacturer of peripherals for

personal computers, was established in the Boston area in 1981. In the intervening years, TEA has expanded its product line to include word processing, desktop publishing, graphics, and other specialized software. At the same time it also expanded services, and now offers on-site classroom and laboratory training in the use of its products, and personalized consulting services such as custom programming, system integration, and one-on-one training. TEA serves customers across the continental United States and Canada through a small network of customer service centers. It now employs 600 workers and has annual revenues in excess of $100 million. Recently, the company has begun to explore overseas markets for its products and services.

Goal Setting

Remember that strategic plans are built on a foundation of the organization's goals, which are statements of desired long-term results, expressed as improvements—how much and in what direction. In for-profit organizations goals are typically economic. In not-for-profit organizations, they usually address some aspect of efficiency in operations.

Because they deal with matters that get to the heart of the organization's reason for existence, organizational goals are usually set forth in writing. They relate to such ends as profitability, growth, capital improvements, asset utilization, employee relations and services, market share and new markets, product mix, productivity, energy conservation, product quality standards, customer service, sales volume, return on investment, and the like.

For example, here are some of TEA's organizational goals:

- To achieve maximum return on investment
- To market only top-quality products and services
- To construct a corporate training facility
- To create a product R&D department
- To increase productivity

In addition, individual departments establish goals, end results to be achieved by the department rather than the total firm. Most departmental goals and action plans are designed to serve the total organization, and certainly this is true of the HR department. Therefore, departmental goals must be derived from and support organizational goals. They, too, are usually committed to writing.

For example, to support the company's goal of increasing productivity, TEA's HR department might set a goal of establishing an employee assistance program. Another one of TEA's goals is "to achieve maximum return on investment." One derivative goal for the HR department is "to market to outside customers training programs developed in-house." Another HR goal to promote return on investment could be "to help employees qualify for advancement and improve their long-range potential."

The issue of goals is keenly important in the HR department. If they are to establish credibility as part of the top-management team, HR managers must set clearly stated goals that are adequate to fulfill the responsibilities delegated to the department by top management. The HR department staff must understand the HR goals and their relationship to the goals of other departments and of the organization as a whole. And they must be committed to their attainment. Today's highly competitive environment demands that HR departments take on bold goals and pursue them aggressively.

The HR department of TEA, Inc., has set these broad goals:

- To serve the needs of the company by:
  —Meeting projected requirements for skilled managers, supervisors, and technicians
  —Improving the job performance of employees in their present positions
  —Increasing the pool of promotable employees
- To serve the needs of employees by:
  —Increasing employee job security and job satisfaction
  —Helping employees qualify for advancement and improve their long-range promotion potential
  —Enhancing the skills, upward mobility, and status of minorities

Approaches to Planning

A plan is a guide to action. It is a map the organization uses to get from where it is to where it wants to be. It involves all elements of the company, and it requires the full support and commitment of employees at all levels.

It also requires a systematic approach. Strategic planning is too complex, and too important, to be done haphazardly or casually. Most organizations have developed a formal system involving two phases: strategic corporate plans, which deal with the next five to ten years, and operational plans for the various departments and operating units, covering the coming year.

Although no two organizations are exactly alike, and for that reason are likely to approach the business-base planning function somewhat differently, some features of good planning are generally applicable across the full spectrum of private and public organizations.

Strategic plans. Strategic plans are future plans. They define the broad direction of what the corporation should become in five to ten years—financial position, organizational structure and culture, products and services, market position, facilities, personnel, and so on. They are based on economic and environmental assessment, projections, scenarios, alternative strategies, and corporate goals. They examine the operational demands of both current and new programs and, in a broad sense, the resources and strategies needed to implement them successfully.

Corporate strategic plans should delineate a logical and unifying overall strategy, and should clearly identify mid-range to long-range goals implicit in the vision. Their fundamental purpose: to coordinate and integrate all organizational assets, capabilities, and talents in a concerted effort to achieve corporate goals.

Normally, responsibility for corporate strategic planning resides in a corporate planning staff, although it is not uncommon for an organization to form a task force, made up of key managers, to develop the strategic plan. HR managers should be primary participants in the corporate strategic planning process, either as a member of a strategic planning task force or as a consultant to the planning staff or task force. One way or the other, HR managers must make sure that human resource needs and priorities are fully taken into account in the development and refinement of the corporate strategic plan.

Essentially, the role of HR managers at the corporate strategic planning level is threefold:

1. Serve as a participant in the corporate planning process, either as a member of a planning task force or as a consultant to such committees.
2. Participate in the process of communicating the corporate plan.
3. Train strategic planning teams.

If a company does not permit the HR manager to participate, he or she should actively solicit the backing of the "movers and shakers" in the organization to lobby for such involvement. If good relationships and helpful assistance are provided to key people in the organization as they develop their operational plans, their assistance should be relatively easy to acquire.

Operational plans. Operational plans are derived from the corporate strategic plan. They define the actual resources—human, financial, space, material—that the various departments will need to carry out the work of the organization in the immediate future, usually the coming year. They deal in quantifiable details: what is to be done, by whom, and when, and how success will be measured. Using production or service requirements, staffing requirements, and statistical techniques, and focusing on costs and benefits, department managers determine the optimal numbers of resources of various types needed to support the strategic plan at different stages. At any given point, operational plans describe the departments' near-term thrust and intensity of effort.

For example, one aspect of TEA's corporate strategy deals with creating new customer service centers. To support that, the marketing department wants to establish twenty-five new customer service centers over the next two years. The HR department will "employ and train fifty additional customer engineers during the next twelve months."

Here's another example. You will remember that one of TEA's corporate goals is to maximize return on investment, and that the HR department, looking for ways to increase return on the company's investment in its people, established a departmental goal of helping employees qualify for advancement. To support those goals, the HR operational plan includes this: "To develop and operate an assessment center, to identify supervisors who have the potential for training and advancement to middle-management positions." Another part of the operational plan, based on the same return on investment goal: "To develop recruitment and training programs for older workers, minorities, and difficult-to-fill jobs, to take advantage of special tax incentives."

HR managers have two responsibilities in operational plans. They provide advice and assistance to line managers and staff officers on human resources implications as they develop their operational plans. And of course, as managers of a function, they must prepare operational plans for their own department.

First they determine the availability of human resources to support all the operational plans of other functions: measuring supply against demand. Then they develop departmental plans to fill the gap—recruitment, selection, compensation and benefits, training and development, appraisal, promotion, and so on.

The sequence. Ideally, the draft corporate strategic plan, which defines output requirements for five to ten years and the corporate strategies and resources needed to achieve them, is produced first.

The HR department develops the "people" requirements of the plan, the controller develops the financial requirements, the marketing department develops the marketing requirements, and so on. And the final corporate plan takes shape. Then the specific resources needed to support the plan are defined by the appropriate operating and staff elements in the form of annual operational plans. It would be senseless to develop departmental operational plans without knowing what the total organization plans to do and become in the years ahead.

The HR connection. Now, where does the HR department fit in the scheme of things? Ideally, the HR manager is a full partner in the strategic planning process, and is either a member of the planning task force or a consultant to the corporate planning office. When that happens, the HR component of the corporate plan is itself a complete strategic plan, but integrated with the plans of other departments and with the overall company thrust. As we have seen in the examples so far, TEA, Inc., is one such company.

Unfortunately, that ideal has not been widely achieved. Although corporate strategic planning is commonplace in modern organizations, participation of HR managers is far from the norm. A recent survey of some 2,100 organizations disclosed that only one-fifth have a formal human resources planning process, and 30 percent of the HR professionals surveyed reported that their planning process was "underdeveloped or rudimentary."[1] All too often, the "people" part of the strategic plan is tacked on to the corporate plan after the fact by non–HR personnel and passed on to the HR department for implementation.

If you find yourself in this situation, you cannot simply dismiss the issue of strategic planning, and leave the decisions to others. You must undertake the delicate task of producing a strategic plan for the department, using whatever means you can devise to blend in the general direction set by the corporate plan. Your responsibilities to the organization will permit no less. The job of the HR manager is to make sure the company has the people with the skills and talents it needs to meet the operating and competitive requirements of the future—and that takes planning. If the HR planning cannot be conducted as part of the corporate process, you must do it on your own.

Then too, we occasionally see organizations that do not do

---

[1]Kenneth Martin, Vice President and Director of Human Resources, The Hay Group. Reported in "HR Planning Process Lacking, Study Shows," *Employee Benefit News,* July 1988, p. 24.

corporate strategic planning, and thus there is no automatic mechanism for HR planning. In this situation too, the dedicated HR manager simply goes ahead and develops a strategic plan for the department. The human resources plan, which will have both strategic and operational components, is developed within the department and implemented there—and all the while the HR manager continues the work of convincing corporate officers of the need for a complete and integrated corporate strategic plan.

Thus, HR managers could conceivably face any of these three scenarios: an enlightened organization that includes the human resources function in the corporate strategic planning process; an unenlightened organization where this sort of participation is shallow or nonexistent; or an organization that does not do strategic planning at all. In any case, the HR manager must undertake the very same stategic planning process. The end product—the full HR strategic plan, with its supporting operational plan—will then either be integrated into the corporate plan, or used separately to guide the activities of the department.

All of which means that HR managers must learn how to do strategic planning—a field that is alien territory to most of them. They must learn what the components of a plan are, how the information is gathered and processed, and what are their multiple layers of responsibility and authority. And that is the focus of the rest of this chapter.

Problems and Pitfalls

There are many snares ready to trap unwary HR managers as they undertake the formidable task of developing and implementing a strategic human resources plan. Here are some of the most common ones.

Disinterest. Some HR managers demonstrate a monumental lack of interest in the economic, bottom-line, results-oriented aspects of business and an almost exclusive focus on people-oriented relationships, services, and processes. They prefer to leave "business" to the CEO, the financial department, and the line managers, and instead concentrate their efforts on purely HR issues.

Lack of knowledge and skills. Too many HR managers lack the knowledge and skills needed to deal effectively with mathematical simulations and with quantitative methods in general and financial concepts in particular. Not only has their formal education over-

■ ■

STRATEGIC PLANNING IN A NUTSHELL

CORPORATE STRATEGIC PLANS

Primary author: Corporate Planning Office or Task Force.
Main purpose: To define the broad organizational direction and focus of a "vision" of what the corporation should become in three to five or more years. It delineates a logical and unifying overall strategy and clearly identifies mid-range to long-range goals implicit in the vision and, in general terms, the resources needed to achieve them.
Contents: Organizational mission, goals and constraints (including financial); economic and environmental conditions; marketing situation, status, prospects, and plans; business scenarios, strategies, business plans, and data base. Component plans from key departments, including human resources.
HR manager's roles: Active participant as either a member of the planning task force, as inputter of HR considerations, or as reviewer and commentator on the draft strategic plan. Salesperson and communicator of the benefits of strategic planning to line managers and staff officers. Trainer of corporate strategic planning teams.

OPERATIONAL PLANS

Primary authors: Line managers and staff officers.
Main purpose: To define the demand side of the equation: the actual resources, human, financial, space, material, and others, needed to carry out the work of the organization in the immediate or near-term future.
Contents: Current output requirements (products or services), scheduled output requirements (products or services), potential output requirements (products or services).
HR manager's role: As a functional manager, define current, scheduled, and potential output requirements for the HR department. As an internal consultant, provide advice and assistance to line managers and staff officers on HR implications as they produce their operational plans.

HR PLANS—STRATEGIC AND OPERATIONAL

Primary author: HR manager with the assistance of department staff.
Main purpose: Using recruitment and turnover statistics (transfers, terminations, and retirement), personnel inventories, performance appraisal reports, and management succession programs, determine the variance between demand and availability of the human resources required to support strategic and operational plans. Then to provide the staffing plans to close the gap between the demand for human resources and their availability.

Contents: Tabular comparison of demand and availability of human resources. Identification of systems and programs to fill the gap between demand and availability: recruitment, selection, compensation and benefits, training and development, evaluation and appraisal, management succession, promotion, and so on.

HR manager's role: Prepare both strategic plan and operational plans for the department. Oversee the definition of requirements for systems and programs, supervise the design of those systems and programs, and manage their development and implementation.

■ ■

looked mathematical and financial concepts, but many have consciously avoided those subjects in their on-the-job activities as well.

CEO vision–strategic plan disconnects. Formal strategic plans are sometimes out of sync with the informal strategic plan that is envisioned by the chief executive officer. The formal plan is usually developed in a rational, linear fashion and focuses on quantitative and therefore measurable factors. The informal plan is based on intuition, political considerations, negotiation, and compromise, and it centers on qualitative factors. A related problem lies in planners' failure to study or understand the perspective and goals of the CEO.

Lack of involvement. One aspect of involvement relates to the role of top management. The CEO and top executives must not only be fully committed to and totally support the strategic planning process and the resulting plans, they must also be directly involved in planning for planning and in the planning process itself.

Here is another facet of the problem. Failure to involve all line managers and staff officers in the planning process, whether out of elitism or ignorance, dooms any plan to failure. Sometimes senior executives believe that they alone are capable of developing plans. Or they assume that the planning office, if there is one, should take responsibility for all formal planning.

Time and scheduling problems. Planning requires a reasonably long lead time to permit full consideration of alternative courses of action, to accommodate the involvement of all organizational constituencies, and to communicate the plan and its results. Strategic planning cannot be a seat-of-the-pants operation. It must be done systematically, in phases or steps, and the timing of each step must be appropriate.

Inadequate communication. From the very beginning of the strategic planning process, efficient communications must be established and maintained. Through oral briefings by managers and senior executives, discussion groups, bulletins or newsletters, and formal reports, people at all levels must be kept informed of what is planned, what is accomplished, what the problems are, and what corrections are being made.

Contents of a Strategic Plan

Although there is no standard format for a strategic plan, most plans contain these common elements.

- *An executive summary.* A "snapshot" of main ingredients of the strategic plan: goals, challenges, risks, options, strategies, and tactical plans.
- *Mission and goals.* Statement of the company's mission: the purpose of the company and the function it performs. Statement of companywide long-term goals.
- *A vision statement.* A copy of the corporate vision statement is included.
- *Environmental scan.* A survey of the external and internal circumstances that affect how the organization functions.
- *Forecast.* Describes the challenges and changes that lie ahead— risks and options, opportunities and threats—and names the ones most likely to affect the organization.
- *Resource analysis.* As planning issues and alternatives are identified, planners must analyze the resources currently available and projected, and compare them with those that will be needed in the five- or ten-year period. The object: to determine shortfalls.
- *Master strategy.* In terms of the entire organization, defines how resources will be deployed and how allocated among the various departments.
- *Supporting operational plans.* Tactical plans detail what each department will do in the short term, and how: identify objectives, describe and evaluate alternative actions, select and develop the best alternatives, implement action plans, and monitor and control them.

- *Financial summary.* Budgets and financial reports detail the dollar aspects of the plan.
- *Implementation and control procedures.* Schedules and task assignments are defined, and a process for review and modification is explained.

HR Plan Components

HR strategic plans follow the format just described for strategic plans in general. In addition, most HR plans include sections on staffing, compensation and benefits, succession, training and development, and marketing. Figure 2-1 is a sample format for HR departments.

Staffing planning. Staffing planning is concerned with

1. Inventorying the kinds, numbers, and skills of employees currently on board
2. Determining the employees the organization needs now and in the immediate future to accomplish its objectives
3. Identifying the gaps between available skills and those required
4. Identifying the resources needed to recruit, train, and develop the people needed to fill the gap
5. Developing and implementing an action plan to acquire the people needed

Compensation planning. Compensation planning focuses on

1. Identifying and analyzing compensation issues and costs
2. Developing and implementing a framework and strategy to determine compensation schedules (job analysis and job descriptions, job evaluation, job pricing, and pay structure)
3. Developing and installing the compensation system and appropriate controls

Benefits planning. Benefits planning is concerned with

1. Identifying and analyzing current and potential benefits issues and costs
2. Developing a strategy to determine the policies, types, conditions, and procedures for awarding benefits
3. Developing appropriate controls to monitor the benefits program

Employee services planning. Employees services planning focuses on

1. Inventorying and evaluating current services
2. Determining requirements for employee services now and in the near term
3. Developing, implementing, monitoring, and evaluating the new or modified services

Succession planning. Succession planning, invariably aimed at company executive positions, focuses on

1. Forecasting requirements, in terms of numbers, kinds, and skills, for executive positions in the near and long term
2. Inventorying current fill of executive positions
3. Determining gaps in kinds, numbers, and skills
4. Developing, implementing, and controlling programs and strategies to search for, attract, recruit, develop, and retain people in the required numbers at the right time

Training and development planning. Training and development planning centers on

1. Analyzing employee training and development needs
2. Designing, developing, and validating training and development systems and programs
3. Conducting and evaluating training programs
4. Calculating the costs and benefits of training and development systems

It may also include the design, implementation, and evaluation of such other training-related programs as tuition-aid plans, organization development programs, and contract training.

Marketing planning. Marketing planning centers on the development of strategies and tactics to

1. Identify what current and prospective customers of HR services want and need
2. Define objectives and potential barriers to their achievement
3. Develop strategies and tactics to overcome the obstacles and a time-phased schedule

(*Text continues on page 50.*)

Figure 2-1.   HR department strategic plan format.

I. Organization

   A. Letter of transmittal
   B. Table of contents
   C. Executive summary (distilled snapshot of goals, threats, challenges, risks and opportunities, strategy, and tactical plans)

II. Introduction

   A. Corporate
      1. Corporate mission (a statement of the purpose of the company as a whole and the function it performs)
      2. Vision statement (a copy of the corporate vision statement)
      3. Policies (a general statement designed to reveal management's basic philosophy and to identify the means by which the mission will be achieved)
      4. Goals (overall, long-term desired results)
         a. Core goals (profitability, sales, market share, ROI, etc.)
         b. Other (R&D, productivity, facility development, social responsibility, and so on)
   B. Human resources department
      1. Mission
      2. Vision statement
      3. Philosophy and policies
      4. Statement of current situation
      5. Statement of trends, issues, and opportunities
      6. Goals
         a. Core (human resources development, compensation and benefits, employee services, and so on)
         b. Other (technical training, executive development, quality circles, marketing training programs, and the like)
      7. Overall strategy
         a. Narrative discussion
         b. Planning assumptions
         c. Desired results
      8. Objectives

III. Summary of business-related HR strategic analysis

   A. Summary of past and current situation
      1. Environmental factors
         a. Political
         b. Social/cultural/demographic
         c. Economic
         d. Technological
         e. Regulatory/governmental

      2. Internal factors
        a. Resources (people, funds, facilities, equipment, and so on)
        b. Organization structure
        c. Personalities/power centers
        d. Significant accomplishments
        e. Significant shortfalls
    B. Future trends, issues, challenges, threats, and opportunities
      1. External/environmental
      2. Internal
    C. "Gap": goals versus forecast
    D. Master HR strategy
      1. Narrative discussion
      2. Expected results
      3. Revised gap analysis
      4. Summary of major action steps
        a. Define
        b. Develop
        c. Implement
        d. Evaluate
      5. Personnel requirements

IV. Detailed marketing strategy by segment (internal and external)

    A. Analysis covering topics in item III
    B. Typical subsections
      1. Each product or service/market segment
      2. Regions, branches, and units/organizational elements

V. Summary of HR-related tactical or operational plans of other elements of the organization

    A. Manufacturing/production/distribution
    B. Engineering
    C. Marketing and sales
    D. Research and development
    E. Finance

VI. Financial summary

    A. Pro forma income and balance sheets
    B. Budgets
      1. Capital
      2. Operating

VII. Implementation and control procedures

    A. Schedule
    B. Task assignments
    C. Review procedures

VIII. Appendix (documentation)

4. Design measures of progress and accomplishment and a supporting budget
5. Implement, monitor, and evaluate the plan and its results

See Chapter 4 for a full discussion of the process of marketing HR products and services.

Sources of Information for Planning

Planning is not done in a vacuum. It must be based on solid information. Fortunately, there are many sources of information available to the HR manager and the strategic planning team.

Information services. Several reputable information services can provide in distilled form voluminous data that would be expensive and time-consuming for an organization to try to research, collect, tabulate, organize, analyze, and digest in-house. You can either subscribe to their services and receive their periodic reports, or make use of them in local university libraries, usually at low cost (you pay only for the actual time the data base was used in your search). A few of the many information services are listed here (see Appendix for address details).

Member Information Exchange, from American Society for Training and Development
Business Software Database, DIALOG, and ABI/Inform, all from UNI/Data Courier
Dow Jones News/Retrieval, from Dow Jones & Company
Educational Resources Information Center (ERIC), from National Institute of Education
Human Resource Information Network (HRIN), from Executive Telecom
National Technical Information Services (NTIS), from U.S. Department of Commerce
New York Times Information Bank, from New York Times
NewsNet
PsycINFO, from American Psychological Association
WILSONLINE, Business Periodicals Index, from H. W. Wilson Company

In-house records and reports. The most readily available and most current source of information for strategic planning is the records, reports, and other documents produced by the organization itself: production, marketing sales, and personnel records; career progression charts; organization development charts; purchasing and receiving records; and equipment inventories.

Among the most useful and usable are documents reporting on MBO programs, organization development, human resources audit, quarterly review and analysis, internal and external financial audit, quality control, contract progress and after-action, annual reports to stockholders and the board of directors, diagnostic summary sheets, and special studies. Also, be sure to tap into the rich material developed in the investigative phase of forecasting (see Chapter 1).

Human resources information system. The information requirements of a human resources planning system are staggering. In addition to basic personnel data, managers need instant information about related corporate financial, planning, business, and operational factors. They also need to update demographic and statistical data, make projections and forecasts, show trends, and test models, perform measurements and statistical analysis, and generate reports, including graphics.

To accomplish all this and retain a measure of sanity, managers need a computerized system, known generically as a human resources information system (HRIS). This is an automated means of collecting, analyzing, and reporting personnel data quickly, inexpensively and safely. A full-function, top-of-the-line personal computer–based HRIS can handle all personnel record keeping and reporting requirements, plus several related functions. It can help HR managers identify future needs and immediate requirements.

Systems may contain 500 or more personnel data fields such as training, education, compensation, payroll data, benefits, attendance and vacation balances, accidents and injuries, parking spaces, and the like. In addition, some systems can produce 100 or more predefined reports (EEO, OSHA, benefits tracking, audits, and so on) and can also create special one-time reports on demand.

HRIS systems invariably contain several application modules, each with numerous data fields. Some of the common modules are listed here (note that most HRIS do not contain all these):[2]

---

[2]For detailed listings of the contents of these and other HRIS data files, see "The Technology of Planning: Today's Human Resource Information Systems," Chapter 3 in Andrew O. Manzini and John D. Gridley, *Integrating Human Resources and Strategic Business Planning* (New York: AMACOM, 1986).

Personnel module
Wage and salary module
Compensation and benefits module
Health claims module
Training and development module
Career development module
Succession planning module
Applicant tracking module
EEO/AA/Government regulation module
Position control module
Word processing module
HR planning module
Networking module

To illustrate the depth of information available, Figure 2-2 outlines the possible contents of just one module: compensation and benefits.

The Strategic Planning Process

Step 1. Plan for planning. It is essential that a planning project must itself be planned. Effective planning occurs only when the proper climate for planning has been established, planning assumptions and policies have been articulated and disseminated, authority and responsibility for planning have been determined and delegated, coordination and communication methods have been worked out, step-by-step procedures for the planning process have been developed, and all that has been communicated to all employees. There are several substeps in planning for planning, but they should all be done expeditiously, and the planning plan should not contain extraneous detail.

• *Get commitment*—of people at all levels. Top management must show support by establishing the proper atmosphere for planning and by providing the resources needed. All other managers and staffers must be made planning conscious. All employees should be informed about the importance of planning and their role in the process.
• *Select the planning team.* Use generalists rather than specialists, representatives from the major constituencies of the HR department. They should be excellent communicators, open-minded, innovative, credible, and able to work with others. Keep the team small—preferably five, but not more than seven.

• *Train the team.* Take the time to engage in team building. Concentrate on defining the ground rules, the roles of participants, the agenda, how decisions and recommendations will be made, and the importance of teamwork. Encourage members to deal with issues, not personalities, to openly confront conflicts and problems, and to avoid scapegoating, putdowns, and mind games.

• *Articulate planning assumptions and rules.* Here at the outset, some of the overall assumptions on which the planning process is based must be clearly stated. Some assumptions may relate to the "real world" in which the HR department operates—the political and economic climate, the actions or intentions of competitors, or organizational realities. Others may relate to methodological premises. Any planning rules must also be set forth now to guide both the planning team and the reviewers of the plan.

• *Set planning goals and objectives.* Here the task is one of defining the objectives of the planning effort: the ultimate purposes of the strategic plan, the specific objectives to be achieved in the planning process, and the relationship of planning objectives to the goals and objectives of the organization. For example, the HR department of TEA, Inc., has identified these objectives of its strategic planning: "To anticipate future needs for human resources, match resources and environmental conditions, and develop innovative approaches to the solution of HR-related organizational problems."

• *Identify data needs.* Determine what information and data will be needed for the strategic planning process and the plan itself— the facts and figures that will provide the basis for analyzing current and future situations—and their sources. Identify the persons responsible for providing the information, the format to be used, and the due dates.

• *Establish schedules.* The planning process must be organized, systematic, and disciplined. That means a planning schedule must be developed. Divide the planning project into several phases and tasks, each with target completion dates. Schedule team meetings, progress reviews by line managers and staff officers, intermediate reviews by top management, and a final review.

• *Select a plan format.* Organize the presentation of the planning document in a logical and easily readable format, complete with summaries that can be used by managers. Include slots for the operational plans of other departments if those plans have implications for human resources.

Step 2. Define the department mission. There are four substeps in describing the mission of the HR department. They follow.

Figure 2-2.   Compensation and benefits module, HRIS.

Compensation

> Automatic pay increase list
> Executive compensation
> Fair Labor Standards Act Classification (FLSA)
> Job evaluation information
> Merit program administration
> Pay grade structure
> Performance appraisal studies
> Salary analysis and review
> Salary budget analysis and administration
> Temporary staffing statistics and tracking
> Wage and salary survey analysis

Benefits

> Benefits tracking
>   Cafeteria plan (Section 125)
>   Medical
>   Hospital
>   Dental
>   Surgical
>   Prescription drug
>   Profit-sharing
>   Stock
>   Life
>   Long-term disability
>   Supplemental life
>   Insurances
> Cafeteria style benefits and health care package
>   administration
> Compensation and payroll management
> Cost containment
> Custom administration package
> Defined contribution [401(k) or ESOP] administration
> Disability claims analysis and case management
> Flexible benefit plan administration
> Health claims analysis and management
> Employee benefits cost analysis
> Employee benefits statements and proof listings
> ERISA vesting schedules
> Generation of annual reports

Historical records and reports
  Compensation
  Incentive awards
  Breaks in service
  Benefit eligibility
  ERISA
Life insurance pricing
Pension projections
Retainment of vested terminated employees' data
Vacation time and sick leave tracking

• *Develop a vision statement for the department*—a description of what the department should be like at the end of the planning period (usually ten years). It should encompass key components of the external and internal environment, the position of the company in its industry, and the role and status of the HR department in that context; and it must devetail with the corporate vision. It should have the potential to inspire people to greater effort.

For example, here is TEA's HR department vision statement:

> By the year 1998, TEA will be a multinational organization with clients and customers in the Far East, Europe, and the Near East. It will have a worldwide reputation for providing top-quality hardware and software, first-rate training programs, and unmatched customer and client service. Its share of the U.S. market will quadruple and its gross revenues will exceed $500 million. The number of employees will increase; however, as a result of austere staffing, novel managerial strategies, and technological innovations, that growth will not parallel the expansion of markets and the rise in gross revenues. Employee turnover will be minimal and job satisfaction will be high because workers will become part owners of the business and have a share in policy making.

• *Articulate a statement of philosophy.* This clearly states the fundamental beliefs, values, and obligations of the HR department, its relationships to the company and its subdivisions, the nature and conditions of employee fair treatment, equity, job satisfaction, and development, the roles and relationships of departmental staff, and the nature and needs of employees at all levels.

Here are excerpts from TEA's statement of philosophy:

> *Production:* Quality controls must be built into production systems to ensure that the systems operate as intended and

produce the kind, quality, and quantity of output that is planned.

Organization: Support elements must be staffed with competent personnel and be given adequate facilities, equipment, and materials to provide quality services in a timely way.

Purchasing: Make-or-buy decisions must be made on the basis of cost-effectiveness analysis.

Human resources: The HR department exists primarily to secure organizational benefits. HR programs and services must make a difference, a measurable contribution to corporate goals and objectives. The effectiveness of all programs must be evaluated by the extent to which meeting the needs of employees also meet the needs of the company.

Training. The HR department must assume responsibility for training and upgrading employees. General, vocational, technical, and higher education cannot provide ready-made inputs to business. Some knowledge and skills are learnable only in the context of company training.

• *Define the department's mission*—why it exists and the function it performs. The mission statement should indicate in reasonably specific terms the department's role in the time frame adopted for the strategic plan—what types of markets, clients, or customers the department wishes to serve and what types of products or services it should offer. It should clearly indicate to all personnel the limits within which the department must operate—where expansion and diversification are acceptable and where they are not. And it should specify the benefits that the organization expects to gain.

For example, TEA's mission statement follows:

TEA was originally established to provide state-of-the-art peripherals for personal computers. Its mission has since been expanded to include the development and marketing of top-quality specialized software and associated training and consulting services to public and private organizations both nationwide and overseas. TEA is a for-profit organization. As such it has an obligation to provide a reasonable return on investment for its owners and stockholders. However, it also has responsibilities to its employees: provision of a safe and comfortable workplace, challenging jobs, fair and equitable compensation and benefits, and opportunities for advancement and self-realization. The mission of the HR department, therefore, is to support the strategic plan, goals, and objectives of the company by ensuring that people in the right numbers and with the right skills are available at all times to produce, market, and deliver quality products and services. To do that, the department must meet its responsibilities to recruit, select, orient, train, assign, develop, compensate, and promote people and, at the same time, help functional managers and staffers meet employees' needs for recognition, advancement in keeping with their performance and potential, safe and healthful working conditions, and job satisfaction.

• *Identify key policies.* Policies are guides to thinking, to discretionary action, to decision making. Policies help ensure coordination before action and provide assurance that recurring problems and issues will be handled with some measure of consistency throughout the organization. Policies should be both responsible and rational. And, in the case of HR department policies, they must be derived from corporate policies, consistent with philosophical underpinnings, and relevant to the HR needs of the organization and its people.

Here are excerpts from TEA's policy manual:

> *Internal control of funds.* The number of fund subdivisions will be kept to a minimum for each section of the department. The objective will be to finance each element at the highest practical level. Fund authorizations and limitations on cost detail accounts, including adjustments, will be made in writing. Control will be exercised by means of budgetary ceilings, centralized verification of funds, centralized accounting records, and advance approval of nonprogrammed expenditures.
>
> *Travel.* Only travel necessary to accomplish the mission will be authorized. In all cases, the most economical mode of transportation will be used. Supervisors will review travel requests and combine trips whenever possible to reduce the number of personnel in a travel status and travel costs. Travel vouchers will be submitted through the HR manager to the controller within five days.

Step 3. Develop the strategic analysis. The strategic analysis has two important parts: external and internal, each one further divided into present and future conditions. Taken together, they constitute the environment in which the HR department now operates and the atmosphere within which it must operate in the future.

The external analysis looks at current and then future conditions in the external environment—the political, social, cultural, economic, and technological—and its impact on the work force, particularly skills requirements.

The internal analysis looks at organizational culture, the quality of work life, and employee participation in goal setting and management. It scrutinizes financial data, the balance sheet, income and profit-and-loss statement, and so on. It examines the consequences over the next five to ten years of changing nothing.

The final part of the strategic analysis involves identifying obstacles, issues, and opportunities, to provide a basis for articulating goals and developing a strategy. Strengths and weaknesses often uncovered during strategic analysis include quality of services, cost effectiveness, contribution to company goals, the education and experience of staff, understanding of company culture, planning ability, availability of resources, coordination, and linkage with company strategic plans.

Common challenges and threats include the department's ability to support the firm's strategic business objectives, getting the management talent needed to meet the operating requirements of the future, customers' perceptions of quality of HR products or services, value of training and development programs, and competition.

Step 4. Determine the department's direction and goals. The mission statement has expressed the real purpose of the department. The analysis has identified major issues, challenges, and opportunities. The planning team can now identify key long-range goals. They do that by determining the HR department's direction—again, linked to corporate goals. The goal statement must be realistic, practical, achievable, and appropriate. It should focus on results rather than on activities, and should provide a firm basis for measuring the department's performance. One of the long-term goals of TEA's HR department, you may recall, is "to help employees qualify for advancement."

Step 5. Develop the master strategy and operational plans. A strategy is best viewed as the continual redeployment of resources to achieve a balanced departmental position of high returns in which benefits exceed, or at least parallel, the investment of resources. The choice of a master strategy, and its supporting tactical or operational plans, will depend on the nature and size of the department and the severity of the difficulties posed by the gaps between current operations and the future as determined by the strategic analysis. In any case, three components are involved: master strategy, objectives, and action plans.

• *Select the master strategy.* A strategy may be aggressive, passive, or something more subtle. Its full statement includes a narrative discussion, expected results, revised gap analysis, a summary of major action steps, and personnel requirements.

For instance, the TEA HR department's master strategy to support the goal of helping employees qualify for advancement is aggressive. In part, it reads:

> First, a projection of position requirements as a result of promotions, transfers, retirements, terminations, and expansion of the company, its branches, and its products and services will be prepared. Then the interests of current employees in pursuing a career development program will be surveyed and a list of committed participants will be developed.
>
> To parallel those actions, a career development program will be developed and implemented. The program will include the preparation of skills inventories for participants, needs assessment, identification of appropriate sources of the needed training (formal training in-house and outside and selected developmental experiences and assignments), provision for funding and the supervision of the program, and followup and evaluation of results.
>
> Expected results include improved employee morale, reduced absenteeism and turnover, greater productivity, and increased loyalty and commitment to the organization.
>
> Additional personnel requirements: one full-time professional to plan, develop, and supervise the execution of the program at headquarters and one part-time person at each branch to manage the program at that location.

• *Identify key objectives.* Objectives are specific targets, either qualitative or quantitative. They focus on critical issues and key result areas—the results of exploiting internal or external opportunities, or both.

Samples of key objectives to support the master strategy follow:

- To develop skills inventories for all career development program (CDP) participants. Action: Manager, Training and Development. Target date: April 1, 1990.
- To prepare needs assessments for all CDP participants. Action: Chief, Assessment Center. Target date: July 1, 1990.
- To budget for training programs for CDP participants for inclusion in the FY 1991 budget. Action: Manager, Training and Development. Target date: October 1, 1990.

Objectives should encompass all major areas in which the HR staff is expected to invest resources. They include managerial and operational obligations of the staff, normal or routine work products and innovative improvement projects, tangible (measurable) and intangible products and services, and focus on critical issues and key result areas.

• *Identify major action steps.* Here the task is to set forth in writing the actions required to implement the plan and achieve the objectives. The operational plan should describe in fine detail what is to be done, who is to do it, and when it is to be completed. It describes specific resources required: personnel, space and facilities, equipment, materials, time, and funds.

For instance, a portion of TEA's HR department operational plan spells out action steps that will accomplish the broad goal of helping employees qualify for advancement and the objective of preparing needs assessments for all career development participants. Other related objectives are as follows:

• Expand the learning center to accommodate ten additional employees.
• Purchase and install ten additional fully equipped learning carrels.
• Increase the budget of the learning center by $10,000 to purchase additional learningware.

Step 6. Staff and win support for the plan. To be successful, a strategic plan must be supported at all levels of organization, from top to bottom. To get that support, several actions are required.

• *Sell managers and staff officers.* To win the support of line managers and staff officers for the strategic plan, make use of their expertise, solicit their assistance, and communicate to them the status of the projects and results as they occur. Be sure to send them proposals, draft action plans, and interim reports for review and comment. Try to get their concurrence in the final product before presenting it to top management for final approval.

• *Sell top management.* Here are some of the things you can do to win the support of the board of control and top executives for the HR strategic plan.

1. Describe the critical issues revealed by the strategic analysis.
2. Select the best time to communicate the critical issues—April or May is usually best so that the issues can be wired into the budget—but don't wait too long.

3. Set realistic goals and objectives based on careful projections of external and internal conditions.

Present regular briefings and status reports to top managers, focusing on the potential contributions of your plan to the attainment of the corporate mission and goals. Translate your operating plans and objectives into measurable financial benefits. When presenting the final strategic plan and its supporting tactical plans, let top management know that the plans have been fully staffed with all line managers and staff officers. Counter all nonconcurrences in the plan with your data and reasoning. Get approval before implementing the plan.

Step 7. Implement the plan. Get the components together and put the plan in motion.

• *Acquire needed resources.* Your action plans should have described the resources required. Now your job is to get the resources and make them available to the people who must implement the plan. Assign people to specific actions and delegate the authority they need to command the necessary space, facilities, equipment, materials, and funds.

• *Launch the plan.* Don't procrastinate by fine tuning the details. When the plan is ready for implementation, move promptly and resolutely.

Step 8. Monitor, assess, and adjust the plan. The strategic planning process is not completed with the implementation of the action plans. Now the task becomes one of monitoring the process, assessing impacts, reporting results, and making needed adjustments.

• *Monitor the process*—to ensure that plans are put into effect by the right people, at the right time, in the right way. Follow up on your instructions to see that they have been received and understood. Don't leave this to chance. Provide guidance and assistance to the people who are implementing the plan.

• *Assess the impact of the plan.* Have some means of tracking progress and accomplishment. Require periodic written reports, make scheduled and unscheduled visits to the areas where plans are being put into effect, and get progress briefings from action officers. Check to see that action plans are carried out as intended, that results conform to what was desired and expected, and that actions are on schedule and within budget.

• *Schedule formal reviews.* Planned, scheduled formal progress reviews are essential. These periodic internal reviews will enable the HR manager to make adjustments to the plan and report to top management on progress and accomplishment. They will also help the HR manager answer some key questions. Is the strategic plan suitable? Appropriate? Achievable?

• *Make adjustments.* If the strategic planning process was well designed and has been carried out conscientiously, there should be no need for drastic changes in the action plans. However, minor modifications are usually required to eliminate small glitches. The managers of the activities involved should review any changes before they are installed.

• *Report results.* This substep is often overlooked, but it is critical. Be sure to report the results of the strategic plan to all concerned. That includes the people within the organization who are either interested in the outcome or are affected by it—and that, obviously, is everyone, from top to bottom, executives to hourly workers. And it also includes other constituencies, people outside the organization who are affected by the changes—customers and clients, suppliers and contractors, consultants, and in some cases, the general public.

Step 9. Review and revise the plan. In this step, the planning cycle is essentially repeated, although now the process should be much simpler. How often the plan should be reexamined is dependent on two factors: the *amount* of change either projected, planned, or in process; and the *rate* at which the change is taking place or is scheduled to occur. In any case, strategic plans should be reviewed at least annually to keep strategic operational plans in sync.

Summary

Strategic planning defines a broad vision of what the organization should be in the coming five to ten years. It is a means of providing direction, dealing with change, enhancing competitive position, and improving operations and results. It considers the probable effects of changes that have been forecast in both the internal and external environments in which the organization must operate—the political, social, cultural, economic, and technological environments. And it also takes into account the probable status and actions of the industry and its main competitors.

The HR manager has the responsibility for developing strategic plans and supporting operational plans that will guide the activities of the HR department during the period. Ideally, this plan will become an integral part of the organization's corporate strategic plan, but even if not it should still be prepared thoroughly and followed conscientiously.

The HR strategic plan rests on a foundation of departmental goals, which in turn were developed to support the company's overall goals. In essence, strategic planning for the HR department involves this sequence: inventory current HR assets; forecast personnel needs; measure the gap; develop plans to fill the gap.

To develop a sound and workable strategic HR plan, the manager must use a systematic process consisting of a series of sequential and interrelated steps.

1. Plan for planning by getting commitment at all levels, selecting and training the planning team, articulating planning assumptions and rules, setting planning goals and objectives, identifying data needs, establishing schedules, and selecting the plan format.
2. Define the mission, supported by a vision statement, a philosophy, and key policies.
3. Develop the strategic analysis, including analyzing external and internal forces, issues, strengths, and weaknesses, and identifying challenges, threats, and opportunities.
4. Determine departmental direction and goals.
5. Develop a master strategy and operational plans with key objectives and major action steps.
6. Staff and win support for the plan.
7. Implement the plan by developing an implementation strategy, acquiring resources, and launching the plan.
8. Monitor progress by assessing impact, scheduling formal reviews, making needed adjustments, and reporting results.
9. Review and revise the plan.

For Further Reading, Viewing, and Listening

Allen, L. A. *Making Managerial Planning More Effective.* New York: McGraw-Hill Book Company, 1982.

Applied Strategic Planning: Executive Briefing (videotape). San Diego, Calif: University Associates, 1988.

Baird, Lloyd, and Ilan Meshoulam. "Strategic Human Resource Management: Implications for Training Human Resource

Professionals." *Training and Development Journal,* January 1984, pp. 76–82.

Barocci, Thomas A., and Thomas A. Kochan. *Human Resource Management and Industrial Relations.* Boston: Little Brown and Company, 1985.

Beer, Michael, and others. *Managing Human Assets.* New York: Free Press, 1984.

Below, Patrick J., George L. Morrisey, and Betty L. Acomb. *The Executive Guide to Strategic Planning.* San Francisco: Jossey-Bass, 1987.

Bruce, Stephen D. *Strategic Human Resource Planning.* Madison, Conn.: Business and Legal Reports, 1985.

Bryson, John M. *Strategic Planning for Public and Nonprofit Organizations: A Guide to Strengthening and Sustaining Organizational Achievement.* San Francisco: Jossey-Bass, 1988.

Delaney, Robert V., Jr., and Robert A. Howell. *How to Prepare an Effective Business Plan: A Step-by-Step Approach.* New York: AMACOM, 1986.

Fombrun, Charles J., Noel M. Tichy, and Mary Anne Devanna. *Strategic Human Resource Planning.* New York: John Wiley & Sons, 1984.

Fray, Lionel L. *How to Develop the Strategic Plan.* 2nd ed. New York: American Management Association Extension Institute, 1987.

Goal Setting (individualized, computer-based lesson). Produced by Addison-Wesley Courseware. Distributed by LEARNCOM, 215 First St., Cambridge, MA 02142, 1987.

Gray, Barbara Jean. "Avoiding the Pitfalls of HRIS," *Human Resource Executive,* July/August 1988, pp. 32–38.

Hax, Arnoldo C. "A New Competitive Weapon: The Human Resource Strategy," *Training and Development Journal,* May 1985, pp. 76–82.

How to Get There From Here: The Strategic Planning Process (individualized, computer-based lesson). LEARNCOM, 215 First St., Cambridge, MA 02142, 1987.

How to Interpret Financial Statements (6-hour audiocassette). American Management Association Extension Institute, 135 W. 50th St., New York, NY 10020, 1987.

How to Prepare a Business Plan (6-hour audiocassette). American Management Association Extension Institute, 135 W. 50th St., New York, NY 10020, 1986.

Holloway, Clark. *Strategic Planning.* Chicago: Nelson-Hall, Publishers, 1986.

Hulett, Daniel G., and Jean Renjilian. "Strategic Planning." Chapter

5 in *Human Resources Management and Development Handbook,* edited by William R. Tracey. New York: AMACOM, 1985.

Karlof, B. *Business Strategies in Practice.* New York: John Wiley & Sons, 1988.

Linkow, Peter, "HRD at the Roots of Corporate Strategy." *Training and Development Journal,* May 1985, pp. 85–87.

London, Manuel. "Human Resources Forecasting and Planning." Chapter 8 in *Change Agents: New Roles and Innovation Strategies for Human Resource Professionals.* San Francisco: Jossey-Bass, 1988.

Manzini, Andrew O. "Human Resources Planning and Forecasting." Chapter 35 in *Human Resources Management and Development Handbook,* edited by William R. Tracey. New York: AMACOM, 1985.

Manzini, Andrew O., and John D. Gridley. *Integrating Human Resources and Strategic Business Planning.* New York: AMACOM, 1986.

Marrus, Stephanie K. *Building the Strategic Plan: Find, Analyze and Present the Right Information.* New York: John Wiley & Sons, 1984.

Michael Porter on Competitive Strategy (90-minute videocassette). Produced by Nathan/Tyler Productions in association with Harvard Business School, 1988. Nathan/Tyler, 451 D St., Boston, MA 02210.

Odiorne, George S. "The Art of Crafting Strategic Plans." *Training,* October 1987, pp. 94–98.

Pattan, John E. "The Strategy in Strategic Planning." *Training and Development Journal,* March 1986, pp. 30–32.

Planning (28-minute videocassette). Produced by Sally V. Beaty. Southern California Consortium, 5400 Orange Ave., Suite 215, Cypress, CA 90630, 1986.

The Planning Environment (28-minute videocassette). Produced by Sally V. Beaty. Southern California Consortium, 5400 Orange Ave., Suite 215, Cypress, CA 90630, 1983.

Planning Techniques (28-minute videocassette). Produced by Sally V. Beaty, Southern California Consortium, 5400 Orange Ave., Suite 215, Cypress, CA 90630, 1983.

Shanklin, William L., and John K. Ryans, Jr. *Planning for Your Company's Future.* New York: Random House, 1985.

Strategic Planning (6-hour audiocassette). American Management Association Extension Institute, 135 W. 50th St., New York, NY 10020, 1982.

Strategic Planning Overview (computer-based training resource).

Training Resource Corporation, Five S. Miller Rd., Harrisburg, PA 17109, 1988.

Strategic Planning Strategies (computer-based training resource). Training Resource Corporation, Five S. Miller Rd., Harrisburg, PA 17109, 1988.

Tregoe, Benjamin B., and John W. Zimmerman. *Top Management Strategy.* New York: Simon & Schuster, 1983.

————. "Needed: A Strategy for Human Resource Development." *Training and Development Journal,* May 1984, pp. 78–80.

What Is Strategic Planning? (individualized, computer-based lesson). LEARNCOM, 215 First St., Cambridge, MA 02142, 1987.

Winer, Leon. "Applying Strategic Planning in Human Resource Development." *Training and Development Journal,* November 1983, pp. 81–84.

3

Budgeting

Dollarizing Plans and Programs

A major problem facing most organizations is the continuing strug-gle of allocating limited resources to achieve maximum efficiency and return on investment. In their search for ways to get the most benefit from each dollar, all kinds of organizations are introducing new methods of programming and budgeting.

In the first two chapters we discussed developing likely scenarios of the future, and using those forecasts as the basis for strategic plans that guide the company's decisions. This chapter deals with acquiring and managing the financial resources needed to put those plans into effect—in other words, budgeting. Its basic objective is to present key budgeting concepts, briefly describe alternative ap-proaches to budgeting, and focus on practical knowledge and skills that HR managers will find useful because they are certain to need them. In budgeting, as in so many other areas, the HR manager has a dual role: influence decisions about the corporate budget, partic-ularly regarding HR-related elements, and prepare, present, de-fend, and manage the budget of the HR department.

The budget is one of the primary yardsticks top management uses to measure the performance of various departments and their managers. Managers who do not know how to plan and use a budget effectively are doomed to failure: They can't achieve what they are expected to achieve, and they rapidly lose credibility.

HR managers are particularly vulnerable. HR department budgets have always come under close scrutiny, especially when budget-cutting efforts focus on activities that are not perceived as contributing to bottom-line results. Why is it, then, that while some HR departments suffer drastic cuts following those reviews, others not only receive continued financial support but also win the battle for larger budgets? The answer lies in the degree to which the HR department is *aligned with and successfully supports* the mission and goals of the organization as a whole.

When corporate resources are divided among the various units, each one vying for a larger share, the managers that come out on top are not the ones that claim a larger *need,* but those whose objectives are wired to the company's objectives, who can demonstrate accomplishments that help achieve the company's goals, and who can make those accomplishments clearly visible to top management. This last point should not be overlooked. Not only must the results be attained, they must also be demonstrated. And, regardless of how effective your managerial style or how creative your ideas, your results are going to be measured in numbers—mainly in dollars.

What Is Budgeting?

A budget is a type of plan—a comprehensive, numerical plan—for the allocation of resources to achieve corporate goals and objectives. To put it somewhat differently, a budget is a statement of expected *results* expressed in numerical terms. It may be financially oriented— as in revenue, expense, cash, and capital budgets—or it may be nonfinancial but still numerical—direct-labor hours, materials, equipment, number of programs and services, trainee output, and so on.

A budget is also a form of managerial control. It is a means of ensuring that results conform to plans by providing a basis for measuring performance against plans, identifying deviations and shortfalls, and remedying those deficiencies or adjusting expectations. The purpose of a budget, therefore, is to make it possible for management to determine what resources *should be* expended, by whom, and for what (planning), and what resources *are being* expended, where, by whom, and for what (control).

Thus one important function of a budget is to help top management decide where to put resources and pinpoint potential threats. But there is more: as control tools, budgets also help managers perform better and help improve the company's overall operation. Here's how:

- Focus managers' attention and effort on *results.*
- Facilitate measuring managers' performance by comparing results with goals and objectives.
- Compel managers to contribute to the attainment of corporate objectives, such as profit, profitability, growth, efficiency, and resource development.
- Provide a basis for assessing the appropriateness of organizational structure, relationships, goals, and objectives.

- Enhance interdepartmental coordination, effectiveness, and teamwork.
- Encourage the use of historical reports and records in the planning process.
- Help identify areas where cost controls and hard-dollar savings can be realized.

Seen from the perspective of the organization as a whole, a healthy and effective budgeting process needs five ingredients:

1. A clearly defined organizational structure: functions, authority, and lines of communication
2. A comprehensive and well-understood planning process
3. A fully developed accounting system, including standard costing, breakeven analysis, and profit-contribution accounting
4. Fixed responsibility for the comprehensive budget program
5. Managers who are knowledgeable about financial planning and the budgeting process

The last item is probably the most important, and particularly relevant for HR managers, who traditionally suffer from a definite phobia about finance.

The Finance Phobia

Finance is the universal language of business, and HR managers must learn to speak it. Unfortunately, all too many HR managers avoid situations where they must discuss or deal with accounting and financial matters. They are often intimidated by financial executives, accountants, even financial reports. Considering their usual educational and experiential background, those shortcomings are not surprising. Most HR managers simply have not had the exposure to financial concepts.

However, in the business world, goals and objectives—and results—are expressed in financial terms. HR managers, no less than any other managers, must be able to conduct the business of their department on sound financial principles. They must approve plans and projects based on their costs and offsetting revenues. They must produce programs that meet financial goals. They must analyze objectives against bottom-line implications.

And so all HR managers must take the steps necessary to take the mystery out of accounting and financial matters. They need to educate themselves about finance, financial documents, and financial concepts and terms. They must understand that financial thinking differs from thinking in terms of marketing, sales, or production. And they must be able to develop more productive relationships with finance professionals. To do those things, they must undertand the key concepts of finance and have a firm grasp of the numbers side of the business and their function in that business. They should know what to look for, and what the numbers are telling them.

HR managers should be able to:

- Read and understand financial statements:
  —The balance sheet, income statement, and profit and loss statement
  —The differences between assets, liabilities, and equities, where they are located on the balance sheet, in what order they are reported, and why
  —The difference between a debit and a credit
  —How revenues, expenses, and net income interact with the balance sheet
  —The meaning of gross margin and why it is critical
- Manage a function according to financial indicators. To do that they must know what the profit and loss statement tells them about the big picture.
- Determine what the various financial indicators tell them about past, present, and future performance and how to use them to develop business strategies.
- Describe how cash is generated, how cash flow is managed, and how profits are determined.
- Define return on investment (ROI) and be able to calculate it.
- Use financial statements to analyze a firm's strengths and weaknesses:
  —Financial statement analysis
  —The meaning and importance of ratio analysis
  —How the income statement is used to gauge performance
  —How to calculate and use price/earnings ratios
  —How to calculate net working capital—and what it means
  —How to perform breakeven analysis
  —How to compare budgeted to actual results and highlight trouble areas
  —Cash reconciliations—what they are and how they work
- Plan future actions based on financial statements and analysis:
  —How to build a budget
  —How to control a budget

Knowledge of financial terms and concepts can be acquired by self-study using the resources listed at the end of this chapter, particularly Droms, *Finance and Accounting for Non-Financial Managers,* and the American Management Association's audiocassette, *Finance and Accounting for Nonfinancial Managers.*

Role of the HR Manager

The corporate budget. Obviously, the managers of all functional areas of an organization should provide input to the corporate budget in terms of the resources needed by their departments to fulfill their assigned functions. They do that by preparing a departmental budget. However, the potential contributions of the HR manager go far beyond presenting the HR department budget.

All budget decisions, no matter which department or function is concerned, ultimately have an effect on the people who work there. Part of the HR manager's job is to bring the "people" aspects of budget issues to the attention of the decision makers, to influence decisions that affect human resources.

To be an effective advocate for HR interests in the budgeting process, the HR manager must operate from a base of credibility. And credibility is built on four foundations:

1. The HR department, its manager, and its people demonstrate their professionalism and leadership by emphasizing performance instead of power, risk taking in lieu of the sure thing, and service rather than prestige.
2. The HR department demonstrates dedication to, and achieves results in, supporting the mission, purpose, goals, and objectives of the organization as a whole.
3. The HR department actively markets programs and services within the organization, by determining what organizational elements need and then meeting those needs.
4. The HR manager and staff are knowledgeable about budgeting principles and the company's budgeting policies.

The credibility of the HR department is never automatically granted; it must be earned.

■ ■

FINANCE IS NOT A FOREIGN LANGUAGE

Here are some key financial terms that HR managers need to understand.

profit. A common financial objective, profit is the excess of income, returns, or gains over expenditures during a specified period of time.

profitability. Another common financial objective, one that focuses on the ability of a firm to produce or create new wealth. It exists when there is a probability (or even a possibility) that resources can be used to yield economic values or outputs that are higher or greater than the combined values of the inputs required to produce them.

return on investment (ROI). Return on invested capital, measured as the ratio of reported income to balance sheet book value. ROI has two components: rate of turnover of total assets and rate of earnings per dollar of sales.

cash flow. Funds derived from operations. It refers to the movement of cash in and out. It is a useful measure of a change in liquidity (convertibility of assets to cash or negotiable instruments).

cash budget. An analysis of the flow of cash in a company over a short or long time frame. It is a forecast of expected cash intake and outlay. It is not an operating statement or an income statement.

balance sheet. A financial document that presents a picture of the status of a company. It essentially presents a comparison of the assets and liabilities of the firm at a given point, usually at the end of an accounting period.

assets. Items (usually tangible and purchased, and backed up by an invoice) owned by a company. They typically include cash and bank deposits, marketable securities, accounts receivable, inventories, investments in other companies, land, plant, and equipment, and sometimes goodwill or other intangibles, all stated on the basis of purchase prices and not on current or market values.

liabilities. Sources of assets, such as accounts payable, and retained earnings, current portion of long-term debt, accrued expenses and income taxes, stockholders' equity (stock issued), and reserve accounts (such as self-insurance, contingency funds, and funds for lawsuits).

profit and loss statement. A financial statement prepared at the end of an accounting period, which provides an indication of the performance of the company's assets during that period. It is a measure of the productivity of the firm's assets.

■ ■

The departmental budget. Within their own departments, HR managers are the budget officers. They must prepare the department's budget, present and defend it to top management, and manage its operation throughout the year.

The first step is to draw up the department's annual budget, using projections from subordinate department managers. Budget preparation must be based on continuous scrutiny of HR programs, operating methods, organization structure, and facilities. It must always be preceded by HR plans, and it must be applied within a framework of corporate and HR goals and objectives.

Preparing the budget is one challenge; getting top management approval is another. Managers in all departments compete with one another for their share of limited company resources. They must be able to justify their requirements clearly and convincingly or fail the competition. The HR manager is the only one who has the stature and knowledge to present the HR department budget to the decision maker authoritatively and persuasively, and win approval.

The budget, once approved and adopted, is not relegated to the filing cabinet. It becomes a management tool. Managers must continuously monitor the budget throughout the year and ensure that policies and rules are followed. And they must be alert to the need for budget adjustments and reprogramming as conditions change.

Key Concepts

Budgeting is a complex science. There are six different basic approaches in use today, and dozens of different types. More than likely you, the HR manager, will not have the discretion to choose which type and which approach to use when you submit your budget to the financial office. Standardization across the company's departments and staff offices is necessary. However, that should not prevent you from applying another approach (in addition to the standard corporate approach) within your department to enable you to achieve better control of your own budget.

Basic Budgeting Approaches

Program budgeting. This system deals principally with broad planning and the costs of programs and services. A great number of detailed cost estimates are distilled into a few categories, each of which represents an objective. The goals and objectives of the organization are defined, and programs are established to achieve them. Each program is broken down into activities, which are costed out and evaluated, and funds are allocated to programs based on benefit-cost analyses. Costs and accomplishments are closely tracked.

For example, the training and development portion of the HR budget may be divided into such categories as executive development, management development, presupervisory training, scientist and engineer development, technical and skills training, safety training, clerical training, and the like. Decision makers can then compare the effort to be made on each category and decide whether to continue, cancel, or modify.

This approach can be used in all areas except direct manufacturing activities.

Incremental budgeting. This system assumes that prior funding levels are required for continued operations, that this year's costs will be at least the same as last year's. New or expanded activities (plus inflation) are evaluated in terms of the costs they add to the prior year's budget. Those incremental costs, and the benefits to be derived, are studied before additional expenditures are authorized.

Incremental budgeting works best in operations where costs are tightly controlled and programs are stable.

Performance budgeting. This approach begins where program budgeting stops. It involves measuring units of work (development hours, instructor platform hours) and output (training programs produced or trainees completing a program) and relating those measures to the amount of input (resources) required.

At the time of budget preparation, output—performance—is compared to input, giving the HR manager important information about efficient use of available resources. To illustrate, just as cost accounting can find the production cost of each dozen widgets, an HR manager can compute cost per presupervisory trainee, cost per trainee hour, or cost per program hour. Actual expenditures can be compared to keep subordinates on target. The performance in those figures is *results*, not merely that employees appeared at their work stations long enough to collect paychecks.

This approach is applicable to situations where costs tend to vary directly with levels of activity and the resulting activity outputs. Work units must be clearly definable and measurable, and systems must be in place to track and tabulate activity volumes.

Flexible budgeting. This system is used to identify how costs should change when output increases or decreases. Flexible budgets require that costs be analyzed and identified as fixed, variable, or semivariable in relation to volume and activity. Authorized expense levels for actual levels of output are set, and variations are analyzed to determine causes.

This approach may be used as a basis for cost control in most areas of business operations; it requires reasonably sophisticated tracking systems.

Planning, programming, budgeting system (PPBS). This approach stresses a longer-term view than more conventional budgets, typically five years, so that it takes account of the costs of present programs in future years. Each major program is analyzed; alternative methods of reaching the same goals and objectives are compared; and ways to minimize cost and maximize return on investment are identified. PPBS, then, is essentially a problem-solving approach in which the manager considers objectives, alternatives, full costs, and future implications.

It is important to note here that although benefit-cost analysis is a valuable tool, it has at least one major limitation in an HR organization. Many of the major HR costs are discretionary—a matter of organizational or managerial choice—and the benefits are not always directly measurable. So the HR manager must often resort to some form of subjective measure of benefits.

Zero-base budgeting (ZBB). Rather than using the previous year's funding levels as a base, ZBB starts with zero, and all activities compete equally for funding. "Decision packages" (definitions of costs, benefits, and alternatives for each activity increment) are developed and ranked by priority; performance measurement and monitoring procedures are set. The approach is highly participative and requires that goals, objectives, and priorities be established for each budget unit. Organizational elements are compelled to justify every item and every dollar in their annual budget request.

Although all six approaches have been used in HR departments, ZBB is the most effective; standard costing, traditional budgeting techniques, and benefit-cost analysis simply do not work well in service functions. The ZBB process is rigorous and time-consuming, but it provides significant benefits in addition to cost control. Properly designed and implemented, ZBB can provide improved linkages between resource allocations and results, encourage staff commitment to specific objectives, enhance the competitive status of the HR department in the allocation of enterprise resources, improve interaction in the decision-making process, enhance planning and control, and provide better feedback to managers and staff.

Types of Budgets

Literally dozens of specific types of budgets exist, but the budgets of HR departments usually fall into two or more of the following four basic categories. As with the budget approaches, you will probably not have the freedom to choose a type for your department. Company policy will probably require you to provide an operating budget because it identifies line items of expense for a companywide tracking and control system. From time to time you may also have to prepare time, space, and materials budgets, which are typically required to support proposals for major programs, and capital expense budgets, which are for major construction or equipment procurement. The actual contents of all types of budgets are outlined in Figure 3-1.

Operating budgets. Operating budgets deal with individual items of expense: salaries and wages, direct labor, supervision, contractual services, utilities (water, heat, power, telephone), rentals and leases, repair of equipment, materials and stock, office and classroom supplies, travel, tuition, conference and membership fees, insurance premiums, and so on.

Time, space, and materials budgets. These are expressed in physical or nonfinancial, rather than monetary, terms, although they can usually be translated into dollar values. Common line items include direct-labor hours, technician, clerical, consultant, trainer, or trainee hours, equipment hours, units of material, square feet of floor space, number of personnel trained, and person-hours or person-days of training.

Capital expense budgets. These deal with capital expenditures—new, upgraded, rehabilitated, or replacement facilities or equipment for which a predetermined dollar value has been fixed and which have a relatively long life expectancy. Budgets for constructing or improving physical plant and facilities (buildings, classrooms, laboratories, conference rooms, shops, libraries, and office space), furniture and furnishings, and equipment fall into this category. Capital expense budgets require long-term planning and a commitment for an extended period (five years or longer) to amortize costs or recover the investment.

Cash budgets. These are forecasts of cash receipts and disbursements against which actual cash experience is compared and measured. This type of budget is particularly important because

Figure 3-1.   Outline of budget contents.

For All Types of Budgets

Statement of goals and objectives
Organization chart
Details of budget items, including justification for each
Department/staff element summary
Signature of department/element head

For Operating Budgets

Receipts
    Depository interest
    Tuition
    Rentals
    Sale of equipment
    Sale of training materials
    Sale of services
    Other income
Cost categories (expenditures)
    Direct costs (salaries, wages, benefits, materials, supplies, consultant fees, utilities, and the like)
    Indirect costs (expenses associated with program development and support activities and services)
    General operating costs (staff training and development, travel and conference attendance, and so on)

For Capital Budgets (long term)

(Includes land, buildings construction or procurement, equipment and furnishings, R&D, major systems development, and significant manpower development programs)
For *each* project
    Internal rate of return
    Payback (in years)
    Net present value
    Date of completion
    Estimated total cost

For Capital Budgets (annual)

For *each* project (in dollars)
    Expenditures from inception to date
    Budget for the current year
    Estimated expenditures for future years
    Estimated total costs at completion
    Original cost
    Project variance

cash must be available in most businesses to meet obligations as they fall due.

Manufacturing vs. Service Industry Budgets

The budget is influenced by the orientation of the enterprise. Most manufacturing organizations are *output-oriented,* so budget preparation is preceded by a sales forecast. Most service organizations are *capabilities-oriented;* they emphasize types and quality of services, rather than the number of services provided, and therefore their budgets are tied to the nature, timeliness, and effectiveness of those services. (A third type is represented by public and private educational, social service, and philanthropic organizations. They are more *input-oriented,* simply because their income is derived from tuition, charges, investments, endowments, and contributions. They can adjust their charges to keep programs and services consistent with available resources.)

Manufacturing budgets and service industry budgets are very different. The budgets of manufacturing firms emphasize inventory, equipment, and standardized products; service industry organizations focus on product on demand, labor, and nonstandardized products.

Although it may appear that HR departments most closely resemble service organizations in their orientation (they do offer services and are concerned about the quality of those services), in actuality they are closer to production organizations. The reason is that a company's human resources—the people who are hired, assigned, motivated, trained, developed, compensated, and led as a part of the HR system—can be viewed as products that will make for greater production, more and better services, and, ultimately, higher profits and return on investment. In that sense, HR activities, programs, and services are output-oriented. When employee records are coupled with forecasts of HR needs, they can be used to develop realistic personnel input figures so that output requirements of the system are met. For that reason, product-centered budgeting and cost-accounting procedures are applicable to HR departments and activities.

In HR budgeting, the basic enigma is balancing relatively fixed resources with variable requirements, and the added problems posed by incremental costs on the one hand, and on the other, thresholds imposed by top management on increases in fixed costs. Input cannot always be adjusted to balance resources and costs unless the organization is willing to pay the price—inadequate HR programs and services that will not support the company's goals and objectives. Historically, during periods of austerity caused by deteriorating business conditions, the training and development budget, which has great cost visibility, has been the first to be cut. Why this area in particular? Because the relationship between training and development and maximum profit, maximum cost benefits, or more efficient services has not been established—at least not to the satisfaction of top management. That shortcoming must be remedied.

Mastering the Budget Maneuvers

You have to know the mechanics of preparing budgets, and understand the philosophies underlying the various approaches and types. You have to become conversant in the language of finance, and comfortable with the numbers side of running a business unit. But in addition to increasing your technical expertise in these areas, you must also become knowledgeable in the more subtle aspects of the budgeting process. You must learn how to recognize budget games that others play, and how to sidestep potential minefields.

Common Pitfalls

Budget problems exist in many HR departments. All too often, people within and outside the HR department play budget games. Other problems are traceable to pitfalls that the unwary HR manager has stepped into. Here are the most common.

Abdicating budget responsibility. HR managers who abdicate their responsibility for budget preparation to the controller or financial department do themselves and their organizations a disservice. The chief financial officer will usually have some authority over all budgetary matters, perhaps even functional authority. Yet it is an unusual controller who really understands HR as a function, and even that rare person has no responsibility for achieving the results HR managers are expected to accomplish. HR managers should use the expertise of their financial officers and get their advice and assistance, but they should never rely on them to prepare their budgets for them.

Excessive budget detail. Too much detail makes a budget cumbersome, expensive, and overly restrictive—a straitjacket rather than a blueprint. It produces administrative nightmares and imposes unnecessary, unproductive operational procedures on those responsible for checking compliance with corporate budget policy. It limits flexibility and responsiveness to changing requirements. A good budget is not an instrument of restriction.

Precedent. Allowing precedent to determine the distribution of available resources subverts good budgeting and, in turn, sabotages efforts to provide effective HR programs. Just because an item was carried in earlier budgets is no justification for including it in future budgets. Nor is the fact that the budget contains an item never before included grounds for deleting the item. Budget line items should be judged on their own merits. If they are reasonable, consistent with goals and objectives, and essential to attaining those objectives, they should be included.

Obstinacy or tunnel vision. To allow budget considerations—particularly restrictive policies and procedures related to use of resources—to override HR goals and objectives defeats the whole purpose of budgeting. For example, some organizations have adopted policies that spell out in excruciating detail the steps that are required to reprogram funds. The steps resemble an obstacle course more than a clearly defined direct route to reprogramming decisions. Other procedures are clearly designed to deny managers the decision-making prerogatives they need to manage effectively. That kind of shortsightedness makes the budget a checkrein rather than a governor. The HR manager has an obligation to bring such obstacles to the attention of the chief financial officer—and, if necessary, to the CEO. Complaints won't suffice; managers must show how the policies impede action.

Mandated budget cuts and bumps. During periods of business decline or financial emergency, many businesses take the drastic step of imposing across-the-board budget cuts. Conversely, when business is booming, top management is faced with the pleasant task of deciding what to do with the profits and sometimes bumps all budgets by a certain percentage.

Neither across-the-board cuts nor bumps should happen. Using a straight percentage increase or decrease to last year's budget as the basic technique is dead wrong. Budget cuts and increases should be based on full consideration of needs and options. Ideally, provisions should be built into the budget to deal with either eventuality—in the form of alternative budgets for bear and bull markets, or contingency "slash" and "boost" lists, each arranged in priority order. Here again, HR managers have no control, but they do have an obligation to try to persuade the chief financial officer to adopt the alternative budget approach.

Throwing budget curve balls. There are countless ways to mislead or deceive decision makers. The arsenal of tricksters is replete with stratagems designed to outwit and delude superiors into believing that managers are on top of their jobs and performing well, maybe better than expected. One of the favorite contrivances is to underestimate sales and overestimate costs. Another is deliberately overestimating the number of participants in a tuition reimbursement or other program and budgeting funds accordingly—a devious means of trying to look good at the end of the year when costs are "saved."

"Spend it or lose it." In many organizations, the homespun philosophy of "spend it or lose it" prevails. Managers, supervisors, staffers, technicians, or others who have the authority to obligate or commit funds have come to the conclusion that any funds that remain unspent at the end of a quarter or the budget year will be reallocated or diverted to another department. Even worse, the conventional wisdom (or past experience) says that if you received an allocation in this year's budget and didn't spend all of it, next year's budget will be reduced by at least the unspent amount.

Padding and hiding. Some other examples of budget folklore: "They'll cut it, so inflate it," or "Conceal it for contingencies." Padding or hiding specific budget line items tends to place the whole budget in question. If the padding is detected—and it probably will be—your credibility will be undermined. The cure is simple: never reward or punish subordinate program managers for either spending their total allocations or returning funds at the end of a budget period. Base your rewards on results achieved, and your admonishments on failure to follow policy and procedures.

Inflexibility. Events often dictate a need for larger or smaller amounts than were originally allocated—changes in the law, for example, or realignment of priorities. Budgets must have a reasonable degree of flexibility, to adjust to such contingencies. The old saw "It's not in the budget" should not be used as the sole justification for denying requests to reallocate funds or make upward adjustments.

Lack of controls. If significant overspending or underspending occurs, budget controls are inadequate. Deviations from planned expenditures should be allowed; but when they are appreciably over or under, they must be completely justified. As much as possible, policies and procedures for handling unplanned expenditures and for adjusting committed funds should be spelled out in writing.

Formula for a Good Budget

Taking into account all we have discussed about the technical knowledge, plus all the subtler operational pitfalls, we can summarize the characteristics of successful budgets.

- *Deals with the long range* (known in some circles as the look-ahead principle). Seat-of-the-pants financial management can only result in substandard programs and missed opportunities. A five-year financial plan, supporting the long-range goals of the department, must be formulated.
- *Considers the full environment* (also known as the cover-the-waterfront principle). The aforesaid long-range plan must take into account all the possible forces: demographic trends, economic forecasts, new markets, organizational changes, company expansion or diversification, projected changes in product and process, new equipment, marketing plans and sales forecasts, prospective staffing policies, personnel needs (numbers, types, and skills), training and development requirements, and desired auxiliary and support services.
- *Reflects a sound forecast* (the crystal-ball principle). Complete, accurate forecasts make for realistic budgets. Forecasting HR requirements is difficult and demanding, but crucial. (Review Chapter 1 for more on forecasting.)
- *Addresses fully developed programs* (the all-bases-touched principle). Hazy programs are totally inadequate foundations for good budgets. You can prepare solid, detailed budgets only when plans and programs are completely worked out.
- *Involves the entire staff* (the bread-spreading principle). There is no better way to get subordinate managers' commitment to managing the budget throughout the year than to have them participate in developing it at budget time.
- *Follows—rather than precedes—programming* (the wellspring principle). Budgets have to be derived from the programs they fund—not the other way around. The practice of first setting an amount of money and then deciding how to divide it up among the department's programs is self-defeating. If that prescribed amount is imposed from top management,

programs will suffer. As before, the solution lies in convincing management that funding should follow program decisions. If that fails, the HR manager can only do his or her best to allocate funds according to each program's priority.

- *Is realistic and achievable* (the do-ability principle). It makes little sense to establish a list of desired results that can never be attained. On the other hand, reaching objectives should not be *too* easy; a judicious amount of stretching is good.
- *Allows for flexibility* (the roll-with-the punches principle). The budget must never be so rigid that it prevents timely decisions in response to change. No manager is clairvoyant enough to foresee everything that might be needed during one budget period, and so she must be given a way to make adjustments as needed.

The Budget Process

Developing a budget actually occurs in three main phases: planning (Steps 1, 2, and 3), preparation (Steps 4 and 5), and control (Steps 6, 7, and 8). Two factors will make this complex process much simpler: sufficient time, and clear areas of responsibility and authority. There will be various deadlines throughout, and you must be sure to allow enough time for review and discussion at each step along the way.

Also, be sure it is clearly defined (preferably in writing) exactly who does what, and make sure all your staff members understand it. The controller or chief financial officer should develop a budget calendar, prescribe procedures, and provide guidance for preparing the budget, for internal control, and for review and analysis. The HR manager (with help from the finance office and contributions from HR staff) prepares the budget and presents it for approval. The financial officer reviews draft budget submissions for accuracy, completeness, and conformance to corporate policies. The HR manager is responsible for monitoring and regulating department expenditures after the budget has been approved. And the controller or financial department reviews budget execution reports.

Step 1. Develop (or review) the long-range financial plan. Five-year plans for the organization as a whole are developed by the chief financial officer, with input from department and line managers. Then all department heads review the corporate financial plan, extract from it the elements that belong to their function, and develop five-year plans for their departments. The departmental plans reflect the department's long-range goals, which in turn reflect the goals of the whole organization.

The long-range HR financial plan must be based on full consideration of all factors:

1. Accurate forecasts of personnel and other types of requirements
2. Current programs, services, and priorities
3. Anticipated organizational changes
4. Projected changes in products, processes, equipment, and services
5. New programs, projects, and strategies
6. Expected procurement, renovation, or replacement of facilities, equipment, or materials
7. Prospective staffing policies

A five-year plan is reviewed in years 2, 3, 4, and 5, and adjusted if need be.

Step 2. Set goals and objectives. Based on the current five-year plan, establish goals and objectives for this year's budget. The task here is twofold. First, determine the nature and direction the budget is to take—the purposes the budget is to serve for the organization, its managers, and its people—stated as goals. For example, one goal might be "To improve the quality of work life for all employees." Second, define the objectives the budget for the forthcoming year is to support—the specific, measurable things the budget is to accomplish. One objective might be stated as "To reduce the costs of employee travel by 10 percent."

Step 3. Establish procedures and schedule. The company's financial officer will probably prescribe the type of budgets you must prepare—operating expense; time, space, and materials; capital expense; or cash—and the approach you will use. If this happens not to be the case in your organization, here you will evaluate the six approaches and four types, and choose the ones most appropriate for your department. In any case, if the corporate approach is program or incremental budgeting, you can also apply the performance or zero-base budgeting approaches within your department to get a better handle on the budget.

The actual format of the budget, its composition and manner of presentation, will undoubtedly be established by the corporate finance office. Study this format; make sure you and your staff understand it and know how to work with it.

Work out a calendar and see to it that it is followed during the entire budgeting process. Include dates when subordinate managers will provide you with their budget input, dates for discussion of various elements, and dates when their final submissions are due.

Now is the time to set up procedures for the reports you will prepare during the budget year as part of your control responsibility. And finally, make provision for a way to revise the budget during the year if needed, and explain the revision guidelines to the staff.

Step 4. Prepare the department's budget. First, the key people in the HR department prepare draft budgets for their areas of responsibility. Give them specific and detailed instructions on how to prepare their contributions; review with them the company's format; check periodically to judge progress and avoid confusion. As an example, Figure 3-2 shows a budget format for the training and development section.

If a zero-base budgeting approach is used, each element's budget submission should include as a minimum:

1. A statement of goals and objectives
2. Details of budget items by cost category
3. A priority listing of projects, programs, and services
4. A statement of impacts if specific cost categories are reduced or disapproved
5. Cost savings or benefits associated with each program or major budget item

Decision packages should be prepared for each discrete activity, program, and service, both current and new, and they should be evaluated and ranked in order of importance through benefit-cost analyses or some other systematic method of evaluation.

If the HR department has sources of revenue (funds not appropriated by the corporation), they should be identified in the budget. Examples are tuition receipts, rental income, and sales of training materials.

To simplify the mechanics of the process, there are now computer programs available (such as Lotus 1-2-3) that can develop effective budgets with fixed, variable, semivariable, and discretionary cost elements; develop, debug, protect, and document budget worksheets; and present budget results. And there are specialized computer programs for individual applications. For example, a

Figure 3-2.   A sample training and development budget form.

Company	Department	Location
Prepared by	Approved by	Date

I. Receipts

Items	Receipts Last FY	Receipts This FY	Estimated Receipts Next FY
1. Depository interest 2. Tuition 3. Rentals 4. Sale of equipment 5. Sale of training materials 6. Sale of training services 7. Other Total			

II. Expenditures

Items	Expend FY 1990	Expend FY 1991	Allot FY 1992	Expend FY 1992	Req. FY 1993	Allot FY 1993

1. General administration
  a. Salary, training manager
  b. Salaries, office force
  c. Office supplies
  d. Other
    Total						

2. Instruction
  a. Salaries, instructor-supervisors
  b. Salaries, instructors
  c. Instructional supplies
  d. Instructional equipment
  e. Contractual services
  f. Other
    Total						

3. Operation of the training facility
  a. Wages, custodians
  b. Contractual services
  c. Fuel
  d. Utilities
  e. Telephone
  f. Other
    Total						

Items	Expend FY 1990	Expend FY 1991	Allot FY 1992	Expend FY 1992	Req. FY 1993	Allot FY 1993
4. Maintenance of training facility						
a. Repair of building(s)						
b. Repair of grounds						
c. Repair of equipment						
d. Other						
Total						
5. Fixed charges						
a. Retirement and social security						
b. Insurance						
c. Rent						
d. Other						
Total						
6. Capital outlay						
a. Land						
b. Buildings						
c. Alteration of buildings						
d. Equipment						
e. Other						
Total						
7. Instructional-support services						
a. Library						
(1). Salaries						
(2). Books						
(3). Periodicals						
(4). Equipment						
(5). Supplies						
(6). Other						
Total						
b. Training aids						
(1). Salaries						
(2). Materials						
(3). Equipment						
(4). Other						
Total						
c. Tuition and fees						
d. Contractual services						
e. Travel and per diem						
f. Conference fees						
g. Professional memberships						
h. Other						
Total						
Grand Total						

budgeting program for training and development can set up budgets for all training activities, perform cost projections, report "actuals" and variations, modify budget allocations, provide cost breakdowns by course, instructor, participant, or department, and evaluate the impact of training budget cuts on organizational effectiveness.

After receiving draft materials from subordinate elements, the HR manager reviews objectives, resource requirements, and resources available, and then prepares a consolidated department budget. This draft document is then sent to subordinate managers for review. They have the opportunity to justify and reclaim deleted items and to discuss the proposed final budget submission. The final numbers are negotiated with subordinate managers.

Usually, the completed draft budget is submitted to another office (central accounting, internal auditing, or financial) for a check of accuracy, completeness, and conformance to corporate formats.

Step 5. Present the budget for approval. Typically, approval is a two-step process. A corporate budget committee, composed of the chief financial officer and heads of other functions, conducts a budget meeting (or a series of meetings), hearing presentations from all department heads, and then makes recommendations to the senior executive. Sometimes the CEO is part of the budget committee, and the final decision is made by the board of directors. In any case, the HR manager's task is to present and defend the department's budget in the most effective way possible.

Essentially, the budget meeting is a decision briefing, and the objective is to obtain a favorable verdict on the HR department's budget submission. A top-notch presentation is critical. That involves several important considerations when you plan your pitch.

- *Keep it brief.* Save the decision maker's time by using concise, simple statements, eliminating excessive words, repetitions, and jargon. Make sure that every statement is important enough to demand inclusion.
- *Keep the decision maker's needs in mind.* Tell only what he or she needs to know to accomplish his job. Try to anticipate probable questions and include the answers in your presentation.
- *Use restraint;* avoid exaggeration.
- *Interpret as well as tell the facts.* Prove the "why" of the facts and lead into the recommended action.
- *Be direct.* Get to the point right away. And stick to the subject.
- *Be thorough.* Make the presentation sufficiently comprehensive

to preclude the need for supplementary explanations or followup requests for additional information.

Step 6. Monitor and report expenditures. The first step in budget control is to establish guidelines for department spending and reporting. Set monthly or quarterly spending targets and dollar limits. Have your section managers prepare expenditure reports at least monthly. Subordinate managers must be held responsible for adhering to those guidelines and accountable for maintaining control over their budget accounts.

Throughout the budget year, the HR manager is responsible for preparing these reports:

- Estimated (budgeted) expenses for the various elements under their control, such as personnel, training and development, and so on.
- Operating reports, usually monthly or quarterly, showing in detail the actual costs along with the budgeted figures.
- Analytical reports showing the breakdown of costs in each element of the department. The training and development manager, for example, may prepare a report showing the costs per trainee or training costs per hour.
- Special reports (most are surveys), prepared at the request of some corporate official or initiated by HR managers in an attempt to improve some phase of their responsibility. For example, a report may be prepared comparing the costs of in-house and outside training.

If budget report formats are well designed, they group costs into categories so that results can be analyzed fairly and efficiently. That makes review of both corporate reports, and the feeder reports submitted to the HR manager by subordinate elements, easy to read and digest. The important thing is that HR managers must take early action on variances, revise estimates of results, or make corrections to prevent additional variations.

Step 7. Conduct quarterly review and analysis. Review and analysis is a control technique used by HR managers to identify and report status, trends, deficiencies, progress, and results to top management and subordinate managers.

There are two basic types of review and analysis: vertical (dealing with one activity or element) and composite (departmentwide). Vertical review and analysis is functional in nature; for example, the review and analysis performed by the manager of the training and development unit in the HR department is a vertical review. Composite review and analysis refers to the evaluation of the HR department's operating program as a whole. The HR manager does the composite review, using the vertical reviews prepared by subordinate managers.

The HR department review and analysis should focus on programs and activities that have a direct bearing on the accomplishment of the HR mission, and it should measure that accomplishment against previously determined objectives. Deviations must be analyzed to determine causes and to evaluate their impact on the HR mission. And, of course, the review and analysis should indicate the actions that have been taken, or will be, to solve the problem.

Step 8. Take corrective actions. Correcting means improving performance. It involves taking action to bring variances into line with plans. Corrective actions depend on the causes of the deviations, and so they can be minor or major, involving special audits or other drastic measures such as the termination of the responsible manager.

Identifying what is wrong is one thing; getting it fixed is quite another. The human element is usually the most critical factor in correction—just as the causes of deviations are usually human in origin. Here are a few suggestions:

- Don't make it necessary for subordinate managers to advertise their failures. Provide them with the means of self-correction so that they can identify and remedy their own deficiencies.
- Correct important deviations first. Small deviations should not receive the same priority. If everything is treated as equally critical, your people will be unable to separate the important from the routine.
- Avoid being dogmatic or arbitrary when deciding what to do. Give your people an opportunity to decide what actions are most appropriate; they are often in the best position to do just that.
- Don't allow staffers, consultants, or your boss to influence your actions too greatly. Their perspectives are likely to be quite different from yours, perhaps even out of line with the realities of the situation.
- Don't procrastinate. Postponing a decision too long often has the effect of eliminating the need for it. That is management by default. It is far better to take action, even if short of the ideal, than be indecisive.

- Avoid precipitate action. Corrective action must be properly timed; take into account the prevailing climate and the readiness of individuals affected by a decision to accept it.
- Take the difficult action when it is necessary. Apply disciplinary measures when they are needed.

Summary

Budgets define areas of activity and accountability, provide needed detail to organizational goals and objectives, and provide the tools managers need to monitor and control performance. Without a firm grasp of programming and budgeting concepts and techniques in general and of the specific budgeting practices of their organizations—and the willingness to apply them—HR managers cannot fulfill their responsibilities. To put it bluntly, managers who cannot perform budgeting tasks cannot manage.

The annual HR budget must be based on a long-range financial plan. And that plan should include full consideration of forecasts of needs, planned organizational changes and realignment, new products, processes, or services, and the impact of such changes on HR programs and services.

To compete successfully with other managers for a share of the funding resources available, HR managers must identify their funding requirements completely and accurately. Unless they prepare and successfully defend their budgets, the funds needed to operate a complete menu of HR programs and services will not be allocated. But the budgeting process must also be sufficiently flexible to accommodate reprogramming or reallocation of resources when that is required by such uncontrollable factors as emergencies or changes in economic conditions.

Although all forms of programming and budgeting have been used in HR organization, zero-base budgeting is potentially the most useful and appropriate. Regardless of the budgeting approach adopted, HR managers, in addition to providing input to the corporate budget, must prepare, present, defend, manage, and control their own department budget. The HR programs and services needed to support the operations of the total organization, its continued viability, and its success in achieving its mission and purposes hangs in the balance.

The steps in the budgeting process are:

1. Develop a long-range financial plan.
2. Set goals and objectives.

3. Establish procedures and schedule.
4. Prepare the department's budget.
5. Present the budget for approval.
6. Monitor and report expenditures.
7. Conduct review and analysis.
8. Take corrective action.

For Further Reading, Viewing, and Listening

Alves, Jeffrey R., and J. David Maupin. *Controlling Financial Performance: Lotus 1-2-3 on the DEC Rainbow.* Bedford, Mass.: Digital Press, 1985.

Amey, Lloyd R. *Budget Planning and Control Systems.* Marshfield, Mass.: Pitman Publishing, 1979.

The Balance Sheet Barrier (30-minute videocassette). Video Arts, Northbrook Tech Center, 4088 Commercial Ave., Northbrook, IL 60062, 1984.

Bell, Chip R. "How Training Departments Win Budget Battles." *Training and Development Journal,* September 1983, pp. 42–49.

Blecke, Curtis J., and Daniel L. Gotthif. *Financial Analysis for Decision-Making.* Englewood Cliffs, N.J.: Prentice-Hall, 1980.

Budgeting (30-minute videocassette). Video Arts, Northbrook Tech Center, 4088 Commercial Ave., Northbrook, IL 60062, 1984.

Camillus, John C. *Budgeting for Profit: How to Exploit the Potential of Your Business.* Radnor, Penn.: Chilton Book Company, 1984.

Clark, Grover M., and Jeanette Perlman. "Budgeting for Human Resources Systems." Chapter 8 in *Human Resources Management and Development Handbook,* edited by William R. Tracey. New York: AMACOM, 1985.

Coleman, A. R., and others. *Financial Accounting for Management.* Old Tappan, N.J.: Reston Publishing Company, 1983.

Controlling Financial Performance With Multiplan. Chesterland, Ohio: Weber Systems, 1983.

Curtin, Dennis P., and others. *Controlling Financial Performance: A 1-2-3 Business User's Guide.* Chesterland, Ohio: Weber Systems, 1983.

———— and Jeffrey Alves. *Controlling Financial Performance: An IBM-PC Business User's Guide.* Marblehead, Mass.: Curtin & London, 1983.

————. *Controlling Financial Performance: Apple Business User's Guide.* Marblehead, Mass.: Curtin & London, 1983.

Droms, William G. *Finance and Accounting for Non-Financial Managers.* Reading, Mass.: Addison-Wesley Publishing Company, 1983.

Finance and Accounting for Managers: Key Concepts, Part I (Service Industries Version) (individualized, computer-based lesson). LEARNCOM, 215 First St., Cambridge, MA 02142, 1987.

Finance and Accounting for Nonfinancial Managers (6-hour audiocassette). American Management Association Extension Institute, 135 West 50th St., New York, NY 10020, 1987.

Frederiksen, Christian P. *Budgeting for Nonprofits.* San Francisco: Public Management Institute, 1980.

Fundamentals of Budgeting (audiocassette and workbook). American Management Association Extension Institute, 135 West 50th St., New York, NY 10020, 1979.

Jones, Reginald L., and H. George Trentin. *Budgeting: Key to Planning and Control.* Rev. ed. New York: AMACOM, 1980.

Kristy, James E., and Susan Z. Diamond. *Finance Without Fear.* New York: AMACOM, 1984.

Long, J., ed. *Budgeting Know-How.* New York: Cambridge Book Company, 1987.

Merchant, Kenneth A. *Control in Business Organizations.* Cambridge, Mass.: Ballinger Publishing Company, 1985.

Murti, V. G. *Budgeting: A Guide for Practicing Managers.* New York: Apt Books, 1984.

Perry, William. *Controlling the Bottom Line.* New York: Van Nostrand Reinhold, 1984.

Ramsey, Jackson E., and Inez L. Ramsey. *Budgeting Basics: How to Survive the Budgeting Process.* New York: Watts, 1985.

Sord, B. H., and G. A. Welsch. *Business Budgeting: A Survey of Managerial Planning and Control Practices.* New York: Controllership Foundation, 1958.

Spiro, Herbert T. *Finance for the Non-Financial Manager.* 2nd ed. New York: John Wiley & Sons, 1982.

Sweeny, Allen, and John N. Wisener. *Budgeting Fundamentals for Nonfinancial Executives.* New York: AMACOM, 1976.

Sweeny, H. W. Allen, and Robert Rachlin, eds. *Handbook of Budgeting.* New York: John Wiley & Sons, 1987.

Vale, Philip. *Financial Management Handbook.* 3rd ed. Brookfield, Vt.: Gower Publishing Company, 1987.

Vinter, Robert D., and Rhea K. Kish. *Budgeting for Not-for-Profit Organizations.* New York: Free Press, 1984.

Welsch, Glenn A. *Budgeting: Profit, Planning and Control.* 5th ed. Englewood Cliffs, N.J.: Prentice-Hall, 1988.

Wildavsky, Aaron, ed. *Budgeting: A Comparative Theory of Budgetary Processes.* New Brunswick, N.J.: Transaction Books, 1985.

4

Marketing

Cultivating Clients and Customers

Too many HR managers run their departments like service stations. They wait for customers and clients to come in with a request for assistance, advice, training, or some other service. But HR departments are not service stations, and no HR manager can afford to be a passive respondent. The high costs of developing HR programs dictate that today's manager actively seek out customers, both internal and external. And that means marketing.

Providing HR programs and services is a people-intensive activity, and the kinds of people involved in providing those programs and services are largely well educated and highly skilled. That adds up to high costs. Beyond costs, there is the imperative of need. HR programs have become an indispensable part of organizational life. They are not frills or luxuries. Without them no organization can remain viable, let alone prosper, in today's highly complex and competitive world.

For those reasons, HR managers must become marketers and competitors—entrepreneurs who aggressively and actively sell their products within their own companies and often to outside customers. Internally, they must ensure that the products and services provided by their departments are fully used, to gain maximum return for the time and resources invested in them. Externally, sometimes HR managers can market some of their products and services to other companies, and in this way can amortize the high costs of producing them for in-house use.

In brief, marketing means going to your customers, finding out what they need, developing a product to meet that need, advertising the product to the people who need it, selling the product, and then delivering it on schedule. All that can be difficult for HR managers, because it requires values and skills not typically found in their repertoires.

Your professional HR expertise can carry you only so far in your role as a marketer. To succeed, you must know how to prospect for clients, both internally and externally, generate leads, get your name and talents known, build your clientele, present a proposal, structure a contract, land profitable accounts, and maintain customer satisfaction.

What Is Marketing, Anyway?

Marketing is easy to define—and easy to confuse. It is not the same as sales, although some people use the two terms interchangeably. It is not the same as advertising. Marketing takes a much broader perspective: the entire process of moving goods from producer to consumer. Advertising is just one part of that overall process. And so is selling. Think of it this way: marketing is long-range product planning remote from the point of sale; selling is usually conducted face to face. Marketing creates the climate in which selling can be effective.

Those who would succeed at marketing must keep one cardinal rule firmly in mind: People do not buy products or services. What they really buy are the benefits they expect those products to provide—the solutions to their problems. Thus, marketing means establishing a relationship between a product and its potential customers, promoting the product on the basis of a set of needs that the customers already have, know they have, or can be encouraged to discover they have.

To put it another way, marketing is the process of finding out what people need or want and then getting it to them—or identifying the people who need what you have and making sure that they *know* they need it, and then getting it to them. It involves research about customers. It involves research about competitors. It involves refining the product to meet customers' needs. It involves describing the product so that it is appealing to prospective customers (that's advertising). It involves establishing a competitive price for the product. It involves selling specific products to specific customers. It involves making sure the means of delivering the product to the customers work well (that's distribution). In short, marketing is a complete system for getting products and services from seller to buyer.

Two Kinds of Marketing

HR managers who set out to be marketers immediately run into a complication: there are two different kinds of marketing involved, and they are different from each other in significant ways—in marketing strategy, tactics, media used, costs, and measures of success.

Internal marketing involves promoting the services of the HR department within your own organization, making sure that all parts of the organization know what you have to offer. The fundamental purpose of internal marketing is to help the organization achieve its goals and objectives, by providing the "people" services it needs to prosper. The resources of the HR department, and you its manager, must be totally dedicated to the success of your primary client: the organization.

Internal marketing is noncompetitive; there is no organizational element vying for "HR business" within the company. The customers are "friendlies" who fully expect to be offered the products and services of the HR department.

To market the right products and services within their organizations, HR managers and their staffs must identify corporate priorities, determine what the implications of those priorities are for HR programs, adjust the talents and skills available within the HR department, deliver learning experiences to their "customers," and evaluate their contributions to the company's progress.

External marketing means taking some HR products originally developed for in-house use—a training videotape, say, or a program for developing managerial talent in technical workers—and selling them to others in the general marketplace. The goal is to generate revenue, to recover part of the cost of producing the materials.

External marketing is highly competitive. You must compete with other vendors of products and services for a share of the market. In fact, with external marketing, you are attempting to take a share of the market *away from* other marketers. That is not an easy thing to do. It is not anything like promoting HR programs within your own company. To succeed at external marketing, you must first figure out who your potential customers are. You must try to learn what they need. You must have a realistic assessment of the value of your own product. You need good intelligence about the products of others. You need a solid, professional marketing strategy, with workable pricing, effective advertising in the right media with the right timing, trouble-free distribution channels, and flawless customer service.

The customers of internal marketing are your co-workers. The customers of external marketing, while not necessarily unreceptive to marketing efforts, must be pursued, wooed, and won.

Requirements for Successful Marketing

Marketing skills and mindset. You, as the HR manager, are the marketing manager for your department's products, and you need the same skill set that marketing managers have. Study this chapter carefully, and spend time with the resources listed at the end of the chapter.

Watch out for some common mental traps that novice marketers fall into. Don't assume your product is so superior to all others that it will sell itself. Don't assume today's customers will buy tomorrow, or that even if they don't, there are plenty of other customers out there. Develop the marketer's mindset: serving the customer's needs is paramount.

Adequate forecasts. Most of the information to develop marketing strategies is based on forecasts of the business environment from political, technological, financial, social, and demographic standpoints. Unfortunately, forecasting remains an inexact science, and many times turns out to be inaccurate. Yet there is no viable alternative; forecasts must be used.

Top management support. No marketing plan can succeed without the total commitment of the board of directors and the top executives of the organization.

Adequate resources. A workable marketing strategy cannot be developed on a shoestring. It requires something more than a modest investment of resources. It demands the talents of many people. And it takes time. Too much pressure to produce a marketing plan in a limited amount of time will doom the effort.

Staff participation. Make all members of your staff a part of the marketing effort. Encourage them to view their jobs in the broadest possible context. Help them to see themselves as marketers or service consultants, people whose job is to ensure that clients and customers receive all the benefits your department and your company can provide. Reward results, not just effort. Keep them informed of the status of all projects. Give them every opportunity to make suggestions and comments—and act on them.

Superior customer service. If your marketing efforts are to succeed, you and everyone on your staff must adopt the basic credo of the marketplace: Serving the customer—internal and external— must be the number-one priority. Here are some specific suggestions for improving your customer service:

- Find out how your customers feel about the quality of your products and services.

- Develop a customer relations program—including the meaning of quality service, customer service policies and standards, means of measuring quality, and an organized visitors' program. Assign responsibility for every action.
- Hire for excellence; identify the qualities you want to see, and select people who meet those requirements.
- Train your people for superior service. Develop specific customer service skills as well as the attitudes needed to support them. Choose your training techniques with care, provide the training, and then evaluate results.
- Establish performance standards and then measure the performance of your people against the standards. Make periodic customer-satisfaction surveys.
- Ask your people for ideas to improve customer relations. Provide rewards for good ideas.
- Reward superior performance in customer service.
- Make it easy for your customers to register their complaints. Keep on top of all complaints; give them personalized attention.
- Convene boards of clients and customers to evaluate your services and to make recommendations for improvement.
- Periodically check your procedures in the role of an outsider. Call your front desk, to hear how callers are treated. Ask a friend to visit your office and report to you on the appearance and comfort of your reception area and the treatment received from your receptionist.

Products for Marketing

What products and services do HR managers have to market, either within their organizations or outside? Plenty! There is a surprisingly great variety of products and services. Here are some of the most common.

Products

Assessment systems
Attitude and opinion surveys
Books, manuals, and
  handbooks
Compensation and benefits
  systems
Computer programs

Evaluation systems
Executive development
  programs
Executive search programs
Films and projectuals
Formal training courses,
  seminars, and workshops

Incentive Systems
Induction and orientation
  programs
Job aids
Management development
  programs
Organization development
  programs
Organization designs
Performance appraisal systems
Productivity improvement
  programs
Publications

Rating scales
Records systems
Recruitment systems
Screening and selection
  Systems
Suggestion systems
Tests and survey instruments
Tuition aid plans
Video and audio tapes and
  disks
Workforce forecasts
Workplace improvement
  systems

Services

Assessment centers
Career planning
Coaching
Consulting
Counseling
Diagnosis
Employee wellness
Executive development
Food
Health
Information
Insurance
Library or learning center
Management development
Marketing
Media production
Medical
Negotiating
Occupational health

Organization design
Organization development
Organization diagnosis
Outplacement
Personnel screeming and
  selection
Physical fitness
Quality circles
Recreation
Research
Retirement planning
Safety and security
Scientist and engineer
  development
Strategic planning
Succession
Travel and transportation
Tuition aid
Workplace improvement

Internal Marketing: The Process

Step 1. Set goals and objectives. In this step, you establish the
goals of the HR marketing effort, what is to be accomplished over
the next three to five years. For instance, one goal might be to
develop a multidimensional program to increase employee participation in problem solving, decision making, and quality control. If

you're uncertain where to begin, go back and look at the list of HR products and services earlier in this chapter. Every single one of them could conceivably be marketed internally. Pick out three or four items where you believe your department has a good program that is not being used to its fullest potential by the employees, and organize your goals around them.

After setting these goals, you move to the task of working out objectives that support these goals. Objectives are usually set for each year. The desired outcomes are described in specific, measurable terms. That is, the objectives describe exactly and quantitatively what is to be accomplished by whom and by when. For example, an objective might be to establish and train ten quality circle groups, one at each branch, not later than April 1, 1990; Action: manager, training and development.

Objectives steer marketing activities so that they stay on target. They deal with important opportunities. But they must be realistic and practical—in terms of both the capabilities of the HR department and their potential for accomplishment. That means they must be attainable.

Never lose sight of the purpose of marketing HR programs internally: to help the organization achieve its overall goals. The goals of the HR department must support the corporate goals, not compete with them. Don't develop your department goals in a vacuum. Instead, work within the framework of the organization's forecasts, its strategic planning, its long-range goals. To develop those plans and goals, the company did a great deal of research on its internal and external environment, industry competition, mission, and so on. Make use of that information.

Step 2. Identify in-house customers. Everyone in your organization is a potential client—executives, managers, supervisors, staff personnel, scientists, engineers, technicians, clerical personnel, and hourly workers. How do you identify the groups and individuals who need your products and services? There are several means of finding out, and you should exploit them all.

Review and analyze company reports and records, they are certain to reveal problems and shortfalls—either potential or actual—that require HR interventions of some kind. So are the reports of managers and supervisors and analysis of their requests for assistance. But the primary means is through formal needs assessment on several levels: organizational, group, job, and individual.

Choose from these approaches:

Advisory committees
Assessment centers

Attitude surveys
Climate surveys
Critical incident surveys
Group discussions
Employee interviews
Exit interviews
Analysis of job descriptions and applicant specifications
Needs inventories
Nominal group technique
Analysis of performance appraisals
Questionnaires
Skills tests
Product or service evaluation
Client reports

And of course there are many informal means—listening, questioning, visiting work areas, and observing people at all levels under all kinds of conditions and in a variety of circumstances. They too will reveal needs for HR programs and services.

Through these various means, you are attempting to learn about the major groups in the company, and the individuals in them.

What values and attitudes are characteristic?
What is their background in education, training, and experience?
What are their professional, technical, and personal goals?
What are the obstacles to the realization of their goals?
What professional, technical, and personal problems do they have?
What kinds of solutions are realistic, practicable, and acceptable?

The answers to these questions will give you the information you need to develop an internal marketing plan and strategy.

Step 3. Write the marketing plan. Once you have learned what your clients need and want, you must develop a written plan defining how you intend to get your product or service to them.

The basic criteria for effective marketing plans are few:

1. Make them measurable so that you can determine how successful they are.

2. Make them flexible so that you can adjust to changing conditions.

3. Make them profitable so that you can accomplish what you set out to do.

A good plan contains at a minimum your objectives, potential barriers to achieving the objectives, strategies, and tactics to overcome the obstacles, time-phased schedules, measures of progress and accomplishment, and a supporting budget. For a full outline, see Figure 4-1.

Step 4. Implement the plan. Now comes the action part—putting your strategies and tactics to work. With the schedule and budget you worked out, start the promotional activities. Design the posters for the bulletin boards. Set up briefing sessions. Make the phone calls. Assign someone to do a writeup in the company newsletter.

Of the many possibilities for marketing HR services, three have proved especially fruitful in recent years: personal contacts, phone calls, and in-house advertising. Let's look at those three for a moment.

You can't sell the HR department sitting behind your desk. Talking informally with people—visiting with them in the shop, on the assembly line, in the training and conference rooms, in the offices, in the cafeteria, and in the field—is one of the best ways for HR managers to market their products and services. Similarly, set up periodic informal briefings for target groups, to let them know about new HR services. Just be sure to keep them *short*. Get out of your office regularly and frequently. Make contact with your "customers" to gain the visibility and credibility you need to be effective.

One of your best in-house marketing tools is the telephone. Never, never drop a lead for a "sale." Always follow up, at least by phone. Call people who have identified problems your department may be able to assist with. And, of course, telephone chats with managers, production facilities, sales offices, and service branches at other locations will often help you identify unmet needs for your products and services. Call your contacts frequently, to stay in touch and to keep your department visible and helpful.

Make full use of all in-house advertising opportunities to inform your customers of your products and services. Use bulletin boards, house organs, special broadsides and fliers, announcements, brochures, course descriptions, and special reports—and make them all high quality.

One source of in-house advertising that you probably have

Figure 4-1. Outline of an internal marketing plan.

- Marketing objectives
    Key assumptions for each of the department's internal markets
    Annual objectives for systems, products, programs, and services
        Financial
        Qualitative
        Quantitative
- Potential problems, barriers, and opportunities
    Capabilities
        Product quality
        Product quantity
        Quality of services
        Quantity of services
    Internal (organizational)
        Staffing
        Funding
        Top management support
        Line managers' and staff officers' attitudes
- Strategy and tactics
    Overall strategy
    Strategies and tactics for each market
        Personal contacts/Inquiring
        Review and analysis of corporate records and reports
        Needs analysis
    Advertising and Media
        Phone calls (Internal telemarketing)
        Personal visits and meetings
        Bulletin board notices
        Company publications and newsletters
        Catalogs and brochures
- Schedules
    Programs
    Services
    Special programs and projects
- Measures of progress and accomplishment
    Number of people served or requests for service
    Feedback from line managers, staff officers, and employees
    Financial statements
    Annual marketing audit
    Other reports
- Supporting budgets
    Operating budget
    Time, space, and materials budget
    Capital budget
    Cash budget

available is your company newsletter. Typically this newsletter is sent to a broad range of outsiders: stockholders, external clients, media representatives, industry leaders, public officials, and so on, and naturally you want it to be impressive. But don't forget that its primary audience is your own "family," the company's employees, and as such it is a prime vehicle for promoting HR programs.

Include stories describing new programs and services, how they came about and how they operate. Whenever possible, include testimonials from employee "customers," explaining how the program saved time or money or solved problems.

To boost your image with all clients, internal and external, make sure your newsletter is top quality; hire a professional to design it. Be sure that every item in it is relevant and interesting; don't use fillers that are of little or no interest to your target audience. Make the lead article an attention-getter. And don't miss an edition!

In all your promotion and advertising, keep your focus on the benefits to the client, not on the features of your products or services. Remember that your product or service exists for the buyer—and not the reverse. Your promotional materials must address the employees in just the right voice, with the right words. Explain what's in it for them, and explain it in their language.

It may or may not be an explicit part of your plan, but one thing you're doing with all your promotions is building a positive image for your department. Every flier, every newsletter, every individual contact is an opportunity to reinforce your identity. Take advantage of that opportunity, and your customers will come to see your department as an expert, caring, problem-solving unit, an organization that wants to help and can deliver on its promises.

However, it's no secret that in some organizations, the HR department has acquired a poor reputation. It might be from failure to support the goals and objectives of the organization, lack of responsiveness to the needs of other departments, botched programs, or delivering ineffective or substandard products. Poor past performance is certain to be extremely damaging to the image of any department.

The simple act of inquiring about the needs and wants of the people in your organization will go a long way toward developing a positive image for the HR department. What else can you do?

- Be results oriented and cost conscious.
- Demand quality—in both the design of HR programs and the materials that promote them. Don't be satisfied with anything less than top-notch work. "Good enough" is not good enough.
- In all contacts with people in the organization—formal or

informal, oral or written, group or individual—speak in nonpsychological terms. Insist that your people always use language that workers at all levels can understand.

Step 5. Track progress and accomplishment. In this step, the marketing effort is monitored, evaluated, and controlled. Your marketing plan should have included controls to identify deviations and shortfalls in your marketing activities as early as possible— preferably before they occur. Here the controls are applied.

Periodically evaluate your in-house marketing by tracking the frequency with which line managers come to your department for help and ideas. Make an annual audit of your marketing functions, following these steps:

1. Define the objectives of the audit; for example, "to measure performance against opportunities, goals, objectives, and resources."
2. Identify areas in which changes to your marketing plan are required; for example, new services needed, where to cut costs.
3. Select and brief the auditing team; be sure that members, whether selected from inside or outside, are independent of the marketing function.
4. Make the arrangements and smooth the way for the auditors to interview clients, customers, suppliers, and company marketing people.
5. Set a report deadline (in weeks, not months).

Step 6. Follow up and revise the plan. The final step is to revise and update your marketing plan in the light of your periodic assessment and the annual audit. Although modifications to the plan may become necessary at any time, it is essential that the plan be systematically examined and revised at least annually.

Internal Marketing: A Mini-Case

To illustrate the process of internal marketing, let's look again at TEA, Inc., the hypothetical company we first met in Chapter 2. You will recall that TEA is a small manufacturer of peripherals for personal computers, established in the Boston area in 1981. In the intervening years, the company has expanded its product line to include word processing, desktop publishing, graphics, and other specialized software. It also conducts on-site classroom and laboratory training in the use of its products and provides personalized consulting services such as custom programming, system integration, and one-on-one training.

Recently TEA's HR manager became convinced that an in-house wellness program for all employees would provide significant benefits for the company. Since such programs are generally managed under the auspices of the HR department, she developed the content of the program and began the marketing process.

Step 1. Set goals and objectives. One of the primary goals of the HR department is to improve the job satisfaction, well-being, and productivity of employees at all levels. That goal can be achieved in part by attainment of this objective: "To establish and operate a corporate wellness program to improve the physical, mental, and emotional health and fitness of employees."

Step 2. Identify the market. The market for the wellness program is identified as employees at all levels. However, to ensure maximum effectiveness, the program is targeted at specific segments of the work force—managers, engineers, salespersons, technicians, clerical personnel, and wage earners.

Step 3. Write the marketing plan. The marketing objective is identified—for example, "to attain an employee participation rate of 75 percent or higher in each of the six employee categories." Potential problems—employee disinterest or objections, top management skepticism, staffing, and costs—are pinpointed. A strategy to overcome objections and costs is developed. To win top management's support, primary focus is placed on collecting and presenting statistical data on absenteeism, drug and alcohol abuse, requests for assistance, counseling, and referrals to clinics and outside health professionals. Wherever possible these statistics are buttressed by hard data. That is, the statistical figures are translated into dollar costs—the costs during the past year of absenteeism, counseling and treatment for substance abusers, operating the drug hotline, accidents and injuries attributable to employee fatigue or drug or alcohol abuse. Employee disinterest and objections are countered by making full use of house organs, newsletters, bulletin board notices, and meetings and briefings, all designed to emphasize the opportunities and benefits the program offers. A series of professionally prepared cartoon posters is displayed on walls throughout the workplace, pay envelopes are stuffed with cleverly written broadsides, articles describing the program and its benefits are placed in the company newsletter, specially printed napkins and low-calorie menus are placed in the cafeteria, employee weight-loss, lowered-cholesterol, and stop-smoking competitions are announced, and a Fitness Freak of the Month award is created. A five-minute briefing about the program is videotaped and shown periodically in the cafeteria and employees' lounge, as well as in classrooms and conference rooms. And a schedule is prepared and published.

Step 4. Implement the plan. The program is activated. Responsibility for various aspects of the program is delegated. Required funding is secured. The advertising element of the company prepares the posters and broadsides, bulletin board notices, and the like. The training and development element prepares a draft of a briefing script, prepares the final script, and develops the videotape. Live briefings are prepared and presented to detail the plans for the program. Informal meetings are held with employee groups to promote discussion and answer questions about the program. The stop-smoking, weight-loss, and Fitness Freak of the Month competitions are launched, and so on.

Step 5. Track progress. The program is monitored in operation. Data on participation are collected and analyzed. Trends—upward and downward—are noted. Problems and shortfalls are identified. Employee comments and reactions are solicited by interviews and questionnaires. What do people like about the program? What requires change? What should be added? Dropped? The program is audited at least annually. All of this feedback is analyzed to identify its marketing implications—to determine what improvements are needed in the marketing strategy and tactics.

Step 6. Follow up and revise. The marketing program is systematically evaluated, revised, and otherwise updated and modified to bring it into line with the results of the assessment, feedback from top management and program participants, and the annual audit. New marketing strategies, media, and approaches are developed and used.

External Marketing: The Process

Step 1. Set goals and objectives. As with the internal marketing process, in this step you establish the goals of what you want the marketing effort to accomplish, and then set specific objectives that will enable you to meet those goals. Because the underlying aim of external marketing is to earn revenue, goals tend to be financial in nature. For instance, one goal might be stated as "to recover part of the costs of developing an interactive project management software package." One objective to help bring that about (and there could be many others) might be "to market one hundred project management software packages to customers and clients over the next twelve months."

Step 2. Identify and segment the market. The step of identifying your market is essentially one of market research—targeting the people who have the problem your product or service can solve and getting to know them. It involves collecting information about your present or potential clients, what they need and want, and how they perceive your organization. You need to know how many prospective customers and clients are out there, precisely where they are, and what is the best way to reach them. It also involves tracking sales (yours and your competitors'), sales costs (cost per product unit or cost per service performed), and other measures of costs, productivity, profit, and return on investment.

Where do you learn all this? Gather data through surveys, interviews, reports, and feedback from customers, prospects, suppliers, and your own employees. Attend trade shows, conferences, and seminars, and talk to as many people as you can. Review competitors' catalogs and brochures. Read reports in trade and professional journals.

In all likelihood, you will identify a market, or more than one, that is impossibly broad. Let's say you have a motivational program for sales personnel that has been tremendously successful and you have decided to market it outside. Who is your market? Every company that has a sales force! Obviously you can't reasonably expect to reach them all, certainly not with the same message. That's where market segmentation comes in.

Segmentation, also called target marketing or niche marketing, divides a large, heterogeneous market into smaller groups, or segments, the members of which have a common interest in a particular product or service. By segmenting your market, you can adjust your promotional and advertising strategies to appeal to the needs of a single audience. That is called positioning—matching your message to the appropriate market segment—and it is segmentation's partner. (By the way, segmentation often is needed with internal marketing too.)

To illustrate the idea of segmentation, let's look at two familiar industries—automobiles and computers. For the computer manufacturer, one market consists of personal computer (PC) users—a very *large* market. That market can be segmented into major categories: users in government, business, industry, education, and so on. In turn, each category can be divided into smaller segments: local, county, state, and federal government; elementary, middle, junior high, and high school, college, and graduate school education; banking, grocery, hardware, and insurance businesses. Another large, undifferentiated market consists of users of personal transportation. That market can be segmented by age groupings (children, adolescents, young adults, older adults, and seniors); by type (standard, economy, customized, and luxury); by use (commuting, business, recreation, sport, competition, and so on). Both the auto maker and the computer manufacturer can now design separate promotion strategies that focus on just what each segment needs to know. And that is what target marketing is all about.

Closer to home, one large market for HR products related to training in basic skills (by means of interactive video) is the federal government. It might be segmented into the major federal departments—State, Labor, Defense, Transportation, Health and Human Services, Housing and Urban Development, and so on. Each of these could be further segmented; for example, Defense could be separated into the Departments of Army, Navy, and Air Force, and each of these could in turn be divided into its major branches and the schools that support each branch. For example, Army schools include aviation, signal (communications), intelligence, armor, infantry, transportation, and finance, to identify just a few. Marketing campaigns could focus on interactive video programs dealing with mathematical skills for personnel preparing for entry into basic electronics training in the aviation, signal, intelligence, and armor schools, emphasizing such features of the program as individualization of instruction, savings in personnel, time, and funds, and reduction in trainee attrition.

Step 3. Analyze competitors. Take a good hard look at how your product stacks up against other similar products—a time-consuming but extremely important step. Carefully evaluate all similar products already available—their characteristics, quality, pricing, appeal, where they're selling and where they're not. Is there a niche your product or service would fill?

You need timely intelligence on your competitors' products—the features, benefits, and shortcomings of those products, territory covered, operations, administration, and financial position. You need that intelligence to make effective decisions, recognize and take advantage of your competition's vulnerabilities, and build your market share by maximizing your strengths and exploiting areas your competitors can't or won't contest.

You need to understand your rivals' current operations and their goals and plans if you are to survive in a competitive marketing environment. You must establish procedures for collecting and analyzing data about competitors, identify their strengths and weaknesses in comparison with your own, and develop cost and pricing strategies that will exploit competitors' weaknesses. To do that successfully, you must explore competitor information sources. So learn from your competitors; analyze their motivations, behavior, strategies, and tactics. Listen to and analyze their assaults on you or your products and services.

Here are some legal sources of information about competitors:

- Articles by their executives, staff, engineers, scientists, and technicians in trade journals and business and professional publications.
- Industry, business, and professional association libraries (for research reports, industry surveys, and product and sales data).
- Industry, business, and professional association conferences, exhibits, and trade shows. Look at competitors' exhibits; eavesdrop. Talk to as many attendees as possible.
- Their annual reports to stockholders, advertising, catalogs, and brochures.
- Their financial statements filed annually with the Securities and Exchange Commission.
- Industry securities analysts.
- Company-conducted or -contracted industry, business, or professional surveys of competitors.
- Review of reports by your company's sales force, franchisees, and dealers.
- Interviews with competitors' salespersons, suppliers, dealers, franchisees, and customers.

Step 4. Forecast sales and market share. In your marketing role, you must have a system for forecasting sales and revenues from HR products and services that is reliable and cost-effective. Unless backed by a corporate forecasting element (usually found only in large organizations), you, and the marketing department (if there is one), must rely on some type of judgmental system for the sales forecast. The most common ones are sales-force estimates, executive consensus, industry-expert estimates, and intention-to-buy surveys.

Market share is a nonfinancial measure of performance. It can be examined nationally, by region or city, or by market segment or type of customer. It is simply the percentage of business (actual customers) that belongs to your product or service (percent of total sales in terms of the volume of goods sold or net dollar volume of sales) in a product category. It represents a measurement at a specific point in time. To determine market share, you need to know how many customers are out there, what they are buying, how much they spend for the particular product or service, how many are sold by your competitors, and how many your company has sold. You also need to know whether your market share and those of your competitors are increasing or decreasing.

Historical market share measurement (over a three- to five-year period) is important because it is a means of gauging progress against the marketing plan. It should be tracked continuously because it will provide valuable information about your own and your competitors' place in the category. It can also provide information on emerging trends and new products. Market share can be determined and tracked through research conducted by your own company's market research department, by outside research sources, or by a combination of both.

Maintaining and increasing market share is always important in a competitive environment. The HR setting today is certainly that. To capture a larger share of the available pool of customers, you need a product that positions well in the market because it provides either unique benefits or more benefits than the products of your competitors.

Step 5. Establish prices. Setting prices on HR products and services is always needed for external marketing, and sometimes for internal marketing too, if the company's departments are organized as profit centers, selling their services to other departments. In any case, the pricing process is part of the total marketing mix. As such, it must be well managed, and it must be integrated with corporate strategy and marketing mix decisions. To do that, HR managers must be fully aware of key pricing issues, be able to determine pricing and target-market objectives, avoid pricing mistakes, and select competitive prices for their products and services. Market analysis, experience, pricing models, or gut feelings are not adequate tools in today's business environment. HR managers need to use a systematic pricing process.

The mechanics of the pricing process generally involve the calculation of the total cost of the product or service, including production costs, all fixed and variable overhead costs, the costs of promoting the product or service, and the margin of profit sought. The sum of these factors equals the selling price—what the consumer pays (except for markups in price set by the distributors, if any). However, price is subject to manipulation.

Historically, the use of price has been the predominant competitive strategy. However, with the increase in the number of competitors and competitive HR products, the product-value relationship has stabilized. Today, the emphasis in competition and promotion is on product quality and customer service rather than on price.

Cost-based pricing is the simplest approach. It involves the basics described above: identifying and assessing all the costs associated with the production, promotion, and delivery of a product or service, adding a factor for profit, and then setting a price based on cost plus profit.

Competition-based pricing is the process of letting competitors establish the prices and then setting your prices low enough to eclipse or keep out the competition to maintain or improve market share. Obviously, price concessions can increase sales. However, irresponsible competitive pricing often results in retaliation by competitors. If carried too far, it can lead to price wars and price attrition.

Customer-based pricing starts with the market and works back into the company. It sees pricing as a function of what the market will bear for the benefits offered by the product or service. Theoretically, there is no limit on either the upper levels of pricing or profitability other than what the customer is willing to pay. Review and analysis of several factors are key to customer-based pricing: the nature of the market, the number, kind, and quality of competitive offerings, the quality of your products and services, and market share.

The intricacies of pricing strategies and approaches are beyond the scope of this volume. You should examine in detail the three main types of pricing just described, as well as breakeven analysis and sales forecasting techniques. Check the resources listed at the end of this chapter, particularly the book by Butaney, Lantos, and Paley.

Develop a fair and reasonable pricing structure. Remember that one of the basic rules of pricing is to compete on value—that is, quality—and not on price. Consider the total operating environment of your company, focusing on those elements that should influence pricing decisions. Some of the most important of these factors are: the size of the market, your market share, customer demands and preferences, the nature of the competition, production, promotion, and distribution costs, new products in development, the life-cycle stage of your product, and the size of your inventory. Factor in all the current marketing conditions you can identify. Use models and matrices to project future market potential. Measure your product's sales potential. Then choose the best pricing approaches for your particular products and services. And keep in mind that people will pay for quality.

Step 6. Write the marketing plan. In this step you will devise your marketing strategy and tactics, and set them formally down in a written plan. It is a precise, specific game plan detailing exactly what you will do, and how, and when. Figure 4-2 outlines the contents of a typical plan. Also, before you start, review the three criteria for successful plans, in Step 3 of the internal marketing process.

Let's review for a moment. You have established goals for your marketing program, and set objectives, involving specific products, by which you intend to achieve those goals. You have reviewed the products of your competitors, and decided you do indeed have something to offer. You have priced the products competitively, and forecast probable sales volume.

You have, through careful market research, identified the potential customers for the products and, if appropriate, segmented that market down into smaller groups, people who are alike in some significant way.

Now the task is to plot out the best ways of reaching those customers, and the best ways of positioning your message for each audience. We can frame the task as a series of questions:

1. What is the best avenue to reach each customer group?
2. Considering our budget, is the best avenue also the most cost efficient? If not, what are some good alternatives?
3. What features of the product are most important to each customer group? What problems does each customer group have that the product will address?
4. What image do we want to project?
5. Are there timing considerations to be taken into account, such as scheduled events in the industry or seasonal shifts?

To answer the first question—how to reach your customers—you must investigate the pluses and minuses of various media: newspapers, radio, television, magazines, trade show exhibits, Yellow Pages, telemarketing, direct response card decks, catalogs, brochures, newsletters, and trade directories. Here is a rundown.

Figure 4-2.   Outline of an external marketing plan.

- Marketing objectives
    - Key assumptions for each of the company's markets
    - Annual objectives for systems, programs, products, and services
        - Financial
        - Quantitative
        - Qualitative
- Potential problems, barriers, and opportunities
    - Internal (capabilities)
        - Product quality
        - Product quantity
        - Quality of services
        - Quantity of services
    - Internal (organizational)
        - Staffing
        - Funding
    - External
        - Social
        - Economic
        - Competitive
- Strategies and tactics
    - Overall strategy
    - Strategies and tactics for each market
        - Management
        - Advertising and media
            - Newspaper and magazine ads
            - Direct mail and brochures
            - Trade shows and exhibits
            - Telemarketing
            - Other
- Schedules and action plans
    - Production
    - Promotion and advertising
    - Sales force
    - Customer service
- Measures of progress and accomplishment
    - Sales volume
    - Profit
    - Return on investment
    - Customer feedback
    - Annual marketing audit
- Supporting budgets
    - Operating budget
    - Capital budget
    - Cash budget
- Summary of plan impact on profit and loss statement

Advertisements in local newspapers, local radio, and broadcast and cable television. Regional advertising is particularly appropriate for promoting events with a geographic focus, such as a workshop on state law relating to health insurance for employees.

Advertisements in trade and professional journals, membership directories, and national magazines. Ads of this nature are suitable for publicizing general-interest seminars, workshops, and training materials to a broad audience.

Audiovisuals. Audiovisuals include projectuals, audiotapes, videotapes, and discs. They can be very effective for promoting products and services and can be designed as either stand-alone or supplementary materials.

Personal contacts. Networking with top-level decision makers and the movers and shakers in organizations can help you gain a hearing for your products and services.

Trade shows, exhibits, and conferences. These group events provide an unsurpassed way to improve company image and recognition, gather information about customers and competitors, and generate sales leads. You have an essentially captive audience of motivated people. See the Appendix for descriptions of appropriate conferences.

Telemarketing. Telemarketing is particularly useful in qualifying sales leads, selling new products to old customers, renewing service contracts, developing prospects, and obtaining marketing research data.

Direct mail. Although direct response techniques are a very expensive means of marketing, they can be exceptionally effective in reaching a clearly defined market segment for HR products and services, particularly workshops and training packages.

Brochures. Brochures are a must for getting leads, describing products or services, and promoting workshops and seminars.

Newsletters. Published monthly or quarterly, newsletters are a particularly useful means of maintaining contact with potential or actual customers in a clearly segmented portion of a market, such as organization development specialists.

News releases. Press releases to local media, focusing on the products, services, and accomplishments of your organization, can achieve maximum image-building impact.

Trade and professional directory listings. Directories provide an especially effective means of gaining nationwide attention among members of the particular group. A list of directories follows; the addresses of the related societies are listed in the organizations section of the Appendix.

ASTD Buyer's Guide and Consultant Directory. ASTD Who's Who Membership Directory. Both from American Society for Training and Development.

Official National Directory of Service and Product Providers to Nonprofit Organizations and Resource Center Catalog. From The Society of Nonprofit Organizations.

Training and Development Organizations Directory: A Descriptive Guide to Firms, Institutes, and Other Agencies Offering Training, Professional, and Personal Development Programs to Business, Industry, Government, and Individuals. From Gale Research Company, P. O. Box 6789, Silver Spring, MD 20906.

Training Magazine's Marketplace Directory: A Comprehensive Guide for Locating Equipment, Programs and Services, Materials, Consultants, Production Facilities, Training Sites, Associations for Training and Development. From *Training* magazine, Lakewood Publications, 50 S. Ninth St., Minneapolis, MN 55402.

Putting this advertising mix together is a complex business. It's more expensive to advertise in some media than in others—a national magazine compared to a community newspaper, for instance—but they may have greater coverage. Some media need longer lead times than others. Some have formats that provide a better fit with your materials. The advertising materials for some media will be more expensive than others (it costs more to produce a television commerical than a two-color brochure) but may provide more "image" impact. A good rule of thumb is to spend most of your advertising dollars on direct response marketing—direct mail, telemarketing, Yellow Pages, newspapers, and magazines.

If the world of advertising is new to you, get some help from the advertising and public relations department of your organization, if there is one, or an outside consultant. An excellent source of information is "Boardroom's Annual Guide to Advertising Media," from *Boardroom Reports,* P.O. Box 1026, Millburn, NJ 07041-9818. Also be sure to include plans for publicity—high-impact promotion ideas that get "free" coverage—in addition to paid advertising.

Still in the planning stage now, move on to questions 3, 4, and 5: features, image, and timing. Isolate the most important concerns of each target group, and decide which features of your product relate particularly to those concerns. Then build your advertising campaigns for each segment around those themes. Emphasize significant strengths, such as

- Success in problem solving for other organizations
- Reputation with other companies

- Diverse staff talents and competencies
- Size (big enough to handle large-scale projects; small enough to respond rapidly and provide personal service)
- Ahead of the state of the art as demonstrated by presentations at professional meetings, journal articles, or research
- Specific business or professional orientation and experience

Spend some time analyzing the image you want to portray. What do you want customers to think when they hear your organization's name? Experienced? Young and dynamic? Small and friendly? Big and expert? You want your materials to reflect that image, consistently, so be clear in your own mind.

Finally, work out a detailed budget and a schedule that takes into account significant events in the industry, in the business cycle of your target customers, lead times for advertising media and conference bookings, and so on.

Working out the details of this plan will take time—perhaps considerably more time than the plan for internal marketing because it involves so many additional factors, many of them new to you. Don't try to rush it. On the other hand, don't be intimidated. It's really a process of moving the parts around until you find just the right fit—what group of customers is the most likely target for your product, what communication channel will reach those customers most directly and most cost effectively, what should the message to those customers be, what media can most effectively display that message, how should the message be framed, and when should it appear?

Step 7. Activate the plan. Now put your plan into action. Reserve the space in magazines, and assign people to work on the advertising copy and design. Design your display at the trade show. Interview outside consulting firms to manage the direct mail campaign. Write the press release. Decide who would be a good "voice" for radio ads. Expand the newsletter. Build a file of good and bad brochures, and look for ideas. Plan what should go in the Yellow Pages ad. And so on.

In every aspect of the marketing effort, in every advertising and promotion piece that you produce, you must be concerned with both content and style. In content, make sure that you focus on the needs and problems of your potential clients and customers. The copy must demonstrate clearly that you understand the prospect's problem, show how your product offers immediate solutions and benefits, tell the prospect exactly how to get the product, and describe the consequences of inaction. Ads must make news verbally, graphically, or numerically; they must have allure, and they must communicate benefits. Keep language simple. Don't use disclaimers. And don't use celebrity endorsements unless the star's expertise directly relates to the product.

The matter of style is at least as important as content. Your ad, your brochure, your mailing piece has to compete with hundreds of others—maybe thousands—for the attention of people who are, for better or worse, profoundly influenced by the output of Madison Avenue's best professionals. Not that you need to hire a famous advertising agency; just make sure that nothing goes out of your department that is anything less than professional quality.

Poor-quality, amateurish materials are worse than ineffective—they can actually cause damage. They will destroy your image and *lose* customers rather than bring them in. If you do not have in your department people with the right talents, look for help. If your organization has a corporate marketing or advertising unit, make full use of the creative talents of the people who staff it. Cultivate them, ask for their advice and assistance, and let them know that their services are appreciated. If no such organizational element exists, use outside designers or advertising consultants to produce materials that are first class in photography, graphic design, layout, illustration, and typesetting.

By way of summary, here are some general guidelines for all your marketing documents, regardless of type.

- Make your marketing documents persuasive and expensive looking—but keep them as inexpensive as possible.
- Use an attention-getter, something that will grab the reader.
- Directly address your clients about a problem they have that you can solve.
- Emphasize the benefits to the reader, the "what's in it for me?" Try to include an *exclusive* benefit; an unmatched, one-of-a-kind advantage.
- Underscore your strengths and neutralize potential weaknesses by proving that they don't exist.
- Use positive terms—action-motivating, power-generating words—and avoid negatives.
- Use effective, relevant, and professional illustrations, with color if possible.
- Give clear, complete, step-by-step instructions for clients to order what you're selling.
- Get the reader to take action by incorporating easy-to-use response vehicles.

Step 8. Track progress. Essentially, the purpose of this step is the same as that in internal marketing: to make sure your goals and objectives are being met. Although the external marketing program typically has more ingredients, in many ways tracking progress is much easier, because the results are generally tangible and quite measurable. How many videotapes ordered? How many registrations for the workshop? How many response coupons from the newspaper ads? How many inquiries from the journal article? How many visitors at the trade show booth?

In addition to checking continually for these individual targets, you should arrange for an annual audit; use the guidelines listed in Step 5 of the internal process.

And be especially mindful of customer service issues. If marketing products outside is a new venture for your department, your people will need training in this area. If problems begin to show up, inadequate customer service could easily be the source.

Step 9. Follow up and revise. Here too, the process is basically the same as with internal marketing. Whatever isn't working, change it. Whatever the audit revealed as a problem, fix it.

Some common problems are cost overruns, poor-quality materials, and trying to spread a budget too broadly. To improve your success:

1. Target market segments and geographical regions very selectively.
2. Minimize promotional support for marginal areas.
3. Maintain tight controls over advertising costs.
4. Improve product manuals and service brochures.

External Marketing: A Mini-Case

Once again we'll look in on TEA, Inc., the Boston-area manufacturer of computer peripherals, software, and related training. Now the enterprising HR manager has decided to focus effort on marketing on-site classroom training in the use of TEA products and personalized service such as one-on-one customized training. Let's follow her through the marketing process.

Step 1. Set goals and objectives. The overall goal for TEA is to remain competitive and show growth in market share, profit, and return on investment in the markets it now serves, primarily educational institutions. It will become more active within the European community as more and more PC systems become common. The following year will see changes similar to that experienced last year in the United States and key European markets.

The following financial targets have been established for this year:

- Total revenues of $1.2 million
- Pretax profits of $170,000
- Return on net capital employed of 11 percent

Although the lion's share of projected total revenues is certain to be provided by the sale of hardware and software, a significant number of dollars can be earned by on-site classroom, laboratory, and one-on-one customized training. The HR manager establishes a goal of "increasing the amount of revenue derived from training services." The specific objective for this year is set at 10 percent of total revenues ($120,000).

Step 2. Identify and segment the market. Major markets continue to experience changes in the amount and types of computer peripherals and the specialized software used, and, as a consequence, the types of training and the media used are changing. Management assumes that these basic changes will continue, as a result of advances in technology and the volume of personal computers in use in all types of industry. The impact of these changes on one of our major markets, educational institutions, is that there is more networking and increased numbers of individual PCs.

Market assessment indicates that the use of PCs will continue to grow in all segments of the market. Since growth in educational institutions will be substantial, the focus of the HR manager's marketing effort will be on educational institutions to complement the thrust of the equipment and software marketing plan.

Step 3. Analyze competitors. Although there are many U.S. firms with the capability of providing the products and services marketed by TEA, only a handful have a comparable mix of products and services. Most domestic firms are primarily targeted at business and industrial markets at home and abroad. Japanese and Korean producers currently dominate the Far East market, although their marketing efforts are targeted mainly at the industrial segment.

More and more training and consulting firms have been established to provide training on computer systems such as IBM and Apple/Macintosh. Their primary marketing targets today are business and industry, but that could change very quickly. The HR manager recognizes this and realizes that she must assess the capabilities, strengths, and weaknesses of these firms so that she will be prepared to counter incursions into the educational market in her territory.

Step 4. Forecast sales and market share. A combination of sales force estimates, managerial consensus, and industry expert estimates, coupled with a recent intention-to-buy survey of clients and potential customers, resulted in a sales forecast that projects the following:

- An increase in our share of the business of U.S. educational institutions from 4.5 to 6.8 percent
- An increased share of the business of the European community's service-oriented companies from 2 to 3 percent

If the company consensus projects increases of from 4.5 to 6.8 percent in its share of the business provided by U.S. educational institutions, it is reasonable to assume that the range is likely to hold firm for training services because the company is the most logical and most visible source of that training and is in a good position to influence that decision at the time the hardware and software are purchased.

Step 5. Establish pricing. The complexities of the pricing process, and the lack of in-house expertise in that art, caused us to seek outside help in the form of a qualified pricing consultant to develop a realistic and reasonable pricing structure for our products and services. The consultant used a combination of customer-based pricing and breakeven analysis to arrive at the pricing schedule. Customer-based pricing was determined to be the most feasible method. It allows the company to set a fair price that customers are willing to pay—one that will yield the desired profit.

Step 6. Write the marketing plan. The marketing objective is identified. It is "to reach prospective customers, promote the company's training services, and deliver a training package with each piece of equipment and software item." Potential problems, such as securing top management support, augmenting staff, and budgeting, are pinpointed. A strategy to overcome problems and concerns is developed. Primary focus is placed on presenting data on costs and potential return on investment to top management. Full use is made of meetings and briefings to inform top management about plans, actions, and progress. The marketing department will be given responsibility for developing promotional pieces for our programs and services, and preparing advertising copy for insertion into appropriate educational, technical, and trade journals. A detailed schedule for the marketing program is developed.

The core of our strategy is to step up our training materials development effort. We propose to take the following steps:

- Establish an educational advisory board comprising specialists in education from grade school to college level, to provide the company with information on how teachers at all levels can better use computer hardware and software in the classroom.
- Add five course-development programmers to our staff.
- Hire two more technicians for our production staff.
- Develop working relationships with universities in each region to gain a competitive edge in referrals to individual companies and institutions.
- Position TEA as a producer of both on-site and mediated training programs for PC systems used for word processing, desktop publishing, and other specialized programs.

Step 7. Activate the plan. The HR manager presents a decision briefing to top management to win its support and funding for the marketing plan. Once the plan is approved, the educational advisory board is established and convened quarterly. Five course-development programmers are selected, hired, and oriented. Initial contacts are made by branch managers with universities in their regions. Promotional materials are prepared and mailed. Customer service representatives emphasize training services in their contacts with institutions.

Step 8. Track progress. Branch managers submit monthly reports on their contacts, their progress in marketing training services, and problems they have identified. In all but one region, reports are positive. The north central office reported a problem with one of its customer service representatives. Apparently the individual lacked initiative and had marginal instructional skills. Those deficiencies resulted in customer complaints, and he was replaced.

Step 9. Follow up and revise. The HR manager examines every aspect of the marketing plan and measures results against the plan. Deviations are identified and corrections are made to the plan and installed.

Summary

Today's HR managers must become entrepreneurs within their own organizations. They can also make significant contributions to their companies by becoming external marketers. Although they may not be able to show a profit from their external marketing efforts, they can amortize the costs of producing HR programs and services by selling them to outside organizations.

Marketing is the function concerned with moving goods and services from producer to consumer. It is the process of finding out what people need to solve their problems and getting it to them—or identifying the people who need what you have, making sure that they know they need it, and then delivering it to them. "Marketing" is not a synonym for "sales," although they are often confused. Marketing is a broad-focus approach to solving customers' problems; sales is but one part of the process.

For HR managers, marketing may take two forms: internal and external. All HR managers have at least one permanent client— their own organization. To be maximally effective, the HR department must actively market its products and services to its internal "customers." It cannot be passive, simply responding to the requests of line managers and staffers for services. The department must actively promote its wares by means of personal contacts, in-house advertising, and telemarketing so that the people served are fully aware of the services available to them and become convinced of their value.

The process of internal marketing takes six steps:

1. Set goals and objectives.
2. Identify the market.
3. Write the marketing plan.
4. Implement the plan.
5. Track progress.
6. Follow up and revise.

The second form, external marketing, poses a formidable challenge to those who have not been prepared by education, training, or experience in marketing. They need to acquire marketing attitudes, perspectives, and skills. They need to learn how to use marketing media—audiovisuals, advertisements, personal contacts, brochures, newsletters, trade and professional directories, trade shows, exhibitions, conferences, proposals, news releases, telemarketing, and direct mail advertising.

The external marketing process has nine steps:

1. Set goals and objectives.
2. Identify and segment market.
3. Analyze competitors.
4. Forecast sales and market share.
5. Establish pricing.
6. Write the marketing plan.
7. Activate the plan.
8. Track progress.
9. Follow up and revise.

The potential return on the investment of time, talent, and other resources in learning and applying marketing expertise both internally and externally can be substantial. Those benefits include lower net costs for high-priced HR systems and programs and, of perhaps more importance, greater visibility for the department and top-management recognition of its contributions and value to the organization and its people.

For Further Reading, Viewing, and Listening

Barhydt, James T. *The Complete Book of Product Publicity.* New York: AMACOM, 1987.

Bencin, Richard L. *The Marketing Revolution: Understanding Major Changes in How Businesses Market.* Philadelphia: Swansea Press, 1985.

Bly, Robert W. *Create the Perfect Sales Piece: How to Produce Brochures, Catalogs, Fliers & Pamphlets.* New York: John Wiley & Sons, 1985.

Butaney, G., Geoffrey P. Lantos, and Norton Paley. *Pricing Strategies and Practices.* 2nd ed. New York: American Management Association Extension Institute, 1988.

Cohen, William A. *Developing a Winning Marketing Plan.* New York: John Wiley & Sons, 1987.

Competing Through Customer Service (60-minute videocassette). Nathan/Tyler Productions, Boston, MA 02210, 1987.

Connor, Richard A., Jr., and Jeffrey P. Davidson. *Marketing Your Consulting and Professional Services.* New York: John Wiley & Sons, 1985.

Customer Service (22-minute videocassette). Produced by WITCOM Associates, 1985. Distributed by American Management Association, Nine Galen St., Watertown, MA 02172.

Customer Service Management Handbook. Waterford, Conn.: Bureau of Business Practice, 1988.

Desatnick, Robert L. *Managing to Keep the Customer: How to Achieve and Maintain Superior Customer Service Throughout the Organization.* San Francisco: Jossey-Bass, 1987.

Edith Roman Direct Mail Encyclopedia: The Intelligent Directory of Mailing Lists. Edith Roman Associates, 875 Avenue of the Americas, New York, NY 10001.

Field, Leonard M. *Competitor Intelligence: How to Get It—How to Use It.* New York: John Wiley & Sons, 1985.

Fuld, L. M. *Monitoring the Competition: Find Out What's Really Going on Over There!* New York: John Wiley & Sons, 1988.

Gosden, Freeman F., Jr. *Direct Marketing Success: What Works and Why.* New York: John Wiley & Sons, 1988.

Kelly, John M. *How to Check Out Your Competition: A Complete Plan for Investigating Your Market.* New York: John Wiley & Sons, 1987.

Knapp, Bonnie Ogram. "Writing a Proposal? No Problem." *Training,* March 1988, pp. 55–58.

Lant, Jeffrey. *Money Making Marketing: Finding the People Who Need What You're Selling and Making Sure They Buy It.* Cambridge, Mass.: Jeffrey Lant Associates, 1987.

LeBoeuf, Michael. *How to Win Customers and Keep Them for Life.* New York: G. P. Putnam's Sons, 1988.

Lele, Milind M., and Jagdish N. Sheth. *The Customer Is Key: Gaining an Unbeatable Advantage Through Customer Satisfaction.* New York: John Wiley & Sons, 1987.

Lyons, John. *Guts: Advertising From the Inside Out.* New York: AMACOM, 1987.

Nash, Edward L., ed. *The Direct Marketing Handbook.* New York: McGraw-Hill Book Company, 1984.

A Passion for Customers (67-minute videocassette). Produced by Video Publishing House. Distributed by Films Incorporated, 5547 N. Ravenswood Ave., Chicago, IL 60640-1199, 1987.

Schrello, Don. *How to Market Training Programs, Seminars & Instructional Materials.* 2nd ed. Long Beach, Calif.: Schrello Direct Marketing (P. O. Box 1610, Long Beach 90801-9990).

Selame, E., and J. Selame. *The Company Image: Building Your Identity and Influence in the Marketplace.* New York: John Wiley & Sons, 1988.

Service Excellence (90-minute videocassette). Nathan/Tyler Productions, 451 D St., Boston, MA 02210, 1986.

Shenson, Howard L., and William R. Tracey, "Marketing Training Programs and Services." In *Human Resources Management and Development Handbook,* edited by William R. Tracey. New York: AMACOM, 1985.

Six Keys to Service (12-minute videocassette). Produced by J. Copeland. National Educational Media, 21601 Devonshire Street, Chatsworth, CA 91311-9962, 1984.

Smith, Ivan Campbell. *How to Analyze the Competition.* Rev. ed. New York: AMACOM, 1988.

Waterman, Robert H., Jr. *Keeping Close to Your Customer* (audiotape cassette). Work Dynamics, 715 Sandor Ct., Paramus, NJ 07652.

Weintz, Walter H. *The Solid Gold Mailbox: How to Create Winning Mail-Order Campaigns by the Man Who's Done It All.* New York: John Wiley & Sons, 1987.

What Is Marketing? (15-minute videocassette). Rank Roundtable Training, 113 N. San Vicente Blvd., Beverly Hills, CA 90211, 1980.

Why Quality? (22-minute videocassette). AMA Film/Video, Nine Galen St., Watertown, MA 02172, 1987.

Winkler, John. *Pricing for Results.* New York: Facts on File, 1984.

5

Innovating
Breaking With Tradition

Today's organizations face very difficult challenges: an expanding global economy, cutthroat competition for markets, drastically shortened product life cycles, rapid technological change, deregulation, mergers and acquisitions, downsizing, and restructuring. To survive in such a world, companies must constantly improve productivity and product quality, develop new products and services, and meet customer demands for service, including custom-tailored solutions to problems. In short, they must be continually innovative.

Innovation has a direct link to two key concerns: competition and profitability. To stay profitable, companies must have creative managers, professionals, and technicians. Faced with tighter time schedules, smaller budgets, and fewer resources than ever before, and with the threat of takeovers ever-present, managers must be more innovative. They must meet those challenges by using new approaches. To remain competitive, companies need an unending supply of fresh ideas. The "business as usual" mentality will no longer cut it. Innovation provides a real competitive advantage.

Here are some other reasons for promoting creativity and innovation:

- To deal effectively with change
- To solve problems
- To respond to new market pressures
- To develop new products and services
- To improve productivity
- To improve product or service quality
- To make use of new information and technologies
- To meet customers' requirements and demands
- To increase options
- To reduce effort and risk
- To create and exploit new opportunities
- To help employees grow and develop

- To enable people to express themselves
- To make people feel better, smarter, and more satisfied
- To survive as a company or a department

So, innovative ability has never been more important to business success, and innovation in the area of human resources is the keystone to that success. Human resources managers play a central role in achieving these benefits. They must serve as catalysts for an organizational climate where new ideas are encouraged. They must create plans to enhance innovation in their organizations. They must develop greater individual and group participation in innovation.

In their own departments, they must recognize that the quality of the products and services they provide depends on the creative capabilities of the people they hire and on certain specific work-related environmental conditions. If HR managers are to become effective managers of creative people, they must find ways to enhance conditions that encourage creativity and minimize those that kill it.

To accomplish that, HR managers must acquire a new mindset, new thinking skills, and novel ways to attack problems and find original solutions. They need to learn to use their powers of logical thinking to make themselves more effective. And, most of all, they need to create an innovative work environment to help transform the whole organization and overcome blocks to creativity.

This chapter has a dual focus. First, it provides a plan and process for increasing your personal creativity and your capacity for innovation. Second, it provides a game plan for developing an environment, both departmental and corporatewide, in which creativity and innovation can flourish—the managerial dimension. Both dimensions should make use of both individual and group approaches to the improvement of creative and innovative capacities. Although the enhancement of personal creativity is certainly a worthwhile project that should be undertaken by all HR managers, the cultivation of an organizational climate that promotes invention and innovation is one area in which HR managers can make a significant contribution because it is directly related to one of their primary functions: the advancement of human potential.

The Nature of Creativity

Creativity—either you have it or you don't, right? Wrong! Everyone has it to some degree. The real differences lie in developing and using it. Creativity is not only the ability to write novels, compose symphonies, or paint works of art. It can be as practical as finding a better way to organize your office.

Creativity is the process of solving problems by adding imagination, invention, and inspiration to logic and competence. Creative thinkers have a different way of looking at things, and they tend to come up with original solutions. Study Figure 5-1 to see how conventional and creative problem solving differ.

That definition of creativity may sound a lot like your idea of innovation. In fact, the two terms are often used interchangeably. For our purposes here, creativity and innovation are viewed as two ends of a continuum: Creativity brings a new concept or idea into being, and innovation makes the idea practical and usable.

What are they like, these innovators? Invariably, they have challenging minds. They are free thinkers. They can dream, but they also turn their dreams into reality.

Creative people are open-minded and mentally flexible. They are able to look at situations from different perspectives without preconceptions or preferences. They play with concepts, ideas, and relationships. They juggle elements into impossible positions, develop wild hypotheses, express the implausible, and think the unthinkable. They are able to suspend judgment when formulating

Figure 5-1. Conventional and creative problem solving compared.

Conventional Problem Solving	Creative Problem Solving
• The problem is well defined and has a definable cause.	• The problem is vague and has no readily definable cause.
• The criteria of solution are clearly identifiable.	• There are few or no criteria of solution.
• Vertical, logical, sequential, convergent thought is used.	• Lateral, nonlinear, illogical, or nonlogical thought is employed.
• Facts are an essential consideration in the process of solution.	• Facts are considered but are not central to a solution.
• Few alternatives are considered.	• A large volume of ideas is sought.
• Critical judgment is brought to bear on alternatives.	• Judgment on the value of ideas is reserved until later.
• The solution is corrective; it fixes something.	• The solution is not necessarily remedial; it may simply identify a new challenge or opportunity.
• The results of applying a solution are predictable, observable, and measurable.	• The results are unpredictable, sometimes unmeasurable, and often involve risk.

alternatives and courses of action. They also tend to ignore convention and precedents when addressing an issue. They have the ability to keep their concentration and tune out distractions. They generate lots of ideas quickly, and more easily from one to another.

Creative people are perceptive and observant. They see problems that have escaped the attention of others. They also have the ability to see the obvious—things that others have overlooked.

Creative people believe in themselves. They trust their intuition, their gut feelings. They don't agonize over tough decisions. They are able to tolerate ambiguity and high levels of risk without losing their composure. They consider their failures as opportunities to learn. They love change and make it happen.

Let's look at some of the specific skills involved.

- *Observational skills*—the ability to collect information using a deliberate and carefully worked out plan, directed toward fact finding
- *Listening skills*—the ability to listen actively, completely, and nonevaluatingly; to listen for meaning, not just words
- *Improvisational ability*—the capacity to ad lib, to use familiar objects, concepts, and ideas in new ways
- *Analytical skills*—using logic and inquiry to solve problems and make decisions
- *Synthetic skills*—combining or merging several facts or ideas to create new or improved concepts
- *Recall or retention skills*—the ability to summon facts for use in collecting data, associating events, solving problems, and making decisions
- *Association skills*—the ability to do "chain thinking," gearing the imagintion to memory, using sounds rather than words, and causing one thought to lead to another rather than concentrating on a sequential series of steps that is characteristic of logical thought
- *Problem-solving skills*—the ability to resolve a troublesome situation by following a reasoned thought process, keeping emotions and personal values in check

The HR Manager's Role

Creativity and innovation are about managing yourself and others in new situations. From that perspective, HR managers have responsibilities for creativity and innovation in three dimensions: personal, organizational, and managerial. All three are critically important to the manager, the organization, and the people managed.

The HR Manager as an Innovator

Successful HR managers are invariably creative and innovative. Hundreds of new ideas are required annually to manage an organization successfully. The margin of success—and, in today's environment, survival itself—depends on the ability of managers and their people to evolve and put to use fresh and workable ideas. HR managers must continually seek new combinations, better ways of doing things, new means of achieving goals and objectives. They must have the will to jettison inefficient, obsolete procedures and replace them with new and better ones, even when it means violating conventions and tradition.

HR managers must be creative and personally productive innovators. Creative thinking and innovation are important skills in carrying out all managerial functions: planning, organizing, staffing, directing, and controlling. They are equally important for managers of all the common functional areas, but are particularly critical in human resources development and utilization, marketing, research and development, and finance.

The HR Manager as an Organizational Advocate for Innovation

HR managers today occupy positions of great influence in organizations. They have high visibility and are recognized as major contributors to organizational well-being and productivity and prime movers in the business of improving organizational performance in all areas. Their focus on the human component of organizational resources gives them a considerable amount of leverage. By sponsoring organizational and management development interventions of all types, they can make creativity and innovation not only acceptable but also demanded. They can improve recruitment and hiring practices so that creative people are employed. They can train employees at all levels in creative approaches. They can help managers structure the work environment and maintain working conditions in such a way that creativity is encouraged.

The HR Manager as a Manager of Innovators

Managers must also be able to identify creative talent, cultivate and tap the innovative abilities of their own people, and encourage them to use those abilities in their work.

The best place to begin is recruiting creative people for the HR department. Hiring people who have a higher than average capacity for creativity and a past record of successful innovation will do more than any other single action to set the stage for generating new ways of doing the HR job. HR managers must systematically identify the personality traits and the specific skills associated with creativity and innovation, seek and attract people with those traits, abilities, and track records, and then hire them.

What should you look for? First and foremost, look for past accomplishments that reveal a creative bent. What has the individual done in earlier positions or in school that is evidence of innovative capacity? Second, during interviews, look for people who are self-confident, patient, and equally adept at objective and nonevaluative thought. Through questioning, estimate their capacity to relate and integrate ideas, to listen and question, to improvise, analyze, synthe-size, and associate ideas and concepts.

But merely hiring people with creative potential is not enough. HR managers must also be able to redesign jobs so that creative talents can be energized and given the opportunity to function. Then they must motivate their people to use their creative talents. To do that, managers must establish and maintain a job environ-ment, working conditions, and a reward system that will encourage the innovative abilities of their people.

Cultivating Creativity

It's no accident that creativity and innovation flourish in some organizations. Look at a company where ideas are swirling, people are charged with energy, and enthusiasm is high, and you'll see an organization with a culture that supports innovation, a management that enhances creativity in its people, and a structure that provides a fertile medium for growing good ideas. Organizations that wish to improve the climate for creativity must make a conscious effort in these areas.

Organization Vision and Commitment

Good strategic plans, abundant resources, and dedicated man-agement are not enough to turn an organization around—to revital-ize it, make it more flexible, innovative, and competitive. That requires organizational vision and commitment. Vision is the ability of top management to articulate a picture of what the organization should be and how it should operate in the future. Without such a picture, the wellsprings of creativity are cut off. The vision should recognize the need for new ways of managing, and it should reinforce those beliefs by rewarding managers for reducing barriers to change and empowering people to create. Rejuvenation is no longer achievable simply by doing the conventional managerial job better. All employees, from hourly workers to top executives, must believe in the vision and be committed to making it come alive.

Organization Climate and Culture

A proper organizational climate is essential for creativity and innovation to flower. An organization where company politics is the way of life—where managers are more concerned about protecting their turf, covering their rears, and enlarging their power than about achieving the goals and objectives of the organization—is one that stifles creativity and innovation. A company whose culture places a premium on conformance, on short-term results, on efficiency above all else, also neglects opportunities to nurture creative people. It will be unable to make the needed adjustments when faced with new competitors or economic change.

Look carefully at the climate of an organization that promotes innovation and you will see:

- Top-level commitment, support, and encouragement
- Psychological safety and freedom of expression and action
- Clear work standards and realistic requirements
- Toleration of failure
- Adequate information and other resources
- Exposure to new experiences, new ideas, and new directions
- Healthy competition
- Positive feedback
- Creative time

HR managers must help their companies break away from old cultural habits—traditional, bureaucratic, product-centered ways of doing business. In their place, they must help other managers and staffers identify focused areas for idea development and then work to establish the climate that promotes innovation. How do they do that? What specific steps can HR managers take?

- Set the example within their own department.
- Refocus executive and management development programs to emphasize items that foster innovation, such as those listed above.

- Initiate organizational development interventions such as training, team building, role analysis, survey feedback, and quality circles.
- Provide specific training in imagineering and creativity for employee groups.
- Improve job descriptions.

Appropriate Organizational Structure

The traditional structure so common in organizations—management centered, hierarchical, and organized by functional specialties—stifles creativity. Structures that promote "doing what we have always done and doing it more efficiently" must be replaced.

One of the most serious structural problems, and one of the most common, is constraints built into jobs. Jobs have been simplified to the point where they are stripped of their challenge. Further damage is done by establishing ultraconservative career patterns for some classes of employees, career ladders that severely restrict progress to more challenging jobs. And performance appraisal systems that reward preset objectives and punish risk taking don't help.

Jobs must be redesigned to include requirements and opportunities for creative activities. People must be given special assignments and independent projects in order to expand their vision and bring them into contact with new people, situations, problems, and ideas—conditions that will build their data bases and stimulate their curiosity and thinking.

Provisions should be made for dual career tracks. Creative people can stay in full-time creative jobs rather than being promoted to jobs they don't like, don't want, and aren't good at. With a dual system, they move up in status and compensation within the organization without abandoning their professional interests or research projects. People who wish to do so can move back and forth between managerial and technical or professional jobs over the course of their careers. Flexible hours and unconventional schedules should be made available to creative people who, for any number of reasons, cannot work regular shifts.

Finally, establishing special committees and task forces, and cross-functional teams, will go a long way toward stimulating innovation and creativity. The opportunity to share ideas and address problems with others often results in novel concepts and ideas—ideas that only synergistic approaches can produce.

Supporting Organizational Systems

Installing specific organizational systems can also be the means of stimulating creativity. Among the most promising are suggestion systems, reward systems, and idea banks. Let's look briefly at these three systems.

A good suggestion system can provide a fruitful source of ideas. Suggestion systems offer employees at all levels a ready means of bringing their ideas to the attention of management.

A well-conceived reward program can also be a boon to the production of new ideas. Giving recognition and awards to employees for their creative products and innovative ideas will encourage others to become creative and innovative. (See Chapter 8 for suggestions.)

Idea banks can take several forms. One of the most useful is the collection of ideas using heuristic computer programs. These programs lead to the development of new ideas and approaches by organizing, processing, and analyzing large volumes of data according to a sequence of operations that combines information in new ways, compares data, and yields relationships and associations previously unnoticed. The program then analyzes its performance, diagnoses its mistakes and failures, and makes corrections to increase the value and feasibility of the information discovered.

Another means of collecting ideas is to establish a file (either manual or computerized) of events that are of crucial importance to the organization, complete with a description of all alternative solutions that were considered and the results of their application. Clues to valuable ideas can be garnered by collecting and studying notes about critical incidents, unusual happenings, or accidental events.

Sensitive Management

Like any other desired result, creativity and innovation don't "just happen." They occur because someone *made* them happen. But creativity and innovation are not universally encouraged. Many executives and managers give lip service to them, but usually end up rejecting new ideas. They are more comfortable with tried-and-true approaches. They emphasize the evaluation of new ideas, not their generation.

Some managers oppose new ideas simply because the organization is operating successfully, the work is getting done, employees are generally satisfied, and customers are not complaining. Others lack the vision to appreciate the potential of a new idea—or fear the risk involved. They don't want to be associated with an innovation that failed, so they become overly cautious. They may inflict punishment for failures, and thereby deter their people from trying out new ways of doing their jobs.

Other managers don't trust their people to get the job done. They impose deadlines that are too tight, shackle their people with red tape, frustrate them with make-work projects, and handicap them with oversupervision. Instead of providing incentives and rewards, they use criticism, coercion, and intimidation to keep people under firm control.

Among the most common putdown techniques are these:

- *Procrastination:* "Let's study this in depth. We don't want to move too quickly and have to junk the idea later." Or "Before I even discuss this, I want you to prepare a complete staff study with supporting cost data and a detailed plan for implementation."
- *Inaccessibility:* "I'm too busy to talk to you right now." Or "Don't bother me with that. You're paid to solve problems, not bring them to me."
- *Blame passing:* "Why didn't you tell me about this before?" Or "How can we explain why we haven't been doing what they want all along? If we do it now, we'll look stupid."
- *Inattentiveness:* "OK. Tell me about it." And then stares at the ceiling, looks out the window, continues writing, or looks bored while the employee attempts to discuss the idea.
- *Discourtesy and impatience:* "Get on with it!" Or "I've heard enough." Or "That's a dumb idea. Come back when you've got something worth listening to."

Managers must seek change, believe in trying out new ways of doing things, and not be afraid to depart from conventional, safe approaches. And they must inculcate those attitudes in their people. They start by believing in the potential of people. They must get rid of the status quo mentality. Dismantle the bureaucracy, burn the red tape, and banish oversupervision. Give people freedom to propose unpopular or controversial ideas—things that go against tradition. Avoid nitpicking their ideas. Give people enough resources to get innovative results—time, equipment, materials, funds—and allow them to control the resources.

Managers of creative people and groups must learn to supervise by persuading, reassuring, stroking, and inspiring confidence, by establishing appropriate and achievable standards, by setting the example, and by leading instead of managing. Those who manage workers not normally thought of as having "creative" jobs should be alert for personal traits that would inhibit an innovative atmosphere. For instance:

- *Poor health*—physical, mental, or emotional illnesses—can steal the energy people would otherwise put into creativity.
- *Bad habits*—inflexibilities and inhibitions—tend to block creativity. Some people seem to have acquired the habit of always taking the easy way out. Others have an overwhelming desire to conform to prescribed ways of doing things.
- *Negative attitudes*—fear of failure or looking foolish, timidity, self-discouragement, and lack of self-confidence—will smother innovation. Some of this may stem from anxiety about loss of status or economic rewards; you, the manager, can ease this worry. A positive attitude, self-confidence, enthusiasm, and willingness to take risks are essential to the release of creative powers.
- *Excuses*—"I don't have time to be creative. I have more important things to do. I'm not a creative person"—indicate a lack of motivation and personal drive.
- *Lack of self-discipline*—which can show up as passivity, apathy, or laziness—is a certain killer of creative thinking. Creativity and innovation require effort—a great deal of effort. Unflagging energy and intense concentration are prerequisites to the generation of new ideas.

Creativity Training

Although many doubt the effectiveness of training in creativity, few would deny that creative problem-solving techniques can produce results. Obviously people can't apply those techniques unless they know what they are and have had some guided practice in using them. Also, there is some evidence that training in creative problem solving unlocks creative talents and helps people discover their creative capacities. Thus, organizations that are dedicated to the notion of creativity and determined to boost it must not overlook specific training programs. The next sections of this chapter describe several techniques, for individuals and for groups.

Individual Creative Techniques

There are many techniques to turn creative power on. To use them you must reserve creative time at least daily. Find your best creative time and location—and then schedule it. The best time and the best place will vary with the individual. For some, it's early in the morning; for others, late at night. Some people generate ideas while exercising—walking, jogging, biking, or even weight lifting. Others do their creative thinking while driving, taking a shower, or just goofing off. When you have found your most productive time, reserve it and use it for that purpose and that purpose only, regularly and religiously.

Many of the group techniques described in the next section can also be used by individuals. Here are some other ways to get your juices flowing.

Browsing and scanning. Faithfully skim books, professional and technical magazine articles, newspapers, advertisements, catalogs, brochures, and the like to get some insights into what others are doing and thinking. Be sure to include materials that are only vaguely related or even totally foreign to your own area.

Document analysis. Analyzing correspondence and reports is another excellent source of ideas—in-house documents and materials from outside, such as travel reports, after-action reports, customer complaints, client requests for assistance, sales reports, and proposals. The object is to read between the lines and garner some tips on what will help improve products, contribute to understanding of customers and competitors, and build a better public image.

Questioning. Many ideas can be generated simply by asking questions—many questions, relentlessly. Why do we do this? Is it really necessary? Why is it done this way? What are the advantages? Disadvantages? Can it be done any other way? How? A checklist of questions can be especially helpful.

Questioning can be used in staff meetings and conferences, at information and decision briefings, during interviews, inspections, and casual walk-throughs, by means of questionnaires and surveys, and by snowflakes or taskers. (The latter two items are short memos, usually less than a page, sent to subordinate managers and staff personnel to get facts and opinions on a specific subject, issue, or problem in writing. Responses are also brief, generally less than two pages.) Questioning provides a valuable means of getting facts and impressions, supplementing your powers of observation, and gaining clues as to what others are thinking.

Journals and note taking. Many people maintain an "idea trap"—a notebook, a set of 3 × 5 cards, or an audiocassette recorder—to jot down ideas whenever or wherever they occur. An idea is a fleeting thing. Unless you record it in some way, you are very likely to lose it forever. Most of us have discovered that it is very difficult to bring back an idea that crossed our minds even a few minutes ago, and almost impossible to retrieve one from yesterday.

Special assignments. People who want to improve their creative problem-solving skills seek out assignments and projects that will build their data base and bring them into contact with new and different people, situations, and problems, and new ideas. Special investigations and studies, audits, quality circle membership, assignment to work teams, task forces, and temporary positions, and travel will provide valuable means of expanding your horizons.

Setting quotas and deadlines. One of the less obvious means of generating ideas is to force concentration on problems by creating quotas and deadlines. Some people maintain that they work best under the pressure of a deadline. If you're one of them, why not impose short deadlines on yourself? Make them even more stress producing (if you can tolerate it) by announcing the deadline to others or promising to deliver something at a specific time. Give yourself a reward for meeting the deadline.

Similarly, you can develop idea fluency simply by establishing numerical quotas for each ideation session. Instead of simply listing all the alternatives or ideas you can think of and then quitting, establish a target number—whether it is ten, twenty-five, or fifty—and then stay with it until you have reached or exceeded that number. Again, give yourself a reward for meeting the quota.

Group Innovative Techniques

The objective of all creative problem-solving techniques is to enable people to break out of their mental strangleholds, clear their minds of traditional thinking patterns, and change their perspectives to see their work environment and problems in a completely different way. That is true for individuals dreaming up new ideas in the shower, and for groups working formally together in a conference room. The group techniques are designed to pile up many ideas about a problem, reserving judgment about their practicality until later. The underlying theory is, the more ideas available, the greater the chance of finding usable ones. The goal is volume. Thus group creative sessions are most successful if they are made up of people who as individuals practice creativity techniques. When people in the group are accustomed to stretching their minds, the results can be positively dazzling.

Regardless of the specific techniques used in problem-solving sessions, the following guidelines apply:

- Participation should be voluntary, and the atmosphere should be penalty free.
- Provide ample time, comfortable facilities, and pleasant surroundings.
- To enhance productivity, in both quantity and quality of ideas, show participants examples of the products or outcomes desired.
- Use warmup activities, involving practice with mundane, improbable, or novel problems. This promotes the quality and quantity of ideas when the real issue is addressed.
- Criticism, including self-criticism, and judgment are suspended while ideas and alternatives are being generated.
- Wild ideas are not only acceptable but welcomed.
- Quantity of ideas is the objective; the greater the number, the better.
- Encourage combining or joining ideas to improve them.

Here are some of the most productive and most commonly used group techniques.

Attribute listing and analysis. Group members start by listing the parts of the problem on a chalkboard or easel for individual attack. Then they write down the characteristics, basic qualities, distinguishing features, or attributes of each one. They then focus their attention on each entry one at a time, using the attribute list as a kind of checklist to force them to look at all aspects of the item. The idea is to systematically generate ways to modify its characteristics to develop a new application for it or to better satisfy its original purpose.

For example, for management development the attribute list might include formal education, in-house seminars, outside workshops, coaching, mentoring, self-development, special assignments, travel, and so on. Now associations between these items can be made—coaching plus special assignments, mentoring plus formal education—with the intention of creating new ideas in management development. For instance, the combination "mentoring plus formal education" might suggest that every employee whose formal education is being sponsored or supported by the company should be encouraged to have a mentor—either a manager or staff officer, not in his direct chain of command, to whom he could go for advice and assistance in matters relating to the educational venture.

Brainstorming and brainwriting. These two similar techniques are designed to produce as many ideas as possible within a short time frame. Both use the principle of free association or "free-wheeling"—purposely permitting ungoverned, uncontrolled, wild thinking, including improbable, impractical, even silly ideas, without attempting to evaluate them. Association works best when people have a large data base—minds well stocked with images gained from varied experiences.

The ideal brainstorming group or panel consists of a leader and seven to ten people of substantially the same rank or status. The composition of the group should be changed when a new problem is introduced, to prevent the development of rigid thinking patterns.

The leader prepares for the session by simplifying and focusing the problem and developing a list of suggested solutions to be used in priming the group when ideas begin to slow down. When the group meets, the leader presents the four basic rules of brainstorming, conducts warmup exercises, poses the real problem to the group, and provides a few examples of solutions.

The four rules of brainstorming are:

1. Criticism of ideas is not allowed.
2. Free-wheeling is welcomed; the wilder the idea, the better.
3. Quantity is the goal; the more ideas you have, the more likely you are to find winners.
4. Combination and improvement are encouraged; combining and building on ideas create even better ideas.

The leader then calls for suggestions and ideas. As each participant presents an idea, a recorder numbers it consecutively and jots it down on a chalkboard or easel or in a notebook. (Ideas can also be taped.) When the flow of ideas slows down, the leader applies pressure and encouragement to the group to get more ideas. At the end of about thirty minutes (or when the idea well has run dry), the leader thanks the participants, asks them to think about the problem until the next day and forward any new ideas, and dismisses the group.

The leader edits the list to ensure that items are clearly and succinctly stated and has the listed transcribed. A second, smaller group, no more than five people, is given the typewritten list of the ideas and asked to select the most promising ones, in terms of appropriateness and workability, and forward them to another small group. That group has the job of developing them for presentation to the decision maker.

Brainwriting is basically the same process but relies on writing ideas down. The group leader describes the problem; participants are given blank sheets of lined paper and are asked to write at least four solutions. They generate ideas by identifying relationships—that is, they relate old to new, associate this idea with that idea, dig for likenesses, similarities, and commonalities, look for causes and effects, contrasts, and patterns. Participants may use similes and metaphors to create interesting, surprising, or preposterous word pictures expressing similarities and differences.

After ten or fifteen minutes, participants are asked to exchange their lists and add additional solutions or ideas suggested by the items on the forms they receive. The exchange process continues until no more ideas are generated.

Checklists. Checklists are sets of specific questions used by participants in problem-solving situations to uncover clues for new solutions. The lists are prepared in advance and used to stimulate ideas. The questions or items on the list are always framed to address a specific problem and are designed to define the problem or develop alternatives for solution. Ideas generated are developed into specific forms at a later time, either by the group itself, or another group or individual.

Scores of ready-made checklists are available in many disciplines to help prod the imaginations of problem-solving teams. For example, Tracey's *Human Resource Development Standards* (see chapter bibliography) is essentially a series of more than 140 detailed checklists for HR managers covering such broad topics as managing the HR function, plant, facilities and employee services, HR program elements and delivery systems. Those checklists could be used by committees, work groups, quality circles, and task forces to address almost any problem concerning human resources. An excerpt from that manual is shown in Figure 5-2.

Another useful checklist procedure that can be adapted to almost any problem is to ask participants to take the concept and then:

Adapt it
Modify it
Substitute something else for it
Make it larger
Make it smaller

Multiply it
Divide it
Add to it
Subtract from it
Rearrange it
Reverse it
Combine it

In addition, the indexes and tables of contents of books and periodicals, encyclopedias, synonym and word-phrase finders, rhyming dictionaries, abstracts, catalog listing, directories, and the like can serve as checklists. And, of course, they can be tailored to fit the problem at hand.

Forced relationships. This problem-solving technique involves squeezing two or more normally unrelated principles together, jamming them into forced relationships. Initially, the relationship may be improbable, impossible, or outright crazy, but the force fitting is modified and continued until the relationship becomes reasonable or at least possible to achieve.

The group starts the process by isolating and recording the essential parts of the problem and facts relating to it. The similarities, differences, and other relationships among the parts are identified and analyzed to determine their patterns. The different parts are then forced into new relationships to develop new ideas.

For example, a committee charged with generating new product ideas for a manufacturer of training equipment might approach the task by listing the items the company already produces: overhead projectors, slide projectors, filmstrip projectors, microfiche viewers, video monitors, cathode ray tube terminals (CRTs), and projection screens. The committee might decide to explore the relationship between overhead projects and CRTs. Free association would almost certainly lead to a product that combines the features of both, so that anything that can be created on a computer screen can be displayed on a large screen for group viewing.

Guided imaging. Sometimes called visualization, guided imaging makes use of the imaging and imaginative powers of the human mind to review the past, contemplate the present, and speculate about the future to create "pictures" of possibilities and improbabilities. The problem may be vague and ill defined, or clear and well described. The task is to perceive it in an open-minded way and to generate images of the situation and mental pictures of the results

(*Text continues on page 146.*)

Figure 5-2.   A sample problem-solving checklist.

B. Career planning
  1. Purposes
     a. Career planning services are provided employees to help them
        to:
        (1) Analyze their values, abilities, aptitudes, interests, and
            potentials
        (2) Plan and implement realistic career development goals,
            objectives, activities, and timetables
        (3) Exploit in-house and outside opportunities to improve
            their skills, knowledge, status, and job satisfaction
     b. Career planning is designed and implemented to achieve the
        following organizational benefits:
        (1) Improve employee motivation, morale, skills, knowledge,
            and productivity
        (2) Reduce turnover
        (3) Improve the utilization of available skills
        (4) Develop a built-in source of supervisors, managers, and
            executives
  2. Policies and practices
     a. Career planning is an integral part of the total HRD program
     b. Career counseling is considered a primary responsibility of all
        managers and supervisors
     c. Career development opportunities inside and outside the orga-
        nization are identified, described, and publicized to all em-
        ployees
     d. Career planning and counseling are closely tied to existing
        personnel systems
        (1) Recruitment practices
        (2) Selection and assignment policies
        (3) Job evaluation procedures
        (4) Salary administration
        (5) Promotion and transfer practices
        (6) Performance appraisal systems
        (7) Rotational assignments
        (8) Training and development programs
        (9) Personnel information systems and skills inventories
        (10) Management succession and replacement planning
     e. The HRD staff provides professional assistance to line managers
        and supervisors in helping employees plan their careers

    f. Career planning is individualized and focuses on systematic self-assessment of the following:
- (1) Values and interests
- (2) Goals and objectives
- (3) Skills, abilities, and aptitudes

3. Resources. The following basic career planning resources and aids are made available to all employees:
    a. Counseling services
- (1) HRD staff
- (2) Line managers and supervisors
- (3) Specialized staff counselors
- (4) Internal and external specialists, such as psychologists and psychometrists

    b. Enterprise communications with regard to the following:
- (1) Training and development opportunities
- (2) Educational assistance
- (3) Job opportunities, requirements, and vacancies, and career ladders
- (4) EEO and affirmative action programs and policies

    c. Psychological testing services
- (1) Aptitudes and interests
- (2) Skills and abilities
- (3) Personality and motivation

4. Strategies and techniques. Career planning and counseling programs make appropriate use of the following strategies and techniques:
    a. Assessment centers
    b. Self-analysis and career planning workshops
    c. Enterprise publications or workbooks directed toward career ladders and job opportunities
    d. Individual career counseling
    e. Outplacement counseling
    f. Special programs for women, minorities, the handicapped, older workers, and potential retirees

5. Evaluation. Career planning and counseling services are evaluated by:
    a. Follow-up of employees
- (1) Interviews and questionnaire surveys
- (2) Reports of supervisors

    b. Measures of bottom line results such as:
- (1) Increased productivity
- (2) Reduced turnover
- (3) Increased number of promotions and promotables, particularly among women, minorities, and the handicapped
- (4) Reduced grievances

of applying various solutions. Descriptive notes are made of these images and are shared with others and reviewed at a later time.

For example, participants in an instructor training session could be asked to deliberately bring pictures back into their minds of the worse or best learning experience, counseling session, or confrontation they ever had. Or a task force working on educational specifications for a new training center may be asked to develop a detailed mental image of the classroom of the future. Or they may be encouraged to convert a two-dimensional drawing of an object into a full-color, three-dimensional construct in their mind's eye—and then verbally describe what they visualize.

Morphological analysis. This is a process of systematically listing and studying all the possible combinations of alternatives that might be helpful in solving a problem. It involves stating the problem as broadly as possible and breaking it into its components for study and analysis. Each of these components is treated as an independent variable and is specified and inserted into a two-dimensional grid or a three-dimensional cube. Each of the intersecting axes of the grid or cube is examined in turn and considered as a possible solution to the problem. The most promising alternative is selected and tested, modified, evaluated, and developed.

Say you're trying to come up with a new instructional strategy. You decide to use a three-dimensional grid (see Figure 5-3). You choose "trainee centered" as a major dimension and list under that heading all the ways trainees can learn without an instructor (role playing, study assignments, games, and so on). That list forms one axis of the morphological grid. Across the other dimension, you write "instructor centered" and list such strategies as team teaching, lecture, demonstration, conference, tutoring, and so on. That gives you a series of boxes where each attribute intersects with an attribute on the other axis. A third dimension could be added under the heading of mediated learning. Attributes might include computer-assisted instruction, interactive video, programmed books, teleconferencing, and so on. Examining the boxes where the three dimensions intersect provides new options.

For example, if you select vertical row A, horizontal row B, and row C on the remaining axis of the cube, where they intersect you have a combination of interactive video, tutoring, and role playing. Another combination would be games, computer-based training, and team teaching. Obviously some of these just don't work; however, continued matching of trials using two and three dimensions will yield many workable combinations.

Figure 5-3.   Example of a three-dimensional matrix.

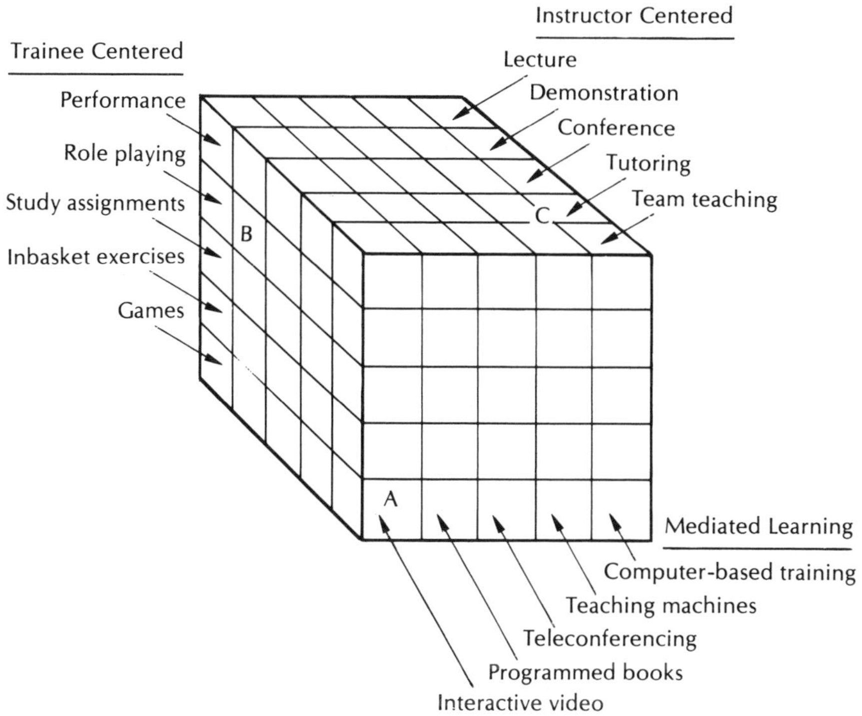

Remodeling. Leads for a new idea can often be generated by remodeling or changing the existing form of a concept. There are many ways to do this. Rearrange—do it backward, turn it sideways, upside down, move it from the end to the beginning, front to back, put it together if it is now separate, separate it if it is joined, and so on. Substitute—use a different material, a different process, a different sequence, different players, and so on. Add—duplicate the program, make it longer, bigger, or more inclusive, add more units. Subtract—reduce the length of the program, make it smaller, leave something out, make it less inclusive, cut the number of units.

The next step. Whatever technique is used, the next step is to record and present the ideas in written form to the person who asked the group for solutions. If the ideas were developed by a group without a specific assignment, or they were a byproduct of an exercise with a different purpose, the ideas should always be forwarded in written form to the managers or staff officers who are responsible for the function involved. For example, training sessions in how to do creative problem solving, conducted by the HR department, invariably address company problems of one kind or another. Although the objective is to train the participants in problem-solving techniques, the products of the sessions are often very valuable and frequently usable by the responsible manager. Send them along, with a cover note explaining why and how the list was produced.

Selling Ideas

A creative idea is worthless unless acted upon. But even a good idea may die unused because it was not sold to the decision maker.

A good idea has two features: it has currency and it provides benefits. An innovative or creative approach must be usable now or in the very near future. An idea that may be of some use to the organization in the distant future is highly unlikely to generate an enthusiastic endorsement by anyone.

A good idea also yields benefits to the organization or one or more of its constituencies (owners, stockholders, employees at all levels, suppliers, consultants, customers and clients, or the public at large). These benefits may be a reduction in absenteeism, accident rates, grievances, lost time, operating costs, rejects, and turnover, or improvements in communication, customer service and satisfaction, employee morale, production, and profitability, to name a few.

One thing more is needed: a good presentation. No matter how promising an innovation is, it will fail if it does not get the support it needs for implementation. That means a well-planned effort to sell the idea to the right people in the right way at the right time. The right way is to base the presentation on facts and logic, even when facts and logic were not the ingredients responsible for the original creative idea. The presentation should focus on what the implementation of the idea will mean in terms of benefits to the organization, its managers, its people, and its customers and clients. Plan to make the presentation to the right person or group, the one with decision-making authority and the power to allocate the resources needed.

Here are some specific suggestions for the preparation phase:

- Develop your presentation thoroughly. Have the idea worked out in fine detail—the what, how, why, when, where, and who.
- Concentrate on the benefits to be derived—by whom, when, and where. But don't fail to identify the costs and risks, and explain how you will minimize them.

- Make the innovation easy to understand; use simple words and, when possible, illustrations, models, and graphics.
- Anticipate negative reactions and questions and prepare your responses.
- Test the idea and your presentation on several people to work the bugs out of it.

The presentation itself is really a decision briefing, since it is designed to obtain a judgment on a proposal from the person empowered to make that decision. Here are some suggestions.

- Have a positive attitude; be bold and self-confident.
- State the purpose of the briefing at the outset: "To get a decision on. . . ."
- Identify the reasons for the briefing—what started the action.
- Outline the organization of the briefing.
- Present the facts that led to a definition of the real problem, sticking to the essentials and getting quickly to the point; include the what, when, where, and who.
- Identify and discuss the facts that bear on the solution of the problem; again include the what, when, where, and who.
- Identify and discuss alternative courses of action, the advantages and disadvantages, costs and benefits of each.
- Present your conclusions, making your statements direct, blunt, and precise; don't hedge. Emphasize benefits and costs.
- Present your recommendations. Put your solutions in such a form that the decision maker can take action. Make them specific, and be sure to identify the kinds and amount of support you will need.
- If you get a turndown, be persistent. Shore up your proposal; remedy the deficiencies; get more people on your side; and try again.

The Innovation Process

Remember that in this area of creativity, the HR manager has three focuses: personal, departmental, and companywide. If you are truly committed to the notion of innovation, you must work on all three: spend some time developing your own creative skills; build an environment in the HR department that makes it possible for the staff to approach their jobs creatively; and help the organization as a whole be the sort of place where innovation is welcomed. In each case, the process has some areas of similarity and some areas of difference. Here's a brief review.

Enhancing Personal Creativity

Step 1. Eliminate blocks to creativity. Stay mentally, physically, and emotionally healthy. Adopt a positive mindset. Get rid of your bad habits. Become self-disciplined.

Step 2. Learn and practice creative techniques. Invest the time and effort needed to fill your toolbox. Practice the techniques described in this chapter; try the group techniques by yourself. Establish personal quotas and deadlines. Set time aside every day for personal ideation, and be sure to record your ideas.

Step 3. Expand and improve your personal idea bank. Browse, scan, question, analyze correspondence and documents, make notes, seek special assignments, attend professional and technical meetings and conferences.

Step 4. Identify focused areas for idea development. Develop written lists of organizational and departmental problems, issues, situations and conditions that either need fixing or can be improved. Put them in priority order for individual attack. Then systematically address each item during your creative time.

Step 5. Sell and install the solutions. Develop your solutions in detail. Get support for the idea from subordinates, peers, and superiors. If you can't make the final decision to implement, sell the proposal to the person who can. When you get the go-ahead, install, monitor, and modify the change as needed.

Managing Creative Effort in Your Department

Step 1. Establish a creative climate. Identify organizational and individual blocks to creativity. Make the modifications required to support innovation. Pay particular attention to reward systems. Check your own managerial attitudes, style, and competencies. Make needed changes.

Step 2. Train your people in the use of creative techniques. As a minimum, include instruction and practice in attribute listing, brainstorming, checklists, and morphological analysis. Acquaint them with the techniques of browsing and scanning, questioning, and notetaking.

Step 3. Identify focused areas for idea development and address them. Set up staff committees to identify and prioritize departmental issues. Provide them with the time, encouragement, and support they need to arrive at novel and workable solutions.

Step 4. Sell and install the creative products of your people. Help your people develop their solutions in detail and prepare them for presentation. Make sure the project is assigned to an individual for implementation. Provide the authority and resources, including start-up, operating, and contingency funding, to carry the project through to completion. Monitor the project and provide additional assistance as needed.

Fostering Creativity Throughout the Organization

Step 1. Get top-management support. Focus the attention of senior management on the value of innovation; start by demonstrating the effectiveness of creative training at the department level. Display the products of those efforts.

Step 2. Teach managers how to build commitment. With team-building exercises and other management development interventions, show them how to develop a high level of trust and commitment within their departments.

Step 3. Encourage managers to let their people be creative. Remind them to assign tasks that offer people opportunities to be creative, and to give them the time, resources, and freedom of action needed to get results.

Step 4. Provide training. Teach managers the key skills and abilities involved in creativity: problem solving, analytical and divergent thinking, use of intuition and gut feelings, and the ability to relate and integrate ideas.

Step 5. Provide personal encouragement. Give managers support and recognition publicizing success stories.

Summary

No organization can prosper without a large amount of creativity and innovation. Competition for markets is too keen, and technology changes too fast, to permit an attitude of "business as usual."

Instead, HR managers must fulfill their dual roles as creative and innovative managers and as managers of creative and innovative people. And they must do everything possible to make the climate of the entire organization amenable to innovation and risk taking.

Creative thinking is unconventional thinking; it adds imagination, inspiration, and invention to more conventional, vertical, and logical approaches. Creativity produces the new concept, product, or idea. Innovation makes the new idea workable.

Creative managers must tear down barriers to the development and implementation of creative and innovative ideas. Organizational barriers include culture, climate, structure, and systems. Managerial barriers include poor management skills, inadequate communication, coercion and criticism, lack of trust, and red tape. Individual barriers include poor health, fear of looking foolish, bad habits, pessimism, cynicism, negative feedback, and lack of self-confidence and self-discipline.

Major stimulants to creative effort are a proper organizational environment, including a structure and systems that complement creativity, managerial encouragement and support, and recognition and rewards. The atmosphere must be psychologically safe, encourage freedom of thought and action, and be tolerant of errors and failures. Managers must show concern for people and provide positive feedback.

Training in creative and innovative techniques should also be provided for employees at all levels. Such training should be voluntary, and it should include a variety of group and individual techniques.

Because most ideas must be sold to a decision maker, it is imperative that proposals be carefully and fully developed into first-rate decision briefings. The thrust of such briefings should be on the benefits to be derived by the organization or one or more of its constituencies.

The process of improving personal creativity involves, in order:

1. Eliminating blocks
2. Learning and practicing techniques
3. Expanding idea bank
4. Identifying areas to work on
5. Selling and installing solutions

Managing the creative efforts of other people means:

1. Establishing a creative climate within the department
2. Training people in creativity techniques

3. Identifying areas for them to work on
4. Helping them get ideas accepted

Fulfilling the responsibility for promoting a creative climate throughout the organization means:

1. Getting top-management commitment to concept of innovation
2. Teaching other managers how to build creative staffs
3. Encouraging other managers to permit creativity
4. Training other managers in creativity techniques
5. Supporting their successes

For Further Reading, Viewing, and Listening

Adams, James L. *The Care and Feeding of Ideas: A Guide to Encouraging Creativity.* Reading, Mass.: Addison-Wesley Publishing Company, 1985.

Albrecht, Karl. *Brain Power: Learn to Improve Your Thinking Skills.* Englewood Cliffs, N.J.: Prentice-Hall, 1980.

———. *Brain Power* (12-minute videocassette). Coronet/MTI Film & Video, 108 Wilmot Rd., Deerfield, IL 60015.

———. *Idea Power* (16-minute videocassette). Coronet/MTI Film & Video, 108 Wilmot Rd., Deerfield, IL 60015.

Amabile, Theresa M. *The Social Psychology of Creativity.* New York: Springer-Verlag, 1983.

Barker, Joel A. *Discovering the Future: The Business of Paradigms* (30-minute videocassette). Produced by Documentary Film Makers. Distributed by Video Publishing, 10740 Lyndale Ave. South, Minneapolis, MN 55420.

Bengt-Arne, Vedin. *Corporate Culture for Innovation.* Brookfield, Vt.: Brookfield Publishing Company, 1980.

Campbell, David P. *The Psychology of Creativity* (52-minute audiotape). Greensboro, N.C.: The Center for Creative Leadership, 1978.

———. *Take the Road to Creativity and Get Off Your Dead End.* Greensboro, N.C.: The Center for Creative Leadership, 1977.

Creative Problem Solving (6-hour audiocassette). American Management Association, 135 W. 50th St., New York, NY 10020, 1978.

Creativity: The Only Way to Fly (8-minute videocassette). Salenger Film, 1635 Twelfth St., Santa Monica, CA 90404-9988, 1982.

DeVito, Frank, and Deidre Sullivan. "Managing Creativity." *Management Review,* January 1985, pp. 42–43.

Drucker, Peter. *Innovation and Entrepreneurship.* New York: Harper & Row, 1985.

Foster, Richard. *Innovation: The Attacker's Advantage.* New York: Summit Books, 1986.

Freedman, George. *The Pursuit of Innovation: Managing the People and Processes That Turn New Ideas Into Profits.* New York: AMACOM, 1988.

Gordon, Jack, and Ron Zemke. "Making Them More Creative." *Training,* May 1986, pp. 30–45.

Innovation: It's Worth the Risk (30-minute videocassette). AMA Film/Video, Nine Galen St., Watertown, MA 02172, 1986.

Kanter, Rosabeth Moss. *The Change Masters: Innovation for Productivity in the American Corporation.* New York: Touchstone Books, 1985.

Keil, John M. *How to Zig in a Zagging World: Unleashing Your Hidden Creativity* (two audiocassettes). Wiley Sound Business, 605 Third Ave., New York, NY 10158, 1988.

———. *The Creative Mystique: How to Manage It, Nurture It, and Make It Pay* (2 audiocassettes). Wiley Sound Business, 605 Third Ave., New York, NY 10158, 1988.

A Kick in the Seat of the Pants (20-minute videocassette). Produced by Century III Teleproductions, 1987. Distributed by AMA Film/Video, Nine Galen St., Watertown, MA 02172.

London, Manuel, *Change Agents: New Roles and Innovation Strategies for Human Resource Professionals.* San Francisco: Jossey-Bass, 1988.

Miller, William C. *The Creative Edge: Fostering Innovation Where You Work.* Reading, Mass.: Addison-Wesley, 1986.

Nirenberg, Gerald J. *The Art of Creative Thinking.* New York: Cornerstone Library, 1982.

Potter-Brotman, Jennifer. "How to Keep Ideas Moving." *Training and Development Journal,* May 1988, pp. 32–34.

Rawlinson, J. Geoffrey. *Creative Thinking and Brainstorming.* New York: Halsted Press, 1981.

Ray, Michael L., and Rochelle Myers. *Creativity in Business.* New York: Doubleday and Company, 1986.

Stein, Morris, I. *Stein on Creativity* (52-minute videocassette). Produced by John McKeithan, 1984. Distributed by the Center for Creative Leadership, 5000 Laurinda Dr., P.O. Box P-1, Greensboro, NC 27402-1660.

Thiagarajan, Sivasailam. "Beyond Brainstorming." *Training and Development Journal,* September 1988, pp. 57–60.

Tracey, William R. *Human Resource Development Standards.* New York: AMACOM, 1981.

Uncover Your Creativity (6-minute videocassette). Produced by Real-time, 1985. Distributed by Salenger Films, 1635 Twelfth St., Santa Monica, CA 90404-9988.

Van Gundy, Arthur B., Jr., *Managing Group Creativity: A Modular Approach to Problem-Solving.* New York: AMACOM, 1984.

Walton, Richard E. *Innovating to Compete: Lessons for Diffusing and Managing Change in the Workplace.* San Francisco: Jossey-Bass, 1987.

A Whack on the Side of the Head (17-minute videocassette). Produced by Carbiner, 1988. Distributed by AMA Film/Video, Nine Galen St., Watertown, MA 02172.

Why Man Creates (25-minute videocassette). Produced by Saul Bass & Associates, 1970. Distributed by Vantage Communications, P.O. Box 546, Nyack, NY 10960.

6

Resolving Conflict
Managing Disagreement

Managing conflict is a tough challenge for all managers—particularly HR managers, the "people experts," because they are expected to play a central role in this area within their organizations. In fact, HR managers have three responsibilities: managing conflict within their departments, serving as internal consultant and sometime mediator of conflicts in other departments, and training other managers and staffers in the process of conflict management.

Most managers don't feel comfortable dealing with conflict because it means that they must deal with emotions. But when there is conflict, the whole department suffers from the resulting tension. When managers handle conflict well, they are rewarded with heightened creative effort, improved morale, and renewed commitment to the organization. When poorly handled, conflict can waste time, talent, and other resources, bruise egos and injure feelings, cause friction or serious lack of cooperation among people and groups, undermine morale and sabotage trust, smother valid dissent, and impede progress. The organization and its management pay the penalty—in wasted resources, lower morale, lack of progress, and decreased productivity.

Conflict management requires integration of several skills: listening, problem sensing, inquiring, problem solving, and negotiating. Managers must learn what causes conflict, how to diagnose the type of conflict, and how to cope with disagreement and controversy. Helping organizations manage conflict is one of the most demanding responsibilities of HR managers—and one of their most valuable contributions.

The Nature of Conflict

There are two fundamental kinds of conflict: interpersonal and intergroup. Interpersonal conflict is any kind of dissension between two people. Sometimes this conflict is open, characterized by overt controversy, argument, hostility, defiance, or fighting. It is readily observable by anyone who is ready and willing to face reality. It is also the type that is most likely to make observers anxious, and eager to withdraw from the scene as quickly as possible. More worrisome is hidden conflict. It is not readily observable; it can be detected only by its symptoms: high levels of employee stress, lowered productivity, poor decisions, apathy, fault finding, complaining, buck passing, defensive behavior, and nitpicking. The level of conflict may range from concealed aggression to sabotage, or anything in between.

Intergroup conflict usually springs from competition, as when departments or staff elements of the same organization vie with each other for recognition, authority, power, or resources. Probably its most serious form is the day-to-day disputes and political infighting of ordinary organizational conflict. It can also be either open or hidden.

Basic Principles

There are certain things we know about conflict.

It is inevitable. Because of the many problems provided by organizational life and the competitive nature of human beings, conflict must be considered a given. Plan on managing, controlling, and channeling it.

It is predictable. Conflict can often be anticipated, since it arises in organizations throughout our society for similar reasons. Your focus should be on anticipating the results of actions, as they relate to potential conflict, determining whether the discontent that may be produced is acceptable, preparing to take compensatory measures, and implementing damage control measures if needed.

It is proportional to the organization. The larger and more complex the organization is, the more frequent, more severe, and more vehement will be its conflicts. Bigness begets strife, complicates communication, and increases competition.

It can be disastrous if excessive. Intense or violent conflict is destructive for any organization. It can destroy relationships, and it always decreases productivity and disrupts cooperation.

It is preventable. Although some conflict is inevitable, much of the most damaging kind is indeed preventable. Preventing destructive conflict is a much more productive strategy than trying to resolve it—and a whole lot easier.

It is complex. Conflict confrontation and resolution are extremely complex strategies. Successful conflict resolution demands a command of many key managerial skills.

It is risky. Conflict resolution involves risks to the manager, the disputants, and the organization. Therefore, not all conflicts should be confronted; some are better left alone. However, conflicts related to corporate goals and employee job satisfaction, morale, and productivity should *always* be addressed.

It is symptomatic. Conflict is a symptom of a problem—not the problem itself. Some of the most common indicators are lower productivity, high turnover and absenteeism, poor decisions, and defensive behavior.

The Positive Side of Conflict

As we said, conflict is inevitable, and all managers need to know how to control it before it destroys employee morale and teamwork. But they also need to know how to use conflict as a positive force for individual and organizational progress. This is a new idea for some—that conflict can have positive results. Wise managers put their energies into learning how to channel conflict, how to manage it, rather than trying to eliminate it entirely.

Discontent with oneself, with one's performance, is a prerequisite for improvement. It's the same for organizations. If it is channeled into useful areas, conflict may:

- Reveal and clarify important issues.
- Increase employee involvement and strengthen cohesiveness and group relationships.
- Promote growth, improve problem solutions, and increase productivity.
- Offer opportunities for managers to learn more about themselves and their attitudes and behavior, explore the perceptions of others, and develop more productive and satisfying work relationships.
- Help managers identify underlying problems, ameliorate or eliminate negative attitudes and feelings, correct misunderstandings, and generate the commitment needed for change.
- Serve as a relief valve for dissatisfaction or strong negative feelings.
- Actuate major changes, innovation, and creativity in finding solutions to problems.
- Goad individuals and groups to acknowledge and deal with difficult problems and situations.

- Expedite the termination of unprofitable or ineffective associations and the breakup of unproductive relationships and subdue disruptive or uncooperative group members.

The Roots of Conflict

In modern organizations, with all their complexities and competing pressures, there is plenty of potential for conflict. Sometimes the situation arises from the character of the organization itself, sometimes from the way managers manage, and sometimes from the way employees behave.

Organizational Sources of Conflict

History and traditions. The way an organization views its role in its industry, how it views competitiveness, the accent it places on profitability, service, or quality can affect job satisfaction and generate discontent.

Mission and purposes. The mission statement can also cause conflict, particularly if it is unclear—there is considerable room for dissension, both internally among organizational elements and externally with other competing companies.

Culture and climate. These factors are the most important determinants of harmony. An excessively competitive organization climate is almost certain to generate both interpersonal and intergroup conflict. A positive climate, an atmosphere of justice, openness, trust, and mutual confidence, must prevail if conflict is to be avoided.

Goals and values. If the organization's values clash with those held by employees or those of other organizations, conflict is created.

Structure. Organization structure provides the framework within which a group of people can work together to attain the goals of the group and the organization as a whole. When the structure is inappropriate or unclear, people will define their own functions. Competition will become the order of the day, and frequent, serious conflict is inevitable. This problem becomes acute when a merger or acquisition creates a new entity out of what originally were two separate companies, each with its own structure and values.

Competitive status. In many organizations, there is a definite pecking order among departments. Often this ranking system results in competition—intense rivalry for the attention of the chief executive, for more power, or for a greater share of the resources available to the enterprise. Departments at the bottom of the totem pole are certain to feel neglected, and that is bound to generate bad feelings and conflict.

Interdependence. Departments are by their nature interdependent. Conflict results when disparity arises from delegations of authority without regard to the needs of specialization. Other problems are informational disparities—the interdependent elements have either no information or different information.

Change. Too often, insufficient thought and attention are given to implementing changes in organizations—with disastrous effects.

Policies. Policies are declarations of what the organization believes are its obligations and responsibilities to its stockholders, customers, clients, suppliers, managers, employees, itself, and the public at large. When policies are vague, imprecise, dogmatic, inflexible, inconsistent, misconstrued, or misapplied, the door is opened for two or more of the organization's constituencies to be at odds.

Managerial Sources of Conflict

Goals, values, and standards. All managers have goals—for themselves and for their departments. If they are not compatible with the goals of the organization or its CEO, trouble is inevitable.

Effectiveness in communication. Communication skills are critical to success as a manager, and are also a key to the prevention of conflict. Communication is the basic process from which most organizational activities derive. Any department is essentially one large communication system through which instructions and guidance from the top are transmitted downward, and information and reports needed for decision are passed upward. Without good communications, it is impossible to reach the goals of the department or to build the spirit of cooperation so essential for productivity and harmony.

Treatment of subordinates. Managers who don't know how to handle people cause inordinate problems. They don't give approval, they never ask for suggestions, and they disregard complaints. Some managers fail to tell their people precisely what they expect and how their performance will be judged. They don't tell them about changes that are going to affect them. When people are ignored or brushed off, they become dissatisfied, and conflicts are bound to arise.

Leadership style. The leadership styles of some supervisors can generate negative reactions among subordinates. For example, some managers espouse democracy but practice authoritarianism. Others engage in punitive or threatening treatment. That is certain to cause resentment—and ultimately, conflict.

Employee Sources of Conflict

Goals and values. When an individual employee's values are at odds with the organization's, conflict is bound to result. For example, an employee who puts a high priority on spending time with family may decline a promotion or resist overtime work.

Job requirements. A major reason why conflict develops in organizations is that employees do not understand their assignments and those of their fellow workers. Conflict can be traced to poorly designed and inadequately defined jobs, overlapping or conflicting duties and tasks, inadequate delegation of authority, and unclear, arbitrary, or overly stringent performance standards.

Competitive status. Competition is yet another major source of conflict. Competition is always keen in organizations, for status, recognition, power, authority, advancement, and the like. When barriers to higher status (whether real or imagined) are encountered, people feel wronged, and the pain is often transformed into negative behavior and either open or concealed conflict with their perceived oppressors.

Job dissatisfaction. Whatever the reason for the dissatisfaction, it is another cause of conflict. Discontent can also be traced to favoritism, whether real or perceived, excessive pressure by managers or supervisors to produce, and differences over job methods and approaches.

Personality clashes. People sometimes instinctively dislike another person, usually because of subconscious stereotyping. Such feelings are common. In any event, personality clashes result in tensions, lack of cooperation, and personal frictions.

Troublemakers. Employees who are preoccupied with enhancing their authority and status at the expense of others are troublemakers. They are disruptive and destructive and are not above cheating, lying, stealing, intimidating, harassing, threatening, or purposely hurting others. They always cause dissension and conflict.

Conflict Management Skills

What knowledge, skills, and attitudes must HR managers bring to conflict situations if they are to have any hope of resolving them successfully?

Self-knowledge. Managers who are effective in resolving conflict know themselves—their strengths and limitations, talents and shortcomings, capabilities and faults. They are able to predict their own reactions and behavior during confrontation.

People knowledge. Managers must have a thorough knowledge of people—their needs and wants, motivations and biases, what makes them do what they do. They must be able to observe and describe behavior in specific, objective, nonjudgmental, and nonlabeling terms. They must always act in ways that preserve and protect the dignity, worth, and self-respect of all parties to the dispute.

Conflict knowledge and skills. A thorough understanding of conflict, its nature, causes, and cures, is also essential to successful conflict management. Managers must also have a complete arsenal of conflict resolution strategies, tactics, and approaches. They must be able to analyze situations to determine what caused the behavior. They must know how to diagnose differences and choose appropriate strategies. They must be able to use more than one strategy and to make adjustments from problem to problem and even during conflict resolution sessions. They must be able to determine the effectiveness of their strategy and identify next steps.

Empathy and fairness. Conflict managers must be able to see both sides as disputants see it but agree with neither. They must be warm and accepting toward disputants but coldly objective toward issues. They must be invariably fair, treating both parties to a disagreement equally. They must be able to recognize and defuse hidden anger or frustration before it is passed on to others. They must be able to lighten up tense situations before they get out of control.

Problem-solving skills. To resolve conflict, managers must have highly developed problem-solving skills: the ability to use observational, inquiring, and probing techniques, to identify the root problem, analyze situations and determine their causes, help the disputants to identify, compare, and select feasible alternative solutions, translate the solution into action, and follow up.

Communication skills. Managers must also have sharply honed listening and persuasive skills. They must be able to listen actively, concentrating on the speaker and the messages. They must be able to listen and watch for meaning, not just the words but the intent, the central theme. Managers must be able to speak clearly and persuasively, using the proper tone, word choice, and body language. They must use the right gestures, movements, and facial expressions to achieve authenticity, credibility, and sincerity.

Negotiating skills. Successful conflict managers are masters of negotiating. They know a variety of negotiating techniques, and they can adjust their techniques to confrontational situations as they develop. They keep people and issues separate. They are patient and never try to rush resolution. They negotiate problems and issues, not demands or requirements. They use questions to get at the facts, give information, control discussion, and supplement their powers of observation for clues as to what the disputants are thinking. They don't enter negotiations with the intent of backing one of the disputants, or with the sole intention of reaching a compromise.

Resolution Strategies and Tactics

Most of the strategies and tactics for resolving conflict rely on oral communications. The characteristics of effective communications—clarity, brevity, simplicity, precision, and integrity—apply to all positive conflict resolution strategies and tactics.

Strategies

Avoidance. There are two forms of avoidance: denial and withdrawal. Both are totally negative strategies. Denial is simply refusing to acknowledge that a disagreement or conflict exists, and withdrawal involves retreating from actual or potential conflict—walking away from it, either figuratively or actually. Denial is never appropriate; it is senseless and childish. Withdrawal, on the other hand, can occasionally be useful. It should be used only when the situation has only minor implications for the organization and its people; when there is little chance for resolution; or when there is a good chance that any form of intervention will only exacerbate the situation.

Prevention. Prevention is a desirable and viable strategy, particularly with potentially destructive conflict. Essentially, prevention involves establishing work conditions that will preclude the onset of incidents that evoke conflict.

Here are four of the most effective techniques:

1. *Participatory management*—giving employees at all levels opportunities to assist in making plans and decisions in areas that they are competent to deal with and in which they have a definite stake
2. *Change management*—always informing employees about forthcoming changes well in advance of their implementation
3. *Team building*—a strategy for helping the work group improve its unity of purpose and functioning
4. *Listening*—asking for and listening to workers' ideas on improving performance and productivity

To use any of these four tactics, you will draw on communication skills and techniques that you have in your tool kit. If you believe you need additional help, you will find useful suggestions in Chapter 12, Managing Change, and in Chapters 1 (Listening) and 15 (Team Building) of the companion volume to this book, *Critical Skills: The Guide to Top Performance for Human Resources Managers* (AMACOM, 1988).

Coercion or force. Force comes in several varieties—some more acceptable and more useful than others. In all its forms it involves use of status or power to resolve differences at the expense of one of the parties—a win-lose alternative. Force can be used when time is short, when you're sure that others cannot change your views, when winning is more important than the risk of making the situation worse, and when there is an absolutely "right" side of the issue.

As a strategy, force comes in several forms. *"Politics"* can be one of the softest and most indirect means of exercising force, but it can also be Machiavellian. In its acceptable form it is a means of influencing people, through tradeoffs or diplomacy, to end their disagreement. In its worst forms it is plotting to bring an individual or group to heel.

A considerably more direct form of force is *domination.* It can also range from "velvet glove" approaches to the "whip hand" approach—the bald exercise of power through intimidation.

Another form of force is *persuasion:* the warring parties are prevailed upon, induced, and convinced to end their dispute. The appeal may be to logic, team spirit, sense of justice, or their own best interests. But persuasion can also be authoritarian. Some managers become very accomplished at using persuasion veiled by threatened use of authority. This style is exemplified by such statements as "You're missing the point," "Now, let's be objective about this," "You've been around long enough to know that . . ." and "You'll do it because I say so!"

Reward is a positive form of force, but it is force nonetheless. Rewards consist of everything from pats on the back, letters of appreciation, and plaques and prizes to promotion—all designed to induce people to remain loyal, satisfied employees.

Threats are still another form of force. While not ordinarily an acceptable strategy, in their "warning" form they have value, particularly as a preliminary step to stop the conflict and preclude the need for more drastic punitive action. In its most acceptable form a threat is an admonition, a fair notice that if behavior does not change for the better, more stringent action will be taken. It should never involve harassment, bullying, or terrorizing tactics.

A final form of force is *punishment,* which can range from an oral reprimand to termination for cause. This is disciplinary action, the most severe of all measures available to the manager.

Neutralization. Neutralization strategies may take two forms: accommodation or suppression. Essentially, both approaches are designed to defuse a conflict situation before it becomes destructive.

With *accommodation,* one side gives in to the other. So the conflict is resolved without meaningful discussion of the positions of the disputants. It is useful only under one of the following conditions: when winning on the issue is critically important to one of the disputants and less important to the other; when achieving amity and accord is paramount; when accommodation on one issue may result in greater flexibility on another issue of far greater importance; when one party wants to be seen as a team player; and when one of the disputants wants to learn more by implementing a different method.

Accommodation, then, is a search for areas of agreement and a means of defusing differences. Although widely practiced, it is not a particularly effective strategy, for one of the parties must be the loser. It is characterized by such words as "You're right," "I see your point," "I never considered that," and "You win."

Suppression is the process of attempting to smooth over a disagreement. It stresses areas of agreement and deemphasizes areas of difference. It downplays arguments that would undermine a position and accents factors that support a position. It is best used when authority over disputants is absent, when time is short, or when the manager believes that others are not prepared to deal with the total situation.

Confrontation. Confrontation is the most widely applicable and undoubtedly the most popular strategy for resolving conflicts. It comes in two types—individual and group—and in several forms: peacemaking, collaboration, compromise, and consensus. In all forms the dispute or disagreement is addressed directly and in a problem-solving mode. The affected parties work through their disagreement objectively—and, ideally, unemotionally and honestly. They attempt to understand the other's position and avoid judgmental comments and behavior. They remain flexible and open and strive for agreement.

In individual confrontation, one of the two parties in dispute, or a third party, decides to bring the issue to a head by bringing the disputants face-to-face to resolve the difficulty, along with a mediator or facilitator. Ideally, this strategy should be applied when the conflict is latent or when emotional tension first begins to build. However, that is not always possible. When the conflict is hidden and develops unnoticed by others until overt action takes place, it bursts into full bloom. But even then, the confrontational approach can still be used.

Peacemaking attempts to get people out of the practice of engaging in destructive interpersonal exchanges. It is essentially a form of group therapy, providing opportunities to discover new and more satisfying ways of relating to others. It employs nondirective approaches—focusing on building a climate of acceptance. It does not make use of diagnosis, but works to help disputants develop positive changes in the way they interact with others.

The peacemaking strategy has one serious drawback. It should be used only by people who have training in individual nondirective or client-centered counseling or in group counseling. Considerable risk accrues to unskilled managers—and participants—who use the approach.

Collaboration emphasizes cooperation and mutual respect, getting the disputants to work together to solve the problem. Essentially, it aims to get the parties to say to each other, either in word or actions, "You're important. You have good ideas." They are encouraged to use questions such as "What do you think?" "Can we agree on . . .?" "Do I understand you to mean . . .?"

It works this way: the views of disputants are presented with the others listening attentively and empathically, underlying assumptions are probed, and disputants seek a resolution of the issue that satisfies the critical concerns of all parties. Collaboration can be used when the issue is vital, too important to be compromised, participants are capable and well intentioned, and enough time is available to explore the situation.

With *compromise,* an attempt is made to identify solutions that give some degree of satisfaction to the conflicting parties. It may be best described as splitting the difference. Compromise usually puts the disputants in a lose-lose or draw situation. It rarely results in a win-win result because both parties must give up something, and both end up feeling that the disagreement has been lost.

Essentially, compromise requires the disputants to put expediency above principle. However, the approach is useful when the issue is not of any great consequence or when the disputants are equal in terms of status, position, aggressiveness, and persuasive powers, or when neither party to the dispute can be moved from their positions. It can also be used when both parties can gain from each other at a cost they are willing to pay or when the cost of not reaching agreement is higher than the cost of a compromise solution.

Consensus applies the approaches used in compromise, but with one important difference: the objective is to achieve common consent, complete accord on the disagreement, rather than compromise. Where achieved, consensus is a totally win-win result because neither party feels that anything has been given up.

Negotiation. Negotiation is either a form of indirect persuasion or a type of force agreed upon in advance by both parties. It invariably involves a third party and comes in three forms: mediation, arbitration, and litigation. Negotiation is another alternative to argument. Because a negotiated settlement of differences is open, it is more likely to be more durable than some means of conflict resolution.

In negotiating, the disputing parties face up to their disagreement openly and directly and work it out in a problem-solving way. It aims to be a win-win approach. It does not make use of power moves, mind games, tricks, or traps. Rather it attempts to make the disputants partners in the venture, and achieve an outcome in which both can become winners.

Tactics

The list of potentially useful tactics for conflict resolution is long, but several are particularly useful for interpersonal conflict in corporate life.

Probing. This is one of the most effective techniques for identifying and clarifying an issue or problem, mitigating emotionalism, and providing feedback to disputants. Essentially, it involves asking detailed and specific questions or making comments to force the disputants to respond and begin to rely on rational behavior rather than emotion.

Listening. If you want to prevent small problems from escalating to something bigger, listen to people. Find out what they want. Listen to them with an open mind and without interrupting. Let them talk freely to you about their worries, fears, problems, and complaints.

Paraphrasing. With this technique, someone—either the mediator or the disputants themselves—restates in different words what was heard, in an attempt to verify that the message was correctly received or to identify where a breakdown has occurred in communications. The receiver uses such introductory words as "If I understand you correctly . . ." or "Are you saying that . . .?" The sender can then either confirm—"Yes, that's exactly what I meant"—or modify—"No, I meant that . . ."

Providing alternatives. One of the best ways to avoid placing disputants in a position where they feel trapped is to suggest alternatives, rather than a single solution, and encourage them to add other alternatives. This puts the disputants in control of the situation—which is particularly important for most knowledge workers. And it avoids the frustration and anger that would be generated by a directed solution.

Providing feedback. Because mutual understanding is so important in conflict resolution, adequate feedback is a very real requirement. Feedback may be positive—affirming that something was done correctly—or negative—pointing out that something has been misapplied and must be corrected. But whether positive or negative, it is extremely important that feedback be provided in such a way that defensiveness, resentment, or anger will not be generated and that rapport and cooperation will be maintained.

Contracting. This simply means getting the parties to arrive at an agreement and a commitment on what each will do to reach a solution or put a solution into effect. The contract gets the disputants to share responsibility for resolving the conflict and to keep lines of communication open.

Deescalating. There are many ways to deescalate conflict. Four of the most successful are depersonalizing the disagreement, making neutral or positive responses, cooling the situation, and giving the disputants a way out. Conflict is depersonalized by concentrating on the facts in the case, by insisting that the disputants discuss the issue and not motives or personalities, and by treating the dispute as a problem for resolution rather than an argument to be won. Conflict can also be deescalated by either not responding to negative comments or answering with a positive or neutral remark.

Many conflict situations can be cooled down by having the disputants put their positions in writing. This gives them a rational outlet for their disagreement and emotions. The effort of writing provides a sort of catharsis that tends to moderate feelings. Sometimes a means can be found to give disputants a way out of their situation without losing face, such as a making a change to another shift, a different work group, or a special assignment.

Pitfalls

There are many traps into which the unwary or inexperienced manager can fall. Here are some of the most common and most damaging.

Precipitate action. Some managers intervene in the situation without first determining whether it is worth the effort. That may cause more damage than leaving it alone. They move the resolution process along too quickly, addressing sensitive issues before people are ready to deal with them objectively and with emotions under control.

Excessive delay. Procrastination can be equally damaging. If the manager waits too long to intervene, the conflict may escalate to the point where it becomes very difficult to get people to address the issue rationally and unemotionally. Its effects may spread to other people and have an adverse impact on productivity. Worse, the conflict may progress to the point where relationships are permanently damaged.

Wrong assumptions. There are several potential trouble spots here. One of the most common is the incorrect assumption that the problem has been defined and may be addressed directly. A companion error is to accept one or both of the disputants' definition of the situation as the root problem. Rarely is either assumption true. In most conflict situations, the real problem is not immediately apparent.

Taking sides. Another serious error, and one that can have far-reaching and long-lasting effects on relationships with subordinates, is to take sides on the issue, or make value judgments about the rightness or wrongness of positions taken by disputants. Managers must be unfailingly impartial when dealing with interpersonal or intergroup conflict. If they show partiality either to people or ideas, they destroy their effectiveness as negotiators—and as managers.

Becoming the "fixer." Some managers develop an unwarranted confidence in their ability to solve the problems of others. Whenever a problem or issue arises, they feel obligated to become the one who puts things right. They fail to realize that most problems can be solved only by the people that have them—and that the job of the managers is to establish the conditions and provide the assistance that people need to identify their real problems and come to a self-determined solution.

The Conflict Management Process

Before you make any attempt to intervene in a conflict, look first at yourself and the situation. Are you the culprit—the cause of the conflict—or a major contributor? Have you failed to define objectives and authority clearly? Are you playing people off against each other? Resolve to look at the conflict dispassionately and empathically, but neutrally.

Then review your options for intervention. Consider the nature of the problem, the people involved, the limits of your authority, and your expertise. If you don't have enough background information about the disputants, do some digging—check personnel records, do some informal questioning. Then decide when and where would be the most appropriate time and place to intervene. But don't wait too long.

Step 1. Get the facts. Identify specifically what triggered the dispute. Exactly what was said and done by whom, when, where, and under what circumstances? What are the consequences of the conflict, in immediate and long-term effects on the organization and the people involved?

Step 2. Define and clarify the problem. This step should be completed with both parties present. Here, the conflict is brought to the surface. The participants explain their perceptions of the problem, what caused it, what it means to them and to the organization, and what they believe is the root cause. Ask questions to diagnose the dispute, identify its source, and determine the stage to which it has evolved. Search for underlying reasons. Isolate specific issues. Determine the real objectives of the disputants. The step is not concluded until both parties agree on the underlying problem and its actual wording.

Step 3. Choose the intervention strategy. Here the manager responsible for helping the disputing parties reach a self-determined solution decides which of the many available strategies offers the most promise. Consider your objective and intent, the degree to which you want to interact with the disputants, your personal style and preferences, your relationship with the disputants, and your conflict resolution skills. It is also wise to have a backup ready, in case the original strategy doesn't get the desired results.

Step 4. Identify the criteria of solution. This step is critical—and usually overlooked. What overall result do both parties want? Do they agree? How will they know when they have reached an action that will give them the results they want? If they cannot state what the solution must accomplish, they cannot reach an accord that will be durable. So, it is essential that they agree on benchmarks against which to measure the worth of each alternative solution.

Step 5. Implement the strategy and brainstorm solutions. Make disputants concentrate on the issue. Brainstorm the problem from both perspectives. Get the disputants to identify at least three means of resolving the dispute that address the concerns of *both* parties. Each disputant, in turn, should be encouraged to identify a solution, and then a second, and a third, and so on. When the alternatives have been exhausted, discuss advantages and disadvantages of each one. What is required to implement the solutions? What are some of the potential consequences?

Step 6. Select the best solution. Here the task is getting disputants to agree on the best solution and identify the specific actions—the who, when, where, and how. Get their commitment on their part of the implementing actions. Strive for consensus or, failing that, compromise.

Step 7. Implement the solution and monitor compliance. Here the parties to the dispute carry out the actions they agreed on. The task of the manager is to monitor the compliance with agreements reached, and provide feedback. Schedule followup sessions to review progress. If necessary, renegotiate the agreement.

Summary

Conflict occurs between individuals and groups. It is characterized by argument, antagonism, and bruised feelings. It may be open and directly observable, or it may be hidden, identifiable only by such symptoms as employee stress, apathy, low productivity, complaints, fault finding, and buck passing.

Conflict in organizations is inevitable, but it can often be anticipated, and sometimes prevented. Its frequency and severity vary in direct proportion to the size and complexity of the organization; bigness results in more serious conflict more often, and excessive conflict is invariably damaging.

Conflict is always a symptom of a problem and never the problem itself. Conflict can come from the character of the organization, the way managers manage, or the way individual employees conduct themselves. Competition, personality, and conflicting goals and values are at the root of many conflicts.

Resolving conflict is a complex skill, a skill that demands mastery of listening, problem solving, and negotiating. To be effective in resolving conflict, managers must know themselves, know people and what makes them behave in different ways, understand the nature of conflict, its causes and cures, and be skilled in using a variety of conflict resolution strategies and tactics.

Conflict resolution strategies include avoidance, prevention, coercion, neutralization, confrontation, and negotiation, many of which come in more than one form. Useful tactics include probing, listening, paraphrasing, offering alternatives, providing feedback, deescalating, and contracting.

When managed poorly, conflict is a totally negative force that wastes time, talent, and other resources, reduces productivity, and damages relationships. When handled well, conflict can be a positive force. It brings employee concerns out into the open where they can be addressed. It releases innovative and creative powers, reduces or eliminates negative feelings, increases productivity, and improves relationships.

The conflict management process involves seven distinct steps:

1. Get the facts.
2. Define and clarify the problem.
3. Choose the conflict resolution strategy.
4. Identify the criteria of solution.
5. Apply the strategy and brainstorm solutions.
6. Select the best solution.
7. Implement the solution and monitor compliance with results.

Although conflict management poses some formidable challenges to HR managers, the development and use of this key skill will provide substantial and durable benefits to the organization, the manager, and employees.

For Further Reading, Viewing, and Listening

Blake, Robert S., and Jane S. Moulton. *Solving Costly Organizational Conflicts: Achieving Intergroup Trust, Cooperation, and Teamwork.* San Francisco: Jossey-Bass, 1984.

Bolt, Robert, and Dorothy Grover Bolton. *Social Style/Management Style: Developing Productive Work Relationships.* New York: AMA-COM, 1984.

Conflict: Causes and Resolutions (24-minute videocassette). Rank Roundtable Training, 113 N. San Vicente Blvd., Beverly Hills, CA 90221, 1975.

Conflict Management (32-minute videocassette). Produced by Program Source, 1983. Distributed by Salenger Films, 1635 Twelfth St., Santa Monica, CA 90404-9988.

Conflict: Managing Under Pressure (25-minute videocassette). AMA Film/Video, Nine Galen St., Watertown, MA 02172, 1986.

The Fine Art of Keeping Your Cool (20-minute videocassette). Produced by J. Copeland. National Educational Media, 21601 Devonshire St., Chatsworth, CA 91311-9962, 1983.

Folger, Joseph P., and Marshall Scott Poole. *Working Through Conflict: A Communication Perspective.* Glenview, Ill.: Scott, Foresman & Company, 1984.

Hocker, Joyce, and William Wilmot. *Interpersonal Conflict.* 2nd ed. Dubuque, Iowa: William C. Brown, 1985.

Johnson, David W., and Frank P. Johnson. *Joining Together: Group Theory and Group Skills.* 3rd ed. Englewood Cliff, N.J.: Prentice-Hall, 1987.

Johnson, John R. "Understanding Misunderstanding: A Key to Effective Communication." *Training and Development Journal,* August 1983, pp. 62–68.

Kahn, Lynn Sandra. *Peacemaking: A Systems Approach to Conflict Management.* Lanham, Md.: University Press of America, 1988.

Kindler, Herbert S. "The Art of Managing Differences." *Training and Development Journal,* January 1983, pp. 26–32.

———. *Managing Disagreement Constructively.* Los Altos, Calif.: Crisp Publications, 1988.

Lippitt, Gordon L. "Managing Conflict in Today's Organization." *Training and Development Journal,* July 1982, pp. 67–75.

Managing Conflict (6-hour audiocassette). American Management Association Extension Institute, 135 W. 50th St., New York, NY 10020, 1981.

Managing Conflict: How to Make Conflict Work for You (15-minute videocassette). Salenger Films, 1635 Twelfth St., Santa Monica, CA 90404-9988, 1978.

Masterbroeck, W. F. G. *Conflict Management and Organization Development.* New York: John Wiley & Sons, 1988.

Organizational Conflict (28-minute videocassette). Produced by Sally V. Beaty. Southern California Consortium, 5400 Orange Ave., Suite 215, Cypress, CA 90630, 1983.

Phillips, Ronald C. "Manage Differences Before They Destroy Your Business." *Training and Development Journal,* September 1988, pp. 67–71.

Pneuman, Roy W., and Margaret E. Bruehl. *Managing Conflict: A Complete Process-Centered Handbook.* Englewood Cliffs, N.J.: Prentice-Hall, 1982.

Poeter, Jack N. *Conflict and Conflict Resolution.* New York: Garland Publishing, 1982.

Robert, Marc. *Managing Conflict From the Inside Out.* San Diego, Calif.: Learning Concepts, 1982.

Tjosvold, D., and D. W. Johnson, eds. *Productive Conflict Management.* New York: Irvington Publishers, 1983.

Turner, Steve, and Frank Weed. *Conflict in Organizations: Practical Solutions Any Manager Can Use.* Englewood Cliffs, N.J.: Prentice-Hall, 1983.

Ury, William L., Jeanne M. Brett, and Stephen B. Goldberg. *Getting Disputes Resolved: Designing Systems to Cut the Costs of Conflict.* San Francisco: Jossey-Bass, 1988.

Walton, Richard E. *Managing Conflict: Interpersonal Dialog and Third Party Roles.* Reading, Mass.: Addison-Wesley Publishing Company, 1986.

Watkins, Karen. "When Co-Workers Clash." *Training and Development Journal,* April 1986, pp. 26–29.

Weiss, Laurie. "Revisiting the Basics of Conflict Management." *Training and Development Journal,* November 1983, pp. 68–70.

7

Disciplining
Changing Behavior

Managers face perhaps no greater challenge in superior-subordinate relationships than the area of discipline. On the one hand, cooperative team efforts toward organizational goals depend on discipline. On the other hand, employees' rights, a growing concern of collective bargaining units, are often at odds with management's needs and options.

Virtually all organizations have written disciplinary policies, rules, and procedures; in unionized companies, they are written into the contract. Disciplinary action by managers is typically subject to appeal by employees through established grievance procedures. In fact, a great many of the disputes that go to arbitration and mediation involve disciplinary cases.

Management has the primary responsibility for developing and maintaining discipline. It meets that responsibility by establishing and communicating standards so that employees will know what is expected of them and what the penalties will be if they violate the rules. But employees should also have a role in developing the disciplinary policy, because they will give more support to standards they have helped create.

Discipline is a complex subject, and most managers know too little about it. Let's start with the question of definition. A fundamental requirement for effective operation is united effort based on the coordinated activities of individuals and groups. United effort requires systematic control of activities, rapid adaptation to changed conditions, and full use of the talents and abilities of each employee. To that end, a first essential is some means of regulating people's behavior and performance. That is discipline in its broadest sense.

Codified rules provide guides for action in organizations, but people must still be impelled to observe them. Even though backed by authority and enforced, rules cannot be effective unless they are reinforced by certain habits and internalized attitudes that are held

176

as common codes of conduct. Those habits and attitudes are what is meant by the term "discipline."

The root of the word more nearly explains its meaning than any definition. It comes from the Latin verb *discere*, meaning "learn." So we can say that "to discipline" means "to teach." In the business world, discipline is the standard of personal behavior, job performance, work habits, courtesy, consideration of others, appearance, and ethical conduct that enables people singly or in groups to perform their duties efficiently and effectively.

In organizational life, discipline has two components: the means by which the organization seeks to influence the individual—such as regulations, procedures, policies, and rules—and the psychological set or frame of reference that determines the individual's behavior, the norms of performance. The first is externally imposed on a person, the second comes from within. Externally imposed discipline makes use of deterrents and penalties to secure compliance. Self-discipline, sometimes called positive discipline, relies on self-motivation, on the willingness of people to do what is consistent with the goals of the organization and the work group. It is achieved when employees know why their jobs are important, how much their fellow employees and the organization are depending on them, and why the organization requires that they do certain things and not do others. Although self-discipline is the preferred type, both forms are needed in organizational life.

Discipline makes specific requirements of the individual, and it has a system of rewards and punishments. A system of formal rules and policies is particularly necessary in large organizations, where coordination from top to bottom cannot be achieved solely by informal means. There are too many chances for confusion of policy, misunderstanding of authority and responsibility, and deviation from common purposes. Such a system provides guidelines for action and sets the boundaries within which individuals can exercise discretion in their behavior. Discipline comes closest to perfection when it assures the individual of the greatest possible freedom of thought and action while promoting feelings of responsibility to the organization and its people.

An effective system of discipline accomplishes many things. It develops employee self-control, enhances cooperation and collaboration in the pursuit of organizational goals, and improves work attitudes and behavior. Overall performance is profoundly affected. So is company loyalty. But a disciplinary system has some secondary objectives that should not be overlooked. It sets an example for employees, deterring those who might be less than willing to subordinate their personal objectives to those of the total organization, and putting troublemakers on notice that their negative behavior will be dealt with promptly and decisively.

A good system will also avert crises and problems; poor disciplinary procedures will exacerbate them. Every time managers interpret disciplinary policy or initiate disciplinary action, they risk a part of the organization's reputation (as well as their own) and open the door to unwanted consequences. Work stoppages, slowdowns, and strikes have been called by unions because a manager made a bad decision in a disciplinary case. The underpinnings for good decisions are sound disciplinary policies and procedures.

Who Is Responsible for Discipline?

All organizational players have responsibilities in the area of discipline. Top management, functional managers, first-line supervisors, and employees all have a stake in good discipline.

Top management's role is to develop and annunciate a philosophy of discipline, including its purpose, a policy framework, and general standards and requirements. It must also actively support managers and supervisors in applying and enforcing policies and procedures.

Functional managers and first-line supervisors are responsible for training supervisors and employees, implementing policies, enforcing rules, investigating offenses, and applying disciplinary measures. They are the people who translate the philosophy of discipline and top management's standards into a workable and working disciplinary system.

Employees should provide input to the system; they should be encouraged to participate in establishing the policies and work rules that will guide their thinking and action. Then they have the responsibility of knowing the rules and regulations and obeying them.

The Role of the HR Manager

The HR manager has four distinct responsibilities in the area of discipline:

1. Participate in establishing corporate policies and procedures.
2. Act as consultant to other managers in disciplinary cases.
3. Teach other managers the theory and practice of discipline.
4. Manage discipline within the HR department.

Let's look at each one for a moment.

Discipline throughout the organization involves the full range of products and services provided by the HR department. Through programs and interventions, such as orientation for new employees, training employees at all levels, guiding and assisting other managers and supervisors, and participating in developing corporatewide procedures for collective bargaining, grievance, and arbitration and mediation, and the establishment of disciplinary policies, HR managers and their staff exert a powerful influence on one of the most challenging aspects of corporate life. They play a major role in molding productive, loyal, and responsible workers.

A fundamental problem for the HR manager is to determine whether different forms of discipline are to be used by the organization—a mix of traditional and self-regulating discipline—and if so, how. Realizing that self-discipline is far more effective and powerful, HR managers must search for ways to develop within all employees a workable frame of reference for regulating their own behavior and performance.

The job of training others is all-important. Specific instruction in disciplinary procedures is a necessary part of the training for all managers and supervisors. To do anything less is to court disaster. HR managers can best help other managers understand the psychology of discipline, and learn how to do a better job of administering it, if they understand some of the problems these managers have.

Some managers find it difficult to discipline their people. Sometimes the underlying reason is that they are unsure of the soundness of their own judgment. Others can't accept the responsibility for what they believe is "playing God." Still others are afraid they will damage the relationships they have built up with their people. It's not uncommon to hear managers say, "I can't discipline anyone until I'm 100 percent sure that I'm right." Or, "I don't have all the facts." Or, "Jones is a great guy and a good worker. So what if he's late sometimes?"

Sometimes managers are reluctant to discipline because they fear the emotionalism of the scene. Unquestionably, disciplinary situations are emotionally charged—for both employee and manager. Managers need to be shown how to face these situations objectively and without loss of emotional control. Decisions and actions taken under the influence of strong emotions are often bad ones.

And occasionally managers need help correcting inappropriate motives. Sometimes they want to acquire the reputation of being strong and unyielding—a force to reckon with. Other times the objective is to curry favor with a higher-level manager who is known to be a hard-nosed disciplinarian. Some managers use discipline to demonstrate their power and authority, or to get revenge for actual or perceived challenges to their status. They all need to be coached in the true objective of discipline: to improve performance.

But the biggest problem is usually simple lack of know-how. All managers must be both knowledgeable about the theory of positive discipline and skilled in its practice. Making sure they are is the job of the HR manager.

To develop a high state of discipline within the HR department itself, it is essential that managers first think through their concept of discipline until it can guide them and their behavior under varying conditions and circumstances, serve as a basis for evaluating their behavior and that of their people, and help them teach the proper standards of behavior, conduct, and performance in their departments.

To help in developing discipline in the department (and the organization as a whole), HR managers have some potent leverage. They control many of the rewards and formal sanctions. More important, they control the two key means of influencing behavior: communication and training.

An Effective Discipline System

It's important to understand that a good discipline system involves more than a package of rules. Ideally, employees set their own standards of behavior, and those standards are consistent with the company's formal policy. When that happens, people are substituting self-discipline for controls previously applied by others. This kind of learning occurs when the disciplinary system, made up of both formal and informal sanctions, rests on a foundation of understanding and confidence.

Good discipline depends on understanding. Each person in an organization must know, understand, and accept the ground rules. When people understand what is required of them, they can usually be counted on to do their job effectively and behave in an acceptable way. Discipline also depends on mutual trust and confidence—managers' confidence in their people, subordinates' confidence in the decisions of their bosses and in their own ability to perform effectively. People must believe that all rules are being enforced, that wrongdoers are disciplined, and that exceptions are not being made for certain individuals or groups. Finally, discipline has to do with informal sanctions within the organization—social pressures generated by employees, based on shared expectations about how people should behave in specific situations. In the best possible case, these informal sanctions dovetail with, and thus reinforce, the organization's formal policies.

Of course formal sanctions are necessary. The concept of organization would be incomplete without some system to hold individual members accountable for their actions. Developing the ingredients of that system, thinking through the full process, is our concern here.

Here's what a superior disciplinary system looks like:

It is constructive. The objective of any disciplinary action is to correct problems—things employees are doing that are interfering with their job or others. The object is not to punish, but to improve. Every step in the disciplinary program should be rehabilitative, positive, and productive. Rare occasions might call for punitive action, but they should definitely be the exception.

It is preventive. The emphasis should be on prevention rather than remediation or punishment. Six strategies will help prevent disciplinary problems:

1. Distribute to all employees written disciplinary policies, rules, and procedures.
2. During new-employee orientation, provide specific instruction about the disciplinary system and its operation.
3. Provide instruction in the do's and don'ts of conduct and performance as a part of both formal and on-the-job training programs.
4. Provide feedback and counseling on the job.
5. Immediately correct errors.
6. Provide recognition and rewards for improvement and for outstanding job performance.

It is job-related. Policies must be clearly, directly, and reasonably related to job requirements. They must *never* deal with personalities, off-the job activities, family, or any other aspects of employees' personal lives that are not clearly related to their ability to function effectively on the job. It is not only damaging but totally futile to try to enforce a rule that most employees consider unreasonable.

It is predictable and certain. Employees must know that when they violate a regulation or policy, they will be called to task. Even if extenuating circumstances make a penalty unnecessary, they must understand that their transgression has been observed and has been judged in accordance with policy. Managers cannot afford to look the other way to accommodate a well-liked employee and crack down hard on someone less popular.

It fits the offense. In general, the penalty must be commensurate with the seriousness of the offense. The concern should be twofold: appropriateness and fairness. That is, the penalty should be reasonably related to the violation and to the employee's past history. Rarely should an employee be discharged for a first offense unless it is extremely serious—stealing, fraud, or negligence resulting in severe personal injury or death. Similarly, it would be inappropriate to suspend an individual without pay for being late to work twice.

It is timely. Disciplinary action should take place as soon after the offense as possible so that it is more easily connected to the violation—rather than the person administering the discipline. Of course you will allow time for a full investigation of the facts. Just don't delay unnecessarily.

It is not imposed without warning. If employees are to accept disciplinary action without resentment, they must regard it as fair. That means that there must be clear advance warning that a given offense will result in a specific disciplinary action. Those specifications must be set forth in writing and distributed to everyone affected by the rules or policies.

Managers also have a responsibility to ensure that employees *really* understand what the rules are and how they will be enforced. That calls for a comprehensive program of communication: explanation and discussion of the disciplinary policy with new employees; bulletin board notices; inclusion in employee handbooks, policy manuals, and union contracts; group meetings when policies are changed; and informal warnings when a manager sees that a rule or policy is about to be violated.

It is consistent. Steady, dependable discipline is fair and more likely to be accepted. When discipline is meted out in a whimsical or capricious way, discontent and charges of favoritism are inevitable. Does consistency mean that punitive action should be determined solely on the nature of the offense, regardless of the background and record of person who committed the offense? Of course not. First offenders are customarily and rightly treated more leniently than repeat offenders, new employees less stringently than old hands, and immature, less skilled, and less intelligent people with greater forbearance than mature, skilled, and highly intelligent people. Every case must be decided on its own merits.

It is impersonal. When workers are disciplined, the relationship between employee and manager is damaged. This can be minimized if disciplining is done impersonally. This means censuring the behavior, rather than the person. If the employee has been warned of the consequences of misconduct, if the disciplinary action is imposed calmly and quietly, and if the employee is treated later as if nothing untoward had happened, relationships are likely to return to an even keel.

It includes an appeals channel. Fairness and equity demand that organizations discipline employees only for just cause, and that any employee who believes that discipline has been unfairly administered may register an appeal for relief through a specific, written grievance procedure. Then, any employee who is not satisfied with management's answer to the appeal should have the right to arbitration. Remember, too, that all employees have the right to counsel, legal or otherwise, when they are charged with misconduct or reasonably believe they might be the recipient of disciplinary action. So, awkward though it may be for management and individual managers, to ensure fair and consistent treatment for all employees, a channel of appeal must be kept open. Before any person is punished, the onus is on management to prove beyond any doubt that a rule or policy communicated to employees has been violated.

Difficult Employees, Common Problems

All disciplinary problems can be cataloged under three headings: attendance, job performance, and misconduct. They are not always related; in fact, they are often mutually exclusive. It is not uncommon to have an employee who is frequently absent, who is an outstanding worker when present, yet who occasionally violates a specific work rule.

In recent years, the most common reason for taking disciplinary action against managers and other employees of relatively high status and position has been betrayal of trust: dishonesty, misappropriation of funds, fraud, stealing, embezzlement, selling company secrets, false statements, and wrongful use of inside information. But those are not the only significant transgressions.

Others include violations of company policy, negligence, conflict of interest, and lying on résumés. Other problems spring from excessive ambition—playing politics, falsification of records, doctoring reports, and spending too much time thinking about the next job. And still another important area, more important today perhaps than in earlier eras, is inappropriate behavior with fellow workers—discrimination, sexual harassment, abrasiveness, bullying, and arrogance.

Lower-level employees commit some of the same violations, but much less frequently. However, they are guilty of many others: loafing on the job, excessive absenteeism and tardiness, absence from regular place of work during working hours without permission, defacing or destroying company property, fighting, lying, cheating, stealing, misappropriating or selling company property, and forging, altering, or deliberately falsifying company records.

Then there are problems of obscenity, verbal attacks, disparaging or otherwise defaming remarks about other employees, malicious use of profane, threatening, or abusive language. Others include violation of safety rules and failure to conform to standards of conduct required of employees when dealing with clients, customers, suppliers, or the general public. Of increasing incidence are reporting to work under the influence of alcohol or drugs, using intoxicating liquor or nonprescription drugs on company premises, submitting false or misleading information to obtain employment or promotion, and insubordination or refusal to follow the instructions of the immediate supervisor.

Difficult employees come in all shapes and sizes and with a great variety of distinguishing characteristics; Figure 7-1 lists some of the most common varieties. But whatever their level in the company difficult employees fall into only five basic types: objectors, complainers, troublemakers, troubled, and careless.

Objectors. Objectors are thoughtful people who question just about anything and everything. They frequently disagree strongly and openly with management actions and decisions—and they often disagree with their fellow workers and even among themselves. They are often the organizational gadflies, inquisitors, and cynics. For that reason they are usually unpopular people. But they can be a very valuable internal source of double checks—a built-in monitoring system—for an organization.

How best to handle objectors?

- Listen to them. Take them seriously. Don't write them off as crackpots or agitators.
- Establish channels for them to voice their objections, to get them heard by the right people.

Figure 7-1. Types of difficult employees.

The absentee	The buck passer
The alcoholic	The early leaver
The aggressor	The bigot
The late arriver	The grumbler
The drug addict	The gossip
The coffee-break addict	The comedian
The meddler	The daydreamer
The sexual harasser	The objector
The brawler	The bottleneck
The rule breaker	The thief
The complainer	The liar
The cheat	The slob
The dress code violator	The slow Joe
The gambler	The accident prone
The phone caller	The perpetually bored
The restroom inhabiter	The goldbricker
The sick-leaver	The bully
The misfit	The troublemaker

- Look into their objections, thoroughly. They usually have a rational basis for their objections, and they could be right.

Complainers. Complainers are an entirely different breed. They are the organizational hand wringers. Nothing is ever quite right, and it is always in danger of getting worse. The chronic complainer is someone who needs desperately to be listened to. Complainers need attention, and they should get it.

Here's how to handle the complainer:

- Listen—carefully and attentively. Don't just pretend. Show your interest by asking questions. How did this happen? How do you feel about it now? What did you do about it? What do you think should be done about this? What can *you* do to improve the situation?
- Don't argue, even if you believe the individual is wrong. Simply state your position and leave it at that.
- Never join the complainer in a gripe session even if you agree that his or her point is well taken. Never get angry.
- If there is a workable solution, identify it and try to get agreement on what is to be done by whom.

- Ask the person to stop complaining. Explain that he or she will be happier by working more and complaining less.

Troublemakers. The misfits, the malcontents, and the inciters are the bane of managers everywhere. These people are disturbed; they mean to cause harm. Unless they can be cured of their disorder, they cannot be allowed to remain in the organization.

There are really only two options for handling troublemakers:

- Help them get rid of their disruptive behavior—or, at the very least, get it under control. Get them professional psychological or psychiatric assistance.
- Get rid of them—fire them.

Troubled employees. Sometimes job performance is adversely affected by personal problems: alcoholism, drug abuse, money worries, illness in the family, marital or emotional problems. Changes in someone's appearance, personality, behavior, or job performance are usually the first signals that the person is troubled. Among the most common indicators are slovenly appearance, chronic absenteeism and tardiness, dishonesty, significant weight loss or gain, frequent hangovers, temper tantrums, insubordination, extreme aggressiveness, disruptive relationships with others, and persistent carelessness. Any of these changes may point to the need for referral to a competent and fully qualified therapist (psychologist, psychiatrist, or other mental health specialist), usually handled through the employee assistance program.

Here's how to handle troubled employees:

- Be understanding and supportive.
- Listen to them carefully and attentively; hear them out completely.
- Be aware of your own limitations. Refer them to specialized sources of help.
- Follow up to be sure that they get the help they need.

Careless employees. Well-intentioned people who violate rules and policies because they are unthinking, scatterbrained, or outright foolish are probably the most common of all. Their transgressions are invariably unpremeditated. They mean no harm. They just seem to be asleep at the switch. But they must be awakened by some mild form of disciplinary action, usually on-the-spot correction. Some inattentive people, however, require more than an oral reprimand to straighten them out because they are guilty of repeat offenses.

Here's how to handle careless employees:

- Never overlook an episode of carelessness; always call attention to the incident immediately.
- If the incident represents a repeat performance, take the culprit aside and give him or her a "Dutch uncle" talk.
- For subsequent episodes, particularly serious violations, impose an appropriate form of disciplinary action.

Taking Disciplinary Action

The best systems are built around what is generally called progressive discipline: each time an employee commits the same or similar offense, he or she receives an increasingly severe penalty. The steps are:

1. Oral reprimand
2. Written reprimand
3. Written warning
4. Disciplinary layoff
5. Discharge

They are almost always delivered to the employee in a face-to-face interview; the exceptions are the written reprimand and written warning, but often they too are presented to the employees in a disciplinary interview. No matter what progressive discipline level is involved, this interview has the same challenges and takes the same skills. Few managers relish doing it, but all must be able to do it successfully. So we'll start with the interview, then take a look at the specifics of the five steps.

The Disciplinary Interview

The disciplinary interview can be and often is an absolute minefield, particularly when emotions like anxiety and anger cause the manager to mishandle the situation. Here are some of the pitfalls.

Incomplete facts. The manager must determine the who, what, where, when, and how of the incident, evaluate these facts, and determine what, if anything, should be done. Without these facts it will be difficult to keep firmly in mind that the purpose of the interview is to close the gap between the expected performance and what was delivered.

Lack of planning. The manager who initiates a disciplinary interview without complete and thorough planning is taking an unnecessary risk. Decide in advance where and when the interview will take place, who will be present, precisely how the violation will be described, and exactly what disciplinary action will be taken.

Failure to anticipate reactions. Try to anticipate the likely reactions of the employee. There are almost certain to be pleas of not guilty, rationalizations or excuses, justification of the act, claims of extenuating circumstances—some accurate and others highly inaccurate. The manager must be prepared to deal with them all.

It may help to remember that even though employees' reactions can take many different forms, there are really only a few very basic emotions involved. One common reaction is hurt, expressed in words or body language or both. Typically, it is followed with practical questions, such as "What are you going to do?" or "What do I do now?" That is, most employees react realistically and rationally after they recover from the initial jolt. The strategy for the manager is to provide the information they need.

A second common reaction is embarrassment, quickly followed by an apology. "I don't know what made me do that. But it won't happen again. I'm sorry." The obvious strategy here is to drop the matter and get back to work.

A third common reaction is shock. It is characterized by expressions of denial, disbelief, and extreme distress. The individual may turn pale, start to shake, or begin to cry. Although this is the kind of response that many managers dread, it is bound to happen, and it must be faced and handled skillfully. The best strategy is to try to get the employee to discuss his or her feelings. Ask questions that will get the person to respond. When control is achieved, the discussion can then move on to what happens next.

A fourth reaction is anger—sometimes noisy and violent, characterized by shouting, countercharges, even physical threats; sometimes quiet fury, bitterness, and resistance to all attempts at rational discussion. The best strategy in this case is to allow the employee to vent his or her feelings and hope the anger will burn itself out. Of course, if the situation appears to be getting out of hand, don't hesitate to call for help.

A fifth reaction, although less common, is suppression of feelings. From all outward appearances, the employee expected the bad news and welcomes it. Actually, the control is a sham. The person is so numbed by the charges that he or she cannot react normally. This is potentially the most alarming and dangerous reaction. The manager must ask enough questions to be sure that the person really comprehends what is happening and understands the seriousness of the situation. Then, and only then, can the discussion proceed.

Mishandling the session. Several things can go wrong during a disciplinary interview. One is to fail to allow the employee to explain his or her side of the story. Another is jumping to conclusions too quickly. Or the manager can make the mistake of skirting the problem or addressing it so timidly, out of anxiety or fear of an emotional confrontation, that the wrong message is sent. Just as bad is delivering an immediate reprimand or precipitously informing the individual of suspension, without going over the facts. And of course there is the potential for becoming angry.

Here are some suggestions to achieve a successful outcome:

- Thoroughly document improper conduct, policy violations, or failure to respond to corrective action. Keep the notes in your files. Ask employees to sign disciplinary reports and performance appraisals to make clear that they have read the documents (not that they agree with them).
- Adhere religiously to company rules, policies, and procedures. They may be a part of the collective bargaining agreement.
- Try to gain the employee's trust. Ask "How did it happen?" Always let employees tell their side of the story before taking action.
- Be fair—and be sure that your action will be perceived as fair by both the offender and other employees (and the union).
- Exercise special care in disciplining women, minorities, the handicapped, and employees over the age of forty.

The Steps in Progressive Discipline

Oral reprimand. This is the "Dutch uncle" talk, and it is by far the most common disciplinary action. Employees whose behavior or performance requires correction must have honest feedback. Managers must do it in a businesslike manner, using a fair, firm, nononsense approach. They must say exactly what they mean, make their point, keep it short, and make it stick.

Here are some rules for the oral reprimand:

- Do it privately—in the employee's work area, if possible, or in your own office if not.
- Choose the time carefully, but make it as close to the time of the offense as possible. Don't schedule the meeting late in the day, and avoid Fridays or the day before a holiday.
- Don't dump on the employee. Don't save all your complaints and criticism until you have a bagful.
- Don't mince words. State your position tactfully in clear and absolute terms. Let there be no doubt as to exactly where you stand and what you mean.
- Concentrate on the job behavior, and avoid saying anything that seems as if you are criticizing the employee as a person.
- Be specific and constructive. Tell the person what you saw— what he did that was wrong—and how you feel about it: annoyed, angry, disappointed, surprised.
- Don't show ambiguity. Avoid smiling or indicating acceptance or approval by body language. Adopt a serious and business-like demeanor.
- Give the employee an opportunity to tell her side of the story. Ask the employee for reasons or extenuating circumstances. Listen with an open mind, but don't accept excuses.
- Tell the person that you appreciate his work in general, but not in this case. But make it unmistakably clear that you are issuing a reprimand.
- Drop the matter and go back to work. Don't repeat the reprimand, and don't hold a grudge against the employee.

The written reprimand. This takes the form of a short memo or letter addressed to the employee. Clearly and succinctly describe the offense, underscoring the fact that this represents *repeat* behavior. In the letter, remind the employee of the previous discussion and any measures recommended and agreed upon. State that additional incidents will result in more stringent action, and note that a copy of the letter will be placed in the individual's personnel file for a specified period.

The written warning. This is actually the first formal stage of progressive discipline. Although their effect may appear to be psychologically similar to written reprimands, written warnings are much stronger. They are usually made a permanent part of the employee's personnel record, and they can be presented as evidence in grievance proceedings or cases involving arbitration, mediation, or litigation. They are usually prepared in four copies—for the manager, union steward, personnel department, and the disciplined individual.

Probationary status is implied in any formal letter of warning, whether or not it is specifically noted. If it is included, the letter should also describe how the probation can be lifted.

Here are some guides for using the written warning.

- Describe the unacceptable behavior or infraction clearly and precisely: the date and time and the circumstances under which it occurred.
- Recount earlier instances of the same behavior or infraction and note that both oral and written reprimands were issued, together with the dates of those disciplinary actions.
- Limit criticism to the primary and repeated shortcoming. Don't bring in new issues.
- Describe clearly, directly, and precisely the consequences of repeating the specific offense.

The disciplinary layoff. This next step usually involves suspension without pay for a specified period, almost never more than one month. Some organizations skip this phase of discipline because it is often difficult to find a suitable temporary replacement. Most retain it, however, because real punishment—loss of income—is convincing proof that the organization means business.

Discharge. Termination for cause is the ultimate penalty, the end of the disciplinary chain—and one that is being used less and less often. Although some maintain that employee termination for cause is evidence of management failure, that is neither necessarily true nor realistic. Some problems cannot be solved. There are limits to what can be corrected or tolerated. Sometimes it's better for the employee to go elsewhere.

Here are some suggestions for the conduct of terminations:

- Never fire on a Friday.
- Fire quickly but not abruptly—within the first two minutes of a five-minute interview.
- Don't show anger or antagonism, and don't ridicule or demean the employee's character, personality, abilities, or behavior.
- Try not to go into the reasons for the termination. Simply state it as a decision that has been made. Reserve the remaining time for the employee's reaction.
- Let the employee express a reaction—the negative spillover

of hard feelings toward you and the company will be reduced. Otherwise the suppressed shock or anger will build and may cause an explosion later—on the way out the door or at home.

- Be in control and stay that way. Don't get drawn into an argument and don't say anything to generate false hopes that the decision can be changed.
- Don't prolong the agony. Keep the meeting brief. Help the individual to accept the reality by repeating, "You're fired."
- After the employee leaves your office, don't discuss the termination with anyone—the case is closed.

One final point: Occasionally you may encounter the suggestion of demoting an employee as an alternative to terminating. As a disciplinary action, demotion is not a good choice, for several reasons: it is a crushing experience for the individual—one that is long-lasting and causes constant humiliation; it is wasteful of talent because it often places an employee in a position that does not make full use of his or her skills and talents; it is expensive, especially when the individual is placed in a dead-end or manufactured job with little opportunity to contribute to the organization. Demotion should be reserved for situations in which an employee has been erroneously promoted or is no longer able to perform the duties and functions of the job because of physical, mental, or emotional problems.

Wrongful Discharge

Possibly no issue in the field of labor today is so filled with emotion nor laden with potential problems for an employer as the discharge of an employee. In our increasingly litigious society, termination is now being accompanied, in ever-increasing numbers, by claims and lawsuits. The historic concept of an employer's unfettered right to discharge at will has come under severe attack, in many instances with growing success. While management still has the right to terminate an employee's position, that right is no longer unequivocal, but is rapidly being modified by exceptions, so that the firing process, once a simple act, is now a potential landmine.[1]

---

[1]From a brochure describing a "Wrongful Discharge Under Massachusetts Law" course. The Cambridge Institute, 1988. Used by permission. (The Cambridge Institute is an organization that provides seminars and workshops on the legal aspects of labor-management relations.)

For centuries, businesses operated under the principle of "employment at will," meaning that the employer has the right to terminate the employment relationship at any time for any reason—or no reason. Then, in the 1950s, state laws began incorporating exceptions that offered employees some protection, and in 1988 the U.S. Supreme Court confirmed the concept of wrongful discharge—terminations made on the basis of discrimination or unfair labor practices are illegal. If an employee can show that one of those factors made a difference in selecting him for termination, he may be entitled to money damages and reinstatement.

Patrick Vaccaro, managing partner of a prominent labor and employment law firm and a writer on legal issues, has summarized three bases for unlawful discharge suits that are recognized by most states:[2]

1. Violation of union agreements or written employment contracts, that is, breach of contract
2. Violation of commonly held principles of public policy, often embodied in statutes or written policies or codes
3. Violation of an implied covenant of good faith and fair dealing

Whenever terminated employees leave the organization bitter, angry, and panic-stricken, our legal system provides a means of getting even, and many lawyers are both eager and willing to take the case.

Your only protection as a manager is full compliance with the law. You need to know precisely where the line is drawn and exactly how to make knowledgeable and legally sufficient termination decisions on the right side of that line. And you need to know how to maintain control should you or your organization be subject to an investigation or a lawsuit. There is a built-in booby trap here: the laws governing terminations are extremely complex and filled with nuances, they are continually shifting and changing, and the laws vary from state to state.

Just Cause

Most wrongful-discharge suits are decided on the concept of "just cause." To win its case, management must prove that it has enforced its rules consistently, that it has made a fair, thorough,

---

[2]Patrick L. Vaccaro, "Speaking to the Law: Wrongful Discharge," *Human Resource Executive,* July–August 1988, p. 11.

and impartial investigation of the facts in the case, that there are credible witnesses to the offense, and that the penalty for the offense is fair under the circumstances.

There are seven tests that should be applied in every case of employee misconduct, whether it potentially involves termination or some lesser disciplinary action. If you can answer yes to all seven, you are well protected against claims of wrongful discharge.

1. *Reasonableness.* Was the employer's rule or order reasonably related to the orderly, efficient, and safe operation of the employer's business, and the performance the employer might reasonably expect?

2. *Adequate notice.* Did the employer give the employee advance warning of the possible consequences of the employee's disciplinary conduct?

3. *Investigation.* Did the employer, before taking the disciplinary action, investigate thoroughly to determine whether the employee violated or disobeyed the rule or order?

4. *Fairness.* Was the employer's investigation conducted fairly and objectively?

5. *Adequacy of proof.* Did the investigation yield substantial evidence that the employee was guilty as charged?

6. *Equal treatment.* Has the employer applied its rules, orders, and penalties evenhandedly and without discrimination to all employees?

7. *Appropriate penalty.* Was the disciplinary action taken by the employer reasonably related to the seriousness of the offense and the employee's record of service with the organization?[3]

Useful Strategies

There are several things you can do to limit your exposure to charges of wrongful discharge and its consequences.

Hire with care. Pay close attention to all elements of the hiring process: recruitment, advertisements, interviews, orientation, induction, and training programs. Monitor the hiring practices of everyone who has a hand in the process—other managers as well as staffers in your department. Review policies, procedures, and practices periodically to ensure that pitfalls are avoided.

---

[3]"How to Avoid Needless Arbitration and Wrongful Discharge Suits," *BNAC Communicator,* Fall 1988, p. 14.

- Don't make (or imply) oral or written promises and commitments that you can't keep. Be especially careful to avoid making oral statements during or following employment interviews. Make sure nothing that appears in employment correspondence, application forms, or salary and benefits statements could be construed as implied contracts.
- Don't make written offers of employment unless you intend to honor them.
- Be sure that application forms contain a disclaimer noting that it is a noncontractual document.
- Be sure that your application forms do not contain implied commitments or contracts. Have your legal counsel check them out and approve them before they are used.
- Get a signed release form from applicants before making inquiries to reference sources.

Keep good records. Keep careful and complete records of all employment contacts: recruitment, screening, selection, orientation, induction, assignment, and performance appraisal documents and records. Review and update them as necessary, but not less than annually.

Review and revise employee manuals. Carefully check all employee handbooks, supervisors' manuals, and policy statements. Eliminate statements that might be construed as implied employment contracts. Build in some flexibility and include disclaimers where appropriate. Control access to all organization documents.

Clean up the disciplinary process. Check all aspects of your disciplinary system and its process to be sure that they meet the tests of effectiveness: preventive, job-related, predictable, fair, timely, consistent, and flexible. The Cambridge Institute suggests these Ten Commandments:[4]

1. Centralize your discipline system.
2. Review every recommended disciplinary action before implementation.
3. Provide industrial due process.
4. Give sufficient notice before disciplining.
5. Use discipline which is progressive in severity when possible.
6. Do not discipline without adequate documentation.
7. Be fair when you discipline.

---

[4]The Cambridge Institute, course description, 1988. Used by permission.

8. Investigate before you discipline.
9. Discipline in a consistent fashion.
10. Maintain flexibility when administering discipline.

Require release agreements. Tightly drawn release agreements can provide protection against litigation. Terminated employees must sign a resignation and release form in order to receive benefits that go beyond their regular entitlements. The company assumes additional expense for the extra benefits, but protects itself against open-ended liability and heavy legal fees should the employee decide to sue.

Include severance pay. Severance payment based on a reasonable formula may lighten the economic and psychological impact of discharge and prevent litigation. For the same reason, health and life insurance coverage can also be continued for a set period after termination.

Provide outplacement services. Outplacement assistance can help prevent litigation by successfully finding the discharged employee another job even before termination. It helps the employee realize that the organization is not trying to "destroy" him. Assistance may include a formal and structured program of résumé preparation, counseling, referral—or it may be simply a matter of allowing the employee to continue to use his office, telephone, and clerical support to look for another job.

The Discipline Process

Developing a Corporate Disciplinary System

Step 1. Think through the concept of discipline. Recognize that the purpose of discipline is to preserve, improve, and enhance the effectiveness of the organization's operations and the performance of employees at all levels.

Step 2. Define unsatisfactory conduct, behavior, and performance. Develop clear and legally defensible descriptions of unacceptable conduct, misbehavior, and rule violations. Describe specifically what the individual would be doing or not doing that would be a violation.

Step 3. Determine the forms of discipline to be employed.
Specify when disciplinary measures will be applied and the extent
to which each form will be used. Make the system progressive, with
increasingly stringent penalties for repeated offenses and more
serious violations.

Step 4. Develop strategies for self-discipline. Define and communicate what is expected. Develop an atmosphere of trust. Encourage the development of informal sanctions.

Step 5. Identify problem people. Note the individuals whose
names are mentioned repeatedly in reports. Document instances of
behavior subject to intervention of some kind.

Step 6. Review and revise. Periodically review disciplinary policies and procedures. Track the types of offenses and their disposition. Make needed changes.

Conducting a Disciplinary Action

Step 1. Respond quickly. When a problem surfaces, respond
quickly and decisively, using the most appropriate intervention
technique. Schedule confidential discussions with the individual.
But don't take any action while you're angry; wait until you cool off.
Criticize the act, not the person. Get the facts. Clearly define what
rule or regulation or policy was broken and how, and explain what
the correct behavior is. Ask the individual for her side of the story—
an explanation and any extenuating circumstances. Provide feedback. Get agreement on needed changes.

Step 2. Select the penalty; inform the individual. Let the
punishment fit the crime. Make it fair and equitable, but don't make
it too severe. And don't agonize about it. Know when you're right—
a rule or policy was broken, adequate warning was given, and the
employee has been granted all his rights. Don't allow yourself to be
talked out of taking the proper action.

Step 3. Take the disciplinary action. Give the oral reprimand
or warning; issue the written letter of reprimand or warning; lay the
individual off without pay. Inform the employee of her rights. Make
a record of the action for file or distribution, with a complete
description of the sequence of events: the specific offense, date,
time, and situation; include reference to previous offenses and
disciplinary actions with dates, and significant comments or agree-

ments made during disciplinary discussions. Get prepared for the grievance.

Step 4. Follow up. Monitor progress and accomplishment following less serious offenses. If the desired changes in behavior and performance have not occurred, schedule and conduct followup discussions. For subsequent discussions, gradually increase the severity of the disciplinary measures.

Step 5. If a grievance is filed, initiate grievance-handling procedures. Follow the published procedures exactly and without deviation. Plan all your moves carefully, and make full use of your documentation.

Step 6. If termination is required, conduct the termination interview. Begin with a simple statement that a decision to discharge has been made. Don't go into the reasons. Spend the remaining time briefly discussing severance pay, insurance coverage limitations and other benefits, and outplacement services, if any. Keep the interview short.

Summary

Discipline is a system of controls designed to get employees to meet organizational standards and requirements. Its specific purposes are to improve organizational performance, avoid crises and problems, and improve worker attitudes and behavior. It comes in two forms: imposed discipline (negative), and self-discipline (positive). The imposed variety uses deterrents and penalties to prevent rule violations and correct employee behavior and performance. Self-discipline, the preferred form, relies on self-motivation and the willingness of people to subordinate their own needs to those of the organization.

If a disciplinary system is to be effective, employees at all levels of organization must understand the requirements, the do's and don'ts, of the system. They must trust and have confidence in their superior, peers, and subordinates. Both formal and informal sanctions must be in place, and all employees must be committed to the achievement of organizational goals and objectives.

Difficult employees fall into five categories: objectors, complainers, troublemakers, troubled employees, and careless workers. Each group requires considerably different handling. The list of potential disciplinary offenses is long, and it differs somewhat for different types of employees. For managers and other professionals, the most serious violations in recent years include betrayal of trust, dishonesty, discrimination, negligence, conflict of interest, sexual harassment, and misuse of inside information. For lower-level employees, the most common types of misbehavior include excessive absenteeism and tardiness, loafing, lying, cheating, and stealing, violation of safety rules, and insubordination.

An effective discipline system is progressive, using increasingly severe penalties: oral reprimand, written reprimand, written warning, suspension without pay, and discharge. Each penalty has its own pitfalls for the unwary manager.

There are several means of limiting exposure to charges of unlawful discharge—one of the most serious consequences of poorly administered terminations. Protective strategies include written grievance procedures, carefully drawn and administered hiring practices, meticulous record keeping, revised employee handbooks and other organizational documents, release agreements, severance pay, and outplacement services.

HR managers have two discipline roles in their organization: help establish the company's policy, and manage the disciplinary system in their own department, taking appropriate action when needed.

Developing the company's policy takes six steps:

1. Think through the concept of discipline.
2. Define what constitutes unsatisfactory behavior.
3. Decide what forms of discipline will be used.
4. Develop self-discipline strategies.
5. Identify problem people.
6. Review and revise procedures.

When a situation requires taking disciplinary action, the process consists of six steps:

1. Respond quickly.
2. Select the penalty and inform the person.
3. Take the action.
4. Follow up.
5. Prepare for grievance filing.
6. Conduct termination interview, if necessary.

For Further Reading, Viewing, and Listening

Abbott, Jan. "How to Say: 'You're Laid Off.' " *Training*, December 1986, pp. 73–76.

Allen, Jeffrey G., Jr., ed. *The Employee Termination Handbook.* New York: John Wiley & Sons, 1986.

Brady, Robert L. *Before You Say "You'll Have to Go . . .": A Termination Decision Tree.* Madison, Conn.: Business and Legal Reports, 1985.

Bramson, Robert M. *Coping with Difficult People.* New York: Ballantine Books, 1981.

A Case of Insubordination (20-minute videocassette). Rank Roundtable Training, 113 N. San Vicente Blvd., Beverly Hills, CA 90211, 1972.

The Correct Way of Correcting (24-minute videocassette). Rank Roundtable Training, 113 N. San Vicente Blvd., Beverly Hills, CA 90211-2387, 1975.

Dealing With Difficult Behavior (6-hour audiocassette). American Management Association Extension Institute, 135 W. 50th St., New York, NY 10020, 1986.

The Disciplinary Interview (16-minute videocassette). Rank Roundtable Training, 113 N. San Vicente Blvd., Beverly Hills, CA 90211, 1974.

The Effective Supervisor: How to Discipline. Madison, Conn.: Business and Legal Reports, 1985.

Ewing, David W. "How to Negotiate With Employee Objectors." *Harvard Business Review,* January–February 1983, pp. 103–110.

Fair and Effective Disciplinary Action (10-minute videocassette). Produced by Business and Legal Reports, 1986. Distributed by American Media, 1454 30th St., West Des Moines, IA 50265.

Feedback: Giving Constructive Criticism (19-minute videocassette). AMA Film/Video, Nine Galen St., Watertown, MA 02172, 1986.

Firm . . . But Fair (15-minute videocassette). Dartnell, 4660 Ravenswood Ave., Chicago, IL 60640, 1980.

Grote, Richard C. "Discipline." Chapter 51 in *Human Resources Management and Development Handbook,* edited by William R. Tracey. New York: AMACOM, 1985.

Handling the Difficult Employee (21-minute videocassette). Produced by Banctraining, 1986. Distributed by Excellence in Training Corporation, 8364 Hickman Rd., Des Moines, IA 50322.

How to Discipline. Madison, Conn.: Business and Legal Reports, 1985.

How to Hire—How to Fire (6-hour audiotape). American Management Association Extension Institute, 135 W. 50th St., New York, NY 10020, 1987.

I'd Like a Word With You (27-minute videocassette). Video Arts, Northbrook Tech Center, 4088 Commercial Ave., Northbrook, IL 60062, 1979.

Kauff, Jerome B., and Practicing Law Institute staff. *Employment*

Problems in the Workplace. New York: Practicing Law Institute, 1986.

Kilmann, Ralph H. "Managing Troublemakers." *Training and Development Journal,* May 1985, pp. 102–108.

Mackey, Daniel. *Employment at Will and Employee Responsibility.* New York: AMACOM, 1986.

Plachy, Roger J. *Performance Management.* New York: AMACOM, 1988.

Ruud, Ronald C., and Joseph J. Woodford. *Supervisor's Guide to Documentation and File Building for Employee Discipline.* Crestline, Calif.: Advisory Publishing, 1987.

Sherman, V. Clayton. *From Losers to Winners: How to Manage Problem Employees . . . and What to Do If You Can't.* Rev. ed. New York: AMACOM, 1987.

So Who's Perfect? (14-minute videocassette). Salenger Films, 1635 Twelfth St., Santa Monica, CA 90404-9988, 1983.

Taking Disciplinary Action (8-minute videocassette). Produced by International Training Consultants, 1981. Distributed by Excellence in Training Corporation, 8364 Hickman Rd., Des Moines, IA 50322.

Walton, Richard E. *Interpersonal Peacemaking: Confrontations and Third Party Consultation.* Reading, Mass.: Addison-Wesley Publishing Company, 1969.

8

Rewarding

Reinforcing Quality Performance

Managers must remember that people are not machines. They need far more than an energy supply and periodic maintenance to function well. Today's workers need personal satisfaction from their jobs, the sense of pride that comes from doing the job well and knowing that others recognize and appreciate it. Managers must be able to say to their people, 'You're important. You matter to me and to this organization." And when people excel, managers must be able to demonstrate that what they have done is of value to the organization.

Why bother with recognizing high performance? From the organization's perspective, because of the profound effect on productivity. At a time when many say that American industry is in crisis because of declining productivity, no organization can afford to ignore this. You cannot motivate people to produce more and better simply by paying them their normal salary. Money alone will probably ensure you their attendance and a reasonably consistent effort, but it will not produce the hustle, high energy, commitment, and total concentration required for outstanding performance. Of all the factors that tend to encourage and develop highly motivated workers, recognizing and rewarding outstanding performance heads the list.

A reward is a special gain given to an individual or a group in return for outstanding achievement. It can be tangible or intangible; it can be monetary or nonmonetary. It is *not* regular compensation for doing a job. One common form of reward is an award, a tangible prize; it may be financial (a bonus or a gift), or nonfinancial (trophy, medal, citation, or plaque). Rewards are given for one of two reasons: exceptional performance of assigned duties and tasks, or unique contributions to the organization, which may or may not be job-related.

A reward tells an employee that someone noticed and someone cares. Because it demonstrates what constitutes outstanding performance, it also creates role models for others to emulate—heroes, in effect. And there are other purposes. Here is a summary:

- To generate, recognize, and reward performance that reflects corporate goals and objectives
- To increase productivity
- To improve the quality of products and services
- To motivate employees, both salaried and nonsalaried
- To improve employee job satisfaction, loyalty to the organization, and morale
- To promote safety and efficiency in operations
- To increase sales
- To reduce costs
- To enhance trainee learning
- To give employees a sense of accomplishment, a feeling of being appreciated

Role of the HR manager. HR managers must take a leading role in designing and developing reward systems. It is their responsibility to be well-informed about the latest research findings on the effectiveness of various types of recognition and awards. HR managers must also educate other managers and staffers in the importance of reward systems in gaining and maintaining a competitive edge, and train them in establishing and using them. And, of course, HR managers must set the example by using rewards in their own departments to influence staff attitudes, boost motivation, morale, and productivity, reinforce desirable behavior and performance, and build employee self-esteem. This chapter describes the HR manager's three functions: developing corporate reward systems of all types (awards and recognition systems), helping managers become better bosses by incorporating reward systems into their way of dealing with people, and setting up systems to reward staff in his or her own department.

Requirements of a Sound System

An effective and workable awards and recognition system has several distinguishing characteristics. All are essential to the acceptance of the system by employees and to its successful operation.

Clear objectives, policies, and procedures. An effective system has a set of written objectives that is clear and specific, complemented by written policies to guide the actions of managers, and a set of procedures describing how the program will be implemented. And, of course, those objectives, policies, and procedures must be understood by employees at all levels. The system must also define the groups of people and the performance that will be rewarded. And, most important of all, the system must reward *results*, not intentions, potential, or activities: rewards must be tied to outcomes that are critical to the success of the organization.

Specific criteria should be clearly spelled out. For example, awards for professional or managerial achievement can be presented for accomplishments that contribute to the efficiency or profitability of the company or a department. More specifically, awards in this category should be given for accomplishments that

1. Result in significant improvements in individual or group productivity.
2. Reduce labor, material, equipment, product service, or other costs.
3. Improve personnel utilization and company operations.
4. Improve services offered to the public, customers, clients, or consumers.
5. Provide significant gains in occupational safety or health.
6. Enhance the image and reputation of the organization in the industry or the community at large.

Another example: awards for technical or scientific achievement can be given for inventions, applications, or accomplishments that contribute to subsequent technical improvements. Awards should be for projects that are significant to the industry or the organization; materially advance the research and development activities or posture of the organization; or make a significant contribution to scientific or technical knowledge.

People-oriented. The plan must focus on people and must be clearly relevant to their needs and values. That means employees must participate in establishing the plan. And, where appropriate, they must also be involved in selecting the recipients. Similarly, first-line supervisors must be completely involved in the program. They must participate in establishing the standards for every form of recognition and reward for which their people are eligible. And they cannot be overlooked when awards are actually made to their people—since they were likely to be participants, if only indirectly, in the achievement.

Competitive. The system must be competitive in either of two senses of the term. It fosters good-natured and friendly competition among individuals and groups of employees—not dog-eat-dog, rancorous rivalries. Or—much more preferable—it encourages employees to compete with themselves, with their own past records.

Achievable. Make the reward achievable and worth getting, but don't make it too difficult to win—or too easy.

Comprehensive. The system must be comprehensive from two standpoints. First, it includes roughly comparable awards and recognition for all levels and classes of employees, discriminating against none. That is, there is something of value in the program for everyone—executives, managers, scientists, engineers, technicians, clerical workers, and hourly employees. Second, it includes both economic and noneconomic, tangible and intangible rewards, again for all types of employees.

Objective, fair, and equitable. Employees must be assured that the recognition program will operate in a way that is proper, fair, and equitable. They must see the plan as directly related to job performance or some other objective of the organization (such as a company's image as a good citizen and good neighbor). Objective performance standards that are regularly updated must serve as a foundation for the program. That means that the system involves accurate measurement of some sort and not just impressions or subjective judgment. And, where judgment is of necessity a factor, more than a single individual should be responsible for making the final decision on the winner. Rewards must be based wherever possible on frequent observation by qualified judges or appraisal by competent evaluators.

Flexible. Some plans do not work because they are inflexible. Management has assumed that the same incentive or reward will work for all levels and types of employees. The fact is that people do not attach the same value or degree of importance to awards or recognition in any form or category. The program must be adjustable so that it will be attractive to all levels and types of employees—managers and supervisors, scientists and technicians, hourly workers and laborers, men and women, young and old. Differences in financial need, marital status, family size, lifestyles, and income level will affect employees' willingness to make the sacrifices necessary to earn recognition and rewards.

Cost effective. Before committing itself to any form of recognition and awards program, top management must determine the cost effectiveness of the system by subjecting it to benefits-cost analysis. The personnel, time, and other resources invested in the system should yield benefits to the organization and its employees that exceed its costs.

Appropriate. Employees will judge awards on the basis of their ultimate value. Reward programs must be seen as worthwhile compensation for the effort and achievement. Rewards must be in proportion to the achievement or contribution to the organization. They must be given only to truly deserving people and must not be too easily won. Awards must be tasteful and of high quality, and they should be individualized. That means that when appropriate, the award is selected to match the specific needs and values of the individual and that the recipient's name appears on the item.

Legitimate and reasonable. Rewards and incentives must be based on the company's (and, where appropriate, the customers') best interests as well as their impact on the recipients. Rewards that could destroy a company's relationships with customers or clients, impugn its reputation, or tarnish its image must be shunned. Excessive rewards, such as expensive cars, lavish vacations, and exorbitant bonuses, tempt people into unethical behavior in pursuit of them.

Timely. Rewards must be presented as soon as possible after the achievement. Ideally, they are almost instantaneous. In any case, the reward should not be deferred until management can spare the time to present it. An award presented weeks or months after the fact loses its reinforcing power.

Accompanied by ceremony. Major and intermediate-level rewards should be presented by an executive or top manager with the recipient's colleagues and, where appropriate, family members in attendance. Newspaper releases or other media publicity, with photographs, should always be provided. Such ceremonies reaffirm to all employees that they are an important and valuable part of an organization that cares about its people.

In summary, we can say that a good reward program must:

- Mirror company culture (core values)
- Be adequately funded (with a realistic budget for administration, materials and services, and awards)
- Be simple and easy to administer (keep the rules brief and clear)
- Be specific (tell everyone exactly what is expected)

- Be achievable (give everyone a fair chance to be rewarded)
- Be measurable (avoid subjectivity by tying evaluation to performance)
- Be appropriate for the achievements being recognized and in good taste
- Be balanced (not so difficult that few people are recognized or so easy that just about everyone is)
- Reflect the employee's or group's status and lifestyle (position, age, career stage, orientation, and values)
- Be personally tailored to the recipient
- Be objective and performance based
- Be actively promoted
- Be adequately publicized
- Be personally delivered by the recipient's manager
- Involve ceremony

And, if a tangible award is involved:

- Have universal appeal and lasting value
- Be something that recipients can't buy for themselves
- Be adaptable to individual personalization

Economic Rewards

One large category of rewards is economic. In this category are included actual cash rewards, like bonuses and merit raises; cash equivalents, like extra paid vacation or company stock; and perquisites that have a monetary value, like company-supported low-cost loans and payment of dues in a professional association. One point is worth repeating: only *extra* forms of compensation can be considered rewards—not regular wages, not overtime pay, not cost-of-living increases.

The company's formal awards program (one element of the overall rewards and recognition system) often includes awards in the form of cash; the employee of the month, for instance, gets her picture on the wall, a nice writeup in the company newsletter—and a brand-new $100 bill. This type of financial reward will be discussed as part of the awards programs, later in the chapter.

The role of the HR manager is to determine the most effective economic reward systems, considering both employee motivation and corporate ability to sponsor, and propose them to top management. Following approval, the HR manager is the one who develops detailed plans for their installation and management—all, of course, with the assistance of the financial department. To do that, HR managers must keep abreast of research and developments in motivational systems in general and compensation and benefits systems in particular.

As you begin developing your plan, you may wish to consider the suggestions listed here, a mix of actual cash and money surrogates. (Some of the key items will be discussed in detail.) One word of caution: Make sure you understand recent federal laws on discrimination in benefits before using them; Section 89 is particularly germane.

Merit raises
Promotions
Cash bonuses
Profit sharing and stock options
Performance-based cash awards
Gift certificates
Membership dues in professional associations
Membership fees in fitness or recreational clubs
Trips to meetings of professional associations, for both employee and spouse
Use of company car or plane
Chauffeured limousine
First-class travel accommodations
Low-cost or no-cost loans
Early retirement with full pension
Free medical exams, free dental care
Business travel insurance
Liberal expense account
In-town apartment
Payment of spouse's travel expenses
Moving expenses
Free financial or legal counseling
Vacation home
Domestic help
Sabbatical leave
Child care or elder care
Personal liability insurance
Tuition payments for spouse or children
Free vacation travel
Tickets to cultural or sporting events

Merit raises. Merit pay is a raise in salary given for outstanding performance of assigned duties and tasks. The approach assumes, or at least implies, that an objective performance appraisal system is in effect to adequately determine the performance of individual employees. If such a system does not exist, merit pay should not be used. And it should never be linked with economic conditions or increases in the cost of living.

If you are considering merit raises as part of the corporate rewards plan, you should be aware of some potential problems. Many employees do not believe that their performance is objectively measurable; they fear that the system will not be fairly administered (favoritism is believed to be inevitable); they believe increases are certain to be skewed (people higher on the scale will receive proportionately larger increases than those below them); and there is potential for employee-manager confrontations and increased numbers of grievances. Despite this, however, merit pay has been used effectively in some organizations.

Bonus plans. A bonus plan provides incentive payments, including lump-sum cash disbursements and savings bonds, in addition to base salary. It is given after the fact to employees who exert greater effort and achieve higher productivity. Bonuses can be used to reward either individuals or groups for improved productivity, greater profit or return on investment, improved operating efficiencies, lower costs, and so on.

Performance-based supplemental compensation. With this reward plan employees who reach quarterly or annual targets are given cash or stock in the company. The target is established before the fact by the manager for individual employees, or jointly with them. The amount of the award is usually pegged to the employee's level of responsibility and the difficulty of reaching or exceeding the target. Usually, such plans are a part of a management by objectives (MBO) program.

Profit sharing, stock options, and deferred compensation. In a profit-sharing plan, qualifying employees receive extra compensation pegged to the company's profits in the period. In a stock option program, qualifying employees can purchase stock in the company for a specified period at a specified price, usually considerably lower than the market price. A deferred compensation plan is a complex program in which the company sets aside a certain percentage of an executive's normal compensation and invests it in a mutual fund or other investment in the name of the corporation. The investment then becomes a corporate investment on the balance sheet. Each year the corporation borrows a certain percentage against the collateral of this investment to buy a cash-value life insurance policy for the employee. Upon retirement, the employee (or beneficiary) receives an annual percentage of the net value of the investment at the time of retirement. The employee gets additional current compensation (subject to annual income tax), a substantial life insurance policy (against which he or she can borrow), and deferred compensation at retirement.

Normally, certain preset conditions determine whether an employee qualifies for these programs, usually related to length of service or rank in the organization. However, all three can be considered monetary rewards in this respect: they are occasionally awarded to outstanding employees who have demonstrated exceptional competence and are considered difficult to replace.

Promotions. Promotion has long been used as a form of reward for achievement and service. It recognizes and repays the person for her accomplishments, and provides an incentive for other employees. Only performance, however, not length of service, can be considered a valid criterion for advancement. Seniority is no guarantee of competent performance in a higher position. It is important to note, too, that outstanding performance in one position is not a certain qualification for success in different and higher-level jobs. Promotion as a reward should be used with care.

Noneconomic Rewards

Economic rewards are indeed important, but they are only one part of the picture. Noneconomic rewards are equally important—in many cases, particularly with knowledge workers, even more valuable than money. Letters of commendation, public announcement of achievements, honorary titles (supervisor of the month), and pats on the back contribute significantly to job satisfaction, morale, and retention of employees. These rewards are particularly effective if they involve the approval of people who "count." For HR personnel and other professionals, this means company executives, other corporate power brokers, and their peers and colleagues both within and outside the company.

Noneconomic rewards also include such things as assignment to prestigious work groups, committees, and task forces, and special individual assignments. There are also nonmonetary perks—special privileges, usually associated with organizational rank and status, granted on an individual basis to recognize high achievement. Examples are reserved parking spaces, plush offices, private washrooms, and access to executive dining rooms and airline VIP lounges.

There is an almost unlimited registry of ideas that enlightened supervisors can use to compliment and reward deserving employees. Many of them are nothing more—and nothing less—than public expressions of respect and appreciation. These various ways of saying "thank you" can be used both with individuals and with groups.

Individual recognition

- Spontaneously reinforcing exceptional performance with smiles, nods, complimentary comments, pats on the back
- Giving direct, on-the-spot public praise
- Recognizing top performance at staff meetings
- Acknowledging contributions by handwritten notes of thanks or commendations
- Issuing formal letters of commendation or appreciation
- Giving individuals special, challenging assignments or independent projects where they will get visibility and potentially more recognition for their efforts
- Providing opportunities for the exercise of leadership
- In reports to top management, identifying outstanding achievers by name
- Making office improvements (furniture, furnishings, and arrangement)
- Providing opportunities for speaking engagements
- Publishing research findings and ideas
- Inserting photographs and writeups in the company newspaper or bulletin or in public press releases
- Holding public recognition programs, banquets, and ceremonies
- Asking people what they want changed in the work environment—and then making the change if at all possible
- Giving people a say in the reward system—what, when, how, and where

Group recognition

- Complimenting work groups or teams at staff meetings
- Charting progress and accomplishment on important projects on bulletin boards
- Holding occasional staff meetings or training sessions in an informal setting away from the workplace
- Hosting informal social gatherings after work

- Sponsoring a special occasion: luncheon, dinner, dinner-dance, picnic, golf, tennis, or bowling tournament, theater party, baseball, football, or basketball outing
- Giving teams special assignments involving visibility and the potential for professional recognition
- Inserting photographs and writeups in the company newspaper or in public press releases
- Publishing research findings
- Holding recognition programs and ceremonies

Praise. For most of today's workers, praise is essential; it is a potent means of recognizing accomplishment and a powerful stimulant for continued improvement.

To be most effective, praise should meet these specifications:

1. It is given *only* when a particularly difficult task has been handled well.
2. It is given prudently and is not exaggerated or excessive.
3. It focuses on the areas the employee or the manager has targeted for improvement.
4. It is given in public, when the accomplishment is truly worthy of public notice.

One of the least expensive and most effective means of rewarding quality performance and exceptional accomplishment is a letter. This can take several forms: letters of appreciation, letters of commendation, thank-you notes, and short memos. Even better, give outstanding work a double recognition: a public pat on the back, followed up by a written thank you that the employee can keep in her personal file.

Special assignments. Special projects, particularly those with high visibility, can also serve as rewards. So can attendance at conferences and conventions. Top performers can be given speaking assignments. They can be encouraged to explore areas of the company that you think could stand some objective appraisal. Make them troubleshooters. Tell them to go to the Seattle office (or New York office if you're on the West Coast) and investigate that nagging problem, write a report outlining their conclusions and recommendations, and present a briefing to the staff.

When you go on a trip to another organization or a branch of your firm, pick one or two of your top performers and take them with you. You'll get a chance to talk to them, learn to know them better, get some of their ideas, and let them know that you are interested in them. They are certain to get the message: they are appreciated, their services are valuable, and they are wanted. That is a reward in itself.

Honorary clubs. A common nonmonetary reward, especially for sales personnel, is membership in a club. Members are inducted at a special ceremony, often involving a dinner, with a great deal of peer recognition. For example, one organization has what is called "The 100-Plus Club," for the salespeople who exceed 100 percent of their sales objectives for two consecutive quarters. New members are inducted, with considerable fanfare, at a banquet during the annual sales meeting, and are presented with a ring valued at approximately $300. The rings (one for men and one for women) are designed with a place for ten small diamonds, and one is added each time the target is reached again.

Humorous awards. A humorous or lighthearted approach to recognition, if done in good taste, can be extremely effective in promoting morale. Examples are coffee mugs with humorous inscriptions, unconventional or outrageous trophies, plaques commemorating such accomplishments as the idea of the month, the sale of the quarter, the blooper of the week, and so on.

In one organization, the "Zot Award" (a monstrosity in shape, size, and composition) is given at the weekly staff meeting to the manager who distinguishes herself in some way at that meeting. In another organization, a "Bomb Award" (a large black bowling ball with a fuse protruding from a finger hole) is given to the manager or staffer who has made himself conspicuous in some manner or fashion during the preceding week. In both cases, recipients are required to display the award prominently in their offices until the next lucky winner is chosen.

Awards Programs

Many companies have included in their overall corporate rewards plan a formalized awards program, incorporating prizes (including cash awards), certificates and trophies, honorary titles, and other symbols of recognition, all systematized into a set program with specific schedules and qualifications. There are awards for individuals and for work teams. There are monetary awards and nonmonetary awards. There are tangible awards like an engraved plaque and intangible awards like the premium parking space reserved for the employee of the month. There are expensive, engraved gifts and inexpensive, perhaps even humorous, items that are treasured for their symbolic value.

Some awards honor achievement on the job: innovation, cost-saving suggestions, safety ideas, production improvements; some recognize long-term achievement, like attendance or years of service. Some are given to employees for activities outside their job: participation in community service, fund-raising campaigns, volunteer leadership in a nonprofit group. All in all, the specific ingredients of an awards program can be anything that has meaning to employees (and is within the means of the organization).

The key is the existence of a program: awards are given on the basis of specific guidelines developed for all employees and communicated throughout the organization; see Figure 8-1 for a suggested format for your organization's plan. Figure 8-2 is a promotional flier that describes the program used by the American Management Association for its employees. For the nomination procedure, you may want to use a form similar to Figure 8-3.

Some of the many possibilities for awards are listed below.

Individual and team awards (financial)

- Cash bonuses and special cash awards (such as the Chairman's or President's Award)
- Gift certificates and merchandise
- Additional education or training
- Travel (cruises, package tours, or independent travel)
- Club memberships
- Time off with pay; extra vacations

Individual awards (nonfinancial)

- Medals, plaques, badges, trophies, pins, and certificates—to honor accomplishments such as supervisor of the month, instructor of the quarter, and employee of the year
- Corporate "Oscars, Emmys, or Nobel prizes"
- Office or work area improvements (furniture and furnishings)
- Testimonials
- Memorials
- Scrolls
- VIP certificates
- Training completion certificates
- Seminar attendance certificates
- Diplomas

- Certificates of appreciation
- Castings and medallions

Group awards (nonfinancial)

- Medals, plaques, trophies, pins, and certificates
- Office or work area improvements and renovations (furniture, furnishing, and decorations)
- Personalized mementoes of many types: calculators, jewelry, wallets, desk sets, T-shirts, paperweights, etc.

Matching Rewards to Employee Values

No system of rewards can be effective unless it takes into consideration the needs and values of the people it was targeted to motivate. Because values are what people consider important, what they will sacrifice for and work diligently to get, rewards must not only be consistent with values but truly represent them. A reward that does not exemplify something of value to an employee will be worthless.

That means that management must consciously develop a profile of employee values by observing the reactions of people to various rewards, interviewing and surveying employees about their preferences for rewards, and conducting tests of the influence of various awards on employee behavior and performance. The most practical means of doing that is to ask groups of workers—managers, professionals, engineers and scientists, instructors and course developers, technicians, salespersons, and hourly workers—to list the kinds of rewards they prefer, in order of priority. That can be done with a simple questionnaire or by group interviews with a random sample of each category of employees. It also means that individual managers must get to know their people and what makes them tick—what motivates them to more and more intensive effort—and then use those findings to make their rewards match the values of individual employees.

Changes in values. Since the 1930s, striking changes have occurred in the values of the American work force. Some of these changes have implications for the type of reward system that will be effective today—values relating to compensation and benefits, recognition, progress and development, jobs and work, career development, and work, family, and leisure. HR managers must make sure they know the extent of these changes in their organization.

(*Text continues on page 219.*)

Figure 8-1. Sample format for a reward system plan.

Policy (*A brief general statement of the company's reward policy*) _____

Objectives (*What the program is designed to achieve*) _____

Responsibilities (*Program director and assistants, awards committee, and functional managers*) _____

<u>Process</u>

Eligibility (*Number and classes of employees*) _____

Nominations (*Sources and procedures*) _____

Awards/prizes (*Types, sizes, and amounts, if monetary*) _____

Requirements/performance levels (*Contributions, achievements, or other criteria*) _____

Schedule (*Dates for nomination, review, approval, and awards ceremony*) _____

Publicity (*Promotional materials and kickoff*) _____

Awards ceremony (*What, where, when, and participants*) _____

Evaluation (*Means of assessing the value of the program and improving its operation*) _____

Figure 8-2.   Description of one company's awards program.

AMERICAN MANAGEMENT ASSOCIATION
ACHIEVEMENT AWARDS PROGRAM
CRITERIA & CATEGORIES FOR AMA ACHIEVEMENT
AWARDS

Categories of Awards:

1. The AMA Award of Distinction, **THE GOLDEN EAGLE:** (Awarded annually)

   Criteria: A person who is good to work with—helpful, supportive, cooperative, caring, dependable, and courteous. An employee, who by his/her **continued extra effort and thoughtfulness:**

   a. Enhances the quality of life for co-workers and other employees of AMA, and/or
   b. Contributes significantly to the operations of his/her departments, and/or
   c. Enhances the AMA image to members, customers, and/or staff.

2. Individual Distinguished Achievement Award: (Awarded annually)

   Criteria: Singular act that enhances AMA's internal and/or external image through outstanding performance **beyond the scope of expected job responsibilities.**

   Nominations will be considered in any of the following categories:

   a. Improving the quality of product, service, or information.
   b. Saving time and/or money.
   c. Producing revenue.

3. Group Distinguished Achievement Award: (Awarded quarterly)

   Criteria: AMA employees, acting as a team, perform a singular act that enhances AMA's internal and/or external image through outstanding performance **beyond the scope of expected job responsibilities.**

   Nominations will be considered in any of the following categories:

   a. Improving the quality of product, service, or information.
   b. Saving time and/or money.
   c. Producing revenue.

Figure 8-3.   One company's nomination form.

AMERICAN MANAGEMENT ASSOCIATION

ACHIEVEMENT AWARDS PROGRAM

NOMINATION FORM

Staff Member Nominated _____

Title _____ Exempt/Nonexempt _____

Department/Accountability Center _____ Location _____

Nominated By: _____ Date _____

NOMINATION CATEGORIES:

     * The AMA Award of Distinction, **THE GOLDEN EAGLE** _____

     * Individual Distinguished Achievement _____

     * Group Distinguished Achievement _____

Provide basis for nomination in space below and/or attach supporting documentation:

_____

_____

_____

_____

_____

_____

_____

_____

_____

_____

_____

Committee Use Only

Received by Awards Committee: _____

Disposition of Committee: _____

_____

Signature of Chairperson: _____ _____

Notified Nominator (Date) _____

Copies to Chairperson of the Awards Committee (white), Nominator (pink)

Compensation and benefits. Although employees have always valued pay and benefits, today's employees tend to consider higher pay and benefits as the natural outcome of superior performance. Earlier, employees saw longevity as the basic determinant of higher pay and more benefits.

Recognition. Today's employees seek out and respond more positively to recognition by the organization and their managers, in contrast to earlier days when employees primarily tried to avoid criticism and expected little praise from their superiors.

Progress and development. Today's workers expect progress and career development as important rewards—a natural consequence of the exercise of initiative and the display of competence and accomplishment.

Jobs and work. Today's workers want jobs and work that are interesting and challenging. They will seek meaningful assignments and accept them as a reward for commitment, effort, and outstanding performance. Earlier counterparts were more likely to accept routine, dead-end jobs and endure repetitive work without complaint.

Work, family, and leisure. Today's employees tend to give high priority to leisure time and family activities, sometimes placing them ahead of work, whereas workers of generations ago invariably placed work ahead of family and leisure. At the very least, today's workers demand a balance between work, family, and leisure.

Reward programs for the HR department. People who work with concepts and ideas (so-called knowledge workers) share the values of other workers described in the preceding paragraphs. However, one additional factor has an important bearing on the types of rewards that will evoke their greatest effort and productivity—the influence of their peers.

Knowledge workers, the heart of the HR function, want and need the recognition of their internal and external peers for technical, conceptual, and human competence, for opportunities to provide professional assistance and leadership to groups of people, and for acceptance and membership in highly select groups. That means that HR personnel are likely to be most receptive to reward systems that include opportunities to be recognized by their peers (attendance at professional meetings and conferences, speaking engagements, publication of their research findings and ideas), assignment to special work teams and task forces, particularly in leadership positions, and nomination for special awards and recognition both inside and outside the company.

The value of self-esteem—a true story. A man I know worked as an HR manager in a medium-size company for ten years. He was senior to all other functional managers. In the community and on the job he was well liked and highly respected. He belonged to two prominent community organizations and several professional associations. Over the years he was honored with several awards for outstanding performance in the company and for extraordinary service to the community.

Recently, he confided to a close friend, "I'm looking for another position—anything to get away from XYZ Company." Naturally his friend asked why. He explained that he had been very satisfied with his job, and still liked it—except for one very important event. A new CEO had been appointed one year before. Shortly after his arrival, and without explanation, the CEO moved the HR manager from his office just down the hall from the CEO's own office, to much less desirable and prestigious office space in another building—and moved a junior functional manager into the vacated office. The senior manager rightly considered himself downgraded and publicly humiliated.

Shortly thereafter, the HR manager found and accepted a comparable position with another organization in a neighboring state. He lost seniority and had to face the problems of moving his family, selling and buying property, closing out his old job, and meeting the challenges involved in starting with a new organization. More to the point, XYZ Company lost a valuable manager.

Do not treat lightly the value of intangible rewards. Our deep needs for recognition, self-esteem, and self-fulfillment are powerful motivators. Organizations that understand this, and use it positively to the benefit of all, will be winners.

The Reward Process

Like any other system, an effective reward system must be developed and implemented systematically and thoughtfully. Here are the steps involved.

Step 1. Determine employee wants. Begin by surveying employees at all levels to find out what kinds of rewards would be meaningful to them. Use a short questionnaire. Follow up with interviews, either individual or group, with a sample of employees in each major category: managers, supervisors, staffers, scientists and engineers, technicians, administrative and clerical, instructors and course developers, sales personnel, hourly workers, and so on.

Step 2. Define system objectives. Determine the purposes and objectives of the reward system and then translate them into a written statement of policies and procedures. It is critically important to know precisely what the reward system is supposed to do for the organization and its people and how it will operate. It is equally important to communicate this information to everyone in the organization.

Step 3. Specify the types of rewards and their requirements. Identify the specific numbers and types of rewards—individual and group, economic and nonmonetary—to be presented each year. Be sure that all categories of employees are covered. Spell out the requirements for each award and publish and distribute them in an employee handbook or some other publication available to all employees. A critical part of this communication involves giving other managers specific guidelines on nonmaterial rewards that employees at all levels want: recognition and praise, special assignments, notes and letters of appreciation and commendation, and so on.

Step 4. Develop an annual schedule of awards. For major awards, develop a schedule that includes the target dates for submission of nominations, review by the selection committee, announcement of the winners, preparation of the award certificate or other item to be presented, presentation ceremony, and release of publicity to news media.

Step 5. Implement and modify the plan. Put the plan into effect, track results, solicit comments and recommendations from award winners and a random sample of supervisors, managers, and employees. Make modifications to the system as necessary.

Summary

People need approval and appreciation. They need to know that they are valued. Regardless of position or status, they are delighted to receive accolades for performance of their duties or for other contributions to the organization. More important, their motivation and morale and, as a consequence, their productivity, will be enormously enhanced.

Among other things, rewards also improve the quality of products and services, promote safety and efficiency of operations, increase sales, and enhance trainee learning. To be effective, the reward system must be understandable and fairly administered, and it must reward results rather than potential or activities. It must be designed and operated in accordance with sound psychological principles.

Rewards are of two basic types: economic and nonmonetary. Economic rewards include merit pay increases, bonuses, stock options and profit-sharing plans, performance-based supplemental compensation, dues in professional and social organizations, and tuition reimbursement, among others. Nonmonetary rewards include pats on the back, letters of commendation, diplomas and certificates, plaques, trophies, and commemorative jewelry, travel, and special assignments, to name a few.

To be maximally effective, a reward system must:

- Have clear and specific objectives, policies, and procedures.
- Be people-oriented, in that it meets the wants and priorities of employees.
- Where appropriate, be competitive.
- Be comprehensive and achievable.
- Be fair, objective, and equitable.
- Be flexible.
- Be in good taste but appropriate and adequate.
- Be accompanied by appropriate ceremony.

Designing and administering the company's reward system is the HR manager's job. The steps in the process are:

1. Determine employee wants.
2. Define objectives for the reward system.
3. Specify the types of rewards and their requirements.
4. Develop an annual schedule.
5. Implement the plan and modify as needed.

For Further Reading, Viewing, and Listening

Collins, Samuel R. "Incentives and Awards." Chapter 43 in *Human Resources Management and Development Handbook,* edited by William R. Tracey. New York, AMACOM, 1985.

Cruden, Herbert J., and Arthur W. Sherman, Jr. *Managing Human Resources.* 7th ed. Cincinnati, Ohio: South-Western Publishing Company, 1984. See especially Chapter 11.

Eichel, Evelyn, and Henry E. Bender. *Performance Appraisal: A Study of Current Techniques.* New York: AMACOM, 1984.

Frechette, Henry M., Jr., and Edward G. Wertheim. "Performance

Appraisal." Chapter 16 in *Human Resources Management and Development Handbook,* edited by William R. Tracey. New York: AMACOM, 1985.

"Getting Results: The Performance Appraisal Process" (audiocassette and workbook). American Management Association Extension Institute, 135 W. 50th St., New York, NY 10020, 1985.

The Go-Giver (30-minute videocassette). American Media, 1454 30th St., West Des Moines, IA 50265, 1981.

Grant, Philip C. *Employee Motivation: Principles and Practices.* New York: Vantage Press, 1984.

Gubman, Edward L. "Getting the Most Out of Performance Appraisals," *Management Review,* November 1984, pp. 44–48.

Hammer, Tove H., and Samuel B. Bacharach, eds. *Reward Systems and Power Distribution: Searching for Solutions.* Ithaca, N.Y.: ILR Press, 1977.

Harper, Stephen C. "Adding Purpose to Performance Reviews." *Training and Development Journal,* September 1986, pp. 53–55.

Henderson, Richard. *Performance Appraisal: Theory to Practice.* Englewood Cliffs, N. J.: Prentice-Hall, 1980.

"How to Motivate for Superior Performance" (audiocassette and workbook). American Management Association Extension Institute, 135 W. 50th St., New York, NY 10020, 1981.

Humorous Awards and Certificates. Westbury, N.Y.: Asher-Gallant Press, 1983.

Jewell, Donald O., and George E. Manners, Jr. *Dynamic Incentive Systems.* Atlanta: Georgia State University Business Publications, 1975.

Kilduff, Martin J., and Douglas D. Baker. "Getting Down to the Brass Tacks of Employee Motivation." *Management Review,* September 1984, pp. 56–61.

Latham, Gary P., and Kenneth N. Wexley. *Increasing Productivity Through Performance Appraisal.* Reading, Mass.: Addison-Wesley Training Systems, 1981.

Leidecker, Joel K., and James J. Hall. "Motivation: Good Theory— Poor Application." *Training and Development Journal,* June 1981, pp. 152–155.

Meidan, Arthur. *The Appraisal of Managerial Performance.* New York: AMACOM, 1981.

Miller, William B. "Motivation Techniques: Does One Work Best?" *Management Review,* February 1981, pp. 47–52.

Myer, Mary Coeli. "Motivation." In *Human Resources Management and Development Handbook,* edited by William R. Tracey. New York: AMACOM, 1985.

Needell, Cheryl K., and George W. Alwon. "Recognition and Reward: Keys to Motivating Supervisors." *Management Review,* November–December 1982, pp. 53–56.

Odell, Carla, and Jerry McAdams. "The Revolution in Employee Rewards." *Management Review,* March 1987, pp. 30–33.

Pinder, Scott C. *Work Motivation.* Glenview, Ill.: Scott, Foresman & Company, 1984.

The Rewards of Rewarding (24-minute videocassette). Rank Roundtable Training, 113 N. San Vicente Blvd., Beverly Hills, CA 90211, 1974.

Rosenbaum, Bernard L. *How to Motivate Today's Workers: Motivational Models for Managers and Supervisors.* New York: McGraw-Hill Book Company, 1982.

Steers, Richard M., and Lyman W. Porter. *Motivation and Work Behavior.* 3rd ed. New York: McGraw-Hill Book Company, 1983.

Ullrich, Robert A. *Motivation Methods That Work.* Englewood Cliffs, N. J.: Prentice-Hall, 1981.

"Understanding Motivation and Behavior." *Training,* July 1985, pp. 12–13.

Vernon-Harcourt, Tony. *Rewarding Management, 1983: The Annual Guide to Remuneration, Benefits, and Conditions for Directors and Executives.* Brookfield, Vt.: Gower Publishing Company, 1982.

Yankelovich, Daniel. *New Rules—Searching for Fulfillment in a World Turned Upside Down.* New York: AMACOM, 1981.

Zemke, Ron. "Rewards and Recognition: Yes, They Really Work." *Training,* November 1988, pp. 49–53.

9

Improving Productivity
Producing More Efficiently and Effectively

It's no secret that American industry is being outperformed by other nations. One recent study showed that from 1972 to 1988 six other countries (Japan, West Germany, Great Britain, France, Canada, and Italy) managed to improve their productivity greater than the United States— *four times greater* (Council on Competitiveness, 1988).

Obviously something needs to be done about productivity. The question is, who should do it? Many believe that the HR function should play a pivotal role in the quest for improved productivity. I would go one step further: The HR manager should *drive* the process. Why? Because major gains in productivity, particularly the component of product quality, will be achieved not by more efficient work methods or more dazzling technology, but by changes in worker attitudes and skills. From the White House Conference on Productivity: "Human resources are the primary factors of economic production. Machinery and financial capital are little more than artifacts of the human imagination. Human resource development is the primary lever for improving the nation's overall economic performance and productivity."[1] And this is the bailiwick of the HR manager.

One of the most important functions of human resources professionals is to design systems that will make it possible for people to be more productive. It may be *the* most important. Unfortunately, too many HR managers think productivity improvement means using a *single*, short-term, quick-fix technique, such as grid organization or quality circles. Or they believe that the responsibility for improving productivity rests exclusively with line managers.

Of course we all know what productivity is. Or do we? It has

---

[1]Quoted in Patricia Galagan, "Staying Alive: Jack Grayson on the American Productivity Crisis," *Training and Development Journal* (January 1984), p. 59.

■ ■

HOW TO RECOGNIZE A GOOD PRODUCTIVITY PLAN

- It is systematic and comprehensive.
- It addresses the company's long-range goals.
- It emphasizes quality control in production processes.
- It springs from genuine concern by company leaders.
- It focuses on areas with high potential for improvement.
- It is led by individuals who have accepted responsibility for improving productivity.
- It involves everyone in the company.
- It uses qualitative and quantitative measure to assess current productivity levels, and analytical techniques to improve them.

■ ■

been narrowly defined as efficiency—the ratio of output to given level of input. It has also been defined more broadly as effectiveness—the extent to which the output of an activity meets a need or solves a problem. In its broadest sense, productivity considers both output production and how well a program achieves its objectives. In the last few years, the definition has been expanded to include the concept of excellence of product or service—quality as well as quantity. In another recent change, the focus of productivity has shifted from blue-collar workers (where improvements have peaked) to the white-collar work force, which is growing much faster and offers greater potential for significant change.

In summary, productivity is not something that is "done to" employees; it is something that is "done by" people. Nor should it be focused on the lower-level people in an organization; it must involve employees at every level. Regardless of the words used to define them, the basic objectives of a productivity improvement system relate to the production of quality goods and services and, at the same time, increased output per hour of work input.

Companies that succeed in improving productivity reap multiple benefits: reduced customer complaints, lower client serving expenses, greater employee commitment, higher morale, a more cohesive and cooperative organization, and increased profitability.

Who is responsible for productivity? Productivity improvement programs—structured, formal plans for identifying problem areas and rectifying them—demand the participation of all elements of the organization: top management, program and line managers, and staff.

Senior management is responsible for providing support for productivity improvement programs and initiatives, and it must be directly involved in the project from its inception. That means that top managers personally kick off the program, participate in planning and training sessions, help determine the objectives and criteria for success, and approve action plans.

Managers of various functions within the organization provide field-level support for the improvement program. They help choose members of productivity improvement teams, and help those teams develop and implement improvement plans and programs. They monitor progress, explore alternative strategies, and recommend subordinates for recognition and awards.

Staff elements are responsible for developing productivity measurement systems, monitoring efficiency and quality of performance, assisting managers and supervisors in solving productivity problems, conducting special studies, keeping abreast of technology and techniques in their functional areas, and preparing periodic progress reports.

In a very real sense, however, everyone in the organization, top to bottom, has a responsibility for productivity. That's because productivity has a new component, something that until just a few years ago would have never been considered part of the equation: quality control. Workers at all levels must accept responsibility for quality, and quality control must be integrated into the production or service process itself.

The role of the HR manager. There are two dimensions of the role of HR managers: their corporate advisory responsibilities and their departmental management responsibilities. Both are important to the organization and its people.

From the corporate perspective, the HR manager has four responsibilities:

1. To sensitize executives, managers, and staffers to the need to emphasize the "people" aspects of productivity improvement strategies and tactics
2. To stimulate productivity throughout the organization, and monitor performance in major programs
3. As a corporate adviser, to help management establish productivity goals, objectives, measurement tools, and action plans
4. As the corporate training expert, to train managers, staffers, and employee work teams in productivity improvement strat-

egies and techniques: basic sampling techniques, flow charts, and measures

As the manager of an organization function, the HR manager is responsible for productivity within the department. This may mean establishing productivity goals and objectives, assigning specific productivity responsibilities and projects, demonstrating concern for the productivity of HR operations, collecting and reviewing productivity data, following up and converting productivity data and strategies into results, and establishing a productivity feedback system for all levels of the department.

In addition, HR managers are responsible for stimulating the commitment of their people to productivity improvement. They do this by soliciting suggestions, publicizing progress toward productivity improvement, posing the most serious HR productivity problems to their staffs to get their ideas, providing ongoing feedback, and establishing monetary and incentive rewards.

Uncovering the Real Problem

The first step in productivity improvement is identifying the problems. If you don't know what's wrong, you can't fix it. But finding out what's wrong is not a simple task because the problems in modern organizations are usually hidden or camouflaged. What you will typically see are indicators, symptoms. When these appear, the task becomes one of identifying the source of the problem. Figure 9-1 provides some examples.

Underlying Causes

Factors that influence productivity are interrelated and interacting. Causes of lower productivity may be controllable (or at least potentially controllable), semi-controllable, or uncontrollable at the organization level. Controllable items are inadequate or inappropriate corporate culture, structure, and processes. Semi-controllable problems include inadequate capital investments in equipment and facilities, excessively high energy costs, inflationary collective bargaining agreements, lack of employee skills, and inappropriate management styles. Noncontrollable factors are changes in the composition of the national work force, a decline in the work ethic, increased growth in service jobs, decrease in manufacturing jobs, increased government regulation, economic downturns, the actions of competitors and suppliers, and changes in customers' needs and

Figure 9-1.   Tracing organizational productivity problems.

Perceived Problem	Related Ripples	Problem Source
Poor departmental budget performance	• Loss of market competitiveness • Intervention (loss of autonomy) • Increased direct management • Reduced design quality	• Poor initial work definition • Ineffective management reporting systems • Lack of supervisory skills
High turnover within junior staff	• Increased use of contract labor • Loss of learning • High recruiting costs • Increasing overtime	• Lack of contribution recognition • Ineffective application of performance feedback system
Increasing hours to complete internal audits	• Poor schedule adherence • Other valuable projects dropped • Lost savings opportunity • Poor audit coverage	• Lack of focus • Unclear audit work methods • Skill and task imbalances
Inadequate resources to produce reports	• Neglect of other assignments • Excessive management data "noise" • Increased distribution costs	• Redundant and unnecessary reports
Poor morale of telephone operators	• Poor service to customers • High turnover • Loss of market share	• Department strategy (efficiency) conflicts with corporate strategy (customer service)

Adapted from Bradford L. Berglind and Charles D. Scales, "White Collar Productivity: Seeing Through the Camouflage," *Management Review,* June 1987, p. 45. Used by permission.

wants. Attempting to address the noncontrollable factors at the company level is likely to be unproductive. They can be cured only by major governmental and business solutions. But the other causes can, and should, be addressed at the organization level.

People. People are a major cause of low productivity. Among the most important factors are these: poor-quality work force, inappropriate attitudes and values, lack of personal drive, low motivation and morale, unrealistic expectations, inappropriate or inadequate skills and abilities, lack of professional norms, and just plain laziness.

Organizational culture. Here the most important factors relate to the quality of work life for employees. The blocks include lack of job satisfaction, high stress and tension, and vague, contradictory, or incomplete job definition. Other common negative factors are an organizational climate that discourages the full use of available skills and talents, and poor or unclear policies.

Organization structure. Here the blocks originate in the infrastructure of the organizations—the means by which the actions of the work force are coordinated, communicated, and controlled. Specific impediments to productivity include overly complex organization with too many levels of management, insufficient delegation of authority, unclear or overlapping duties and responsibilities, employee–job mismatches, and inadequate, inconsistent, or conflicting instructions or standards.

Management. Inadequate management and leadership skills, lack of a model and standard for employees to emulate, and poor management practices are other major causes of low productivity. Some common problems: improper management of the work environment, improper allocation or use of resources, failure to link resources and results, unclear or unrealistic expectations, negative or no feedback, lack of planning, vague objectives, indecision, acceptance of time wasters, inadequate or insufficient delegation, failure to listen to employees and recognize their ideas and concerns, too much busywork and not enough productive work, and excessive negative stress.

Other shortcomings include overworking the best people and underworking the less competent, inflexibility, and failing to keep promises and give rewards. Still others include too much concentration on financial, legal, or public relations goals and not enough attention to human capital and productivity. And of course there are the common human failings of wrong-headedness, lack of sensitivity to potential or actual problems, lack of know-how, and errors of judgment, such as applying blue-collar approaches to white-collar situations.

Organization processes. Impediments to productivity in processes include inappropriate or arbitrary means of planning and goal setting, failure to establish priorities, vague and unmeasurable objectives, and poorly designed work processes and procedures. Others are inadequate systems of communication, decision making, employee evaluation and feedback, recognition and reward, compensation and benefits, and training and development. And still other causes are poor work area layout, substandard tools and equipment, inadequate lighting, and poor materials.

Technology. Here the impediments include outmoded or obsolescent operating systems, insufficient investment in research and development, failure to make full use of technological advances in communications, and training and development systems.

Productivity Audit

To pin down the specific problem areas, to distinguish the real impediments from their symptoms, your organization needs to conduct a productivity audit, a detailed analysis of the company and the way it operates. The means of doing that are quite straightforward: questionnaires, observation, and interviews.

Separate questionnaires should be designed for managers and supervisors and for individual employees. The questionnaire for managers and supervisors should ask such questions as: Are we as competitive, productive, and cost effective as we should or could be? If we aren't, why not? What are the problems and the obstacles? What specifically can we do to improve our competitive status? Productivity? Cost effectiveness? The questionnaire for individual employees should ask such questions as these: What is your job? What gets in the way of doing your best on the job? What do you need that you don't now have to do your job better?

Observation should focus on the job environment, working conditions, work flow, and job processes: it's a search for problems and obstacles to productivity. Then follow up with structured interviews with employees at all levels where observation (or responses to questionnaires) indicates a potential or actual productivity barrier.

Data collected should be tabulated, summarized, and analyzed to develop a priority list of productivity problems for resolution.

This list should be distributed to all employees so that they will know that their input has been used. Then an action plan to address the problems should be prepared.

Designing a Productivity Plan

After the real problems have been uncovered, the task is to develop a plan of corrective action. Because productivity itself is a complex, interactive process, a program to bring about improvements must be planned carefully and systematically. Where to start? What does a productivity plan look like? What does it contain? Fortunately, we have several models to draw upon.

Contents of the Plan

There are several different ways to organize the contents of a productivity improvement plan.[2] One model is built around four components: methods, equipment, resource utilization, and employee performance. Another emphasizes the human dimensions of productivity and sees productivity as a system of components, functions, and processes. A third identifies seven components: resources, employees, products, services, managers, quantity, and quality. A fourth writer describes these ten areas of an organizational productivity model: planning and goal-setting process, organization structure, productivity and performance measurement systems, individual performance feedback, reward systems, management processes, communications and management information systems, operating systems and technology, personnel policies, and training and development.

Although all four of these models have value, in my view the most promising approach for any type of organization, public or private, production-centered or service-oriented, is one that takes the broadest possible view. For that reason, I suggest that a composite of all four be applied. An outline for that system appears as Figure 9-2. The HR manager would, of course, focus attention and efforts on the "people" components of the system—which are not limited to the items with HR in their titles.

---

[2]For details on the four models mentioned here, see (respectively) the works by these authors at the end of the chapter: Bain, Carkhuff, Riggs and Felix, and McDermott.

Figure 9-2.   Components of a corporate productivity improvement system.

Planning and Goal Setting

    Strategic plans and goals
    Operational plans and objectives
    HR plans and objectives

Organization Structure

    Organization design
    Organization development

Management Processes and Policies

    Communications
    Management information systems
    Policies

Financial and Material Resources Utilization

    Funds
    Equipment
    Operating systems and technology
    Methods and processes
    Productivity

Products and Services

    Quality
    Quantity

Human Resources

    Staffing
    Personnel policies
    Productivity and performance measurement systems
    Individual performance feedback
    Compensation and benefits systems
    Training and development systems
    Reward systems
    Workplace improvement

Key Elements of the Plan

Regardless of which model is used to outline the contents of a productivity plan, the approach chosen must address four fundamental elements, in this order:

1. Setting goals and priorities
2. Establishing performance standards and measures
3. Selecting objectives
4. Applying controls

Goals and priorities. Goals must be comprehensive, consistent, and realistic, and must be appropriate to the needs of all organizational consistencies. They must provide an adequate basis for planning and control, and must be communicated to all constituent groups. Some goals are certain to be more critical to the success of the productivity improvement program than others. Those that are most central to the organization's mission and purpose should be given highest priority. Among the leading candidates: organization structure and staffing, employee training and development, communication, physical plant and facilities, cost control, and incentives and reward systems.

Performance standards and measures. Performance standards must be selected or developed for each work activity that is related to a problem area. These standards define the amount of time and resources required under normal conditions to complete one unit of output and the characteristics of the product from the standpoint of quality. Performance measures are the yardsticks that will be applied to gauge whether the product meets the standard. Standards should be objective, reasonable, and attainable.

Standards and measures for production-type jobs are relatively simple to develop. A unit of measure is developed—widgets per minute, letters per hour, instructor contact hours per week—and worker performance is monitored. If appropriate, a work simplification program is used, in which alternative methods to doing the task are tested and the best one applied and refined.

However, it is not so easy to measure the output of knowledge workers; what they do during the typical workday can't really be counted or measured. Staffers in the HR department are an example. Often the results of their work are indirect, an intermediate step toward achieving certain larger objectives, such as promotable personnel. Let's use the HR department as an example to look at measures of intangible productivity (of course when developing a productivity program for your own department, you'll find this example particularly helpful).

Productivity measures for knowledge workers should measure efficiency (the ratio of program inputs to outputs), quality (accuracy, timeliness, and thoroughness of programs and services), and effectiveness (the relationship of program outputs to what the program or service was intended to achieve).

The *efficiency* of HR products and services is determined by analyzing (1) output to input over time; (2) output to input of HR products or services against other organizational elements with similar services or overhead costs; (3) output to input against a standard. The staff can help calculate or estimate the standard in terms of the resources needed to complete a unit (program or service). Alternatively, you can examine historical averages, or in some cases perhaps apply engineering standards, such as work sampling, time measurement, or predetermined work standards.

The *quality* of HR products can be measured in terms of the following:

- *Timeliness.* Log in each unit of work, record completion times, and compute total processing time by subtracting one from the other.
- *Response time.* Determine the time difference between receipt of a request for a product or a service and time when the product or service reaches the user.
- *Error rates.* Determine from a sample of outputs the percentage that has flaws, does not match specifications, and is rejected or reworked.
- *Completeness.* Follow up on a percentage of outputs to determine whether the entire job was completed.
- *Complexity.* Determine the impact of the time standards for the output and, where possible, identify ways to simplify the process.
- *Customer complaint rate.* Tally the number of customer complaints about products or services.

Effectiveness of HR programs and services is measured by (1) comparing what is produced with what was intended (program objectives or desired results); (2) selecting effectiveness indicators (see Figure 9-3); (3) collecting and analyzing effectiveness data. Effectiveness data may be collected from existing departmental records and reports, and from special studies or surveys.

Objectives. After measures of performance have been developed, objectives can be set. The process is far from simple. Possibil-

Figure 9-3.   Sample effectiveness indicators.

- The costs of HR operations compare favorably with those in similar companies.
- The thrust of on-the-job efforts of HR staffers is directed toward company goals and cost containment and profit objectives.
- HR systems, products, services, and operating methods are appropriate for their intended use and achieve the desired results.
- Important deadlines are met or beaten.
- Key staffers are successful in helping their people improve their performance.
- Subordinate managers and staffers have their replacements trained.
- Unit costs—such as cost per hour, cost per square foot of floor space, equipment cost per trainee, equipment cost per hour, and materials cost per product—are reasonable.

ities include eradicating obstacles to productivity, eliminating overlapping or duplicated activities, consolidating closely related activities, balancing work load, simplifying work, and so on. In any case, objectives should deal with important opportunities and critical problems; they should be specific, clear, realistic, practical, and, where possible, quantifiable; and they should include a target date.

Controls. You have identified an acceptable level of performance (the standard). You have established a yardstick (the measurement) to apply to that performance, so that you can monitor whether performance matches what was planned (the objectives). If performance deviates unacceptably, you must initiate corrective action; that's what control is all about. Productivity control depends on both the content of the information about performance, and its timing. Requirements vary widely depending on the degree of control desired, the work activity involved, and the type of resource being controlled. Usually two types of reporting system are needed: One is made up of operational statistics for line managers, and the other is a periodic statistical summary for top management. Both should highlight deviations from productivity objectives.

Example of an HR Department Productivity Problem and Its Solution

Here's an abbreviated description of one facet of an HR department productivity improvement program. The problem is this: Training system development is inefficient and, as a consequence, the department is insufficiently responsive to company training requirements and employee needs. The strategies used to remedy the problem, such as the provision of additional training for system developers, will not be addressed. The general approach used to fix the problem follows.

Goals and priorities. The HR manager actuates staff members' involvement and commitment to improvement by soliciting their appraisal of the responsiveness of the training development system and getting their input on the goals to be pursued and the order of priority for attack. Following discussion, the staff defined the problem and established the goals and priorities for improvement—all in writing. Heading the list were the goals of reducing response time and increasing the trainee pass rate.

Performance standards and measures. Next the staff identified the productivity standards and the yardsticks to be used to measure each. They selected the following:

- *Efficiency,* measured as the ratio of program inputs (hours of professional and clerical effort) to output (the number of instructional modules produced)
- *Quality,* measured by such gauges as trainee performance on criterion measures
- *Timeliness,* measured by the gap between identification of requirements and the availability of a validated training program

Objectives. The group next addressed specific objectives. Among them were reduction in the lead time for system development from its current three to six months to a range of one to three months and a reduction in the trainee failure rate from its current 15 to 20 percent to 5 percent or less.

Controls. The staff then identified the controls to be applied to the project. Among them were the maintenance and daily review of project charts, daily monitoring of training system work teams, review of draft training modules, and reports of validation trials of systems produced.

Finding Solutions: Strategies and Tactics

We have said that HR managers are key players in productivity systems; their role is much broader than improving their own department. They must be able to make substantive suggestions to top management and line managers—which for some may mean improving their knowledge base. That is the purpose of this section: to make HR managers aware of wide-angle approaches to productivity, so they will be able to promote the exchange of ideas and practices that enhance productivity and to recognize conditions that are disincentives.

A plan for improving productivity has to incorporate specific action steps—things that senior leaders, managers, supervisors, and individual employees can do to bring about changes. To a large degree, the actions chosen for a particular plan will depend on the character of the organization itself, and your company may have to devise entirely new approaches to deal with its specific targets. But there is a large body of ideas, both macro-scale strategies and micro-scale tactics, ready to be tapped into.

Macro Strategies

Several far-reaching and long-term strategies have been used to effect improvements in productivity and its partner, product and service quality.

Quality of worklife programs. These programs, known as QWL, are designed to improve both the physical and psychological work climate. Rather than specific tools and mechanisms, QWL programs represent a new way of thinking about organizations and the people who work in them. They focus on making modifications to the job environment and the ways that work is conducted so that people can adapt to changing conditions, perform their functions more efficiently and effectively, and, at the same time, increase their job satisfaction. QWL is a long-term, systemic approach to change and improvement. It involves all organizational constituencies—management, employees, labor unions, and other groups that are a part of the environment of the company. And it affects all aspects of company operation.

Project management. Essentially project management is a means of organizing and managing a complex project on the basis of its technical, schedule, and cost objectives rather than on the basis of existing organizational arrangements and procedures.

A project manager and her team are given authority to draw resources from the various departments and staff elements of the organization; to make contacts with outside vendors, suppliers, contractors, and consultants; to create, implement, and monitor a plan and schedule for using those resources to solve a problem or deliver a product. To control their projects, project managers use a variety of mechanisms—Gantt charts, PERT charts, the critical path method (CPM), and resource allocation scheduling, to name a few (for others, see Chapter 11). All are designed to ensure that a project is started and completed on time and within budget and that the final product, whether a system or a service, meets specifications and quality standards.

Management by objectives. An MBO system is a relatively uncomplicated means of improving management and, in turn, productivity. It is a top-down, sequential, and formal means of developing organizational goals and their supporting objectives at each level of organization. An effective MBO system necessarily and invariably addresses productivity problems and provides solutions because it focuses on key result areas—areas that are important to the individual employee and to the department.

In most organizations key result areas include profitability, productivity, competitive status and market share, customer service and satisfaction, creativity and innovation, cost management, conservation of resources, management development and performance, employee attitude, training, employee services and career development and performance, and corporate image, public responsibility, and ethics.

Participative management. Participative management has enormous potential for raising productivity because it improves employee motivation, morale, commitment, and job satisfaction. Simply stated, participative management encourages employees at all levels to share in formulating policy and in making decisions in areas that directly affect them and their jobs. It is a particularly effective strategy when used with knowledge workers because they have the interests, capabilities, and talents to make substantive contributions to the organization. Mechanisms used include work teams and task forces, committee assignments, quality circles, and special projects.

The primary requirement for shared management is real participation and involvement—not a counterfeit or half-hearted management invitation to participate, which employees will inevitably sense and reject. Nor is participative management a form of brainwashing where the manager decides on a course of action and then tries to persuade his people that it was their idea. It involves a serious and deliberate effort to involve people in the management of a department or organization.

Some key concepts for an effective participative management system:

- Participation means mental and emotional involvement and commitment.
- It motivates initiative, creativity, constructive criticism, and positive contributions.
- It encourages and promotes acceptance of responsibility and commitment to the betterment of the organization.

Suggestion systems. A properly operated suggestion system can pay dividends in any organization. First, it offers a ready way for employees to voice their complaints about situations, working conditions, or policies that affect them and their work. Second, and even more important, it provides a veritable flood of ideas for improving operations. To be effective, the suggestion program must be properly administered. That means:

1. The system must be adequately promoted and publicized.
2. Suggestion boxes and forms must be readily available.
3. Forms must be easy to complete.
4. Suggestions have to be promptly screened, evaluated, and processed.
5. Substantial awards must be given for accepted suggestions, consistent, of course, with the benefits derived from them.

Tactics

Several techniques have proved to be very useful in achieving productivity improvement goals and objectives.

Organization structure. High productivity requires a proper and appropriate organization structure to fully release human talents and skills, coordinate effort, communicate requirements and information, and control results. Look at spans of management, how functions are grouped, how authority is delegated. Check on reporting relationships, departmental staff, and work-team interfaces, resource allocations, and decision-making processes. Study job descriptions, looking particularly at the clarity of duties, functions, and authority.

Streamline the organization. Diagram work flow as a first step in cutting out unnecessary functions, jobs, or steps. Scrutinize staff jobs. Rewrite job descriptions that contain such duties as "coordinate," "review," "advise," "act as liaison to," and other imprecise, equivocal, or meaningless terms. Change the duties and tasks to outputs rather than activities. Simplify the work. Be sure that people are doing the right things *and* doing things right. Both are important, but the former is paramount. Eliminate tasks that do not contribute to the mission or do not add value to the product or service.

Organization climate. An organization climate that emphasizes doing the right things as well as doing things right, product quality rather than employee happiness, decision and action rather than "further study," and manager responsibility for cost management and results rather than activities, is likely to be highly productive. The tactic here is to analyze the climate in your organization from the productivity perspective.

There are four dimensions of organizational competence, an important part of organizational climate: commitment, collaboration (teamwork), creativity, and responsibility. Every organization needs to look carefully at what it is doing to promote those elements, and what it is doing to inhibit them.

Personnel selection and assignment. The hiring and assigning processes are so important to the achievement of optimum productivity that they justify as much time and effort as HR managers can give to them. No amount of training can make productive employees out of people who shouldn't have been hired in the first place. Even when selection and assignment decisions are made by another manager, the HR professional should be a major participant in the screening, selection, and job placement processes. HR managers should work with other managers throughout the organization to ensure that effective procedures are established and followed.

Communication. One of the most important keys to managing people effectively and achieving maximum productivity is open and effective communication. Getting people to be more productive involves a rather straightforward process: setting mutually acceptable goals, giving people the information they need to perform their jobs, providing day-to-day feedback, reviewing performance, and paying continuous attention to employee motivation. Much of this is achieved by skilled communication.

Training and development. Training and development provide employees with the knowledge and skills they need to do the work assigned to them and achieve the performance standards established for their jobs. It also enables them to make the needed adjustments when their jobs change in some dimension.

Productivity improvement and training are inextricably related and mutually dependent. You can't have one without the other. Part of the training will focus on the individual manager, supervisor, technician, or hourly worker. Another aspect of the training must focus on the development of work teams since so much of the operation of today's product and service companies are conducted by teams and task forces. In both cases, training must include clear definition of what productivity is and what it is not, why it is critical, how it is achieved, how it is measured, and when and how it is reported.

Some of the primary means of increasing productivity are applying "speed-up" tactics (getting people to produce more efficiently or produce more output per unit of time), installing new equipment, establishing new procedures, and redesigning the work area. All these measures require training *before* they are put into effect, because at least some changes in abilities and performance are required.

In most organizations, training is a two-step process: first-line supervisors are trained and they, in turn, conduct on-the-job training for their people to ensure that the new system works as intended. The adequacy of the training is your responsibility; whether the vehicle is coaching, team building, or formal instruction, you may need to train the trainers. This means that the HR manager must have a comprehensive understanding of modern, systematic approaches to training: the rationale for training as it relates to productivity; quality and costs; fundamental principles of adult learning; needs assessment strategies and techniques; tests and measurements; designing the training environment; using appropriate instructional techniques; and assessing and evaluating results.

Performance appraisal. Improved performance involves much more than providing encouragement for greater and more consistent effort. Managers must measure, evaluate, and reward performance. A sound, professionally administered performance appraisal system has enormous potential for improving the productivity of individual employees and, in turn, the organization's total work force.

Effective performance appraisal is structured and formal. It is designed to eliminate subjectivity, bias, inconsistency, and unfairness. It includes what is expected of employees, what aspects of their work will be evaluated, when the work is to be completed, how much they should accomplish, and how well the product or service stacks up against standards of quality. It involves frequent observation and measurement of performance against the standards, feedback to employees, and written records of the process and results.

Managerial productivity. Don't overlook the importance of improving the productivity of managers. It often is more productive than shop-floor programs and office-procedure remedies. Be sure that executives and managers articulate and commit themselves to annual, measurable, and time-phased management improvement objectives and track their accomplishments and shortfalls.

Motivation. One of the most effective means of achieving gains in productivity is to analyze the work environment and the mechanisms used to promote motivation and morale. Use written surveys, interviews, and suggestion systems to solicit employee attitudes about the workplace, organization policies, and work processes. Then act on whatever you learn.

Work procedures and processes. The methods, procedures, and processes used to produce the end products—the goods and services of the organization—must be studied. The adequacy of the resources provided to individuals and work teams—the people, funds, equipment, materials, supplies, information, direction, time, space, and facilities—must be examined.

Look at the documentation of operating policies and procedures—their availability, clarity, and accuracy. Review work flow from individual to individual, individual to work team, and work team to work team. Can improvements be made? Examine the use of manual and automated production, communication, and control systems—the processes that transform the inputs into outputs—with an eye to improvement. In short, take a close look at work methods and work flow, resource coordination, sequencing, handoffs, and controls, and all other facets of the output process to identify ways to improve the procedures.

Environment. This factor is often overlooked. Does the work environment facilitate productivity, or does it impede performance? Are human–machine–technology interfaces structured properly? Ergonomics is the science of making places, furnishings, equipment, and products fit people. When planning a new facility, or when it's time to invest in new office furnishings, consider this: a well-designed work station can save money by increasing worker productivity and decreasing employee turnover. A poorly designed work station decreases productivity and increases errors, and it also increases use of sick leave and workers' compensation claims. The most important aspects of work station design are comfort, flexibility, attractiveness, quality, durability, and cost.

Feedback and reward systems. Effective feedback and reward systems are probably the most important productivity improvement strategies of all. What makes a good feedback system? It makes use of planned (but seemingly spontaneous) reinforcement; it pinpoints key measures of performance but keeps them simple, straightforward, and easily seen and counted; it involves work-related discussions with employees about their performance; it uses charts and graphs displayed on bulletin boards where performance is plotted for all to see; it identifies specifically what was good or bad about performance and gives credit and correction; it involves periodic, honest summary evaluation by means of detailed performance reviews; and it doesn't accept excuses such as "the union won't let us," "the equipment malfunctioned," "supplies were late," or "my partner didn't show up."

A sound reward system is equally important. A productivity improvement program that does not include a recognition and reward component is certain to fail. People need incentives and rewards to invest the time, talent, and effort to produce goods and services faster and better than ever before. And rewards should be both economic and psychological, for individuals and groups. They should include merit pay, performance bonuses, gains sharing, suggestion awards, job enrichment opportunities, and public recognition. (See Chapter 8 for details.)

Celebration. Celebration is probably the most overlooked tactic. Ceremonies are important to people—particularly ceremonies that recognize accomplishment. Significant achievements should always be acknowledged by some observance or company ritual. It doesn't have to be an extravaganza. When a major productivity target is achieved, call all participants together and compliment them for their accomplishment. Encourage employees to express their ideas on why and how the goal was achieved. For major accomplishments and breakthroughs, plan and conduct a real victory celebration—a picnic, dinner dance, or something similar.

The Productivity Improvement Process

Step 1. Get the commitment and support of all concerned. Get involvement and action from everyone—top management to hourly workers. If you don't, the program will be just another boondoggle, doomed to failure from the outset. Get top management *deeply* involved. Visibly demonstrate your commitment by making improvements in your own office, and your personal performance. Don't forget to get the cooperation of the collective bargaining unit. Enlist the help of clients and customers, supplies, and consultants in identifying problems and solutions.

Step 2. Appoint and train a productivity improvement team. Make productivity improvement the responsibility of a carefully selected team, with a leader who is senior, competent, and experienced. Choose as members people who are good team players: people who have demonstrated their willingness to accept responsibility and contribute ideas and suggestions for the solution of problems, who are able to concentrate on issues instead of personalities, who can listen attentively and critically, and who are self-disciplined, forceful, and positive.

All need training in using data-gathering instruments, identifying obstacles to productivity, and developing solutions. In addition, the team members need an orientation to the principles and processes of teamwork.

Step 3. Identify and define the problems. Administer questionnaires, surveys, and interviews to all constituencies to identify, categorize, and prioritize productivity shortfalls and problems. Supplement these approaches with planned observations. Study the facts collected. Examine all criticisms, complaints, and suggestions. Judge the validity of each item by checking it against other sources. Summarize the deficiencies in simple terms. Determine the underlying causes of the problem or shortfall. Clarify the conditions that led to it and are sustaining it.

Step 4. Formulate criteria for judging solutions. How will you evaluate proposed solutions? Establish standards of acceptability, and state them in terms of end results to be achieved. Include comprehensiveness, quantitativeness, work-relatedness, repetitiveness, consistency, timeliness, and completeness. Develop realistic and, where practical, quantifiable measures of productivity.

Step 5. Establish productivity improvement goals and objectives. Spell out the end results to be achieved by the improvement program. Establish specific objectives and milestones for departments, branches, and individuals so that they know what results are expected of them. Maintain your focus on the real goal of productivity improvement: to satisfy your customers and clients so that the company can grow and prosper in the long run.

Step 6. Develop action plans. Develop action plans, including sequencing and timing, to remedy productivity problems. Be systematic. Determine what is to be done, who is to do it, when, and (sometimes) how. List all the positive things that should be initiated along with the negative things that should be curtailed, weigh each item in terms of importance, rank items by the ease with which they can be accomplished, and match the ease with the importance, and you'll know which ones to work on first. Consider both macro-strategies and less global approaches. Remember that people—not equipment, new procedures, or capital expenditures—are the key to improved productivity.

Step 7. Install the improvement systems and procedures. Put your action plans into effect. Give people the tools and gauges they need to measure quality and quantity themselves. Encourage people to set their own performance standards. Hold managers accountable for results. But be sure to give them the authority and resources they need to achieve the goals.

Step 8. Track progress and measure results. Monitor the implementation of your plans and provide feedback to all participants in the process. Be hard-nosed about productivity. Cure procrastination by helping people see the underlying reasons for their faulty behavior; give them support and feedback in overcoming this disabling habit. Compare results with baseline data collected before the system was installed. Focus on results rather than on how people work—on quality, quantity, and timeliness, rather than neatness, orderliness, or approach.

Step 9. Reward productivity. Publicize achievements and reward them. Give people recognition, rewards, a voice in decisions, and opportunities to grow and develop. Tie extra compensation to productivity. Rank employees by effectiveness and give large merit raises and bonuses only to the top performers.

Summary

If human resources is to be successful in gaining and maintaining a position of importance in the organizational scheme of things, productivity improvement must be an integral part of its management philosophy and a major planning target. For that reason, HR managers must provide the leadership both within and beyond their departments to develop understanding and use of productivity measures and strategies at all levels of the organization and in all functions. They must reassess the value of past programs and revitalize those that have improved productivity in the past. And they must be more aggressive in exploring, developing, and exploiting new initiatives and technologies that will produce future improvements.

Productivity improvement consists of measures to make the process of converting resource inputs into *quality* products and services more effective and efficient. It is not the same as cost reduction or cost control, although it does include better cost management, improved performance of people, and wiser use of resources. It is something done *by* people, not *to* people.

Traditional methods of measuring productivity were largely limited to the production of blue-collar workers, where the outputs were countable. In recent years, however, interest and attention have shifted to productivity measures for white-collar, knowledge workers. Now, measures of efficiency, effectiveness, and quality, instead of quantity, are the focus of interest and attention.

An effective productivity improvement plan includes goals and priorities, performance standards and measures, and management controls. It exploits contemporary broad-scale strategies, such as quality of work life programs, project management, management by objectives, participative management, quality circles, and suggestion systems. It also makes optimum use of changes to the organization climate, personnel selection and assignment processes, communications, training and development systems, performance appraisal, managerial productivity, employee actuation and motivation, work processes and procedures, the work environment, and feedback and reward systems.

HR managers must remember that people—not equipment, new procedures, or capital expenditures— are the key to improved productivity. Therefore, sound, disciplined management of people is the top productivity improvement strategy.

Improving productivity involves the following steps:

1. Get commitment from everyone in the organization.
2. Appoint and train a productivity improvement team.
3. Identify the problems.
4. Set criteria for evaluating suggested solutions.
5. Establish goals and objectives.
6. Develop action plans.

7. Put the plans into effect.
8. Track and measure progress.
9. Reward results.

For Further Reading, Viewing, and Listening

Bain, David L. *The Productivity Prescription: The Manager's Guide to Improving Productivity and Profits.* New York: McGraw-Hill Book Company, 1986.

Beatty, Richard W., H. John Bernardin, and James E. Nickel, eds. *The Productivity Sourcebook.* Amherst, Mass.: Human Resource Development Press, 1987.

Belcher, John G., Jr. *Managing for Productivity.* Houston, Tex.: Gulf Publishing Company, 1987.

Better Productivity Is Not by Chance (60-minute videocassette). Video Education Network, 1550 Northwest Highway, Suite 108-C, Park Ridge, IL 60068, 1986.

Blake, Robert R., and Jane Srygley Mouton. *Productivity: The Human Side.* New York: AMACOM, 1981.

Carkhuff, Robert R. *Sources of Human Productivity.* Amherst, Mass.: Human Resource Development Press, 1983.

The Competence Connection: Managing for Productivity and Health (60-minute videocassette). Telometrics International, 1755 Woodstead Ct., The Woodlands, TX 77380, 1988.

D'Aprix, Roger. *Communicating for Productivity.* New York: Harper & Row, 1982.

Doyle, Robert J. *Gainsharing and Productivity: A Guide to Planning, Implementation and Development.* New York: AMACOM, 1983.

Gregerman, Ira B. *Knowledge Worker Productivity.* New York: AMACOM, 1981.

Guaspari, John. *I Know It When I See It: A Modern Fable About Quality.* New York: AMACOM, 1985.

Heisler, William J., W. David Jones, and Philip O. Benham, Jr. "Performance Management Methods: Enhancing Employee Productivity." Chapter 8 in *Managing Human Resources Issues: Confronting Challenges and Choosing Options.* San Francisco: Jossey-Bass, 1988.

Holoviak, Stephen J., and Susan Stone Sipkoff. *Managing Human Productivity: People Are Your Best Investment.* Westport, Conn.: Greenwood Press, 1987.

I Know It When I See It (18-minute videocassette). Produced by Century III Teleproductions, 1986. Distributed by American

Management Association, Nine Galen St., Watertown, MA 02172.

Improving Employee Productivity, I and II (individualized, computer-based lessons). LEARNCOM, 215 First St., Cambridge, MA 02142, 1987.

Managing for Productivity (28-minute videocassette). Produced by Sally V. Beaty. Southern California Consortium, 5400 Orange Ave., Suite 215, Cypress, CA 90630, 1983.

McDermott, Lynda C. "The 'Productivity Bandwagon'—The Hottest Game in Town?" *Training and Development Journal,* April 1982, pp. 72–73.

Monson, Robert L. "Productivity Improvement." In *Human Resources Management and Development Handbook,* edited by William R. Tracey. New York: AMACOM, 1985.

Morf, Martin. *Optimizing Work Performance: A Look Beyond the Bottom Line.* Westport, Conn.: Greenwood Press, 1986.

Nadler, Leonard. "HRD and Productivity: Allied Forces." *Training and Development Journal,* August 1988, pp. 25–29.

Nash, Michael. *Making People Productive: What Really Works in Raising Managerial and Employee Performance.* San Francisco: Jossey-Bass, 1985.

Ozley, Lee M., and Judith R. Ball. "Quality of Worklife." In *Human Resources Management and Development Handbook,* edited by William R. Tracey. New York: AMACOM, 1985.

People and Productivity: We Learn From the Japanese (28-minute videocassette). Produced by Chuck Olin & Associates, 1985. Distributed by Britannica Training and Development, 1488 S. Lapeer Rd., Lake Orion, MI 48035.

Productivity and the Self-Fulfilling Prophecy: The Pygmalion Effect (30-minute videocassette). CRM Films, 2233 Faraday Ave., Suite F, Carlsbad, CA 92008, 1987.

The Productivity Dilemma (28-minute videocassette). Produced by Sally V. Beaty. Southern California Consortium, 5400 Orange Ave., Suite 215, Cypress, CA 90630, 1983.

The Pursuit of Efficiency (25-minute videocassette). Rank Roundtable Training, 113 N. San Vicente Blvd., Beverly Hills, CA 90211, 1982.

A Question of Management (35-minute videocassette). Salenger Films, 1635 Twelfth St., Santa Monica, CA 90404-9988, 1986.

Riggs, James L., and Glenn H. Felix. *Productivity by Objectives.* Englewood Cliffs, N. J.: Prentice-Hall, 1983.

Sears, Woodrow H., Jr. *Back in Working Order: How American Institutions Can Win the Productivity Battle.* Glenview, Ill.: Scott, Foresman & Company, 1984.

Shetty, Y. K., and Vernon M. Buehler. *Productivity and Quality Through People: Practices of Well-Managed Companies.* Westport, Conn.: Greenwood Press, 1985.

Stanton, Erwin S. *Reality-Centered People Management: Key to Improved Productivity.* New York: AMACOM, 1982.

Weisbord, Marvin R. *Productive Workplaces: Organizing and Managing for Dignity, Meaning, and Community.* San Francisco: Jossey-Bass, 1987.

Why Quality? (20-minute videocassette). Produced by Century III Teleproductions, 1987. Distributed by American Management Association, Nine Galen St., Watertown, MA 02172.

Working Together (18-minute videocassette). Produced by J. Copeland. National Educational Media, 21601 Devonshire St., Chatsworth, CA 91311-9962, 1988.

10

Managing Costs
Providing Products and Services Economically

In this era of economic uncertainty, high costs, and rising employee expectations, companies must spend only what their business positions and their projected revenues can justify. For their part, HR managers must be able to demonstrate their dedication to the challenge of managing costs, both in their own departments and in the organization as a whole.

The primary thrust of the HR manager's corporate responsibility is to help line managers and staff officers control "people" costs, focusing their efforts on systemwide opportunities rather than isolated events. In this area of people costs, the HR manager often does not have the authority to create and enforce policy, but serves in an expert advisory capacity to the board of directors and top management.

In the HR department, the manager must look for ways to promote cost savings and economical use of enterprise funds. HR managers are responsible for communicating goals and encouraging cost management efforts by all personnel. Successful execution of a cost management program depends upon the commitment of HR managers and their people.

In the chapter on budgeting, we noted that budgets are both managerial plans and controls, that the purpose of a budget is to determine what resources *should be* expended by whom and for what—the planning component—and what resources *are being* expended where, by whom, and for what—the control component. Obviously, one of the primary means of achieving control of costs is through the budgeting process—budget preparation, execution, monitoring and control, and adjustment. For all functional managers, including HR managers, the starting point for effective cost management must be the budget, because it is there that the roots of overspending are planted—whether in unrestrained personnel

251

authorizations, poorly controlled obligation and commitment authority, inadequate cost accounting, ill-conceived expenditure rules, or untimely or incomplete budget execution reports.

Although they must cut back wherever possible, HR managers must retain the integrity of their programs. A "meat ax" approach to cost containment is a bad mistake. Costs should rarely, if ever, be slashed. Instead, make a careful review and analysis of past and current operations, to identify potential areas for savings.

One problem for some HR managers is understanding the terminology. The lexicon of cost management has grown rapidly in recent years, and many terms with discrete meanings have been (incorrectly) used interchangeably. That has often resulted in misunderstanding, confusion, and false starts. Here are definitions of some common terms: names of processes, and names of tools.

Systems and Processes

Cost management is the process of tracking and analyzing expenditures with a view toward eliminating, reducing, or containing the costs associated with all aspects of company operations or, at the very least, maximizing the value derived from capital and operating expenditures.

Cost analysis is a process used to identify and track the costs of a department's activities, programs, and services: personnel, contractors, consultants, temporary employees, real property, space and facilities, equipment, materials, supplies, and services.

Cost-benefits analysis is a technique used to compare total resources required with total benefits received from each program or unit.

Economic analysis is a systematic approach to a given problem, designed to help the manager solve it. The full problem is investigated, and objectives and alternatives are searched out and compared in the light of their benefits and costs through the use of appropriate analytical techniques.

Life-cycle cost analysis is applied to the costs of a system, organization, or item of equipment that will be incurred throughout its entire life, from R&D through phasing out.

Direct costs are expenses associated with specific projects or activities. They include out-of-pocket expenses and salary costs.

Indirect costs are those not associated with specific programs. Examples are fringe benefits and overhead costs.

Total costs are the sum of direct and indirect costs.

Analytical Tools

Program evaluation review technique (PERT) is a statistical procedure used to predict the amount of time required to complete any element or aspect of a job or project.

Critical path method (CPM) defines the tasks that need to be done to complete a job or project, determines the sequence in which they must be completed, and estimates the time needed to finish the project. The sequence of tasks that take the longest time to complete is called the critical path, and all scheduling decisions are made on the basis of this critical path. CPM charts can provide an accurate picture of the time that can be saved by allocating extra resources to critical areas, thereby saving funds.

Gantt charts are simple bar graphs showing tasks, start dates, completion dates, and the status of projects between starts and completion. A clear bar represents a total task for a project. As time elapses, the bar is filled in to show the time remaining for completion.

Linear programming uses a linear (straight-line) programming model to produce a minimum-cost solution to a problem. It can also be used to determine the marginal profitability of adding people, facilities, or equipment.

Simulation typically involves a computerized model of a large, complex, nonlinear problem. The technique simulates operations and responses to situations to test the ability of a procedure to overcome obstacles and meet variations. The simulation is used to predict results or provide answers to "what if" questions.

Work distribution charts are used to improve work flow, allocate time to work processes, distribute work evenly, and reduce employee boredom or fatigue. The charts are developed by determining what tasks are being performed in a work area, who specifically is doing them, and how much time is spent on each one. A knowledgeable supervisor analyzes the chart to improve task assignment and performance.

A *work process chart* is a simplification technique that documents the flow of a single unit (form, document, equipment part, component of a system) through an operation. The chart is used to analyze the process and improve efficiency. Symbols are used to show stages in the work process: operation, transportation, inspection, and storage or delay.

Line of balance is a monitoring tool that uses the concept of control by exception. It focuses on major checkpoints in the overall project schedule and monitors progress as compared with plans.

Analysis provides information on elements that are ahead, behind, and on target.

Critical incident involves collecting statements based on direct observation of job incumbents or recall of job behavior by employees that typify both competent and incompetent performance of a job or task. The technique underscores critical job behaviors for emphasis in training and supervision.

Developing a Cost Management System

Requirements for success. Success in cost management hinges on four factors:

1. Developing improvement plans, listing projects to be undertaken, assigning responsibility for each project, and establishing target dates for project completion
2. Motivating subordinates to improve their own work methods
3. Providing the means and incentives for all personnel to participate in the effort
4. Implementing improvement actions in a timely way

The most promising areas for cost reduction are the ones that involve waste in some form. Some of the most common are employee benefits, expenses for travel and training, duplicate functions, people idle time and equipment downtime, and unnecessary equipment and materials.

A proactive approach. Companies and HR departments that have formal cost management programs and are continuously sensitive to costs are in the active mode. During good times they are alert to cost containment opportunities. They anticipate future business conditions and have plans to deal with them. So during bad times they are able to confront the situation effectively, without panicking.

A reactive approach, in contrast, has no formal cost management system but simply reacts to every situation. The result is crisis management, focused on damage control.

To implement a proactive cost management program:

1. Establish specific written, quantitative objectives for each cost management area.
2. Formally report dollar savings quarterly.
3. Encourage personnel to keep up a continued effort by assigning a high priority to implementing cost management proposals.
4. Give appropriate rewards for cost reduction ideas.

Guiding principles. HR managers should be guided by these four principles when developing their cost management programs.

1. *Attention/effort principle.* The costs of doing business tend to decrease in direct proportion to the effort and attention given to cost containment.

2. *Bull market principle.* When business is good, the economy is healthy, and inflation rates and unemployment are low, there is more to be gained by cost control and cost reduction efforts than during periods of business decline.

3. *Bear market principle.* When business is bad, the only way to increase profits and return on investment is to reduce costs, improve quality, and increase productivity.

4. *Paralysis principle.* Excessive pressure on managers and other employees to cut costs while increasing productivity often results in paralysis, stress reactions, and other indicators of impaired, rather than improved, performance.

Cost-Reduction Opportunities

Opportunities abound in all organizations to control costs and effect substantial savings. HR managers need only to look around, encourage their people to be alert to cost improvement possibilities, and apply the appropriate techniques and tools to reap the benefits. Some of the areas listed below relate specifically to your management of your own department; others are corporatewide areas where you can exert positive influence, helping other managers control their "people" costs.

Absenteeism and tardiness [corporate]. There is much you can do to reduce absenteeism and tardiness and cut the horrendous costs associated with them. Here's how to improve the record.

- Publicize attendance and tardiness policies and stick with them. If sick leave is unapproved, don't pay for it. If there is a penalty for tardiness, impose it. Let people know that you are serious.
- Set the example. Be on the job on time every day—even when you run into problems.
- Require employees to call their immediate supervisors when they are unable to report for work. Require supervisors to ask

what the problem is and how long the person expects to be away from work.

- Watch for absentee patterns—the day following holidays, Mondays or Fridays, the day fishing season opens. Is the pattern job related?
- Install an attendance control module on your computerized HR system to document employee attendance, spot previously conscientious employees whose records are deteriorating, and highlight poor attendance records.
- Show interest in employees' personal problems and concerns; learn the names of their spouses and children.
- Try to find out why employee attendance deteriorates. Is it because of conditions at home? On the job? Can you change those conditions?
- In your department, keep track of what's going on in each subordinate's job and have a backup available to reduce the impact of an absentee worker. Visit the work areas daily to show interest in what's going on and to learn what is happening.
- Welcome each person in your department back early in the morning when he or she returns to work. Ask returnees how they feel and listen attentively to their responses. Tell them that they were missed.

Accidents [corporate]. Accidents are very costly events. Not only do they cause pain and suffering for victims and their families, they also cause serious financial wounds and serious distress to the organization: compensation and medical payments, increased insurance premiums, lost time (victim, co-workers, and investigators), production slowdown, and often litigation expenses and repair of damaged equipment. To protect employees and organizations from these devastating effects, install an effective safety program:

- Train employees in safe practices and emphasize preventive measures.
- Publicize specific safety rules, regulations, and instructions.
- Hold employees responsible for obeying safety rules and regulations.
- Ensure prompt corrective action when safety rules and regulations are violated.
- Conduct frequent, thorough inspection of equipment, facilities, and devices to identify potential hazards.
- Investigate all accidents and injuries to determine causes and prevent recurrence.

- Remedy hazards at once.
- Track and report lost-time accident rates and costs.

Communication systems [departmental]. Efficient communication systems—using telephones, intercoms, Telex, facsimile equipment, satellites, conference calls, teleconferencing, and electronic mail (computers connected by modems)—can speed up communications to a degree never before possible, bringing substantial savings in time.

To control telephone, modem, and fax costs, adopt the following policies and procedures:

- Periodically ask the phone company for an equipment inventory—a list of every item included in the local-service portion of your bill. Investigate any discrepancies and request refunds where errors are found.
- Maintain records of all service changes ordered—instruments and services, moves, installations, and disconnects. Get refunds for unused service.
- Require that all long-distance calls be routed through the company operator.
- Assign identification numbers to employees who make long-distance calls and require the operator to reject calls without an ID.
- Assign someone the task of monitoring and analyzing phone bills and checking out anomalies and departures from the norm.
- Train employees to exercise telephone discipline.

Compensation [corporate]. Compensation is the obvious place to begin cost control. Look first at your organization's staffing needs as determined by technology, quality, competition, and costs. Check out and apply one or more of the various approaches to job evaluation. Identify the sources of the information you need to price jobs realistically and competitively: benchmarks, wage surveys, market analysis, and the like.

Most people have grown up with the notion that they are entitled to annual raises regardless of business conditions or their own productivity. That entitlement mentality must be eliminated. Instead of automatic salary increases, introduce lump-sum payments and incentive programs to tie salary increases to competitive performance. (See Chapter 8 for more on performance-based systems.)

Here are some of the other things you can do to reduce compensation costs.

- Hold across-the-board pay increases to the minimum needed to meet inflation.
- Recognize contributions to the organization through development opportunities and job security in addition to reasonable merit pay raises and salary increases.
- Use lump-sum merit increases instead of salary adjustments.
- Instead of merit raises use overtime pay for employees who are normally exempt.
- Make job-title "promotions"; they are sometimes more rewarding than pay increases.
- Increase the number and value of one-time (that is, not built into base salary) incentive awards.
- Review your compensation program regularly. Continually monitor market trends and changes in your organization. Adjust compensation to shifts in supply and demand and changing technologies.

Contracting out [departmental]. Save the cost of fringe benefits by contracting with, rather than hiring, salespeople, consultants, physicians, psychologists, instructors, computer programmers, designers, drafting technicians, photographers, and freelance writers and artists. Here are some more cost control suggestions:

- Get expert legal help before negotiating a contract.
- Be careful in choosing the type of contract; learn the difference between firm fixed price, fixed price with incentive, cost plus fixed fee, cost plus fixed incentive, cost-sharing, and cost contracts.
- Avoid short contracts and fixed-price contracts with escalation clauses or redetermination-of-price clauses.
- Include provision for termination of the contract, for the convenience of the company (reduced need or no further need) or for cause (default of the contractor).
- Have signed contracts with workers in which they acknowledge their status as contractors and their responsibility to pay their own taxes.
- Require the contractor to submit a full account of costs plus projections of remaining costs at least monthly. This will help prevent cost overruns.

Defects [departmental]. If your department's materials are marketed outside, be aware of the costs associated with defects.

Anything that you can do to prevent substandard products or services will not only result in direct savings but will also repay you in the form of customer good will and repeat business. Here are some steps you can take.

- Institute quality control mechanisms, both during production and when the product is being used by the customer.
- Establish responsibility for quality; designate those responsible for inspecting, measuring, and reporting compliance with quality standards.
- Concentrate on prevention; make it right the first time.
- Get customer feedback, evaluate it promptly, and respond to it quickly.

Downsizing and delayering [corporate]. To remain competitive, many American companies have closed plants or downsized their work force in recent years. Although this may have had the desired effect on the company's financial position, the human costs have been significant. As HR manager, you can help top management take a balanced approach.

- Don't get obsessed with the idea of getting lean and mean. Don't make so many layoffs that the work load of those remaining becomes too heavy and their productivity drops because of exhaustion, bitterness, or paranoia.
- Examine the needs of the company over the long term, decide which functions are essential and which are no longer necessary, and then decide which employees are best prepared, by training, experience, and performance, to do the jobs that remain.
- Use an objective means of determining which employees will be retained, such as a review committee of managers representing all company functions and areas of activity.
- Terminate unproductive people.
- Effect the reduction in force by attrition, voluntary layoffs, and early retirements.

Employee assistance programs [corporate]. Traditional employee assistance programs (EAPs) have been credited with reducing absenteeism and offering employees help with personal concerns like substance abuse, financial management, and marital counseling, accidents, increasing productivity, decreasing disciplinary problems, lowering turnover, and improving morale. In addition, controlled studies have shown hard dollar savings in medical costs, particularly in the area of chemical dependency treatment. However, as EAPs become more popular and expand into other areas—mental health services, eating disorders counseling, weight control, smoking cessation, health education, bereavement counseling—some companies are becoming concerned about increased costs.

What can you do to reduce EAP costs? Here are some suggestions.

- Assess substance abuse in your organization.
- Develop and implement a substance-abuse policy.
- Implement employee and supervisory training programs.
- Install a help line or hot line staffed by specialists.
- Help employees resolve their personal problems by establishing first-level (supervisory) in-house counseling services.
- Contract out for complex problems and expensive services, such as psychological counseling.
- Track and analyze the costs of EAP both ways: nonprovided (absenteeism, turnover, low production, poor quality) and provided (in-house specialists, hot lines, training, and contractual services).

Equipment downtime [departmental]. When equipment of any kind goes down, production stops. Schedules are disrupted, delivery dates are missed, and customers are lost. What can you do to reduce equipment downtime?

- Train all equipment operators in preventive maintenance procedures.
- Set up daily, weekly, and monthly equipment maintenance checks—and follow them.
- Contract with equipment suppliers for periodic alignment and maintenance of equipment; preventive maintenance pays for itself many times over.

Executive perks [corporate]. Executive perquisites are costly and should be carefully assessed and constantly monitored. Here are some suggestions:

- Determine how your company's perks stack up against those offered by your competitors of comparable size and market position. If they are out of line, reduce them over time.
- When you cut perks, grandfather current employees but withhold certain perks when new people are hired.

- Replace expensive perks with less costly but attractive expansions of others.
- Review executive and managerial perks and practices at least annually.

Flexible staffing [corporate]. Use overtime, temporary and permanent part-time personnel, and consultants to effect substantial savings in salaries and fringe benefits, reduce vulnerability to periodic or seasonal layoffs, and cut turnover. When you need additional secretarial, accounting, or technical help to accommodate vacations, prolonged illnesses, or peak work load periods, hire temps. But be sure to provide the employment service with accurate job descriptions so that you won't be paying for an accountant or secretary when all you need is a clerk or a typist. To gain maximum productivity from temps, analyze your peak work load periods so that you can determine exactly how often and how long you will need the additional help. That way, you may be able to get the same person for subsequent periods and avoid retraining.

Insurance [corporate and departmental]. Insurance is an important purchase in any organization, requiring considerable knowledge and expertise. HR managers have a dual role here. Life, health, and accident insurance are employee benefits, and as such are part of the HR manager's job responsibility. Other forms of insurance—fire, theft, liability, business interruption, property damage—will probably be purchased by another department for the company as a whole, but HR managers need to be on top of costs as they occur in the department.

Medical benefits and health care [corporate]. Health care costs continue to rise, and companies must find ways to reduce the impact of these increases.

A good cost control system can reduce payment error and lower administrative costs. To achieve those objectives, you need detailed claims data. Unless your company is very small, that means a computerized system. Only a fully automated system can provide all the information and services you need: monitoring eligibility, calculating benefits, tracking claims from submission to payment, detailed statistics on claims management, in-depth data gathering, and tailormade reporting systems to support management decisions.

Here are some other ways to control the costs of health care, for both current and retired employees.

- Consider pooling—two or more businesses combine their employees to attract health care programs at competitive rates.
- Encourage competition among health care providers.
- Encourage enrollment in health maintenance organizations.
- Require employees to get second opinions (and provide incentives for getting them) on surgical procedures.
- Establish or raise per-person and per-family deductibles, and institute reimbursement on the basis of reasonable and customary charges.
- Perform case management or utilization reviews on hospital claims.
- Establish outpatient mental health and substance review programs.
- Audit health care costs.
- Hire medical experts to monitor treatment.
- Institute a health risk screening program for current employees.
- Contract out for EAP services; hire only fully qualified professionals.
- Employ independent third-party reviewers of EAP services.
- Emphasize outpatient treatment, where appropriate.
- Establish cost containment committees to monitor authorization programs, utilization review, mandatory second-opinion programs, case management, alternative delivery systems, and discharge planning services.
- Consider establishing flexible benefits and employee option plans where employees can adjust their benefits to meet their needs.
- Establish medical case management programs for catastrophic illnesses, such as AIDS and other terminal diseases.
- Develop training and education programs to make employees more knowledgeable health care consumers.
- Develop safety training programs to reduce accidents.
- Encourage employees to report suspected cases of health care fraud or abuse (billing for services not rendered) to their claims offices.
- Require co-payments (cost sharing) for in-hospital, outpatient, and physicians' services. Compensate by providing higher levels of coverage, unlimited lifetime maximum benefits, emphasis on preventive care, choice of personal physician, quality providers, and hassle-free claims procedures.
- Contract out for medical efficiency experts (physicians and

registered nurses) to monitor the progress of hospitalized patients and oversee employee treatment.

- Require regular health checkups of all employees (pay part or all of the cost).
- Establish a nonsmoking or restricted-area smoking policy.
- Establish fitness programs (require blood pressure tests and physical exams, including stress tests, prior to participation). Offer incentives for participation: membership fees in health clubs, weekend vacations for two for workers who quit smoking, and so on.
- Consider implementing a hospital reimbursement system based on diagnosis related groups (DRGs).
- Conduct workshops on relaxation techniques, positive coping strategies, nutritional guidelines, exercise routines, and other similar programs.

Project management [departmental]. Improved project management will keep costs down, meet deadlines (missed deadlines represent unnecessary costs), schedule people and activities more efficiently and minimize confusion and errors (again reducing costs), and bring projects to completion on time and within budget. To gain those benefits, use project management strategies like these.

- Select qualified project managers and team members carefully, give them enough authority to draw on the resources they need from all company sources, and hold them accountable for performance.
- If team members are not experienced, give them team-building training.
- Require the potential user to define the objectives of the project and the operating characteristics of the system to be developed.
- Prepare a preliminary financial analysis of the project.
- Make the system designer responsible for exploring all reasonable alternatives for satisfying user requirements.
- Plan thoroughly. Don't start any major project until every subordinate manager has signed off on the design and detailed plans for its conduct. This will forestall costly design changes later.
- Schedule the entire project: display the schedule with graphs, charts, and project boards.
- Monitor the progress of the project. Require periodic status reports.

• Require final testing of the system and its documentation before it is turned over to the user.

Purchasing [departmental]. One of the most neglected areas in management is the buyer-supplier relationship. Closer attention to that relationship offers an opportunity to improve product quality, profitability, and costs. Even if a company has a purchasing department, the HR manager must be involved in the purchasing function to some degree. To maximize return on every purchasing dollar, you must locate qualified suppliers, communicate your requirements clearly, and do your homework on current prices and value. Make detailed cost comparisons (see Figure 10-1). Then negotiate to get the best possible price. Try to get a "most favored user" clause in written contracts with suppliers, guaranteeing that products will be sold to you at the lowest possible price and that if another user gets a lower price you will be refunded the difference.

Here are some of the things you can do to reduce purchasing costs.

• Persuade other departments to coordinate their needs with yours and then place larger orders.
• Discourage the use of nonstandard items, and try to order items in standard packages.
• Never buy quality you won't use, such as one-time film typewriter ribbons for draft reports.
• Shop for the best prices.
• Inspect and reject all faulty goods; return them for credit.
• Take advantage of cash discounts whenever possible.

Figure 10-1.   A sample price cost comparison.

	Dealer A	Dealer B
List price per binder	$200.00	$200.00
Discount	10%	15%
Net price after discount	180.00	170.00
Quantity rebate/discount for 10	15.00	None
Price each after quantity discount	165.00	170.00
Price for 10 binders	1,165.00	1,170.00
Early payment discount (1%)	116.50	None
Cost after early payment discount	1,048.50	1,170.00
Shipping charges	18.50	None
Final Real Cost	$1,067.00	$1,170.00

- Avoid short-term buying; begin negotiating long-term buying agreements.
- Identify and cure the mistakes you're making in determining and stating requirements, writing specifications, requisitioning, qualifying suppliers, identifying sources, negotiating processes, ordering, receiving, inspecting, and handling invoices.

Records and reports [corporate]. Although they are essential management tools, records and reports are expensive, and personnel reports are no exception. To control the costs of records and reports, try these ideas:

- Ensure that reports are a part of the overall plan for information processing.
- Focus reports on managerial evaluation and decision-making requirements.
- Develop standardized records and format them so they can be prepared by automated systems.
- Make reports flexible enough to adjust to changes in the organization and the requirements of managers.
- Schedule reports for annual review, evaluation, and improvement. Eliminate costly and unnecessary reports (ones that probably no one reads).

Security systems [departmental]. Employee theft represents substantial costs in most businesses. Although it is probably impossible to eliminate completely, a great deal can be done to reduce losses. The first step is to identify indicators: frequent complaints of shortages in shipments, different entries on original and duplicate copies of the same form, frequent replacement of tools and equipment, storage of materials in an unusual place, files out of sequence, or documents in possession of people who don't need them.

The second step is to develop procedures to prevent theft. Consider these possibilities: improved disbursement and accounting procedures, preemployment personnel security checks or background investigations, distinctive "picture" identification badges, security guards and watchdogs (not attack dogs), proximity alarms, key control, magnetically coded (credit-card type) keys, three-combination locks, detailed inventories of all valuable tools and equipment, and engraving serial numbers on tools and equipment. Set up special security measures in vulnerable areas—warehouses, tool bins, storage areas, computer room, and audiovisual equipment rooms. Limit access to those areas. Inventory the areas periodically on a random schedule and let everyone know it. Install a sign-out system for tools and equipment.

Technology [departmental]. The rapid growth of techology and its applications provide many opportunities for substantial savings in HR-related programs and activities. Microcomputers have many applications that will save substantial amounts of money. In addition to word processing and spreadsheet applications, there are now on the market many computer-based systems that can save time and money by automating many of the tasks of training management. Other computer applications include accounting, budgeting, financial analysis, and desktop publishing systems for newsletters, forms, reports, and marketing materials.

Advances in telecommunications and audiovisual equipment provide many opportunities for cost savings in the training and development area. Interactive video, color video copy processors, laser graphics, computer-generated graphics and transparencies for large-screen presentation, and desktop presentation systems are only a few of the innovative products now available.

Training and development [corporate]. Well-designed training and development systems not only produce better-trained people but also reduce training time, trainee attrition, and on-the-job training requirements, and improve employees' promotability, productivity, motivation, and morale—all of which have a positive cost outcome. The key is using a systems approach to designing the programs.

Cost containment for training and development programs should focus on the following areas:

- *Training and development programs.* Look for ways to reduce the cost of training employees and the cost of managing training programs. For example, one company saved $113,000 a year after it decided to work on trainee retention and managed to decrease attrition from 10 percent to 5 percent (see Figure 10-2). Another organization packed its twenty-session training program into fourteen weeks instead of sixteen, and saved $241,000 a year (see Figure 10-3).
- *Major items of training equipment.* Can you decrease either the number of items or the total cost?
- *Supplies.* Investigate ways to reduce the supplies, the unit price or total cost of supply items, or associated costs such as receipt, storage, and distribution.

Figure 10-2.   Calculation of savings resulting from a reduction in trainee attrition from 10 to 5 percent.

	1989 (10 classes)		1990 (15 classes)	
	Number	Costs	Number	Costs
Trainees enrolled (14 weeks @ $15 per hour)	20	$1,680,000	300	$2,520,000
Trainees graduating	180		285	
Labor hours and costs	5,600	112,000	8,400	168,000
Equipment costs				36,000
Total Costs		$1,792,000		$2,724,000
Cost per Graduate		$ 9,955.56		$ 9,557.89

Savings per Graduate	$ 397.67
Savings per Year	$113,335.95
Three-year Effect	$340,007.85

Figure 10-3.   Calculation of savings resulting from a reduction in training time.

	1989 (20 classes/ 16 weeks)		1990 (20 classes/ 14 weeks)	
	Number	Costs	Number	Costs
Trainees enrolled ($15 per hour per trainee)	400	$3,600,000	400	$3,360,000
Labor hours and costs per class	640	12,800	560	11,200
Total Costs		$3,612,800		$3,371,200
Cost per Trainee		$ 9,032		$ 8,428

Savings per Trainee	$ 604
Savings per Class	$ 12,080
Savings per Year	$241,600
Three-year Effect	$724,800

- *Transportation management.*
- *Communications systems management.*
- *Maintenance of training equipment.*
- *Training property and facilities.* This area includes real property and installed equipment (buildings, road, pavement, and grounds); operation of utility plants and electrical, heating, fuel, water, waste, and pollution control systems; and facilities support such as fire protection, refuse collection and disposal, recycling, and custodial services.
- *Storage, packaging, and packing.*

Travel [departmental]. For HR organizations that provide seminars, workshops, and other training and development programs, travel is an important and necessary cost of doing business. New technologies such as teleconferencing are not always an adequate substitute for face-to-face contacts. Fortunately, travel costs are among the most controllable costs in most businesses. Most departments can trim their travel costs by at least 10 percent, and many can do far better.

Controlling travel costs starts with your organization's corporate travel policy. Know the corporate guidelines, and structure departmental policies around them. Don't make the rules so strict that they demoralize employees; the policies should be fair and flexible enough to accommodate exceptions.

One excellent way to control costs is to have an in-house travel office, staffed by an experienced, knowledgeable and committed travel manager. Encourage senior management to establish such an office, and use it faithfully. However, if each department makes its own arrangements in your organization, here are some suggestions for reducing travel costs:

- Interview travel agencies. Look for ones that offer automation, lowest-fare scans, frequent-flyer bonus tracking, management records and reports, value-added services such as expense report analyses, and cost savings studies. Settle on one or two aggressive travel agencies to handle all your travel arrangements. Negotiate preferred-vendor agreements.
- Use travel management software, turnkey packages that manage travel expenses, direct employees to preferred vendors, conduct on-line audits of your travel agency, and provide up-to-the-minute flight schedules and fares.
- Develop clear, detailed, and enforceable departmental policies. Check employee handbooks and other documents for outdated or conflicting policies. Set rules on class of service,

meals, car rentals. Distribute the policy to all employees; include a form for them to sign and return stating that they have read and agree to follow the policy.

- Require pretrip authorization for all travel.
- Prevent "frequent flyer" abuse. Use low-cost airlines.
- Time side trips around low fares and fly at off-peak hours. Combine trips. Use discount ticket brokers. Get rebates.
- Negotiate car rental contracts.
- Investigate direct deals with airlines for cost-effective arrangements, such as point-to-point discounted fares, discounts for group travel, and negotiated fares on highly competitive routes.
- Negotiate special rates with airlines for repetitive or pattern travel, for your frequent workshops and branch office visits.
- Monitor vendor compliance with your travel policies (audit lowest fare, hotel rates, and so on).
- Negotiate with hotels to ensure maximum value in room rates, food and beverages, extra services, and the like. Search out hotel chains that offer special corporate rate programs such as "super saver" advance purchase discounts, frequent guest programs, and upscale amenities.
- Use charge cards for travel, entertainment, and phone calls.
- Require travelers to attach hotel receipts to their expense vouchers. Check to ensure that travelers are selecting moderately priced (rather than luxury) hotels and are getting the lowest corporate rate for single rooms.
- Reimburse employees at a flat rate, based on an average cost, for meals enroute to their destination and return and for employees who work on Sundays or holidays. Do not reimburse for meals unless an overnight stay is involved.
- Require employees to take advantage of (and report on their travel vouchers) meals included in the price of a seminar or conference, or in the price of transportation (complimentary breakfasts, luncheons, and banquets).
- Reimburse employees for business entertainment on an actual expense basis. Require written justification for the expense and receipts.
- For attendance at seminars, workshops, and conferences, where more than one employee attends, double up attendees in one or more rooms. When several people travel together, book them into "all-suite" hotels and use the suites for small-group meetings instead of reserving a separate function room.
- Require travelers to use public transportation or taxis instead

of rental cars for local transportation. Require written justification for exceptions to the policy.
- Monitor compliance with your travel policies and institute a disciplinary system for employees who violate them.

Wellness programs [corporate]. Any organization that is serious about managing costs must include wellness programs as part of the solution. These programs, usually designed and administered by the HR department for all employees of the company, have demonstrated undeniably the logic of this simple truth: if you teach your people how to stay healthy, you save a bundle on medical benefits—not to mention high morale and productivity.

Here are some specific suggestions for employee wellness programs:

- Provide periodic medical evaluation of employees, at company expense.
- Evaluate the work environment and eliminate health hazards.
- Conduct frequent and regular inspections of restrooms, change rooms, showers, food and water supplies, vending machines, lunchrooms, work spaces, and the like.
- Establish voluntary employee wellness programs to reduce the high costs of absenteeism and medical payments. Include such programs as stop smoking, fitness, diet, nutrition, and stress management.
- Establish a fitness center in-house or provide inexpensive memberships at local community fitness centers.

The Cost Management Process

Step 1. Identify major cost areas. In human resources, high-dollar costs are typically found in labor, compensation and benefits, medical benefits and healthcare, training and development, contracting out, materials, travel, purchasing, and reports and records.

Step 2. Determine cost management targets. Here specific expenditure areas are identified and dollar cost-reduction targets are set for the coming month or year. Two of the primary means of setting targets are analysis of records and reports and brainstorming. The important thing is to set specific, realistic, reachable, and measurable objectives. Without such dollar targets, little will be accomplished because the value of the program will be shaded, perhaps invisible.

Step 3. Collect and analyze cost management data. The next step is to break the cost target areas into their component parts (cost elements) and analyze each element. Using budget variance analysis (a detailed comparison of budgeted and actual costs of items of expense) or statistical analysis of individual elements (accidents, absenteeism and tardiness, grievances, turnover, rejects, and so on), determine what the root problems are and where, when, and how they originate.

Step 4. Establish cost target priorities. At this point, using either judgmental procedures (panels of experts, brainstorming, or committees) or more sophisticated techniques (such as line of balance or linear programming), rank targets in order of importance. Because all cost management strategies have a price tag in people-hours (collecting and analyzing cost data, developing policies, monitoring progress, and reporting accomplishment), the areas with the greatest potential for cost savings should be addressed first.

Step 5. Develop and implement cost-management action plans. Essentially, this step involves the problem-solving process, whether conventional, creative, or analytical. Use a systematic approach—identify the problem, establish solution criteria, analyze the problem, identify alternative solutions, and select the best ones. All solutions should include updating mechanisms and should emphasize means of strengthening cost control strategies. The resulting action plans should describe the who, when, where, what, and how of the cost management program.

Step 6. Track progress and accomplishment. No cost management program can succeed unless it is closely monitored. Objective, systematic followup answers some very basic questions: Are people meeting their responsibilities for cost containment as defined in the plan? Is the program producing the results intended? What gains have been achieved? What glitches have developed? What needs to be done to shore up the program so that results will be worth the time and talent invested?

Step 7. Provide feedback and rewards to deserving employees. Publicize accomplishments through such formal and informal means as staff meetings, memoranda, daily bulletins, bulletin board notices, and house organs. Each individual or group that makes significant gains in the cost reduction program should receive recognition and reward.

Step 8. Report and document savings. The company controller or budget officer should report, document, and validate savings, naming the budget activity area that is affected. Savings from all validated actions should be consolidated on a summary report and distributed to management and to departmental personnel.

Summary

Effective cost management is one of the prime indicators of a manager's competence because it has a direct impact on the corporate goals of profitability, productivity, efficiency, and return on investment. HR managers must be successful in stimulating and encouraging actions, both within their departments and throughout their organizations, to achieve company goals and objectives with the lowest possible expenditure of resources and the highest possible dollar savings.

To achieve cost management objectives, HR managers must master several systems and practices such as cost analysis, cost-benefits analysis, and at least a few of the many analytical tools currently available. But mastery of the tools alone cannot guarantee adequate management of corporate costs. A proactive posture—a formal cost management program with well-conceived plans, realistic and measurable objectives for each cost management area, high-priority management attention, employee encouragement, involvement, and incentives, and an effective reporting system—is also essential. A proactive stance also means that HR managers emphasize cost control tactics during good times and bad, increasing their efforts during periods of business decline.

The HR manager has cost responsibilities both within the HR department and in HR-related programs that serve the entire organization. In both cases, the manager must search for opportunities to control costs; that means looking at a wide range of activities and services with a fresh eye. Success in achieving cost objectives will show up in the department's and the company's balance sheet, and that in turn will bring enhanced image for the department and its manager and greater top-management support for HR programs.

The process of cost management includes eight critical steps:

1. Identify the major costs involved in company and departmental operations.
2. Determine dollar targets.
3. Collect and analyze cost management data.
4. Establish cost target priorities.

5. Develop and implement cost management strategies, tactics, and action plans.
6. Track progress and accomplishment.
7. Provide feedback and rewards to deserving employees.
8. Document and report savings to management and employees.

For Further Reading, Viewing, and Listening

Bellingham, Richard, and Barry Cohen. *The Corporate Wellness Sourcebook.* Amherst, Mass.: Human Resources Development Press, 1987.

Brown, Gordon C. "Leasing Your Staff to Cut Costs." *Management Review,* December 1984, pp. 19–21.

Counting the Cost (20-minute videocassette). Rank Roundtable Training, 113 N. San Vicente Blvd., Beverly Hills, CA 90211, 1988.

Day, Denis. *How to Cut Business Travel Costs.* New York: John Wiley & Sons, 1986.

Frederickson, Jack M. *Cost Reduction in the Office.* New York: AMACOM, 1984.

Getting Started With Project Management (individualized, computer-based lesson). LEARNCOM, 215 First St., Cambridge, MA 02142, 1987.

Getting the Slack Out of Your Project Plans (individualized, computer-based lesson). LEARNCOM, 215 First St., Cambridge, MA 02142, 1987.

Head, Glenn E. *Training Cost Analysis: A Practical Guide.* Boulder, Colo.: Marlin Press, 1985.

Health Care Costs: Where's the Bottom Line? (30-minute videocassette). BNA Communications, 9439 Key West Ave., Rockville, MD 20850-3396, 1986.

Hirsch, William J. *The Contracts Management Deskbook.* Rev. ed. New York: AMACOM, 1985.

How to Meet Project Deadlines (individualized, computer-based lesson). LEARNCOM, 215 First St., Cambridge, MA 02142, 1987.

Kearsley, Greg. *Costs, Benefits, and Productivity in Training Systems.* Reading, Mass.: Addison-Wesley Publishing Company, 1982.

———. *Calculating Human Resource Costs and Benefits: Cutting Costs and Improving Productivity.* New York: John Wiley & Sons, 1986.

Kirrane, Diane E. "Cost Accounting Today." *Training and Development Journal,* September 1986, pp. 24–27.

Kozlowski, Joseph G., and Walter Olesky. *A Guide to Cost-Effective*

Employee Benefit Programs. Englewood Cliffs, N.J.: Prentice-Hall, 1987.

Managing Health Care Costs: An American Management Association Research Report. New York: American Management Association, 1988.

Masi, Dale A. *Designing Employee Assistance Programs.* New York: AMACOM, 1984.

McIntyre, William, and Jack Gibson. *101 Ways to Cut Your Insurance Costs Without Sacrificing Protection.* New York: McGraw-Hill Book Company, 1987.

Pitone, Louise. *Absence and Lateness: How to Reduce It—How to Control It.* Madison, Conn.: Business & Legal Reports, 1987.

Rutigliano, Anthony J. "Surgery on Health Care Costs: A Checklist for Health Activism." *Management Review,* October 1985, pp. 24–32.

Rx for Absenteeitis (15-minute videocassette). Dartnell, 4660 Ravenswood Ave., Chicago, IL 60640, 1976.

Spencer, Lyle M. "Calculating Costs and Benefits." Chapter 108 in *Human Resources Management and Development Handbook,* edited by William R. Tracey. New York: AMACOM, 1985.

Tagliaferri, Louis E. "Cost Improvement." Chapter 21 in *Human Resources Management and Development Handbook,* edited by William R. Tracey. New York: AMACOM, 1985.

Tomasko, Robert M. *Downsizing: Reshaping the Corporation for the Future.* New York: AMACOM, 1987.

The Troubled Employee (25-minute videocassette). Dartnell, 4660 Ravenswood Ave., Chicago, IL 60640, 1982.

"Wellness" Programs Work!—The Benefits of Working Well (50-minute videocassette). Produced by Video Education Network. Distributed by Dartnell, 4660 Ravenswood Ave., Chicago, IL 60640, 1987.

Zetlin, Minda. "Grounding Corporate Travel Costs." *Management Review,* November 1985, pp. 26–34.

11

Managing Time
Working Smarter, Not Harder

Do you come in early, leave late, skip lunch, take work home night and weekends, and still feel overwhelmed by your work load? Do you think you need more time? You don't. The time is already there. You just need to manage it more carefully. With time management skills, you can save a minimum of one hour per day. Even more important, you can improve productivity and efficiency, avoid the chaos of missed deadlines and unfinished tasks, and gain more time for your family, your friends, and yourself.

Time management is really about productivity, because productivity is directly related to how well people use every hour of their work day. And because productivity is directly tied to your reputation and credibility, it behooves you to master the skill of time management. As HR manager, you actually have a threefold job in time management: Improve your own use of time, teach your staffers how to do it, and, through special in-house workshops, train employees throughout the company in the techniques of working smarter.

Time is very much like money, and often more valuable. You can save it, spend it, invest it, loan it, waste it; the only thing you can't do is borrow it. Time management is the art and science of using those valuable hours prudently and well to achieve personal, professional, and organizational goals. It is the practical and effective system of taking time to save time, so you can get more of the things done that have to be done and have time left over to do some of the things you want to do. It involves a systematic approach to managing your programs, projects, activities, priorities, and schedules.

Proper management of time, both yours and that of your people, yields many benefits. You will handle more work with less staff, develop your subordinates, eliminate productivity bottlenecks, avoid missed deadlines, and increase job satisfaction and enjoyment—all of which ultimately shows up on the balance sheet in terms of higher return on investment and greater profits.

275

If control of time can yield so many benefits, why isn't it practiced more often and more successfully? Much of the fault lies with managers, who for whatever reason—unclear goals, lack of planning, misplaced priorities, or failure to delegate—are unable to maintain proper control over the use of their own time or that of their people.

Some other familiar problems that beset people at all levels are procrastination, inability to say no, lack of organization, excessive socializing, inaccessibility of people or information, impulsiveness, lack of concentration, and outside distractions.

Surprisingly, many managers appear to be totally unaware that they have serious time problems. Yet a little bit of reflection usually quickly reveals the indicators—and sometimes the causes—of time mismanagement. Here are some of the most common.

- *Missed deadlines.* You simply cannot afford to miss deadlines and retain your credibility. Being late with important commitments has been the downfall of many otherwise excellent managers.
- *Excessive stress.* When people become overloaded with work or begin to miss deadlines, the pressure starts to build. They believe the situation is getting beyond control—and that generates further stress and more problems.
- *Self-doubt.* Given enough pressure and tension, people are almost certain to develop doubts about their ability to do the job. Having control of time creates enthusiasm and confidence; loss of control produces pessimism and diminished self-confidence.
- *Sleepless nights.*
- *Exhaustion.*
- *Working long hours.* Putting in ten- or twelve-hour days *regularly* is a sure sign that something is wrong. So is working on weekends to catch up. Too many managers have the mistaken notion that working through lunch hours is a sign of efficiency and strong dedication to duty. Every person needs at least a thirty-minute break in the day. If you find it impossible to do that, you have time problems.
- *Constant interruptions.* You may mistakenly believe that maintaining an open-door policy during the entire workday speaks well for your managerial style and your concern for people. It doesn't. A parade of visitors and lots of phone calls really mean that you are misusing your time.
- *Frequent and drawn-out meetings.* If you have more than one meeting a day, and if they take more than thirty minutes on

average, you have some major adjustments to make in management style.
- *Overstuffed in-basket and briefcase.*
- *Numerous crises.* Crises are a way of life in today's tumultuous business environment, but they should not occur daily—or even weekly. If they do, something is definitely wrong.

Buy Yourself Time: Strategy and Tactics

The only effective way to cure your time management problems is to look for the source—not the symptoms—and the source is your management style, the way you plan, organize, and carry out your functions. HR managers need to develop strategies and techniques for time management that complement their management style and, at the same time, permit them to put all their functions and activities in perspective and in priority order. Here are some ideas; some of these techniques are managerial only, but many can be shared with your staff.

Maintain adequate staffing. Sometimes the underlying problem rests with improper staffing levels. With the current emphasis on downsizing and delayering, some organizations have become so lean that some managerial jobs are too much for one human to handle. You may need additional help, a deputy or an assistant. But first look for other means of reducing your work load.

Redesign your workplace. Good workspace design blends human needs with the tasks to be performed. To create an environment that facilitates efficiency, your office layout should optimize work flow and minimize unnecessary activities and distractions.

Organize your office and desk. Make your office conducive to concentration and unfavorable to interruptions. Sit where traffic will be outside your line of vision; don't face a window or an open door. Shut off your phone ringer and have your secretary or receptionist screen calls. Use sound baffles to reduce ambient noise. Keep reference materials, writing instruments, and forms handy. Organize your desk. Keep everything you use frequently close at hand and in its regular place. File materials not used often, or place them in a credenza or on a shelf away from your desk.

Control paper. It has been estimated that at least one third of the paperwork generated in modern business is unnecessary. Resist the temptation to save all the materials that you receive; probably 80 percent of the paper that is filed is never used. Always open your mail near a large wastebasket—and use it. You can also reduce your contribution to the paper battle by using the phone instead, selecting the easiest format for the task (note, memo, letter, and so on), jotting handwritten replies on internal memos, using form letters for routine correspondence, and outlining your reply before writing to keep your response as brief as possible.

Limit interruptions. Unexpected visitors and phone calls are responsible for much of the time lost by managers. You can do much to control the time-wasting aspects, and still build strong personal relationships.

Establish and publicize blocks of time when you will be available for visits by staff and outside visitors. Set aside two special one-hour open-door times, one in the morning and one in the afternoon, for anything your people want to discuss. Of course, make it clear that you are available at any time for emergencies. Clearly state times when you will *not* be available. Keep social visits to a bare minimum. If you don't want to be interrupted, tell visitors politely but firmly that you can't see them right now and ask them to come back at a specific time.

Insist that your people think through beforehand what they want to discuss before they pay you a visit. Whenever you can, ask visitors how much time they need and then tell them how much time you have—and stick with it. A useful tactic is to talk with people in their own offices rather than yours; it's easier to cut off lengthy conversations.

Handle phone calls efficiently. Establish criteria for the calls you want to take—spouse or boss, customer or client, supplier or contractor, and so on. Have your secretary or receptionist screen all other calls and then return them when it's most convenient for you. Ask your secretary to find out what the caller wants so that you can be prepared when you call back. Set aside specific times for making return calls, and make them in batches, four or five back to back. Try to call when people are most likely to be in. Have phone numbers handy. Plan specifically what you are going to say before you place the call. Don't allow yourself to be placed on hold for more than a minute or two. If you are unable to speak to the person you are calling, leave complete messages so that she will be prepared when she calls back. When you do get her on the line, keep small talk and general conversation within bounds. Use your notes. Get to the point quickly but not bluntly. Take followup action immediately after completing the calls.

Control meetings. Keep departmental meetings to a minimum. Hold them in a conference room (not in your office) and only when they're absolutely necessary. Invite only the people who have something to contribute. Publish an agenda in advance and adhere to it. Start on time. Establish time limits for each agenda item and stand firm with them. Stop on time. As soon after the meeting as possible, distribute written summaries of decisions and assignments to all who are interested or affected. To emphasize the need to save time, occasionally hold two-minute "stand-up" meetings; comfortable seats in a conference room tend to prolong meetings. Another tactic is to hold small meetings in someone else's office, where it is much easier to cut off discussion once the problem has been solved or a decision has been reached.

Meetings with individuals, either your own staff or people from other departments, are a different story. These one-on-one or two-on-one meetings are almost impossible to control. You can't turn people away when there is a crisis that needs resolution. You can't set a deadline in minutes for arriving at a solution. The best you can do is to discover as quickly as possible what the real problem is and then identify and evaluate alternative solutions. The main thing is to keep participants on the subject and avoid buck passing, blame placing, argumentation, and recrimination.

Improve your reading and scanning skills. Considering the variety of content and formats you must deal with on a daily basis, you must be a rapid reader and you must also be able to shift gears quickly and smoothly. A course in speed reading may be the answer. But, even if you don't need formal training, there is a lot you can do on your own to improve your reading speed and comprehension. Consistently try to *force* an increase in reading speed, develop a few simple scanning techniques, and practice, practice, practice. Learn to read headlines, centerheads, paragraph leads, and topic sentences. Of course the starting point in saving time is to be very selective; read only what is useful.

Overcome procrastination and paralysis. Procrastination is one of the foremost causes of executive time wasting. The reason for procrastination is simple human nature. People tend to do first those things that have the greatest personal appeal, and to put at the bottom of their "to-do" lists the things that are difficult or uninteresting, regardless of their importance. That's at least part of the answer to the question of why the important work doesn't get done.

How do you avoid procrastination and indecision? Persuade

yourself that the task is not as onerous or as difficult as it appears—that it is do-able. Examine your excuses; find the flaws in your reasoning. Force yourself to do the task that needs to be done. Set a time limit for completion and then reward yourself for completing it. Above all, don't reward yourself for procrastinating; make procrastination unpleasant and unrewarding.

Closely akin to procrastination is the problem of paralysis—you feel so overwhelmed by the volume of the work you have to do or its difficulty that you don't know where to start. So you fumble and flounder around and accomplish nothing. The solution is just the opposite of the procrastination strategy: do something easy or enjoyable first, to jump start yourself. Your feelings of accomplishment and satisfaction will overcome your mental block.

Delegate. You should be delegating all routine actions and repetitive tasks to your staffers. As they become competent through your training, delegate even more complex tasks. That way, you reserve your valuable time for the critically important, goal-oriented tasks and decisions.

Determine which tasks you should delegate to others, either because you don't have the time to complete them, other people are more capable of doing them well, or people need to learn to perform them for the sake of their own development as professionals. Then inform them, brief and clarify the tasks, establish the time target, train them, set standards, be ready to assist, check on their progress and accomplishment, and praise and reward them for achievement.

Insist on completed staff work. Does delegated work arrive at your desk ready for your signature, or at the very least, in final draft, ready for review? If not, you have a great deal of on-the-job training and coaching to do. When your people prepare reports on projects involving work units they supervise, do they summarize and consolidate all reports from subordinates into a single report for you? If not, you are on the receiving end of incomplete staff work, and the stack in your in-basket is needlessly high.

Plan for your best work hours. All of us have a time of day when we are at our best, when our alertness, energy, and enthusiasm are at their highest. It could be early in the morning, noontime, early afternoon, or in the evening. As much as possible, schedule your most important and most difficult activities for your best hours. Reserve the low-energy times for simpler, more routine tasks.

Simplify your day. Don't overschedule yourself or overtax your capabilities. Be realistic. Organize your time around goals, objectives, and priorities, not around hours and minutes. Group recurring and similar tasks, such as dictating letters and memos, returning phone calls, conducting interviews, and so on, and assign them to the same block of time. Do them in a single sitting.

Use gimmicks to keep you on course—a red-bordered file folder for top-priority tasks, a blue checkmark for less important ones, a green folder for nice-to-do tasks, and so on. Post a project chart where you can see it from your desk; note progress on each item at least weekly. Divide incoming paperwork into four piles: must do now (keep on desk), must do soon (place in suspense file), should read (put in "read" file or briefcase), nice to read (bottom drawer); unimportant or duplicate notices or items that are simply a waste of time go in the circular file.

Handle each item only once; file it or send it to someone else. Discard what you don't need immediately. For large reports, read the executive summary and then skim the rest; highlight important parts. Place a "destroy date" on every item in your file. Clean out your desk and your files regularly.

Develop "to-do" lists, including alternate activities. At the end of each day, develop a list of activities for the next day, based on your goals and objectives, and assign a priority ranking to each item, perhaps 1 for "must do," 2 for "should do," and 3 for "nice to do." Write time estimates for the items on your list, and set deadlines for completion. Give yourself the satisfaction of crossing items out as they are accomplished, but don't be concerned if you don't complete every single task—few people ever do.

What kind of activities should you include on your to-do lists?

- *Critical tasks,* the ones that are central to your job—the ones by which your competence and dedication will be judged.
- *Appointments and meetings.*
- *Routine tasks and correspondence.* Maintain a file of routine "to do's"—sign letters, review agenda and minutes of meetings, and the like. Do them while you're waiting in someone's office or on hold on the phone.
- *Self-development activities*—a minimum of one a week.
- *Creative tasks.* Be sure to block out specific hours each week for creative and innovative tasks, the ones that produce new ideas, projects, and products.
- *Rest, relaxation, reflection, exercise, socializing, and spiritual renewal.*

Save time while traveling. Consolidate trips; travel only when necessary. When you do travel, do so in off-peak hours and use direct flights. Use a written itinerary and stick to it. Maintain a packed bag, ready to go at a moment's notice. Package a section of your briefcase with homework items you can do on your trip. Have your secretary or assistant sort and prioritize your paperwork. Use airport hotels for appointments and meetings to save travel time in congested downtown areas. Use a taxi rather than a rented car; you'll save time finding your destination and locating a parking space. Carry a pocket audiocassette recorder; use waiting time to process reports and dictate correspondence.

Ride the train, subway, or bus to the office rather than drive. Use the commuting time to read reports and correspondence. If you must drive, use audiocassettes to dictate notes or to listen to self-development tapes. Keep a notebook or audiocassette recorder with you at all times—including bedtime—for recording notes and ideas as they come to you.

Use productivity tools and systems. Many of the tools and processes described in the chapter on productivity can also be considered time management tools; here are a few others with a specific time management role.

Time management software. There are PC programs that maintain daily diaries and office schedules, track appointments, provide ticklers for correspondence, schedule meetings, track the scheduling of facilities, equipment, or projects, monitor resource use, and print reports. Other information organizer programs record names, dates, key facts and figures, and comments on contacts or events in up to a dozen different customized views, merge data from other programs, and print calendars, updates, and an unlimited array of reports, form letters, and memos. And there are other programs that let you create, retrieve, and fill in forms quickly and easily.

Display project boards. With a visual planning board (such as a six- or twelve-month schedule board, assignment control board, progress board, or planners) on your office wall, you can check on the status of plans and projects with just a glance from your desk.

Communications equipment. State-of-the-art communications equipment and capabilities—"smart" telephones, conference calls, teleconferencing, electronic mail, fax, Telex, and PC modems—can put information into the right hands quickly. Electronic mail software systems for your PC will let you create, send, and receive memos, graphics, spreadsheets, and files from within any application without leaving your desk.

Data bases. Data bases can be used to keep track of detailed data such as names and addresses, personnel information, supply inventories, programs, costs, expenditures, other records. They can supply just about any kind of information, readily available by the stroke of a key and easily updated. Electronic spreadsheets can perform time-consuming functions quickly—calculating budgets, making projections, developing forecasts, tracking progress on projects, calculating running statistics and percentages. All these are big, big time savers.

Word processing hardware and software. Text and graphics manipulating equipment and programs with more than 120 features are now available in many forms. They can be used to do both simple and complex tasks—from composing and revising letters to desktop publishing, including imaging. Some programs include an electronic thesaurus with up to 220,000 synonyms, and general-purpose, medical, and legal dictionaries. Other programs include a fully interactive editor that checks written documents for spelling, punctuation, hyphenation, abbreviations, sexist and racist language, confusing or improper word usage, vague or overworked words, and structural errors.

Information systems. Computerize your human resources information systems, so you can respond quickly and accurately to management requests for reports and give your staff the information they need when they need it. What should be computerized? Basic recordkeeping, compensation and benefits, EEO and attendance reports, code tables, and the like.

Computer-based training management systems. Many computer-based systems now on the market can save time and simplify the tasks of training administration and reporting. These systems maintain an enrollee data base, schedule classes, instructors, resources, and locations, check prerequisites and enroll qualified participants, prevent overbooking, establish wait lists, dispatch course notifications and correspondence to participants and their supervisors, generate itemized checklists for each course or seminar, and log course cancellations with reasons. Companion reporting systems produce training calendars, list participants' training histories, print attendance rosters, calculate statistics, link to word processing, spreadsheet, and graphics packages, and produce reports.

Help your staff people improve. Start by having them maintain time logs and then analyze their own use of time. Have each person come up with suggestions for improvement. In addition you, as manager, should study how groups of employees use their time, analyze the data, and take remedial actions: policy changes, reassignment, and training.

Discuss time management at a departmental workshop. Share the techniques you have learned. Identify and change policies that result in time wasting. Train your people to provide completed staff work. Periodically, take a short break to review how things are going. Ask yourself, Are we using our time to best advantage? Should we be doing this now? Should we be doing this at all?

The Time Management Process

The two keys to effective control of time are setting up a systematic time management process, and developing the habit of following it conscientiously.

Step 1. Examine your values, goals, and priorities. The focus of your efforts to improve your management of time must be on doing the *right* things—not on keeping lists, making notes, or following suggestions for doing things right. In other words, the key to time management rests in spending your working hours on activities that relate to your goals—and your organization's. So the first step is to be clear about what matters to you.

Is your work meaningful and satisfying? Is your off-the-job life enriching? What aspects of your work life and home life need improvement? To what extent to your personal values dovetail with corporate values? Are you happy with your career goals and the progress you are making toward achieving them? Look at long-term goals (ten years), midrange (three to five years), and the near term (one to two years). Now set your priorities. Decide which goals (long range, midrange, and short term) are the most compelling, and assign numerical priorities to each goal in each category.

Step 2. Identify and analyze your time problems. You need to become keenly aware of time and how you use it—or waste it. There are three aspects of time wasting: how you waste your own time, how others waste your time, and how you waste the time of others (boss, peers, subordinates). You need to find out where, how, and why all three occur. To compare how you *think* you use your time with how you *actually* use it, do a time utilization study. On a form similar to the one shown in Figure 11-1, record your estimated and actual time for at least one full (and typical) week. Include all activities and how much time you spend on each one: meetings and conferences, phone calls, paperwork, research and reading, talking with your boss, helping your people, seeing visitors, traveling, commuting, calling on clients, counseling, instructing, eating, exercising,

Figure 11-1.   A sample time utilization log.

	Activity	Estimated Time	Actual Time	Analysis (Reason for Difference)	Corrective Action
Monday					
6:00					
6:15					
6:30					
6:45					
.					
.					
.					
8:00					
8:15					
8:30					
8:45					
7:00					
7:15					
7:30					
7:45					
.					
.					
.					
10:00					
10:15					
10:30					
10:45					

reading, daydreaming, and whatever else you do. Compare estimated and actual times. Analyze the results. Determine the reason for the differences between your estimated and actual times. Note what you need to do to remedy the differences.

Step 3. Establish your objectives and schedule. Objectives are important because they enable you to focus your activities and your time attaining desired results. Without them, your decisions and actions will be made in response to immediate pressures and short-run advantages. Objectives must be specific, realistic, meaningful, and measurable, and must cover key result areas. Your objectives should specify what you intend to change or improve about your use of time and by how much and by when. Write down your objectives—the specific results you want to achieve in the next week or month. For example, if one of your personal goals is to spend more time with your children, then you might select as an objective "No work at home after noon on Saturday."

Step 4. Develop an action plan. Identify the steps required to accomplish each objective. Use your analysis of your time usage and change your time-wasting habits. Remember that you cannot change your level of efficiency without changing your actions. Determine what you and your people need to do to allow you and them to spend time most profitably. Establish priorities for your actions and those of others, and determine the time needed to accomplish each item or establish a deadline for completion.

To continue with our example, an action plan to reduce the hours you now spend working at home on the weekend could include several specific targets: save all noncritical correspondence for the week and dictate responses on the train ride home Friday evening; start work one hour earlier on Fridays; get up at normal workday time on Saturday; no business calls from home telephone, no matter what.

Step 5. Implement your plan. Put your improvement plan into effect. Regulate your activities and those of your people.

Step 6. Review and revise your plan. Periodically review the effectiveness of your time management plan. Are you achieving the objectives you set for yourself? For your people? Do you feel less harried and more in control? Are your people using their time to best advantage? Check the indicators of time problems identified earlier in this chapter. Do any of them show up? Keep a time log for a week and reanalyze how you are spending your time and where you can make further improvements. Then make needed adjustments to your plan.

Summary

Time management is an important skill for today's HR manager. Anything you do to improve your management of time is actually an improvement in productivity. Unfortunately, many managers do not realize they have severe time problems. They do not recognize the symptoms: excessive stress, strong feelings of self-doubt, sleepless nights and exhaustion, the habit of working late, through lunch, and on weekends, constant interruptions, correspondence backlogs, and frequent crises.

Most time-management problems are self-inflicted wounds. They are the results of managers' failure to establish and maintain control over their own use of time or that of their people. The underlying causes are often lack of clear professional and personal goals and objectives and misplaced priorities. They are a reflection of poor planning, inadequate delegation, procrastination, too many distractions and interruptions, and the inability to say, "No, not now."

Managers must overcome barriers to getting things done. They must learn to concentrate, commit to the work at hand, establish completion deadlines, and stick with them. They must learn to handle paperwork only once—read, sign, file, delegate, or dump.

Some of the specific things you can do to cure your time management problems are redesign your workplace, organize your office and your desk, get control over your paper, empty your in-basket, limit interruptions by visitors and phone callers, control the frequency and length of meetings, improve your reading and scanning skills, overcome procrastination, delegate more tasks to your people, insist on completed staff work, use productivity tools and systems, plan and schedule your workday, and train your people.

To spend your valuable time more wisely, follow these steps:

1. Examine your values, goals, and priorities—personal as well as professional.
2. Identify your time problems.
3. Set objectives and a deadline for accomplishing them.
4. Develop an action plan.
5. Put your plan into effect—stick with it.
6. Review and revise as needed.

For Further Reading, Viewing, and Listening

Douglass, Merrill E., and Donna N. Douglass. *Manage Your Time, Manage Your Work, Manage Yourself.* New York: AMACOM, 1985.

Drucker, Peter F. *The Effective Executive.* New York: Harper & Row, 1967.

Haynes, Marion E. *Personal Time Management.* Los Altos, Calif.: Crisp Publications, 1987.

The Juggler: Concentration and Time Management (28-minute videocassette). Cally Curtis Company, 1111 N. Las Palmas Ave., Hollywood, CA 90038-1289, 1985.

Kobert, Norman. *Managing Time.* Millburn, N.J.: Boardroom Books, 1980.

Lakein, Alan. *How to Get Control of Your Time and Your Life.* New York: NAL Penguin, 1974.

LeBoeuf, Michael. *Working Smart: How to Accomplish More in Half the Time.* New York: Warner Books, 1980.

A Perfectly Normal Day (27-minute videocassette). Cally Curtis Company, 1111 N. Las Palmas Ave., Hollywood, CA 90038-1289, 1978.

Phillips, Steven R. "The New Time Management." *Training and Development Journal,* April 1988, pp. 73–77.

Scott, Dru. *How to Put More Time in Your Life.* New York: NAL Penguin, 1981.

Smart Tools II: An Introduction to Databases. Smart Tools III: An Introduction to Spreadsheets. Smart Tools IV: An Introduction to Telecommunications (individualized computer-based programs). LEARN-COM, 215 First St., Cambridge, MA 02142, 1987.

Stokes, Stewart L., Jr. *It's About Time: A Practical Guide to Managing Your Most Important Resource.* Available from Organization Design and Development, 101 Bryn Mawr Ave., Bryn Mawr, PA 19010.

Stretton, Barbara. *BLR Handbook of Practical Time Management Techniques.* Madison, Conn.: Business and Legal Reports, 1986.

A Team of Two (30-minute videocassette). Cally Curtis Company, 1111 N. Las Palmas Ave., Hollywood, CA 90038-1289, 1987.

Time Management (60-minute videocassette). Produced by Levitz-Sommer Productions, 1986. Distributed by Alessandra & Associates, P.O. Box 2767, La Jolla, CA 92038.

Time Management (30-minute videocassette). Produced by International Training Consultants, 1984. Distributed by Excellence in Training Corporation, 8364 Hackman Rd., Des Moines, IA 50322.

Time Management: Beat by the Clock (30-minute videocassette). Van Dyck Communications, 822 Folsom St., San Francisco, CA 94107, 1987.

The Time of Your Life (27-minute videocassette). Cally Curtis Company, 1111 N. Las Palmas Ave., Hollywood, CA 90038-1289, 1985.

Time to Think (23-minute videocassette). Rank Roundtable Training, 113 N. San Vicente Blvd., Beverly Hills, CA 90211, 1985.

The Time Trap (28-minute videocassette). American Media, 1454 30th St., West Des Moines, IA 50265, 1981.

Total Time Management (6-hour audiocassette). American Management Association Extension Institute, 135 W. 50th St., New York, NY 10020, 1983.

The Unorganized Manager. Part I, Damnation. Part II, Salvation. Part III, Lamentations. Part IV, Revelations (videocassettes). Video Arts, P.O. Box 508, Northbrook, IL 60065-0578, 1983, 1985.

Winston, Stephanie. *The Organized Executive: New Ways to Manage Time, Paper, and People.* New York: Warner Books, 1985.

12

Managing Change
Dealing With the Inevitable

Change is an organizational fact of life. If an organization is to survive today, its managers must be able to handle change positively—to alter policies, structure, and products in time to meet new conditions—and do it with a minimum of resistance and disruption. It is far better to deal with change—to modify it, redirect it, or disarm it—than to ignore or fight it.

Organizations can't change until individuals change. Without employee support, new ideas and new technology become unworkable. So, organizational change must be linked to individual change. Many well-intentioned change efforts fail because critical issues at the top, middle, and bottom of an organization are not addressed in time—or not at all. What is needed is a well-coordinated HR support system that will enable organizations and their people to successfully mount ambitious change projects with potential for high payoff.

The key to acceptance of change is effective communication. That involves intensive efforts to promote trust and ensure that managers share information honestly and on a timely basis with employees. And that's where the HR department comes in. When change causes resistance in an organization, as it inevitably will, the HR function must be capable of stepping in and guiding other managers and staffers, as well as senior executives, in developing strategies and teaching the skills needed to integrate the change.

Think of change as the flip side of innovation. In the context of organizational life, change refers primarily to the work environment—a planned or unplanned alteration in the way work is performed. It can be a distortion or an improvement; it can bring either deterioration or growth.

Innovation results in one form of change. But it is not the most traumatic simply because it is deliberate, planned. Innovation invariably is an attempt to improve operations, productivity, profitability, products, services, or the quality of work life for employees. But there are other kinds of change—some deliberate and some unexpected, some welcome and some unwelcome.

Forces outside the organization can cause many changes: ownership (takeovers, acquisitions, and mergers); the composition of the work force, the economy and the money supply; technology; types of equipment, materials, and processes; the needs and wants of customers and clients; the amount and kind of competition; the law, government regulations; and the political landscape.

Changes are also caused by internal forces. They may involve such specific factors as company philosophy, management style, mission, purpose, goals and objectives; systems, products, and markets; communications networks and the relationships between employees and managers; restructuring and downsizing; competitive status; and financial stability, profitability, and return on investment.

Who Is Responsible for Change?

People at all levels of organization have some responsibilities with regard to change. Senior executives are key players. They are often the sponsors of change and have the primary responsibility for identifying and championing the new vision that must accompany substantive change in an organization. They must also assume the responsibility for building an environment where employees at all levels feel free to improve operations, innovate, and make changes. They must relate practical plans for change to strategic plans and organizational problems and issues.

Line and functional managers are the planners, implementers, and facilitators of change. They must prepare employees for change, overcome their fears of new systems and processes, and develop in them total commmitment to the new way of doing things. They must develop a comprehensive implementation plan for the change. They must clarify plans, integrate new processes and practices into operations, encourage employees to accept ownership of the change, and provide feedback to their people, the inventors of the change, and top management. And they must develop teamwork within their organizational elements.

Role of the HR Manager

HR managers share with line and other functional managers responsibility for creating and maintaining a climate in which change can be accepted rather than resisted. In their own departments, and with respect to the HR function in other elements of the organization, they are responsible for introducing and evaluating change; they must develop detailed plans for making change happen. In addition, HR managers have another significant responsibility: They must help other managers and staffers to effect changes of their own, primarily by training.

Training senior executives. The primary task here is to help executives understand the importance of preparing employees for change. They need to know why people resist change, and the costs attributable to that resistance. And they need to learn the skills involved in determining *when* change should be implemented and *how* to manage human factors to gain the support of employees.

Training line and functional managers and staffers. The real thrust of the training effort must go to line and functional managers and staffers because it is they who must become the enablers and facilitators. The plain fact of the matter is that many managers are not knowledgeable change managers. They need training in such skills as goal setting, communicating, consulting and negotiating, overcoming resistance to change, evaluating, training, and team building. Instead of focusing exclusively on the technical aspects of new systems, managers and staffers must prepare employees for the change, recognize the symptoms of resistance, develop strategies to overcome that resistance, and integrate and build commitment to the change.

Training work teams. In training employees, much of the emphasis will be on work teams. Team members will need training in the various roles (leader, member, recorder, process observer, and resource person), in sensing problems, resolving conflicts, and overcoming barriers to change.

Understanding the Nature of Change

If they are to do a complete job of helping their companies through the process, HR managers must be aware of some fundamentals about the psychology of change. As "climate control" officer, the HR manager, even more than others, has to understand the forces that cause people to resist change, and the predictable cycle of reactions they go through.

Why People Resist

Economic fears. The most obvious reason for resistance is economic. Employees resist reorganization, downsizing, and automation because they fear they will lose their jobs, be demoted, or have their pay and benefits reduced. Their primary concern, and the underlying reason for their resistance, is their anxiety about the economic welfare of their families.

Personal anxiety. Employees resent the implied criticism that their methods are wrong or inadequate. Or they fear that their hard-earned skills will not be used in the new structure. Still others are just emotionally unprepared to accept change; they need total stability in their lives.

Threats to relationships. Anything that has the potential to disrupt existing work associations and social relationships is typically viewed with alarm. Employees strongly oppose changes that threaten to jeopardize their status, power, or authority or break up long-established and tightly knit groups and work teams. And they invariably dislike having to make new social adjustments.

Union objections. Unions have a role to preserve—protection of their members from actions that will adversely affect them. Collective bargaining units are likely to resist change and promote employee protests unless they have been informed well in advance of the change, asked for suggestions, and asked for their support.

Common Reactions to Change

Each change situation is interpreted by people according to their attitudes, and that determines how they will respond. However, there appears to be a predictable sequence of feelings aroused by workplace change.

Denial or disbelief. The initial reaction to change, particularly change that is unwanted, is denial. The meaning of the change doesn't sink in immediately, so nothing changes—people work very much as they did before. The solution to denial is to get past it as quickly as possible. Don't prolong it by encouraging a "business as usual" approach. That will only result in bigger problems down the road. Instead, encourage people to react to the change. Help them to understand that what they have heard is true—that the change is happening. At the same time, be open to and accept expression of negative feelings.

Resistance. As people begin to perceive the potential impacts of the change on them, their jobs, their families, and their well-being, anxiety, depression, self-doubt, fear, and hostility appear. Job performance and productivity begin to decline. Absenteeism, tardiness, rejects, reworks, and customer complaints are likely to skyrocket. So are threats of resignation and requests for services in the employee assistance program.

The most effective strategy is to accept what's happening. Let employees openly share their feelings with management and with others. They need a catharsis, a means of venting their negative emotions. Some experts advocate planning picnics, parties, and dances to contain or flush these normal but negative responses.

Exploration and investigation. If all goes well, most employees move on to the next phase. They take renewed interest in their work, and productivity improves. People then begin to turn their attention to the future. They ask questions about directions, how to achieve their goals, how to relate and interact with their colleagues, and how to move the organization in the right direction.

Acceptance and commitment. At this point, the transition is complete. Employees buy into the new way of doing things. They have learned new ways to interact and relate to their peers, superiors, and subordinates. They are eager to develop new plans and to adopt new procedures and processes.

The Effects of Change on People and Organizations

People Issues and Impacts

When employees begin to sense that a significant change is about to take place, their outlook and frame of mind are immediately altered. Their focus of attention turns to self-preservation. Some employees may decide the game is not worth playing and bail out on their own. Others suffer severe psychological damage.

Climate of uncertainty and suspicion. Even positive proposals for change can result in uncertainty and ambiguity. People start wondering about the future of the organization and their place in it. Sometimes they are simply incapable of performing at their customary level of competence because of the personal tension and distress they feel.

Radical change makes people suspicious. Although their first reaction may be surprise or disbelief, they soon realize that it is for real. It is then that they begin to wonder what top management is up to. When they can't get all the information they want, their suspicion evolves into mistrust.

Self-centeredness and nonadaptive behavior. When employees begin to believe that management has no concern for their welfare, they start looking out for themselves. They may become aggressive, even belligerent, in their attempts to acquire power. Or they may become apathetic, passive, or unresponsive.

Some people react to change with totally damaging behavior: alcohol and drug abuse, child and spouse abuse, feigned illness, or withdrawal, and, less common but not rare, suicide threats and even actual suicide. Immediate professional counseling is needed.

Loss of job. The most serious consequence of structural change, from both human and economic standpoints, is lost jobs. Terminations have a heavy impact on the psyches of employees, the security and well-being of their families, and even the economic health of communities.

Organizational Issues and Impacts

We must not lose sight of the fact that change will always have an impact on the organization itself. Here are some of the most common consequences.

Pressures on management. Not only must managers adopt a new system, they must also sell it to their people. There is also certain to be considerable pressure from top management to implement change quickly and cure the problem that made the change necessary. Managers are then under severe pressure to succeed.

Power plays. Restructuring and downsizing almost always result in at least some jockeying for position. Power and authority change hands. Some managers lose their punch; others lose their ability to influence the action. Unfortunately these tussles often result in permanently damaged relationships, wasted time and effort, and squandered resources.

Communication breakdown. When significant change takes place in an organization, communication problems intensify. Finding out what is really going on becomes next to impossible. The grapevine runs rampant. Employees tend to share a minimum of information with others, and look at information passed on to them, particularly from the top, with suspicion.

Team disintegration. Regardless of the type of change—a new boss, new people on the work team—people tend to begin to think about themselves, and teamwork begins to self-destruct.

Morale problems. Change begets rumors, restlessness, fears, and resistance. Unchecked, these attitudes can cause widespread tension, disrupted relationships, and lost commitment. The ultimate result is total demoralization of the work force.

Productivity decline. The combination of all these negatives invariably results in plummeting productivity. Communication glitches and clogged channels make it difficult to get information and impossible to get timely decisions. Employees waste hours worrying, discussing, and thinking about what is happening and how it affects them and their families.

Strategies for Handling Change

There are two basic approaches to solving the problem of employee resistance to change: overcoming it and reducing it. In overcoming resistance, management tries to apply enough pressure to induce resisters to do what is wanted—for example, threatening discharge if they don't adjust, or promising pay raises if they do. In reducing resistance, management tries to convince employees that their fears are groundless, that their job security is guaranteed, that their earnings will not be reduced, that their work environment will be improved, and that their opportunities will be expanded.

Several change strategies can be used to smooth the change process and prevent negative effects. The first two strategies we will examine are clearly the direct responsibility of the HR manager. The remaining nine strategies are normally controlled by senior management. Here the HR manager's job is to use his or her position, influence, and skills to ensure that plans for change are built with careful consideration of their impact on employees. Of course all eleven are the responsibility of the HR manager within his or her own department.

Build a climate for change. Successful change is mainly the result of a climate that welcomes, initiates, and manages change. In such a climate, risk is accepted as a natural part of doing business. A premium is placed on innovation and creativity. People are encouraged to try new and different approaches to the job. Al-

■ ■

THE FIVE C'S OF SUCCESSFUL CHANGE

Help people cope with change by teaching these five C's. Start with yourself:
set the example.

1. **Commitment.** Build in employees a sense of meaning and purpose in
   their jobs; get them to be totally involved in their work.
2. **Confidence.** Develop employees' self-assurance in their own abilities
   and trust in their teammates' competencies.
3. **Control.** Encourage people to take charge of their jobs—what they do
   and how they do it. Give them independence and as much personal
   power and authority as they can handle.
4. **Challenge.** Help people see the change as a challenge, not a catastro-
   phe, and as an opportunity to develop and learn new skills.
5. **Collegiality.** Teach employees to value their colleagues, respect themselves, and feel the common bond that exists between themselves and
   their co-workers.

■ ■

though mistakes are not encouraged, they are not punishable offenses—at least not the first time around.

Protect employees. To gain support for change, managers must
give employees assurances that they will be protected from economic
loss. Such things as seniority rights, opportunities for advancement,
training, and development may be guaranteed. Some organizations
offer retraining; some absorb displaced workers in other jobs without loss of pay, prestige, or opportunities; others defer the change
until the problems of displaced workers are solved.

Provide outplacement services. Outplacement services can go
a long way toward cushioning the blow of termination. Usual services
are skills assessment, job market information, help in preparing
résumés, assistance in enrolling in government-sponsored retraining programs, in-company redeployment, employment interview
training, time off for job searches, benefits counseling, and personal,
financial, and family counseling.

Improve communication. This is probably the most important
strategy; it will do more to overcome resistance than anything else.
Employees need information—not only *what* is going to happen but
also *why*. The information should be communicated to the entire

organization, and it must be done in such a way that the facts will be clearly understood.

Encourage participation. Today's employees have a strong desire to participate in making the decisions that affect them. They are confident that they know the critical operational problems and want to share their insights. Managers should tap this source of help. Participation in making decisions helps those involved to understand the situation, assures them that management is not trying to bamboozle them, and makes use of the contributions of those who must implement the change. Companies can also gain invaluable assistance by encouraging employee participation in developmental activities such as quality circles or training.

Share benefits. Another strategy is to permit employees to share in the economic and nonfinancial benefits derived from change. Profit-sharing and production-sharing plans are examples. Where changes make the employees' jobs easier, less stressful, or less time consuming, organizations show that they are concerned about the total job environment. Installing employee comforts and conveniences is another way of telling employees, "You count."

Avoid trivial change. People can tolerate only so much change, and if they are peppered with many irritating small changes, they will rebel. Managers must strike a balance between excessive change, which results in organizational instability, and insufficient change, which causes organizational stagnation. Managers must encourage support for change by preventing trivial and unnecessary change.

Make change tentative. When employees are allowed to participate in making decisions involving change, it is sometimes possible and desirable to implement the change on a trial basis. That strategy allows employees to check their reactions to the change and to determine whether the change is workable. But when employees have not participated in the decision, it is imprudent to make tentative changes; to do so will only prolong the period of uncertainty, increase tension, and almost certainly increase resistance.

Make change gradual. If possible, critical changes should be introduced gradually. Slow changes are usually less disruptive, generate less resistance, and provide much greater opportunity to fine tune. But slow change also has its dangers. The change may be so gradual that people continue to act as if no change had occurred, or may begin to wonder where the change is leading.

Provide training. Change requires people to unlearn old habits, skills, and attitudes, and then learn new ones. Unfortunately, it is possible to learn new skills, habits, and attitudes and still retain the old ones. People must be taught new skills and habits in familiar contexts so that they will be able to accept, install, and use them consistently. And then they must be given reinforcement in a supportive climate. That is one of the primary tasks of leadership—to provide that supportive climate.

Imposed Change: Special Situations

Much of this chapter so far is directed to managers as they initiate change. But what about change that is dictated, either from outside the organization or at the corporate level? Two very common, and very difficult, situations are mergers and takeovers, and restructuring and downsizing.

Mergers and Takeovers

What can managers do to ease the pain and smooth the way for themselves, their people, and their organizations when a merger or a takeover occurs? Here is a condensed version of the suggestions given by Price Pritchett, an expert on communications programs for companies being acquired or merged.[1]

1. Control your attitude. Don't let negative attitudes develop. Try to find the positive potential in the merger. Get involved. Don't wait to be asked. Seek opportunities to be helpful to the people managing the merger. Welcome the challenge to your professionalism and competence. That's why you were hired. Maintain your composure even when the going get tough.

2. Expect change . . . and be a change agent. Recognize that change is inevitable. Be prepared for it by being flexible. Accept the fact that you're going to have to adapt to new bosses, policies, procedures, and even standards. Acknowledge that there is more than one way to run an organization successfully. Don't be an observer. Get involved in the change. Make suggestions. Become a change agent.

---

[1]Price Pritchett, *The Employee Survival Guide to Mergers and Acquisitions,* copyright 1987 by Pritchett and Associates, Inc., Dallas, Texas. Used by permission.

3. Be tolerant of management mistakes. Be sympathetic, supportive, and helpful to your boss and other managers. Always give the new management the benefit of the doubt. Constantly exercise restraint. Try to be a part of the solution rather than a part of the problem.

4. Don't blame everything you don't like on the merger. Avoid finger pointing. Don't try to pin responsibility for bungles and mistakes on the new managers or the new organizational arrangements. And don't make the mistake of assuming that all the changes you are seeing are a result of the merger. Remember that problems and issues arise in every organization and that the structure, the leadership, and the processes cannot be held accountable for every unwelcome event.

5. Be prepared for "psychological soreness." Be ready for unhappiness, distress, sensitivity, and other negative feelings in yourself and your people. Pritchett says, "Expect your psychological muscles to get sore" when changes are made in your work environment. But don't let the soreness incapacitate you.

6. Get to know the other company. Try to overcome all negative impressions you had about the other company before the merger. Study the other firm in detail. Read its history. Learn about its culture and its accomplishments. Learn about its people, its executives, managers, scientists, and staffers—who they are, what they have done, and what they plan to do. In short, learn how they do business.

7. Use the merger as an opportunity for growth. Make the merger a career milestone. Get a fresh start. Rethink your values, goals, and priorities. Take a hard look at your job performance, your strengths and deficiencies. Set new personal and departmental goals and objectives. Make productive use of your time.

8. Keep your sense of humor. Keep things in perspective. Nothing is ever quite as bad as it seems at first glance.

9. Practice good stress-management techniques. Take care of yourself physically. Get enough sleep. Learn relaxation techniques and use them. Engage in a regular program of physical exercise. Learn to control your emotions.

10. Keep doing your job. Try harder. Work smarter. Use all the resources that are available to you. Don't let up on your work, and don't become passive. Invest yourself totally in your work and your assigned mission.

Restructuring and Downsizing

Most restructuring actions today fall into the category of downsizing, resulting in a reduction in force. How should it be managed? Before implementing layoffs, companies must plan carefully, to minimize the shock, confusion, and anger that inevitably follow. Managers have key responsibilities: to perform an internal impact assessment, to create policies and timetables, to plan for severance pay and relocation counseling—a complete package of services to help employees.

Here are some suggestions when downsizing is imminent and unavoidable:

Be prepared. Study past changes and their impacts in your own organization and others. Identify the lessons learned. Do some networking with your HR colleagues in other companies. Think through your policies and procedures well before they are needed. Get input from your staff. Check the collective bargaining agreement carefully. Anticipate all the potential adverse effects—on management style, communication networks, quality of work life, employee motivation and morale, and work team and individual productivity. Plan to counteract them.

Organize the process. Systematically identify which functions, jobs, and people are to be reduced or eliminated, in what order, and when. Determine how functions will be handled once they have been cut back. Don't make across-the-board reductions. Target functions and jobs on the basis of your strategic plans and the bottom-line results you are seeking to achieve. Then, once you have built the climate, clarified the change, and identified the primary impacts on people and the organization, get on with the downsizing action.

Address sensitive communication issues. Determine what employees need and want to know, develop a communications plan to provide that information, and then implement the plan. Communicate completely, honestly, openly. Announce the change at a meeting—never in a newspaper release, on a bulletin board, or in a company publication. Give people an opportunity to ask questions and listen carefully to their concerns. Install and publicize a hot line for instant, clear, and accurate information about the change.

Provide options and assistance. If employees are to be given choices of any kind, give them access to the information they need to make informed decisions. If loss of job is involved, provide outplacement services to help people locate new jobs. Identify employees who are too shocked by the change to make the decisions they need to make, and give them special help through the employee assistance program or professional counseling. Where possible, use alternatives to layoffs—job sharing, performance-based pay, early retirement incentives.

Apply damage-control measures. Monitor events closely. Identify glitches as early as possible and do something to minimize the damage they can cause to the organization and its people. Modify your plan and make it work better.

The Change Process

There are several things you as HR manager can do to initiate and manage change in your organization and in your department.

Step 1. Get yourself ready. If you have negative attitudes toward change, change them. Expect change and use it as a means of improving your department and the organization it serves. Be sensitive to the various dimensions of change, but keep your perspective and your sense of humor. See change as an opportunity to achieve personal growth. Use stress-management techniques when the tension builds. Above all, keep doing your job.

Step 2. Establish goals and objectives. Choose an area for change where success is assured. Be sure that it is compatible with organizational goals. Ask yourself what you want to change and why. Define the proposed change in detail. Develop written goals and objectives for the change project. Keep them easy to understand but challenging.

When you are not the initiator of the change, your responsibility is to identify and, where necessary, clarify the goals and objectives of the imposed change. Why is the change to be made? What is to be gained? By whom? When?

Step 3. Select and train change agents. The change process is too big for one person, or even one management level, to handle. One of your earliest tasks is to choose a change team, people from any level of the organization who are able to anticipate, accept, sell, and use change to make the company and its people more productive, more profitable, and more satisfying. In essence, their function is to identify blocks and establish action plans. Choose the team carefully. Team leaders must be skilled, open-minded, and able to obtain the full participation and involvement of group members. Group members must be committed to the resolution of differences, open-minded, knowledgeable about the organization, and willing to state and defend their convictions in the face of opposition; they need to be skilled in problem solving, conflict resolution, and evaluation. Train the group in the change process.

If the change is imposed, you still need to select and train the people who will be directly involved in the change—the people who will make it work.

Step 4. Formulate and implement the plan. Identify the players and their roles—the who. Then determine how the project will be structured and managed—the how and the when. Develop a written master plan for the change effort—the time schedule, the deadlines, the right resources, and the means of measuring progress and accomplishment—with specific milestones for each phase. Your objective throughout is to ensure that you maintain control over the process so that the focus and direction of change will be what was intended.

Step 5. Sell the change. In implementing the plan, you of course have communicated the ingredients of the change to all concerned. Now the task is a bit different: sell them on the value of the changes. Resistance to change is a lot like sales resistance, so use the tools of the professional salesperson: persuasion and negotiation. Warm up the "prospects," describe the "product" (what the change is all about) and the benefits "buyers" will gain, identify the obstacles they are likely to face, use the wide variety of strategies available to overcome objections, and "close" the sale (get acceptance of and commitment to the change). Regardless of whether the change is imposed or self-generated, the focus in selling must be on overcoming the really critical barriers to change in the organization: the fears, attitudes, and values of employees. Help your people develop a positive attitude toward change, to welcome it and accept it.

Step 6. Manage the ongoing process. Now the focus shifts to direction and control. Whether the change is initiated or imposed, the task is keeping the project on track and achieving the results intended. Directing involves guiding, motivating, encouraging, communicating, coaching, and inspiring. The controlling function focuses on actions designed to ensure that events, progress, and results match plans. It is achieved by establishing measurable standards, comparing performance with the standards, identifying deviations and shortfalls, and applying corrective strategies.

Step 7. Evaluate results and revise as needed. Don't lose interest in the project when the change has been installed. Be alert for glitches in implementation and new problems. Look for ways to improve on the change, make it more effective and less costly. Again, get the ideas of the users. And provide continuous feedback throughout the organization.

Summary

Change in any system is inevitable. Competition, economic and social factors, legislation, technology, human values, and a host of other things constantly and inexorably alter the organizational scene over time. Managers, particularly HR managers, have only one option. They can't decide *whether* to change; they can only decide *how* to change. They must either accept change as a normal and natural process and exploit it for competitive advantage, or perish under the weight of the status quo.

Change is brought about by forces within and outside the organization. Internal sources include changes in ownership and top management with their inevitable consequences: changes in philosophy, mission and purposes, goals and objectives, management style, communication, employee relations, new systems, processes, products, and services, and the quality of work life. External sources of change include demographic shifts, changes in the economy, customers, and clients, competition, the law and government regulations, the political scene, and, of course, technology. Among the more dramatic and disturbing changes currently affecting many organizations are downsizing and restructuring caused by takeovers and mergers.

Change sometimes produces adverse effects on the organization, such as intense pressures on managers, destructive power plays, communication breakdowns, team disintegration, morale problems, and subsequent productivity decline. It also affects people, often resulting in feelings of uncertainty and ambiguity, suspicion, self-centeredness, resignations, nonadaptive behavior, and job loss. Employee resistance to change has its roots in potential adverse economic impacts, such as loss of job security, pay, and benefits, and negative attitudes, such as skepticism, threats to established interpersonal relationships, and union objections.

The most effective strategy for managing change involves building an organizational climate for change, protecting employees from adverse effects, improving communication, encouraging participation in decision making, using consulting and negotiating tactics, sharing benefits derived from the change, avoiding trivial change, making change tentative and gradual, and providing training for all levels of employees.

To manage change successfully, HR managers must:

1. Get themselves ready for change.
2. Establish realistic and attainable goals and objectives.
3. Select and train the team of change agents.
4. Formulate and implement the plan.
5. Sell the change.
6. Manage the ongoing change process.
7. Evaluate results and revise the plan as needed.

For Further Reading, Viewing, and Listening

All Change (The Management of Change) (two videocassettes). Produced by Video Arts. Distributed by Films Inc., 5547 N. Ravenswood Ave., Chicago, IL 60640, 1988.

Allen, J. G. *Surviving Corporate Downsizing.* New York: John Wiley & Sons, 1988.

Bell, Robert. *Surviving the 10 Ordeals of the Takeover.* New York: AMACOM, 1988.

Bohl, Don Lee, ed. *Responsible Reductions in Force: An American Management Association Research Report on Downsizing Outplacement.* New York: AMACOM, 1987.

Conner, Daryl. "Introducing New Technology Humanely." *Training and Development Journal,* May 1985, pp. 33–36.

Dalziel, Murray, and Stephen C. Schoonover. *Changing Ways: A Practical Tool for Implementing Change Within an Organization.* New York: AMACOM, 1988.

Davy, Jeanette A., Angelo Kinicki, John Kilroy, and Christine Scheck. "After the Merger: Dealing With People's Uncertainty." *Training and Development Journal,* November 1988, pp. 57–61.

Egan, Gerard. *Change-Agent Skills. Part A: Assessing and Designing Excellence. Part B: Managing Innovation and Change.* San Diego, Calif.: University Associates, 1988.

Fink, Steven. *Crisis Management: Planning for the Inevitable.* New York: AMACOM, 1986.

Gilmore, Thomas North. *Making a Leadership Change: How Organizations and Leaders Can Handle Leadership Transitions Successfully.* San Francisco: Jossey-Bass, 1988.

Goodman, Paul, and others. *Change in Organization: New Perspectives on Theory, Research and Practice.* San Francisco: Jossey-Bass, 1982.

Goodmeasure, Inc. *The Changing American Workplace: Work Alternatives in the 1980s.* New York: AMACOM, 1985.

Hutchinson, Frank, and Greg Gilbert. "Readying Your Company for Change." *Training and Development Journal,* May 1985, pp. 28–30.

Jacobs, Dorri. *Change: How to Live With, Manage, Create and Enjoy It—At Work.* New York: Programs on Change, 1988.

Jemison, David B., and Sim B. Sitkin. *Acquisitions: The Process Can Be a Problem.* Boston: Harvard Business School Publishing Division, 1986.

Kanter, Rosabeth Moss. *The Change Masters: Innovation for Productivity in the American Corporation.* New York: Touchstone Books, 1985.

Kirkpatrick, Donald L. *How to Manage Change Effectively: Approaches, Methods, and Case Examples.* San Francisco: Jossey-Bass, 1985.

Lippitt, Gordon L., Petter Langseth, and Jack Mossop. *Implementing Organizational Change: A Practical Guide to Managing Change Efforts.* San Francisco: Jossey-Bass, 1985.

London, Manuel. *Change Agents: New Roles and Innovation Strategies for Human Resource Professionals.* San Francisco: Jossey-Bass, 1988.

Managing Change (28-minute videocassette). Southern California Consortium, 5400 Orange Ave., Suite 215, Cypress, CA 90630, 1983.

Morgan, Gareth. *Riding the Waves of Change: Developing Managerial Competencies for a Turbulent World.* San Francisco: Jossey-Bass, 1988.

Overcoming Resistance to Change (16-minute videocassette). Coronet/MTI Film & Video, 108 Wilmot Rd., Deerfield, IL 60015.

People at Work (15-minute videocassette). Rank Roundtable Film & Video, 113 N. San Vicente Blvd., Beverly Hills, CA 90211-2387, 1987.

Pritchett, Price. *Making Mergers Work: A Guide to Managing Mergers and Acquisitions.* Homewood, Ill.: Dow Jones-Irwin, 1987.

————. *After the Merger: Managing the Shockwaves.* Homewood, Ill.: Dow Jones-Irwin, 1985.

————. *The Employee Survival Guide to Mergers and Acquisitions.* Pritchett and Associates, 350 Campbell Center, Dallas, TX 75206, 1987.

————. *Making Mergers Motivate: A Conversation With Dr. Price Pritchett* (audiotape). Dallas, Tex.: Pritchett and Associates, 1987.

————. *Merging! The Challenge of Change* (16-minute videocassette). Dallas, Tex.: Pritchett and Associates, 1987.

————, and Fred W. Cover. *The Human Resources Planning Guide to Mergers and Acquisitions.* Dallas, Tex.: Pritchett and Associates, 1987.

Tomasko, Robert M. *Downsizing: Reshaping the Corporation for the Future.* New York: AMACOM, 1987.

Walton, Richard E. *Managing Change in the Workplace.* San Francisco: Jossey-Bass, 1987.

Wilkins, Alan L. *Developing Corporate Character: How to Successfully Change an Organization Without Destroying It.* San Francisco: Jossey-Bass, 1989.

Woodward, Harry, and Steve Buchholz. *Aftershock: Helping Your People Through Corporate Change.* New York: John Wiley & Sons, 1987.

13

Managing Ethics
Championing Moral Values

Ethical issues are a daily component of business, and they are more important today than ever. Ethics are involved in all facets of a business: decision making, arbitration, marketing and sales, financial reporting, personnel, appraisal, and leadership. Managers must be able to see the ethical issues in the choices they face, make decisions within an ethical framework, and build and maintain an ethical work environment. HR managers must be especially sensitive to ethical issues because of their key role in the development of "people" policies and programs.

There are a lot of stakeholders in the game of ethics: corporate boards of control, the company itself, executives, managers, and supervisors, employees, customers and clients, suppliers, competitors, the industry at large, the community, and the nation. At one time or another, ethical decisions involve all these constituencies, and have a profound impact on market share, competitive position, profitability, image, job satisfaction, and morale.

The crux of the matter is that ethical behavior often collides with the bottom line—at least in the short term. But things are changing. The word is getting out: ethical behavior is good business; it contributes to success in the marketplace. A reputation for honesty and integrity attracts and holds customers, and will ultimately show up in the bottom line.

Organizations that have strong ethical values and consistently display them in all their activities derive other benefits, too: improved top-management control, increased productivity, avoidance of litigation, and an enhanced company image that attracts talent and earns the public's good will.

The question of business ethics focuses on business practices in light of some concept of human value. Thus, traditional business goals—profit, growth, or technological progress—are evaluated not for their own sake but for their contribution to some basic human good, such as investor satisfaction, improved services, or better working conditions. The ethical, the *right* thing to do in business is that which best serves the ideals of morality *and* good management practice. The highest moral good is what professional ethics is all about. An ethical dilemma occurs when two or more values conflict. The best solution to any problem almost always involves a cost of some kind.

In the arena of human resources, the most significant contemporary issues of ethics center on the employees' relationship with the firm, the organization's relationship to its employees, and the firm's relationship with its outside constituencies: unions, suppliers, competitors, and customers. In any of those areas on any given day, you as the HR manager might face a situation calling for a tough decision. Here are some examples.

Employees' relationships with the firm

Conflict of interest
Fair day's work for a fair day's pay
Honesty and integrity
Loyalty
Moonlighting
Privacy
Theft (time, materials, products, or funds)
Travel vouchers
Whistle blowing

Organization's relationships with employees

Clarity of communications
Code of ethics
Due process
Enforcement of corporate policies, rules, and regulations
Equal employment opportunity
Affirmative action
Compensation and benefits
Grievance procedures
Management competency and leadership
Personnel records
Sexual harassment
Conditions of work

Firm's relationship to unions, suppliers, competitors, and customers and clients

Good-faith bargaining
Grievance procedures

Strikes
Union busting
Conflicts of interest
Fair bidding
Kickbacks
Denigration of competitors
Unethical competition
Advertising
Fraud or deception
Quality control (products and services)

Ethics in Our Time

Roots of Ethical Behavior

The ethical behavior of HR managers has its roots in several aspects of contemporary society: the general culture of our society, values of the organization they work for and the profession they are a part of, and their own personal values.

The culture. American society, the culture itself, has established fundamental norms and values that undergird our behavior as a people. They are encompassed in our basic values and community standards, and formalized into law.

The foundation is the basic American values established by the Constitution and Bill of Rights, Declaration of Independence, and other traditions: democracy, freedom of speech and assembly, free enterprise, free public education for all, nondiscrimination, respect for work, and the like.

To this broad foundation we have added community standards, values established by custom and accepted by the majority of a region or individual community as right and proper behavior. Examples are respect for the aged and infirm, concern for wildlife, participation in community affairs, protection of the property of neighbors, and support for youth activities. Community standards reflect the values held by individual community members, value systems developed over a lifetime of experiences dominated by three basic social institutions—family, church, and schools.

Finally, as a nation we have created a body of legal standards that codify our ethical values into law: the federal constitution, state constitutions, and the statutes. Examples are Title VII of the Civil Rights Act of 1964, the Occupational Safety and Health Act of 1970, the Equal Employment Opportunity Act of 1972, and the Ethics in Government Act of 1978.

The organization. The values of an organization—as reflected in its management philosophy, its culture, and the products or services it offers—echo the values of the individuals who make it up: employees, supervisors, managers, and, most significantly, the CEO and top leaders. Some commonly held organizational values are the importance of resources, return on investment, the welfare and well-being of employees, service to customers and clients, and loyalty to the organization.

Although the goals and values of an organization may be implicit or explicit, to a growing extent they are being placed in writing. Many companies have adopted codes of ethics or include sections in their policy statements that relate explicitly to the ethical realm. They address such issues as leadership, integrity, equity, employee rights, employee development, participation in policy formulation, nondiscrimination, quality of work life, and the like. Specific suggestions for developing a code of ethics are presented later in this chapter.

The individual. People's own values are a reflection of their home life and rearing, education and training, and religious beliefs. They bring these values to the performance of their jobs. Examples are competence, honesty, a sense of personal responsibility, completing a task on time, and pride in workmanship.

The profession. Although at present there are no universally accepted ethical standards for the HR profession, professional associations have established codes of ethical conduct that members must follow. They typically emphasize desirable standards of service and performance and deemphasize remuneration. Because they are voluntary, enforcement is difficult. But they are a deterrent to unethical conduct because members want to keep the confidence and respect of their peers and retain the right of continued affiliation.

The American Society for Training and Development has adopted the code of ethics and rules of behavior shown in Figure 13-1.

Pressures and Temptations

How would you rate your own standards of ethics in business? Are you always ethical? Are you ethical except in situations where

Figure 13-1. ASTD code of ethics and rules of behavior.

ASTD Code of Ethics

The ASTD Code of Ethics provides guidance to members to be self-managed human resource development professionals. Clients and employers should expect from ASTD members the highest possible standards of personal integrity, professional competence, sound judgment and discretion. Developed by the profession for the profession, the ASTD Code of Ethics is the Society's public declaration of its members' obligations to themselves, their profession and society. I strive to . . .

- Recognize the rights and dignities of each individual.
- Develop human potential.
- Provide my employer, clients and learners with the highest level quality education, training and development.
- Be a good citizen and to comply with the laws and regulations governing my position.
- Keep informed of pertinent knowledge and competence in the human resource field.
- Maintain confidentiality and integrity in the practice of my profession.
- Support my peers and to avoid conduct which impedes their practicing their profession.
- Conduct myself in an ethical and honest manner.
- Improve the public understanding of human resource development and management.
- Fairly and accurately represent my human resource development/human resource management credentials, qualifications, experience and ability.
- Contribute to the continuing growth of the Society and its members.

Rules of Behavior for National Members

Members of the Society shall . . .

- Refrain from any overt statement or pointed humor which disparages rightful dignity and social equity of any individual or group when presenting from any Society platform.
- When using the Society's name or in introductions to presentations, make clear the ideas presented are personal and do not represent those of the Society.
- Refrain from using the Society's platform to directly sell, promote, or otherwise encourage participants to purchase or use the speaker's products or services.

ASTD Code of Ethics and Rules of Behavior for National Members, *1988 Who's Who in Training and Development: The Official Membership Directory, American Society for Training and Development* (Alexandria, Va.: ASTD, 1988, p. iv). © 1988 by the American Society for Training and Development. Used by permission.

you can't possibly be found out? Are you ethical except when you are under pressure from your boss or your peers? Are profits more important than your personal values? Do your career goals sometimes take precedence over principle? Anyone can be ethical when there is no pressure to act otherwise. Pressures to be unethical come from many sources—yourself, your boss, your peers, your subordinates—but true professionals are able to resist.

Personal ambition and self-interest are probably the most common causes of unethical behavior. To improve their personal situation, to gain advancement, higher income, or reputation, or to avoid criticism or punishment, people do self-serving and unethical acts.

Your peers can also put pressure on you to behave unethically. It is always difficult to turn down a request for help, especially from a colleague, yet abandoning your own standards serves neither one of you. Unpleasant though it may be, the right thing is to decline. Say something like "I appreciate the difficulty of the situation you face. I would like to be able to help you, but I cannot."

At some point, all managers face pressure from their subordinates to be unethical. People might ask you to cover absences, to overlook infractions "just this time," or to help them cover up a near-accident. As a professional manager, you should never give in to such requests. Not only would it be unethical, you will also destroy their respect and ruin your power as a manager and leader. The difficult but right thing to do under these conditions is to get the group together and talk to them along these lines: "I understand that you're not asking me to do this out of self-interest. But I will not tolerate dishonesty. We are going to abide by the code of conduct of this organization. We're going to do our job properly."

Pressure to be unethical can also come from your superiors, usually stemming from their desire to look good to *their* superiors. "I don't care how you do it, but I want that contract."

Pressure from a superior is extremely difficult, particularly since it is often accompanied by a threat, either direct or implied, of some adverse action, such as a poor performance report or denial of a bonus. But the fact that the pressure comes from your boss is not an excuse to behave unethically. Don't deceive yourself into believing that you are doing something to make your department look better; recognize that your motivation is self-protection. It's a tough thing to do, but as a true professional you must refuse to compromise your values.

The culture of the organization is still another source of unethical conduct. And it is not only the organization that engages in questionable practices. Organizations that place too much emphasis on managerial aggressiveness and corporate expansion, competitiveness, and profit are just as likely to stimulate unethical actions.

Identifying Ethical Problems

In most organizations, ethical choices revolve around recurring problems. It is critically important that these problems be identified, so that policies to resolve them can be developed.

Clark Moeller suggests asking the following questions to decide if a particular issue is relevant to your organization.[1]

1. Do you think the issue is important to the maintenance or improvement of the corporate atmosphere?
2. Has the issue been mentioned in talks or papers given or issued by the CEO or a member of the board of directors?
3. Is there a corporate policy that clearly addresses this issue? And has it been consistently enforced?
4. Although there may be no formal policy on the issue, is there an understanding on the issue? What is it?
5. Have there been either grievances or instances in which this was raised as an issue?
6. Has the issue surfaced in exit interviews, performance evaluations, quality circle discussions, or suggestion boxes?
7. Has the question surfaced as an issue in management meetings?
8. Have shareholders' resolutions on the issue been voted on at the annual board of directors meeting?
9. Is the issue addressed in federal or state legislation?
10. Could you develop a good case study on the issue that would stimulate seminar participants to examine their own attitudes and practices?

Generally, the kinds of issues that present problems in business ethics revolve around competition, both corporate and individual, and the potential disparity between corporate profitability and social responsibility.

Corporate social responsibility. Most HR managers today are very much aware of their responsibilities as a part of an organization designed to serve certain needs of society and as an employee with

---

[1]Clark Moeller, "Ethics Training," Chapter 84 in *Human Resources Management and Development Handbook,* edited by William R. Tracey (New York: AMACOM, 1985), p. 1206.

power to use resources to make a profit. They recognize that numerous groups in society can be benefited or harmed by the organization and by their actions as managers. The potential dilemma is this: are HR managers bound to use the resources of the organization directly for the interests of owners only or do they have the obligation to promote the good of the company or of society? HR managers making decisions for their companies face problems where guidelines are either unclear or missing. Not everything that is good for the organization is good for people or for society at large. Almost all decisions contain a mix of benefits and liabilities to the many constituencies of an organization.

Corporate competition. Competition for market share, for talent, for resources, for funds, and for customers is much more intense today than it has ever been before; in many cases, it borders on cutthroat. Within the United States and abroad, companies battle each other for customers and clients. Within organizations, departments compete with each other for resources—people, time, space, equipment, and funds. With organizational competition at such an acute level, it should come as no surprise that some managers have stepped over the line between ethical and unethical practices. What is surprising is the extent to which that continues to happen, and the identity of the many prominent organizations in all fields caught with their moral standards below their knees.

Individual competition. There has always been intense competition among managers and other professionals for employment, advancement, monetary gain, recognition, status, and personal prestige. Today, in an environment poisoned with mergers, takeovers, restructuring, and downsizing, one-on-one struggles for supremacy (perhaps even survival) have become not only more earnest but also much rougher. These new organizational arrangements prompt fear and anxiety, and people who are normally honest and considerate suddenly become unscrupulous and uncaring.

Judging Behavior and Making Decisions

People often find themselves in complex situations where the ethical alternative is not clear. Those are the real ethical dilemmas. In these situations people need a reasoning process to help them decide what course of action will result in the greater good. Similarly, it is not always easy to judge whether a particular action is ethical or unethical. In both cases—evaluating your own behavior and that of others—analyzing all factors of the situation should make the right course of action clear. Here are some ideas.

- *Learn the facts.* Before a decision can be reached, or a judgment made, the judge must know the facts about the behavior and the person involved, with due consideration of that person's age, status, intelligence, maturity, and educational level.
- *Learn the circumstances*—the what, where, when, and how. Make sure you know the probable mood or disposition and intent of the person; the degree to which the act was voluntary or involuntary, deliberate or accidental, imposed or inadvertent, premeditated or spontaneous; in short, the why.
- *Be aware of the ethical principle violated.* Is the decision or behavior well within the law, or does it violate a law or corporate policy?

When the individual making the judgment is also the person who performed the action or must make the decision, there is one other test.

- *Evaluate your emotional reaction.* If I take this action or make this decision, will I feel good, satisfied, pleased? Or will I feel guilty? Would I be glad to have my boss, my family, my friends know what I have done?

Role of the HR Manager

HR managers play several important roles in the area of ethics. At the corporate level, they have a responsibility for exerting a positive influence on the moral tone of the organization. Within their own departments, they have several responsibilities and many opportunities to develop and maintain an ethical climate.

Corporate Level

HR managers exert influence by:

- Encouraging executives and senior managers to demonstrate concern for ethical practices
- Engaging in discreet discussion, making executives aware of how their actions affect employees at all levels

- Assisting the board, the CEO, and senior executives to integrate ethics in all activities of the company—strategic and operational planning, human resources, finance, purchasing, marketing and sales, distribution, advertising, and so on
- Helping senior management to integrate values into the policy process—ethical codes, social audits, changes in organization, and widening and deepening the involvement of employees in making value judgments
- Persuading senior management to address ethical issues as a part of the strategic planning process
- Encouraging senior managers to provide specific answers to ethical questions posed by operating managers, staff officers, and other employees
- Enlisting the help of managers and representatives of other employee groups in developing a strong corporate moral code of ethics
- Encouraging top management to empower people to influence those who make policy by holding policy formulation hearings with representative groups of employees
- Participating in setting and communicating standards relating to ethical conduct
- Developing guidelines for screening and selecting employees
- Providing training in ethical behavior for employees at all levels
- Recommending naming a corporate ombudsman (an older, highly respected manager, close to retirement, relieved of operating responsibility) to hear complaints from individuals, investigate them, and resolve them as quickly and as satisfactorily as possible
- Suggesting a mentoring program
- Proposing annual ethical audits, carried out by an outside consultant but overseen by the HR department
- Suggesting a hotline that can be used by anyone at any time to air a grievance, blow a whistle, pose a question, or discuss a problem
- Advocating input lines where employees, clients and customers, suppliers, and the general public can make known to top management their concerns, perceptions, and demands

Departmental Level

Within their own departments, HR managers have these responsibilities:

- Observing the highest standards of personal ethical conduct
- Developing a support network—associates inside and outside the company with whom they can discuss ethical issues
- Tapping the expertise of professionals who understand the problems of ethics and their implications
- Building employees' self-esteem (people who like themselves and feel good about themselves can resist pressures to do the wrong thing)
- Being cautious in their use of power and authority because they often produce negative side effects, such as "getting even"
- Reducing the pressure on staff to "obey" or "win"
- Providing staff with positive, growth-producing experiences
- Taking positive actions to build and maintain a strong moral climate by providing guidance and support to their people in making ethical choices
- Communicating the corporate code of ethics
- Conducting staff meetings and workshops devoted exclusively to departmental business ethics
- Monitoring compliance with corporate policies and standards by maintaining a system of daily supervision, periodic performance appraisal, and audits
- Providing channels by which any employee can file an ethical concern and get a fair hearing without fear of negative consequences
- Establishing channels and procedures for accountability
- Imposing sanctions appropriate to the offense promptly when serious infractions occur
- Reinforcing ethical behavior by providing financial, positional, or personal rewards that are appropriate for the decision or action

Ethical Issues of Modern Corporations

What kinds of ethics problems crop up in the business world? Hundreds, of course; maybe thousands. Here are some of the more common, particularly those that affect HR managers.

Employees' fair share. Equity and fair share for employees are issues of increasing concern. Confronted by rising inflation and higher prices, employees want to see more of company profits expended on things that will benefit them—health and accident coverage, employee services, child care, improved working conditions, and so on.

Employees' rights. The issue of employee rights centers around the relationship between employers and employees. There are two types: legal rights, which are specified or protected by law, such as the rights of due process, free speech, to vote, and to form unions, and moral rights, which are not necessarily specified or protected by law, such as the right to be treated with dignity and respect. Since employees have voluntarily entered into a relationship with an employer, do they have the right to refuse a test for AIDS? A lie-detector test? Blow the whistle on a dangerous product or defective equipment? Participate in managing the organization? Most HR managers would answer yes, but many others disagree.

Affirmative action. The affirmative action issue has to do with the right of employees to be treated equally and without discrimination in matters of hiring, pay, and promotion. Discrimination, actions taken against protected groups, such as women, minorities, and the disabled, is one aspect of people–organizational relationships. Affirmative action is something quite different. Affirmative action policy has taken two forms: favoring qualified minorities when hiring or promoting employees, and establishing quota systems to regulate the proportion of minority members hired or promoted in accordance with an ideal distribution of employees on the basis of sex, race, creed, or ethnicity.

HR managers can exert considerable influence in the area of affirmative action since they, with the advice and assistance of legal counsel, develop policies with respect to employment, pay, benefits, training and development, promotion, and so on. And they are the prime movers in implementing policies in these areas.

International trade. The growing number of American businesses engaged in international marketing and trade poses some new problems. Managers are being forced to deal with difficult cultural enigmas and dilemmas—including U.S. laws forbidding actions that are acceptable ways of doing business in foreign countries.

HR managers are playing an increasingly critical role in training managers, technicians, and other employees for service overseas and for staffing joint foreign–U.S. manufacturing ventures within the United States. They can do much to prevent unethical decisions and actions through these programs.

Doing business with the government. With the expansion of the government's "contracting out" programs, which is now being extended to services as well as products, many companies are dealing with the government for the first time—and with the ethical issues posed by these new relationships. Here again, HR managers can influence the moral tone of doing business—and even have a direct impact. Many requests for proposals issued by local, state, and federal government departments and agencies are for training programs of one kind or another. Literally dozens of private corporations, through their HR departments, bid for these contracts.

Financial reporting. In recent years, fraudulent financial reporting by individuals and companies have posed a very real threat to the integrity of the business world. The HR manager's responsibility here is to monitor financial management and financial reporting within his or her department, with special attention to the control of funds, purchasing matters, and travel vouchers.

Advertising. Although there are state and federal laws and several agencies created to protect consumers, unfair and deceptive advertisements are not uncommon. HR departments are not immune, particularly as they begin marketing their materials and services outside their own company. HR departments have been known to make exorbitant claims about their products, particularly training programs. Their promises of reductions in trainee time, attrition, and costs and increases in skill and productivity are misleading, if not outright falsehoods.

Confidentiality. There are at least two aspects to the issue of confidentiality: corporate (goals, financial status, product development, and company documents) and personal (information about health conditions, family status, career goals and objectives, and job performance found in appraisals and other personnel records). Obviously, the HR department is deeply involved in collecting information about employees—from personal data about their background and health to job performance data. This is a sensitive area, one that requires carefully developed policies and continuous monitoring of procedures.

Treatment of employees. Despite the gaggle of laws guaranteeing equality in regard to recruitment, screening, selection, assignment, transfer, promotion, compensation, benefits, training and development, discipline, and layoffs and termination, discriminatory practices continue. Regardless of statutes prohibiting it, sexual harassment remains a serious problem. And though labor laws have done much to protect the rights of employees and to ensure safe and healthful working conditions, violations continue to occur.

So, to ensure fair treatment for all, the conditions of work require continuous assessment. Obviously HR managers must be deeply involved in the process.

Graft and kickbacks. Today's headlines are full of stories of monumental bribery and payoffs, but HR managers face more ordinary forms of graft. A common one is the practice of taking free familiarization trips, ostensibly to evaluate a facility as a potential seminar site, when the traveler has no meeting-planning responsibilities, accepting trips to exotic locations knowing full well that such facilities will never be used. Another common problem is accepting extravagant gifts (bribes, not incentives) from contractors, clients, customers, or suppliers.

Building an Ethical Organization

Talking about ethics is a bit like preaching to the faithful: people with clear and consistent values don't need a dissertation; they need solid ideas on exerting a positive influence on their work environment, enhancing and enriching the moral climate of the organization. In practical, tangible terms, what can be done? In particular, what can HR managers do?

Top-Management Example

Probably nothing is more important to an ethical corporate atmosphere than the moral tone and example set by top management—the chief executive officer and the board of directors. The personal values of the CEO and other top executives, powered by their authority, set the ethical tone of an organization. For that reason, standards of ethical conduct must be formulated systematically at the top level of management. And HR managers must assume responsibility for convincing top management of the importance of the example they set for other managers and lower-level employees and for influencing them to demonstrate their concern for moral values and ethical practice.

Management must make certain that every department plays a role in fostering employee compliance with corporate ethical standards. It must oversee the development of policies to fit each department, focusing on things that are likely to crop up as moral or ethical dilemmas in connection with the activities of the department, rather than generalized, "one size fits all" policies.

Top executives must insist that managers tell their people clearly and explicitly what is expected of them in the way of ethical behavior. They must tell employees not only what to do and what not to do but also how to deal with violations. They must encourage line managers and workers at all levels to spot and report potential ethical problems. They must conduct climate and attitude surveys and provide feedback on results. They must get as much help and input as possible—ask their people for recommendations for changes in policies and procedures. And they must establish a hotline for anonymously reporting unethical behavior.

Written Codes and Standards

If management is to build ethical relationships with all its constituencies, it must constantly test its own values and the policies that result from them. And then take the next step: articulate and disseminate its ethical values in written form. HR managers should play leading roles in developing and communicating ethical codes, rules, and standards: convincing top management of the need for such documents, establishing and supervising a task force to draft the documents, and communicating the finished product to all employees, after it has been approved by the board of control.

Code of ethics. An effective code of ethics is clear, specific, positive, and direct. It communicates in unmistakable terms what is to be done—the ethical standards that the organization demands be met. Ideally, the code is developed by a group of employees representing the various levels and functions of the organization. Also, a corporate code of ethics should be

- Reasonably consistent with reality
- Not in conflict with the values of the organization, the top management group, company employees, or its various constituencies
- Reasonably consistent internally
- Not arbitrarily imposed on employees
- Subject to debate or change, not carved in stone

What topics should be included in a corporate code of ethics? Here are some possibilities.

Acceptance of costly entertainment, gifts, travel, payments, loans, services, or favors
Advertising
Affirmative action

Business with foreign governments
Commercial espionage
Compliance with corporate policy
Compliance with laws and regulations: antitrust and trade regulation, election campaign, and securities
Conduct of business with subcontractors and suppliers
Conflicts of interest and outside activities
Corporate hospitality to public officials
Corporate political contributions
Discovery and reporting of violations
Employment by or receipt of compensation from other organizations
Environmental compliance
Equal opportunity
Fair competition, bargaining, and bidding
Extortion and kickbacks
Fees to consultants and agents
Financial interests in franchises of the corporation or its subsidiaries
Financial interests in or indebtedness to other organizations
Foreign Corrupt Practices Act of 1977
Foreign boycotts and restrictive trade practices
Full communication with management and auditors
General integrity
Hazardous waste and pollution
Insider information
Loans and borrowing
Moonlighting
Political activity of employees
Political contributions
Pricing, negotiation, and performance of contracts
Privacy
Protection of confidential information
Preservation of assets
Public relations
Purchase and sale of stock by officers and directors
Quality and testing
Recording of funds, assets, and disbursements
Relationships with government officials
Relationships with suppliers
Reports and assurances
Technology, information and security
Theft
Transactions with agencies of the U.S. government
Whistle blowing

A portion of one company's code of business conduct and ethics is shown in Figure 13-2.

Employee handbooks. A good way of informing employees of the ethical standards they are expected to meet is a booklet of guidelines for ethical conduct. It should contain materials such as:

- The importance of honesty and integrity to the individual and the organization
- Policies about giving and receiving gifts and gratuities
- The pitfalls of coverup, deception, and coercion
- How to set a model of probity and acceptable conduct for subordinates to emulate

Figure 13-2.   Sample code of business conduct and ethics.

Summarized below are Sundstrand's commitments, which are a prime element in conducting our business with integrity:

- We will conduct ourselves in a legal and ethical manner in all aspects of our business.
- To our customers, we are committed to providing value through quality products and services which meet or exceed requirements and specifications, delivered according to agreed schedules.
- To our suppliers, we are committed to being a good customer and will emphasize fair competition, a sense of responsibility, and long lasting relationships.
- To the communities in which we are located and to society as a whole, we are committed to responsible corporate citizenship.
- To our shareholders, in pursuit of our growth and earnings objectives, we are committed to keeping the highest standards of integrity at the forefront of our activity and exercising prudence in the use of Company assets and resources.
- To our employees we are committed to provide employment, compensation, training, promotions, upgrading and other conditions of employment without regard to race, color, creed, sex, age, physical handicap or national origin and, to take affirmative action, as appropriate, to ensure the meeting of these objectives and employment of Viet Nam era veterans; and to maintain safe and healthy working conditions.

From *Business Conduct and Ethics Reference Manual*, Sundstrand Corporation, January 1989, p. 2. Used by permission.

- Proper relationships with clients, customers, dealers, suppliers, contractors, and consultants
- Responsibilities with respect to funds, plans, facilities, equipment, supplies, products, merchandise, and other company assets
- Time, property, and fund accountability, including protection of company property, commitment of funds, and travel and expense accounts
- Responsibilities for the conduct of inspections and the validity of reports and records
- The consequences of avarice, dishonesty, misconduct, disobedience, or deviations from policies and regulations, and toleration of these violations by subordinates

A useful format employs questions and answers. For example:

Q. A travel agency has given me a leather briefcase as a holiday gift. May I keep it?
A. No. You may keep a gift only if it is of nominal value. Otherwise, you must return the gift with a polite thank-you letter and an explanation that company policy prohibits accepting gifts of more than nominal value.
Q. A tennis tournament is being sponsored by a supplier of training materials. May I play and keep any prizes I might win?
A. That depends on the location of the tournament, how often it is held, the value of potential prizes, and your responsibilities in dealing with the supplier. Although participation may be appropriate in some circumstances, you should only do so after approval of your superior.
Q. My supplier of computer-based instructional software is in town for a meeting and has invited my husband and me to dinner. May we accept?
A. You must always avoid even the appearance of impropriety. Expensive dinners and luncheons or other forms of lavish daytime, evening, or weekend entertainment should be shunned. If you are visiting a supplier's factory, you may accept a modest working luncheon in the company cafeteria or a nearby restaurant so long as they are inexpensive and infrequent. Of course you are expected to reciprocate should you be visited by the supplier at one of our facilities.
Q. Our current insurance adviser has asked me to assist her in a consulting capacity to develop a training program for another client. The program would be of no interest to our firm. Would this represent a conflict of interest?

A. Our conflict of interest policy requires you to get permission in advance. However, approval is unlikely because this consulting assignment could create the appearance of a conflict of interest.

Countermeasures

There are several effective countermeasures HR managers can marshal against unethical behavior, measures that can reduce the chances of violations and the opportunities for wrongdoing.

Employee screening and selection. First and foremost is careful screening and selection of employees. Hiring ethical people in the first place is perhaps the best way to ensure that employees will consistently make the right choices when confronted by moral dilemmas.

For extremely sensitive positions, where the costs of selection errors are totally unacceptable, such as in national or corporate security matters, accessibility to drugs, and law enforcement, stringent screening is indicated. That kind of screening typically involves checks of FBI, police, school, and financial records, or even a complete background investigation involving interview of former employers, peers, colleagues, and friends. For most positions, such in-depth screening practices are not required. Nevertheless, for even routine hiring this is a potential minefield. Ask the wrong questions or use the wrong procedures and you run the risk of violating the law. So, be sure that your recruiting advertisements and guidelines and your screening and selection policies and procedures will pass muster from EEO standpoints.

Although a few "honesty tests" (psychological tests) are available for job applicants, they should be used with caution, if at all. In any case, they must be professionally developed and validated, and they must be administered and interpreted by trained psychologists or psychometrists. Avoid the use of lie detectors. Although they may be legally used under certain conditions, they are too controversial and unreliable for most business situations.

So, what can you do in the hiring process? Although it is difficult to distinguish the ethical from the unethical job applicants, there are a few indicators. Here are a few suggestions that may be of some help.

Always review application forms and résumés carefully and never fail to follow up by making telephone checks with applicants' immediate supervisors in their last few jobs. That tactic alone will often identify truly unethical people, those with a track record of unprofessional practices or unacceptable standards of conduct.

During employment interviews, look for clues that signify the applicant's potential for engaging in unethical behavior. Ask questions such as the following: Who has served or is now a role model for you? Is it ever appropriate to break a rule or violate a policy? Of the groups you belong to, which one gives you the most satisfaction? Why? Have you ever made waves? What were the circumstances?

Throughout the interview, listen carefully. Use not only your ears but also your eyes, watching facial expressions and body language. Attend to verbal and nonverbal clues that communicate passivity about moral dilemmas. Be sensitive and alert to signs that people:

- Appear to have difficulty empathizing with others
- Show prejudices and engage in stereotyping
- Place obedience to authority over involvement, fairness, and justice
- Talk in absolutes, hyperbole, and generalizations
- Are totally absorbed in their own interests—what they will get from the position in salary, benefits, and promotion—rather than in what they can contribute to the company

Look for people who:

- Show loyalty to and trust in others
- Have uncompromisingly and sincerely adhered to a moral code or set of values
- Have demonstrated that they are good employees, neighbors, and citizens—people who have shown that they care by providing service to their organizations, their communities, and other people
- Have proved their ability to love, to work, and to form commitments

Fair and equitable treatment. Employees who are satisfied with their jobs, their status, compensation, benefits, job security, and their prospects for advancement are likely to be loyal to their organization. Employees who believe they are overworked and underpaid, are not given the recognition they deserve, or are dissatisfied with their working conditions are likely to become disgruntled and angry. They may, and often do, develop a desire to "get even" or strike back. The result is all too often dishonesty, stealing, or some other unethical act.

HR managers can make a big contribution here. They can provide training for supervisors and managers, the goal of fair and equitable treatment of employees. And they can be the impetus for corporatewide programs to improve working conditions, such as quality circles, quality of work life, compensation and benefits, counseling and career development, and employee assistance programs.

Personal mental strategy. Managers must develop and apply major mental and emotional strategies to counter the blandishments and allure of ethical snares. They need something to help them overcome the temptation to defy the odds, to disobey the rules and not get caught, to try to bend the laws to their own advantage. Here are some ways to counter these tendencies.

- Remember that testing situations in life are inevitable. There will always be pressures from seniors, peers, subordinates, or people outside the organization to take shortcuts or yield to baser instincts. Even minor defeats are humbling, but they can be helpful if they result in new resolve to persevere.
- Learn to spot the big lie in temptation and corruption. They promise more than they can possibly deliver—and they always leave behind more complex problems than existed before. Don't fall into the trap of self-justification for errors of judgment: "I don't know what got into me. I guess I just wasn't thinking." Be honest with yourself. Become realistic and self-disciplined.
- Remember that feelings and emotions flow from actions and not the reverse. Take charge of your feelings by acting in accordance with standards of rightness, goodness, and ought-to-ness.
- Replace your bad habits with good ones. Stay away from people and situations where your standards can be defeated. Avoid being idle, that's when you are most vulnerable. Stay physically and mentally active.

Physical security. Limiting employees' access to valuable documents, products, information, corporate plans and forecasts, and other "trade secrets" is a wise protective strategy. If your organization does not have a physical security system, propose it without delay. It should have these features:

1. A written and strictly enforced policy on access to valuable items, including information, published and distributed to all employees

2. Storage of documents or other valuable items in locked containers, filing cabinets, or vaults
3. Controlled access to storage areas
4. Strict document control: every document prominently stamped RESTRICTED or CONFIDENTIAL in block letters at the top and bottom of each page in a dark color, numbered, signed for upon receipt, logged in and out, and shredded or burned when no longer needed

Internal accounting and administrative controls. Effective internal accounting and administrative control systems will do much to prevent violations of ethical standards. Although HR managers can do little to determine the controls of the organization as a whole, they do have a responsibility for installing such systems within their own departments. Accounting controls should be designed to protect corporate assets from misuse and assure the accuracy and authenticity of financial records. Administrative controls should be structured to make certain that corporate policies regarding the management of assets are being observed by all employees. Both types are needed to protect corporate and department assets.

Disclosure agreements. A well-designed and solid confidentiality or disclosure agreement should be prepared, signed by new employees, witnessed by a corporate official, and filed. The document should be a part of the hiring package prepared by the HR department (with the advice of legal counsel) and administered to all entering employees. The agreement should clearly describe the responsibility of the employee to protect secrets or other items of value to the organization, define what items are included in that category, and identify the penalties for violations.

Also, when employees leave, whether through resignation, layoff, firing, or retirement, a portion of the exit interview should be devoted to reminding them of their obligation to keep confidential information to themselves.

Education and training. People are more often nonethical than unethical; that is, they lack ethical standards and values. Can nonethical or unethical people learn to behave ethically? Yes, they can. People are not born with values and standards. They are learned (or not learned) at home, in the church, synagogue, or mosque, at school, and in the workplace. Inappropriate standards can be replaced with worthier values. Voids in standards can be filled. More and more organizations are now conducting their own ethics workshops and seminars for employees, sending them to public seminars, or contracting with ethics training specialists for tailored courses. What are the objectives of such training?

- To sensitize people (particularly managers and supervisors) to ethical dilemmas
- To define business ethics
- To enhance managers' ability to recognize and analyze ethical problems
- To improve managers' capacity for ethical decision making
- To help managers understand the corporation's policies and obligations to its employees, suppliers, customers and clients, and the public at large
- To help managers learn how to integrate ethics into management practice, particularly in planning, policy making, and organization change

HR managers, in their capacity as primary training agent for the organization, play a significant role here. Their first job is to gain enthusiastic top management support for ethics training for employees. Next, they must locate a credible and qualified seminar leader or team of instructors. The next step is to identify and analyze the specific ethical issues, problems, and opportunities that exist. That step is essential if the content of the training is to be relevant to those who attend. Using those problems and issues, the task becomes one of selecting or developing case studies and role-playing skits of realistic, work-related situations and using them as the basis for discussion and resolution by participants in the training program.

The experience of many companies in recent years has taught us that certain conditions are essential to the success of ethics training. Here are some of the most critical.

- If possible, conduct the workshop away from the plant or office—in neutral territory.
- Allow enough uninterrupted time for the sessions.
- Bring in a knowledgable resource person unconnected with the company, a consultant.
- To emphasize the importance of the training, get the CEO to participate in the kickoff ceremony.
- Don't preach; allow people to identify their own ethical values and level of ethical behavior; challenge their reasoning; make them aware of different viewpoints.
- Teach people the processes of analysis leading to higher levels of ethical behavior.

- Use realistic ethical dilemmas, problems, and cases—issues that are likely to arise in the organization—for presentations, discussions, simulations, and role playing.

Internal audits. The internal audit is one of the most potentially productive means of monitoring the ethical culture of an organization. An audit is a planned, systematic means of assessing the extent to which corporate codes of ethics and policies on ethical behavior are being carried out. Clearly, this strategy is an HR responsibility. The HR manager should propose the audit, plan it, report its findings, supervise its conduct by an independent consultant, and develop and implement remedial strategies.

An audit invariably involves interviewing and observing, reviewing records and reports, administering questionnaires and surveys, identifying and analyzing deviations, determining causes, taking remedial actions, including improvements to systems and procedures, and following up.

To be successful, an audit must have several critical items:

- The unqualified support of top management and managers of the organization
- The resources needed to launch the project and see it through to completion
- Skilled, competent, credible, dedicated, and independent auditors
- Thorough advance planning and communication and coordination with all parties involved—management, workers at all levels, customers and clients, suppliers, consultants, and vendors
- Coverage of all key ethical issues
- Objectivity in data collection and analysis
- Complete candor by everyone who deals with the auditors
- Conscientious written reporting of findings and feedback to all constituencies

Enforcement and sanctions. Although the most effective form of control is self-control, a sense of personal responsibility for one's own conduct and behavior, there are circumstances that demand sanctions or censure. When employees have been told the ground rules of acceptable behavior and the consequences of failure to conform, and they still choose to violate those norms and standards, formal sanctions must be imposed.

The HR manager is responsible for formulating draft policies regarding sanctions and getting them approved by the board of directors. Within his or her own department, the HR manager is responsible for implementing the policies and handling violations.

Before sanctions are applied, the following conditions must exist:

- Prior identification of employees to whom the policies apply
- Provisions for expeditious handling of violations
- Advance identification of managers or supervisors empowered to take specific actions
- Consideration of all the facts and circumstances surrounding the behavior
- Provision that employees be informed of their transgressions and given an opportunity to respond
- An appropriate and progressive sequence of adverse or disciplinary actions for repeated offenses: oral admonition, written warning or reprimand, probation, reduction or discontinuance of performance award or bonus that might otherwise be granted, cut in salary, suspension without pay, demotion, or termination (except in cases of gross misconduct or grave violations or rules, where immediate discharge is justified)
- The right to appeal a finding or adverse action

As a working manager, let this be your guiding principle: reprimand people immediately when you discover that they are doing or have done something unethical. If the offense is serious enough, fire them.

Reporting violations. In a well-run organization, employees never go over their immediate supervisor's head with a complaint or a problem. They have no need to. They go straight to the supervisor, who invariably listens, responds to the complaint, and takes the action that is required. But that kind of situation is far from universal. In many organizations, there are supervisors and managers who, for one reason or another, either can't or won't listen, or listen and then take no action.

People are justified in bypassing their superiors when ethical or moral issues are involved. They have a duty to themselves, the company, and to the public to disclose situations involving fraud, public health or safety, or the public interest. Therefore, all employees should know their responsibility to report a violation of company policy either to their immediate supervisor or to someone higher in the chain of command, and they should also be given guarantees of anonymity and immunity from retaliatory action.

Recognition and rewards. Just as sanctions are an unequivocal requirement for violations of ethical standards, rewards for ethical conduct are equally imperative. It takes more than a modicum of courage to face an ethical dilemma squarely, and it takes guts to make the right decision or take the correct action.

Unfortunately, too often people pay a high price for taking an action that is right but unpopular, or one that adversely affects an individual or group. Management must even the score by rewarding the action with recognition, commendation, compensation, and other forms of reward. Moral and ethical contributions to the company's reputation are no less important than accomplishments of other types.

Here again, the HR manager is responsible for sensitizing top management to the need for using recognition and rewards to reinforce ethical conduct, and recommending the types of rewards that are appropriate. And, within his or her own department, the HR manager has the duty of carrying out the program.

Summary

Ethics in business is concerned with dilemmas—the clash of two or more moral values. It relies on reason and not on religion. It focuses on business actions and practices, and it makes judgments about those actions in the light of some human value. The ethical act is the one that best serves the ideals of honesty, integrity, morality, and good management practice.

The roots of ethical behavior can be traced to our culture, the law, basic American and community values, organization culture and atmosphere, social institutions, the values of the chief executive officer and top managers, the standards of friends and colleagues, work and careers, individual personal values, and professional codes.

The sources of ethical dilemmas are legion: corporate social responsibility, corporate competition, individual competition, and human frailty. Pressures to behave unethically come from several sources: self-interest, superiors, peers, subordinates, and the organization itself. Professional managers should never give in to these pressures, or they risk losing their effectiveness as leaders.

HR managers have a dual role with respect to ethics: to exert a positive influence on the tone of the organization, and to develop an ethical climate in their own department.

Those who want to help build a strong ethical culture in their organization have several avenues. They can convince senior management to be visible examples and actively demonstrate their concern for ethical business practices. They can guide the process of developing and communicating the company's code of ethics. And they can activate a number of countermeasures, including training, independent audits, sanctions, and rewards for ethical conduct.

For Further Reading, Viewing, and Listening

Abelson, Raziel, and Marie-Louise Friquegnon, eds. *Ethics for Modern Life*. 3rd ed. New York: St. Martin Press, 1986.

Bahm, Archie J. *Ethics: The Science of Oughtness*. Albuquerque, N.M.: Bahm, 1980.

Baumrin, Bernard, and Benjamin Freedman. *Moral Responsibility and the Professions*. New York: Haven Publications, 1983.

Bayles, Michael D. *Professional Ethics*. Belmont, Calif.: Wadsworth Publishing Company, 1981.

Blanchard, Kenneth, and Norman Vincent Peale. *The Power of Ethical Management*. New York: William Morrow and Company, 1988.

Brody, Baruch A. *Ethics and Its Applications*. San Diego, Calif.: Harcourt Brace Jovanovich, 1983.

Business Ethics (58-minute videocassette, 68-minute audiocassette). Produced and distributed by Kantola Productions, 152 17th Ave., San Francisco, CA 94121, 1988.

Donaldson, Thomas, and Patricia H. Werhane, eds. *Ethical Issues in Business: A Philosophical Approach*. 2nd ed. Englewood Cliffs, N.J.: Prentice-Hall, 1983.

Gandossy, Robert P. "The Tough Job of Shutting Down Corporate Fraud." *Management Review*, September 1988, pp. 39–43.

Goodpaster, Kenneth E. *Ethics in Management*. Boston: Harvard Business School Publishing Division, 1985.

Halberstam, Joshua. *Virtues and Values: An Introduction to Ethics*. Englewood Cliffs, N.J.: Prentice-Hall, 1988.

Hayes, James L. "Ethics." Part 4 in *Memos for Management: Leadership*. New York: AMACOM, 1984.

Hoffman, Michael, and others, eds. *Corporate Governance and Institutional Ethics*. Lexington, Mass.: Lexington Books, 1984.

Johnson, Oliver. *Ethics*. 5th ed. New York: Holt, Rinehart & Winston, 1984.

Management Ethics: A View From the Top (14-minute videocassette). Ethics Resource Center, 600 New Hampshire Ave., N.W., Washington, DC 20037, 1984.

A Matter of Judgment: Conflicts of Interest in the Workplace (30-minute videocassette). Produced by Jacoby/Storm Productions, 1986. Distributed by Ethics Resource Center, 1025 Connecticut Ave., N.W., Suite 1003, Washington, DC 20037.

Moeller, Clark. "Ethics Training." Chapter 84 in *Human Resources Management and Development Handbook,* edited by William R. Tracey. New York: AMACOM, 1985.

Nolan, Richard T., and Frank G. Kirkpatrick. *Living Issues in Ethics.* Belmont, Calif.: Wadsworth Publishing Company, 1982.

The Parable of the Sadhu (30-minute videocassette). Harvard Business School Publishing Division, Boston, MA 02163-1098, 1987.

Pastin, Mark. *The Hard Problems of Management: Gaining the Ethics Edge.* San Francisco: Jossey-Bass, 1986.

Shea, Gordon F. *Practical Ethics.* New York: AMACOM, 1988.

Srivastva, Suresh, and Associates. *Executive Integrity: The Search for High Human Values in Organizational Life.* San Francisco: Jossey-Bass, 1988.

Toffler, Barbara Ley. *Tough Choices: Managers Talk Ethics.* New York: John Wiley & Sons, 1986.

Wasserstrom, Richard A. *Today's Moral Problems.* 3rd ed. New York: Macmillan Publishing Company, 1985.

White, Louis, and Kevin Wooten. *Professional Ethics and Practice in Organizational Development.* New York: Praeger, 1985.

White, Thomas I. *Right and Wrong: A Brief Guide to Understanding Ethics.* Englewood Cliffs, N.J.: Prentice-Hall, 1988.

Yezzi, Ron. *Directing Human Actions: Perspectives on Basic Ethical Issues.* Lanham, Md.: University Press of America, 1986.

14

Developing Yourself
Commanding Your Own Destiny

Career growth and development are vital to your well-being and your survival in the business world. Shifting work values, technological change, organizational downsizing, takeovers, and a host of other dramatic changes—most of which are beyond your control—demand that you be ready to change jobs, if not careers, without missing a step.

In this era of frequent mergers, it's not enough to be good at what you now do; you must have new skills if you are to remain competitive. You'll need a broader range of knowledge and skills so you can adjust to a wider range of duties and responsibilities. To complicate matters, information in most fields today is growing at an increasing rate. In human resources management, the amount of knowledge has probably doubled in the last five to seven years. If you think you are keeping pace by standing still, watch out—you are actually moving backward.

Most HR managers have hopes and dreams for their own future as professionals. The trouble is that too few have made a commitment to their own personal and professional development, and still fewer have standards against which to measure their own progress and accomplishment. That shortcoming must be remedied if career dreams are to be realized.

What does it take?

It takes planning. You need to figure out where you have been, where you want to go and who you want to be, and how to get there. You must select meaningful goals for your life and take the career and self-development actions that will get you there. To do that you need to identify your values, preferences, abilities, and disabilities, make choices and set goals, take the actions required to achieve those goals, and plan for contingencies and blocks to progress. Self-development is planned, not coincidental. Take another look at the homework you did in Step 3 of Chapter 11.

It takes knowledge and skills. You need to improve yourself, develop your people, get work done, and handle difficult situations—and all that takes knowledge and skills. You need to stay current with HR issues and developments, expand your knowledge of HR practice, and improve professional performance. You need to be able to design and develop effective training and development programs, along with other HR strategies and techniques.

It takes self-assessment. You need to step back from the stress of your position and reexamine your style, strengths, and weaknesses. Then develop a plan to exploit the strengths and shore up the weaknesses. So your first step in self-development is to prepare an accurate self-assessment and then follow up with specific development goals and objectives.

In this process you may uncover some surprising things about yourself. A man whose career had flourished for some years in an industrial company volunteered to be a "loaned executive" for his area's United Way committee, and discovered that the nonprofit sector provided him a great sense of accomplishment. Doing his self-assessment, he realized that a high level of personal satisfaction was important to him—and that it was missing from his current position.

It takes redefinition of "success." The more talents you develop, the more skills you acquire, the more opportunities will be open to you. But you must keep one important fact of organizational life firmly in mind. Promotion, once considered inevitable for solid performers with high potential, is now becoming relatively uncommon. Flatter corporate organization charts, slimmer top management levels, fewer vice-presidents, and more and more outside consultants are the way of the corporate future, as companies cope with downsizing and restructuring. For many, that means premature structural job plateauing and shattered career expectations.

You need to consider seriously the opportunities and challenges presented by job enrichment and enlargement, temporary positions, and lateral transfers, with their ability to prevent content plateauing. You will need to redefine success, to see it in terms other than promotion—in the forms of new challenges, new experiences, new contacts, new outlooks, new satisfactions.

It takes commitment. Who's responsible for your career development? You are. You must take charge of your own career direction, and not expect your boss to provide the direction and the answers. That's why this process is called *self*-development.

What do you need to do? Identify your career options both within and outside the organization. Weigh and compare the trade-offs of different career paths. Then develop your action plan, both long term and short term.

If it is to do any good, a self-development program must be tailored specifically for the individual. For this reason, it's not possible to describe a model or a "typical" program. However, all good programs do share these traits.

Self-directed and managed. This means that you assume full responsibility for your own learning, change, and development by bringing to bear all your personal and organizational resources. You, and not the organization, are in charge of setting goals, identifying and using sources of information, defining and evaluating success.

Goal-driven. Self-development programs must be directed toward the attainment of clearly stated, realistic, and achievable personal and professional goals. They must be future oriented, and they must be thoroughly planned and sharply focused. Goals should be set forth in writing, reviewed at least annually, and revised as needed.

Flexible. Situations change constantly; so do challenges and opportunities. A self-development program set in concrete cannot be responsive to such changes. You can't afford to lock yourself into a program that may become impossible to achieve or inconsistent with organizational realities.

Professional. A viable self-development program should contribute to the reputation and improvement of the HR profession. It does not protect the status quo; rather it accommodates and welcomes change. It provides the basis for creating new theories, new methods and approaches, and improved practices and thereby advances the profession.

Efficient and cost-effective. Waste in any form—time, energy, funds, materials, and people—is scrupulously avoided in a good self-development program. Resources are selected carefully and used wisely.

Relevant to career stage. An effective self-development program must be relevant to the status you have reached in the profession, your current career stage.

Assessing and Analyzing Yourself

One of the first steps in self-development is to conduct a thorough and honest self-analysis. Take a good hard look at your career status, personality, abilities, interests, and needs. Let's see what is involved in those various areas.

Career Status

First, analyze where you are now in your career.

- Identify and define the major problems in your career and your job. As things stand, where will you be in five years? Ten years? And where do you want to be? The gap is the problem.
- Look at the environment from several perspectives—personal, social, financial, and cultural. What are the challenges, threats, and risks in your piece of the world? What are the opportunities?
- List the critical issues and problems that must be considered in developing a long-range career development plan. Rank them according to importance. What actions can you take that would produce success? What actions would prevent failure?
- Do you feel stuck in your present job? Is your career path clear? Do you know what career opportunities are available to you?
- Are there other blocks to your self-development, such as lack of self-confidence, an inclination to overlook shortcomings, indecision about personal goals, or reluctance to change? Begin by comparing your performance against your own past achievements rather than against those of colleagues or competitors.

Personality Self-Analysis

One of the hardest things to do is to look at ourselves objectively and realistically, without self-lionization, deception or hopelessness. But it must be done if we are to achieve self-understanding—a balanced picture of our failings and imperfections, feelings and emotions, flairs and talents, and biases and predispositions. What are the requirements for gaining such insights? Psychological wellness, an open mind, determination to find and accept the truth about ourselves, a belief in our capacity to change, and the ability to think logically.

How do you find out the truth about yourself? Here are some approaches.

Questioning. Ask yourself some tough questions and give honest answers. Here are a few samples:

Why am I here? What is my purpose in life?

Why do I work for this company? Does my job match my purpose in life?

What has the company done to help me achieve my purposes? What else can it do?

How can I help in that endeavor?

Put your answers on paper. Read and think about them. Put them aside for a day or two, then, read them again. You're sure to learn a great deal about yourself from this simple exercise.

Reflection. Systematically probe your past. Reflect on your memories of relationships, your conflicts, your experiences, and your successes and failures. Your goal here is to identify the critical incidents that made you what you are today. What were your parents like? Your teachers? How did you react to them? How did you get along with your friends and neighbors? What successes in school and college made you the proudest? What were your biggest disappointments? Write down your answers; think about them. Take the time to write an autobiography; it will give you insights into yourself that no other activity can provide—and it will be something your children will treasure.

Daily journal. Keep a daily journal for one week; record a variety of situations and your reactions to them. Include descriptions of at least five highs and lows—situations that caused you to feel elated, depressed, angry, pleased, frustrated, or satisfied. At the end of the week, analyze them carefully. Is there a pattern, a certain type of situation, a particular individual, or special time of the day when you react in a certain way? Were you an active or passive participant? Did you contribute to the satisfying situations? What would have happened if your role in the situation were changed? Try to put yourself in the other person's place. Can you now predict your behavior better than you could before?

Comparative ratings. Develop a list of personality traits, descriptive terms that could be applied to you, and place them vertically on a sheet of paper as shown in Figure 14-1. Across the top, make columns labeled Self, Boss, Subordinate, Spouse, Best Friend, and Judgment. In the "Self" column, place a check mark opposite each trait that you believe applies to you. Next, put yourself in the shoes of your boss, your subordinate, your spouse, and your best friend. Put a check mark for the traits they would say you have. Be

Figure 14-1.   A comparative rating scale.

Trait	Self	Boss	Subordinate	Spouse	Best Friend	Judgment
Aloof						
Aggressive						
Argumentative						
Arrogant						
Cautious						
Confident						
Dreamer						
Eager						
Easily swayed						
Easygoing						
Efficient						
Egotistical						
Fair						
Firm						
Friendly						
Generous						
Grouchy						
Hostile						
Hotheaded						
Humble						
Impulsive						
Kind						
Lenient						
Observant						
Optimistic						
Pessimistic						
Reliable						
Selfish						
Sentimental						
Shrewd						
Slow						
Sociable						
Stubborn						
Tactful						
Talkative						
Tense						
Truthful						

Adapted from *Effective Psychology for Managers* by Mortimer R. Feinberg, Ph.D. © 1965. Reprinted by permission of the publisher, Prentice-Hall, Inc., Englewood Cliffs, N.J.: Prentice-Hall, Inc., pp. 46–47.

sure you have included roughly the same number of negative and positive traits. If your list leans heavily toward positives or negatives, you are probably not being objective enough.

Then evaluate the check marks. Put a plus sign in the "Judgment" column for each trait on which there is general agreement between your evaluation and the theoretical verdict of others; these represent your core personality. Put a minus sign where you and others generally disagree. If there is a strong thread of difference, try to determine which response is closest to the truth, and try to figure out why those people see you differently.

Skills and Abilities

New skills represent "value added" for managers. Skill requirements vary from position to position and organization to organization. However, there are many benchmark skills that must be a part of the repertoire of any competent HR manager (or any other manager, for that matter).

Develop a list of the skills that you believe are the most critical to success as a HR manager. (The table of contents of this book and its companion volume, *Critical Skills*, may serve the purpose quite nicely.) Then rate yourself on each one; are you proficient, or does that skill need improvement? (See Figure 14-2.) Be honest with yourself. Cross check your evaluation against the comments of your boss in your last performance appraisal.

Knowledge

To be competitive, HR managers must have a much broader range of knowledge than was expected of their predecessors even five years ago. They must know the principles, concepts, and facts that will enable them to handle a broad range of assignments and to work for more than one company and one boss.

Go back to your self-analysis in Figure 14-2. For each skill that you feel needs some improvement, work up a list of all the knowledge you would need to acquire. For example, suppose you checked that budgeting needs improvement. Your knowledge list would include:

Key financial terms and concepts
    Balance sheet
    Assets, liabilities, and equities
    Debit and credit
    Profit, profitability, and return on investment

    Revenues, expenses, and net income
    Gross margin
Financial indicators
    Cash flow
    Ratio analysis
    Price/earnings ratios
    Net working capital
    Breakeven analysis
    Cash reconciliations
Basic budgeting approaches
    Program budgeting
    Incremental budgeting
    Performance budgeting
    Flexible budgeting
    Planning, programming, budgeting system
    Zero-base budgeting
Types of budgets
    Operating budgets
    Time, space, and materials budgets
    Capital expense budgets
    Cash budgets

Interests

Make a list of your career direction options: HR management, human resources development, general management, needs analysis, career development, counseling, instructional systems development, instructing, assessment and evaluation, marketing, media production, task and skill analysis, organization development, research, entrepreneurial pursuits, and independent consulting. Add any others you may have considered in the recent past. Which ones clearly attract your interest? Use the process of elimination to develop a "short list" of three to five choices. Set the list aside for a week or two and come back to it for another look. Place the options in order of priority and file the list for future reference.

Needs

Needs are the essentials of life: physiological, security, and, most important of all, psychological—the need for acceptance, attention, affection, self-esteem, achievement, independence, freedom, recognition, approval, prestige, self-realization, and self-fulfillment. All are important underpinnings of motivation and personal drive.

Figure 14-2.   A scale for rating professional skills.

Skill	Proficient	Need Improvement
Appraising performance		
Budgeting		
Coaching		
Counseling		
Decision making		
Delegating		
Developing yourself		
Disciplining		
Forecasting		
Hiring		
Improving productivity		
Innovating		
Inquiring		
Leading		
Managing change		
Managing costs		
Managing ethics		
Managing time		
Marketing		
Motivating		
Negotiating		
Problem sensing		
Problem solving		
Resolving conflict		
Rewarding		
Speaking		
Strategic planning		
Team building		
Writing		

Again, make a complete list of the needs that are, in your own judgment, the most potent sources of your motivation and behavior, see Figure 14-3. Include all categories—physical, security, and psychological. Even include some special ones that are characteristic of you; for example, self-confidence, decisiveness, or spirituality. Then evaluate how important each one is and determine whether it is being met.

Setting Personal Goals

A necessary step in the self-development process is to define where you want to be and what you want to be doing five or more years in

Figure 14-3.   Self-analysis of needs.

Need	Being met	Unmet and critical	Unmet and unimportant
Nutritious food			
Exercise/fitness			
Fun			
Recreation/hobbies			
Sufficient sleep			
General good health			
Pleasant place to live			
Financial security			
Social acceptance			
Help with personal problems			
Physical safety			
Adequate transportation			
Respect of co-workers			
Professional recognition			
Increased compensation			
Opportunity for advancement			
Love of family members			
Support of spouse/partner			
Spiritual sustenance			
Private time			
Recognition by boss			
Track record of accomplishments			
Time to think			
Time to play			
Approval of supervisors			
Expressed appreciation			
Others:			

the future. You need to set your career goals and make decisions about family, geography, training and education, experience, position, and salary that are appropriate to those goals.

The process involves asking yourself some hard questions—and taking your time with the answers.

Do you want to remain in human resources development, if that is your present field, or do you want to expand your horizons and get into the broader area of human resources management and utilization?

Do you want to move into the line organization as a manager of a function such as marketing?

Do you want to remain in your current geographic location or are you willing to move your family to another part of the country?

Do you want to remain with an established organization as an employee or do you want to become an entrepreneur, an owner of your own consulting business, for example?

As you begin the work of pinning your thoughts down into concrete goals, you may find some helpful ideas in these three references (see end of chapter): Ford and Lippitt, *Planning Your Future;* the videocassette *Goal Setting for Fun, Health and Profit;* and *Setting and Achieving Personal Goals.* The following suggestions may also be helpful.

- Determine whether you are more interested in planning your career within your present organization, helping to create an organization by planning your career, or planning your career advancement without restrictions on the type or location of organizations.
- Decide whether you want to create opportunities for career advancement rather than merely looking for those that exist.
- Develop a sequence of goals—short-range, intermediate-range, long-range, and ultimate—to establish a ladder reaching from where you are now to where you ultimately want to be.
- Take the time to think things through. The importance of career decisions demands careful thought and deliberation.
- Set increasingly high but realistic goals.

And, to make achievement of these future goals more likely, resolve to make some changes in the way you do things now. Consider these:

- Be willing to go the extra mile, ready to do whatever it takes to get the job done (short of totally selfish, unethical, or illegal behavior). "Good enough," "That'll do," "What difference does it make?" "So what?" "What's it to me?" "Who cares?" do not belong in your vocabulary.
- Be your severest critic. Check yourself on everything you do. Double check your work products before submitting them. Be sure that everything measures up to your standards and your company's.
- Keep physically and mentally fit. A high level of physical and

mental energy is essential to deal with the pressures of the modern organization.

- Improve your communication skills. Learn to listen, speak, and write better. Critique yourself regularly and get feedback from your superiors and peers.
- Restore curiosity. All of us were very curious about things as children, but somewhere in the process of growing up, we lost that sense of wonder.
- Increase sensitivity. Most of us need to improve our ability to sense the needs and emotions of other people—family, friends, bosses, subordinates, and colleagues.
- Don't get uptight. Work calmly, steadily, and easily. That doesn't mean loaf. It means taking the time to do it right the first time. Don't create unnecessary tension for yourself. You'll live longer and happier and enjoy your job more if you work calmly and with composure.

Resources to Call On

Resources for both aspects of self-development—personal and professional—are many and varied. Personal growth and development encompasses three general areas—intellectual, physical, and emotional—and includes such diverse elements as individual and group learning experiences, health and fitness programs, recreational activities, stress management, and assertiveness training, to name but a few.

Personal Development

Intellectual. No matter how much formal education you have acquired, there is always room for more learning. It can be gained individually through formal and informal courses, seminars, workshops, reading and study, and in group experiences, such as games, exercises, problems, and tests. The objective here is learning that is not directly professional or career oriented.

Physical. A comprehensive physical health program should include regular physical checkups, nutrition and weight control, exercise and fitness, and recreational activities.

Many organizations now have on-site physical fitness centers. Others provide health club memberships or group rates at nearby facilities—and even daily time off with pay to use them. If your company does not offer such services, it's up to you to incorporate a fitness program into your regular routine.

Emotional. Managers are not immune to stress-related illness. If you think you need help here, one of the first steps is to examine the possible sources of stress and explore methods of self-protection. A second essential step is to locate potential sources of assistance. Today there are many, and some are in-house programs. Employee assistance programs (EAPs) provide professional, confidential diagnosis and counseling and make outside referrals for such problems as alcoholism, substance abuse, family and financial problems, and mental and emotional illness.

Professional Development

The other big area to concentrate on is professional development—the continuous process of improving performance and potential. This includes all strategies and tactics that can contribute to technical, conceptual, managerial, and human competencies.

Formal training. Formal opportunities for continuing education and training abound, and they may take several forms: enrollment in college or university degree, nondegree, or certificate programs, evening and continuation school study, correspondence and home study courses, and attendance at public and in-house short courses, seminars, and workshops sponsored or conducted by government agencies, chambers of commerce, private institutions, professional associations, training firms, and corporate training departments. Many companies encourage participtation by granting time away from the job with pay, full or partial tuition reimbursement, grants and loans for study, and free books and instructional materials. There are numerous opportunities and options, and you should exploit them to the fullest.

To identify degree and certificate programs, consult the catalogs of colleges and universities in your area, and the *ASTD Directory of Academic Programs in Training and Development/Human Resource Development.*

Dozens of reputable organizations offer professional seminars and workshops. Most are nondegree and noncredit programs, although many offer continuing education (CEU) credits. Here are four excellent sources; where addresses are not included, consult the Appendix.

ASTD Buyer's Guide and Consultant Directory, published by the American Society for Training and Development

Training Magazine's Market Place Directory, published by *Training,* Lakewood Publications, Inc., 50 S. Ninth St., Minneapolis, MN 55402

The Select Guide to Seminars: The Quarterly Journal of Business Training and Development Courses, published by Skeibo, 44 Forester Ave., Mount Vernon, NY 10552

American Management Association Catalog of Seminars

In addition, informal development opportunities abound.

One-on-one training. One-on-one, on-the-job, day-to-day learning experiences, under the tutelage of a conscientious and experienced coach, are powerful means of learning. All of us have had experience with it because it is probably the earliest way we learned anything. More important, this method is potent because it involves learners directly, continuously, and intensively with the trainer and the skills to be learned.

Advisers and mentors. One of the most productive things you can do is select a few advisers and one mentor, people you respect and who know you and your capabilities but are not directly involved in your personal or work life. They should be winners: senior people who are good at their jobs, are highly respected in their organizations, and can serve as role models because they exemplify professional skills, beliefs, and values. Because they are experienced, they can provide advice, assistance, and career perspectives that are beyond the grasp of less experienced professionals. And because they are detached, they can offer objective evaluation of your career development plans and activities.

Learning centers. One of the easiest ways to stay current in the profession is to make use of the individualized learning centers that are rapidly becoming an important learning resource in many organizations. They permit a self-directed approach to learning that combines all the best elements of educational technology and adult learning principles.

The typical learning center offers materials in a variety of formats: audio- and videocassettes, computer-assisted and computer-managed instruction, interactive video, 8mm. and 16mm. film, programmed and conventional books and workbooks, periodicals, organization documents, and a large number of programmed materials in audiovisual forms (sound filmstrip, slides, overhead projectuals, and so on). Other delivery systems on the horizon are compact laser discs, 9mm. video, and satellite communications. You can tailor your program to fit your individual learning styles. More important, you can decide for yourself what, when, where, and how to learn.

Research. HR managers cannot rely completely on the efforts of other researchers to provide them with data for decision making. Every HR department is unique enough to warrant a modest but continuing research effort. An HR research program involves logical, reflective, systematic investigation and thinking to find the best solution to a specific problem. Research studies provide benefits to the individual conducting it as well as to the organization, the main one being that research is a development activity. It does more than produce knowledge; it also enhances careers. For that reason, in addition to encouraging and supporting a realistic research program, HR managers should become actively involved in research projects to develop themselves.

Data bases. In a growing number of organizations it is now possible to tap into on-line automated data bases. These systems can search for journal articles, newsletters, doctoral dissertations, research studies, conference reports, and books on subjects of interest. Some provide full texts of journals and newsletters; others provide information on computer software and other nonprint learning materials. If your own library or information center doesn't have access to these systems, larger public libraries and college and university libraries can often provide it.

Here are some of the reference data bases currently available; addresses for associations are located in the organizations section of the Appendix.

> *ABI/Inform,* produced by UMI/Data Courier, Inc., 620 S. Fifth St., Louisville, KY 40202.
>
> Educational Resources Information Center (ERIC), National Institute of Education, U. S. Department of Education, 1200 19th St., N.W., Washington, DC 20208.
>
> Human Resource Information Network (HRIN), Executive Telecom System, Inc., College Park North, 9585 Valpariso Ct., Indianapolis, IN 46268.
>
> *PsycINFO,* American Psychological Association.
>
> National Technical Information Service (NTIS), U.S. Department of Commerce, 5285 Port Royal Rd., Springfield, VA 22161.
>
> *TRAINET* seminar data base (for ASTD members only), American Society for Training and Development.

WILSONLINE, Business Periodicals Index, H. W. Wilson Company, University Ave., Bronx, NY 10452.

Reading, viewing, and listening. Of course, the lack of an individualized learning center or an on-line data base should not keep you from individual reading. Professional managers make regular use of books, newsletters, and periodicals, both popular and professional, to keep up to date. A list of some of the more useful publications in the field is provided at the end of this chapter.

Printed materials, audio- and videocassettes, and PC discs can be borrowed from corporate and public libraries and used at home or in the office. Audiocassettes can be used in the car or on the train on the way to and from the office.

Networking. In this context, networking refers to the process of using a community of professionals to get advice, information, and referrals. Some networks are electronic, tying members together by computers and modems. Networking is a productive strategy for expanding your learning resources. It can provide insider information on the latest developments in the field, expert opinion and advice, moral support, and access to other networks. Through contacts with knowledgeable and experienced professionals and practitioners, you can ask questions and almost immediately get answers.

One of the most useful networks to HR professionals is the Member Information Exchange (MIX) of the American Society for Training and Development (ASTD), administered by ASTD's Information Center, and available only to ASTD members.

Speaking and writing. Although often viewed as threatening situations, speaking engagements offer another important avenue for self-development. Membership in such personal-improvement groups such as Toastmasters and Junta also provide a valuable and inexpensive means of developing public speaking proficiency.

One young manager in an engineering consulting firm traces her rise in the company back to the time she was called in to pinch hit for her boss in a speaking engagement. It wasn't luck—it was her astuteness in recognizing the opportunity and her hard work in preparing an outstanding presentation on short notice.

Writing for publication provides another opportunity for career enhancement. Although few writers in the HR discipline or related fields have made it big financially (most professional journals do not offer payment for articles), peer recognition for their contributions to the professional literature has been reward enough for many.

Professional associations. Membership in professional groups is a must for career development. Although they are time consuming and involve some cash outlays for dues, registration fees, travel, and subsistence, they are worth every dollar spent for the contacts and information they provide. Many consider the opportunities to interact with peers and more experienced specialists and to share experiences with other professionals the most valuable aspect of membership.

To gain the most from professional groups, be an active member. If there is a local chapter, join it and participate regularly. Attend local, state, and regional meetings and the national conference if at all possible. Read the organization's publications. Make use of the membership directory to establish networks. If the opportunity presents itself, assume a leadership role and hold office in the organization.

Here are some of the most useful professional associations for HR managers and practitioners (see Appendix for address details).

American Association for Adult and Continuing Education
American Management Association
American Society for Training and Development
Association for Educational Communications and Technology
Association of Human Resource Systems Professionals
Human Resource Planning Society
International Personnel Management Association
National Management Association
National Society for Performance and Instruction
Northeast Human Resources Association
The Organization Development Institute
Society for Human Resource Management (formerly the American Society for Personnel Administration)

Conferences and expositions. Of course priority for attending national and regional conferences and expositions goes to organizations you belong to. But it's a good idea to attend annual meetings of other professional groups at least occasionally. The conferences of these organizations (see Appendix for details) are of special interest to HR managers.

American Association for Adult and Continuing Education's annual conference, a six-day meeting that attracts approximately 2,000 professionals
American Association for Counseling and Development's an-

nual convention, three and a half days, with between 4,000 and 5,000 counselors and human development specialists

American Management Association's annual Compensation and Benefits Update, a two-day conference; also annual Human Resources Conference and Exposition, 1,200 human resource executives and practitioners

American Psychological Association's annual convention, five days, 12,000 members

American Society for Healthcare, Education, and Training's annual Conference and Trade Exhibition, two days, 500 health care professionals; contact American Hospital Association

American Society for Training and Development's annual Conference and Exposition, six days, 6,000 business, industrial, and military HR managers and practitioners; also, National Conference on Technical and Skills Training, three days, 1,000 professional trainers

Association of Human Resource Systems Professionals annual conference, three days, 800 HR and personnel managers

Benefits Expo—National Conference and Exposition for Employee Benefits Decisionmakers, three days, 500 benefits managers

International Training Conference on Public Personnel Administration, five days, 800 senior-level human resource professionals; contact International Personnel Management Association

Management Training Conference and Exposition, four days, devoted to those who train executives, managers, and supervisors

Meeting World, three days for conference, convention, trade show, and travel planners and consultants

National Society for Performance and Instruction's annual Conference and Expo, six days, 1,200 human resource professionals

Organization Development Institute's national conference, two and a half days, 1,000 organization development practitioners

Society for Human Resource Management's National Conference, four days, 2,500 participants

Training magazine and *Personnel Journal*'s annual Training Conference and Expo, five days, 6,000 personnel and training professionals; also, annual cost-effective training conference, three-day conferences held in three locations for training and HR executives and managers

Marketing Yourself

Marketing was defined earlier in this book as the process of finding out what people want or need and then getting it to them, or identifying the people who need what you have, making sure that they know they need it, and getting it to them. That definition also fits the concept of self-marketing. To move upward in your career, you need to identify the organizations that need your skills and talents, get them to know they need them, and then deliver them. To do all that, you need a winning game plan.

The self-marketing process involves a series of seven steps. They are briefly described in the following paragraphs.

1. *Set your goals and objectives.* Convert your self-assessment into goals and objectives. Decide where you want to be and what you want to be doing three, five, and ten years from now—for example, are you aiming for vice president, human resources; corporate manager, training and development; independent HR consultant; researcher? Develop your objectives—the things you must do to get to where you want to go. Make the objectives specific and measurable—for example, "to learn the financial terms and concepts needed to perform the budgeting function by June 1990."

2. *Survey the job market.* Take a wide-angle look at the entire human resources discipline both in-house and outside. What kinds of jobs are available now? How many? Where? What positions show promise as far as having vacancies or being in demand during the next three to ten years? Are there new jobs in the offing? Where are these positions? In a particular region of the country? Overseas? In what kinds of companies? In which industries? Private organizations? Public? Government agencies?

3. *Identify your marketing targets.* Select one or more targets for your campaign. First, settle on the types of organizations, including your own, that are likely to have the position or positions that you have identified as your short-, mid-, and long-range targets. Then look for companies or agencies in locations where you would accept a position, if offered. Do some networking; check with your advisers and mentor. Develop a long list. Then consider the probabilities—the odds of getting a position in those organizations and the potential demand for people in the target positions. Following your evaluation, develop a short list.

4. *Analyze the competition.* Now compare your current talents and the formal and informal credentials you will have in the next three, five, and ten years with the projected supply of job applicants for

the targeted positions during that time frame. Are you competitive? What do you need to do to make yourself more competitive?

5. *Design your strategy and tactics.* Next focus on the means of achieving your goals and objectives to give yourself a competitive advantage. Look for ways to enhance your knowledge and skills, increase your responsibility, and enlarge your current job. If you are an HR manager, seek opportunities to participate in corporate-level task forces such as strategic planning teams. Search out promising lateral moves and special assignments. Check out vacancies in other companies, other industries, other locations, and public agencies; look primarily for new challenges and opportunities—ones that represent a step toward your ultimate goal. Continue your formal education. Pursue an M.S., M.A., M.B.A., Ph.D., or Ed.D. degree. Engage in regular self-study. Register with a job search firm. Study the "positions available" section of professional journals.

6. *Promote, advertise, and sell yourself.* Get visibility within your own company by performing all jobs and tasks in a professional and outstanding manner. Take advantage of opportunities to present briefings to top management, make public presentations, and write for publication. Become involved in community activities. Become active in a professional association and seek leadership positions. Prepare carefully for every activity, not just for those that have high visibility. When a position becomes available, whether inside or out, be fully prepared before applying. Learn as much as you can about the organization and the job, double check your résumé, rehearse your answers to the questions you expect to be asked, be on time, and look your very best.

7. *Modify your plan.* Periodically update your market survey and, as needed, make changes to your marketing targets and reanalyze your competition. Evaluate your strategy and tactics and your success in accomplishing what you set out to do. Again, make needed alterations to your plan.

Here are some aspects of marketing yourself that deserve special attention.

Image. The image you project to a prospective employer is made up of many things:

1. Your written self-description—the résumé
2. Your telephone image—your voice, speech, tone, and style
3. Your in-person impact—your appearance, speech, dress, posture, body language, neatness, personality, attitudes, and ability to respond to questions and sell your package, what

you say, what you wear, what you say and how you say it, and how you act—all these definitely communicate who and what you are

4. Your reputation
5. Your past accomplishments

Ideally, you want to be seen as an ethical, professional, competent, responsive, caring, personable, problem-solving person—a person that wants to help and can tailor his or her skills and competencies to satisfy needs and solve problems. So emphasize your strengths in all your correspondence, résumés, and telephone and personal contacts.

And don't overlook the importance of projecting an impressive image of your current position. This is particularly vital if your goals involve advancement in your present organization, but it is also a key to career development in general. If you want to get ahead, you have to get noticed. You must create and maintain a higher profile and greater visibility with those who count in your organization.

One very smart young man, then a training consultant on a one-year contract with a communications conglomerate, came to the attention of the organization's CEO when he presented him with a copy of a book he had found particularly stimulating. He is now president of one of his company's subsidiaries.

It's not enough to be competent and make contributions to your organization. You must also position yourself so that your achievement can be seen. You do that by creating a favorable personal and professional impression, projecting a sense of confidence and authority, and communicating more powerfully and effectively.

Marketable achievements. Every professional should have a written inventory of marketable accomplishments, a journal of professional and technical achievements maintained over a period of years. It provides a structured method of identifying and quantifying the level of your experience, knowledge, ability, interest, and success in areas of consequence in modern organizations. It is invaluable when you're planning a career change. More and more prospective employers are requiring applicants to submit descriptions of major accomplishments, either as a part of their résumés or as a separate attachment. Your inventory will also be useful when you're preparing qualification briefs, personal marketing letters, and newspaper ad replies; it's a good review tool when you're getting ready for job interviews. A complete and well-written inventory will also help you be more objective and believable when completing job performance self-appraisals.

One career strategist suggest you go one step further and create a notebook highlighting your professional accomplishments, with separate sections for your full résumé, descriptions of successful projects, letters of recommendation and commendation, relevant certificates, newspaper and journal clippings about activities you organized, and so on.

Interviewing. It is beyond the scope of this book to teach you how to conduct yourself in a job interview; many excellent references (see end of chapter) can help you here. You'll also get positive ideas by sharing experiences with other professionals in informal networking situations; don't forget, too, that you get better at interviewing with practice.

But one aspect worth discussing, because it is too often overlooked by ambitious professionals, is this: interviewing is a two-way street. While you are being evaluated as a potential employee, you should also be evaluating the organization as a potential employer. Some organizations are mismanaged, poorly staffed, underfinanced, unproductive, and occupy inferior competitive positions in the corporate scheme of things. Accepting employment with the wrong company can cause major setbacks, possibly even a fatal blow, to your professional career and your personal life.

Many factors have to be considered before accepting employment offers, and much of the needed information can be gained through the job interview. Use the interview to learn about company climate, competitive position, problem-solving style, and most important, the status accorded to the HR department.

Here is a sample of some of the questions you might ask to get some perspective on the organization and how it operates:

What are your company's major strengths? Greatest limitations?
What are the strengths of the HR department?
How many professionals are assigned to the HR department? How many support people?
What was the total budget for the HR department last year? What is it this year?
Please describe your planning system, budgeting system, performance appraisal system, promotion policy, reward system, staff training and development policies, and so on.

Executive search firms. Executive search firms are an important resource because they can give you access to organizations that do not advertise positions. They can provide you with details about prospective employers and positions and they often offer assistance in tailoring your résumé to the positions available.

So, for success in landing a high-visibility executive position with a six-figure salary, marketing yourself effectively to executive search firms is a must. To do that successfully, you must be able to locate appropriate companies and then to identify the reputable ones. It is not an easy task, for the number of companies is growing so fast that many emerging but competent organizations are not listed anywhere. Check with your professional association; networking can also help here. Another source of names is the Association of Executive Search Consultants; also check *The Directory of Executive Recruiters* in your library or its digest-sized edition for job-seekers.

These search companies deal in the human resources area, and you may want to contact some of them. (I present the names for your convenience, but neither endorse nor recommend any of them.)

Abbott Smith Associates, Inc.
P.O. Box 318
Franklin Ave.
Millbrook, NY 12545
914/677-5051

The Adler Group
1560 Broadway, Suite 1100
New York, NY 10036
212/764-4678

Corporate Recruiters
201 Summit View Dr., Suite 303
Brentwood, TN 37027
615/377-1940

Executive Search, Inc.
Gateway One
Newark, NJ 07102
201/621-1920

Reinhardt and Associates
8902 N. Meridian St., Suite 238
Indianapolis, IN 46260
317/846-7655

Sheridan Search
27853 Berwick Dr.
Carmel, CA 93923
408/625-1474

Vogel Associates
P.O. Box 269
Huntington Valley, PA 19006
215/938-1700

The Self-Development Process

Step 1. Assess your assets and limitations. Evaluate your knowledge, skills, abilities, habits, attitudes, and learning style to discover assets, strengths, and weaknesses. Then analyze that information and use it to develop realistic goals and objectives and workable action plans.

Step 2. Determine your status and opportunities. First establish where you are in the HR field, then determine the realistic opportunities for your status, either now or in the near future, both within your present organization and on the outside. Look for newly created positions, promotion, job enlargement, special assignments, lateral transfer, temporary positions, a bigger job elsewhere, an entrepreneurial job, and so on.

Step 3. Identify your career goals. Taking into account your assets and liabilities, and your opportunities, select a career goal, a statement of where you want to be and what you want to be doing five to ten years from now. Goals should consider professional challenge, job satisfaction, opportunities for recognition, achievement, self-realization, self-esteem, and job and financial security.

Step 4. Identify your learning needs and objectives. What professional and personal knowledge skills do you need to achieve your goals? Consider such things as effectiveness in needs assessment, managing people and situations, coaching and counseling, HRIS system selection, implementation, and management, marketing, financial, and auditing skills. Make a list of your needs and then translate them into a priority list of objectives—what you plan to accomplish over the next one to two years.

Step 5. Develop your strategy and supporting action plans. To achieve each objective, you need to develop strategies and supporting action plans. Put them in writing and have a backup plan.

Step 6. Execute your plan. Now put your plan into effect. Schedule periodic get-togethers with an adviser or your mentor.

Join professional organizations and participate in their conferences. Network. Search out opportunities to speak to live audiences. Set aside time weekly for research and writing. Get published.

Step 7. Monitor, evaluate, and modify your plan. Monitor your progress. Are you carrying out your plan as originally envisioned? Evaluate results. Are you making any progress in improving your learning skills and professional knowledge? Get feedback from your advisers, mentor, superiors, and subordinates, and modify your plan as needed.

Summary

Career development is not a matter of choice. It is vital to your personal well-being and your success in the professional world—even your survival as a manager. Constant change, the rapid growth of information in the HR field, and the demands of the HR managerial job demand continuous attention to personal and professional development.

Self-development is the process of improving yourself in all dimensions: personally, professionally, physically, mentally, socially, emotionally, experientially, and even spiritually. A successful self-development plan requires thorough planning, development knowledge and skills, self-assessment, redefinition of "success," and commitment. Your program should also be goal-driven, flexible, professional, efficient and cost-effective, and relevant to your career stage.

Self-assessment is an integral part of the process, and can be accomplished by questioning, reflection, a daily journal, and comparative ratings (by self and others). A key step is to identify realistic and attainable goals, for it is certain that if you don't know where you want to go, you'll never know when you get there. So, think things through, know what you want, work at it, check on your progress, and be your severest critic.

Resources for personal and professional development abound: formal and informal training and education, on-the-job training and experiences, the use of advisers, mentors, learning centers, data bases, research, reading, listening, and viewing, networking, speaking and writing, membership in professional associations, and attendance at conferences.

You must also be able to market yourself. That means that you must identify the organizations that need your skills and talents, get them to know that they need them, and then deliver them. To be a successful marketer, you must have a winning game plan—a strategy for describing what you can do that will appeal to prospective employers.

The self-development process includes seven sequential steps:

1. Assessing your assets and liabilities
2. Determining your status and opportunities
3. Identifying your career goals
4. Identifying your learning needs and objectives
5. Developing your strategy and supporting action plans
6. Executing your plan
7. Monitoring, evaluating, and modifying your plan

Human Resource Journals and Newsletters

Adult Education Quarterly. American Association for Adult and Continuing Education, 1201 16th St., N.W., Suite 230, Washington, DC 20036.

Annual: Developing Human Resources, University Associates, 8517 Production Ave., San Diego, CA 92121.

ASTD National Report on Human Resources (eight times per year). American Society for Training and Development, 1630 Duke St., Alexandria, VA 22313.

Bulletin on Training. Bureau of National Affairs, 9439 Key West Ave., Rockville, MD 20850.

Canadian HR Reporter (biweekly). Corpus Information Services, 1450 Don Mills Road, Don Mills, Ontario M3B 2X7.

Communication Briefings: Ideas that Work (monthly). Encoders, 806 Westminster Blvd., Blackwood, NJ 08012.

Compensation and Benefits Review (six issues per year). American Management Association, P. O. Box 1026, Saranac Lake, NY 12983-9986.

Compflash (monthly). American Management Association.

Corporate Travel (monthly). Gralla Publications, 1515 Broadway, New York, NY 10036.

Creative Training Techniques: A Newsletter of Tips, Tactics and How-tos for Delivering Effective Training (ten times yearly, plus quarterly supplements). Lakewood Publications, 50 S. Ninth St., Minneapolis, MN 55402.

Education Communications & Technology Journal (monthly). Association for Educational Communications and Technology, 1126 16th St., N.W., Washington, DC 20036.

Employee Benefit News: The News Source for Group Benefits Decision-

makers (monthly). Enterprise Communications, 1483 Chain Bridge Rd., Suite 202, McLean, VA 22101.

Employee Benefit Notes and EBRI Issue Briefs (semimonthly). Employee Benefit Research Institute/Education Research Fund, 2121 K Street, N.W., Suite 600, Washington, DC 20037-2121.

Executive Development: An International Publication (semiannually). MCB University Press Limited, 62 Toller Lane, Bradford, England BD8 9BY.

Harvard Business Review (bimonthly). Harvard University Graduate School of Business Administration, Soldiers Field, Boston, MA 02163.

HRD Quarterly. Organization Design and Development, 101 Bryn Mawr Ave., Suite 310, Bryn Mawr, PA 19010.

HRD Review (monthly). 105 Berkley Place, P. O. Box 6, Glen Rock, NJ 07452.

HRSP Review (quarterly). Association of Human Resource Systems Professionals, P. O. Box 801646, Dallas, TX 75380-1646.

Human Resource Development Quarterly. Published jointly by ASTD and Jossey-Bass. Available from Jossey-Bass, 350 Sansome St., San Francisco, CA 94104.

Human Resource Executive (monthly except August and December). Axon Group, 1035 Camphill Rd., Fort Washington, PA 19034.

Human Resource Management (quarterly). John Wiley & Sons, 605 Third Ave., New York, NY 10158-0012.

Human Resource Management News (weekly). Enterprise Publications, 20 N. Wacker Dr., Chicago, IL 60606.

Human Resources Professional (bi-monthly). Faulkner & Gray, 106 Fulton St., New York, NY 10038.

Info-Line (monthly). American Society for Training and Development.

Journal of Management Development (six issues per year). MCB University Press Limited.

Management Review (monthly). American Management Association.

Supervisory Management (monthly). American Management Association.

Meeting News: Facts, News, Ideas for Convention, Meeting and Incentive Planners (monthly). Gralla Publications, 1515 Broadway, New York, NY 10036.

Organization Dynamics (monthly). American Management Association.

Performance and Instruction (monthly). National Society for Performance and Instruction, 1126 16th St., N.W., Suite 214, Washington, DC 20036.

Personnel (monthly). American Management Association.

Personnel Administrator (monthly). Society for Human Resource Management, 606 N. Washington St., Alexandria, VA 22314.

The Prior Report (monthly). Prior Resources, 405-13 College Ave., Clemson, SC 29631.

Public Personnel Management (four issues per year). International Personnel Management Association, 1617 Duke St., Alexandria, VA 22313.

Top Performance (monthly). The Zig Ziglar Corporation, 3330 Earhart, Suite 204, Carrollton, TX 75006-9685.

Trainer's Workshop (bimonthly). American Management Association.

Training and Development Journal (monthly). American Society for Training and Development.

Training Directors' Forum Newsletter (ten issues). Lakewood Publications.

Training: The Magazine of Human Resources Development (monthly).

For Further Reading, Viewing, and Listening

Acumen: Developing the Personal Insight That Leads to Professional Effectiveness—A Comprehensive Computer-Based Self-Development Tool for Managers. Human Synergistics, 39819 Plymouth Rd., Plymouth, MI 48170.

American Society for Training and Development. *Models for Excellence: The Conclusions and Recommendations of the ASTD Training and Development Competency Study.* Baltimore, Md.: ASTD Press, 1983.

Bard, Ray, Chip R. Bell, Leslie Stephen, and Linda Webster. *The Trainer's Professional Development Handbook.* San Francisco: Jossey-Bass, 1987.

Bardwick, Judith M. *The Plateauing Trap: How to Avoid It in Your Career . . . and Your Life.* New York: AMACOM, 1987.

Beilke, Ines. *Career Motivation and Self-Concept.* Dubuque, Iowa: Kendall-Hunt Publishing Company, 1986.

Bolles, Richard N. *What Color Is Your Parachute?* Berkeley, Calif.: Ten Speed Press, 1987.

Brown, Duane, Linda Brooks, and Associates. *Career Choice and Development.* San Francisco: Jossey-Bass, 1984.

Career Management: When Preparation Meets Opportunity (20-minute videocassette). AMA Film/Video, Nine Galen St., Watertown, MA 02172, 1983.

Chakiris, Betty June, and Gilbert M. Fornaciari. "Self-Development." In *Human Resources Management and Development Handbook*, edited by William R. Tracey. New York: AMACOM, 1985.

Chapman, Elwood N. *Be True to Your Future.* Los Altos, Calif.: Crisp Publications, 1988.

————. *Plan B: Protecting Your Career from the Winds of Change.* Los Altos, Calif.: Crisp Publications, 1988.

Davidson, Jeffrey P. *Blow Your Own Horn: How to Market Yourself and Your Career.* New York: AMACOM, 1987.

Falvey, Jack. *What Next? Career Strategies After 35.* Charlotte, Vt.: Williamson Publishing Company, 1987.

Ford, George A., and Gordon L. Lippitt, R. *Planning Your Future: A Guide for Personal Goal Setting.* San Diego, Calif.: University Associates, 1988.

Fritz, Roger. *Rate Your Executive Potential.* New York: John Wiley & Sons, 1988.

Getting Ahead: The Road to Self-Development (28-minute videocassette). Rank Roundtable Training, 113 N. San Vicente Blvd., Beverly Hills, CA 90211, 1970.

Getting Fit: Balancing Your Physical Health and Lifestyle Needs (55-minute videocassette). Produced by Video Education Network, 1986. Distributed by Dartnell, 4660 Ravenswood Ave., Chicago, IL 60640.

Goal Setting for Fun, Health and Profit (17-minute videocassette). Salenger Films, 1635 Twelfth St., Santa Monica, CA 90404-9988, 1980.

Gutek, Barbara A., and Laurie Larwood, eds. *Women's Career Development.* Newbury Park, Calif.: Sage Publications, 1987.

Hall, Douglas T., ed. *Career Development in Organizations.* San Francisco: Jossey-Bass, 1986.

Hornstein, Harvey A. *Managerial Courage* (two audiocassettes). Wiley Sound Business, 605 Third Ave., New York NY 10158, 1988.

I Want to Change But I Don't Know How (29-minute videocassette). Cally Curtis Company, 1111 N. Las Palmas Ave., Hollywood, CA 90038-1289, 1983.

Kaplan, Robert E., and others. *High Hurdles: An Inside View of Executive Work, Character, and Development.* Greensboro, N.C.: The Center for Creative Leadership, 1988.

McCullough, Richard C. *Planning Your Professional Development in Human Resource Development.* Alexandria, Va.: ASTD Press, 1987.

Mepham, John. *Your Guide to Job Promotion.* New York: State Mutual Book and Periodical Service, 1987.

Newman, James A., and Roy Alexander. *Climbing the Corporate Matterhorn* (two audiocassettes). Wiley Sound Business, 605 Third Ave., New York, NY 10158, 1988.

Norris, Kenneth E. *Winning at Work: The Road to Career Success.* Summit, Penn.: TAB Books, 1987.

Potter, Beverly A. *The Way of the Ronin: A Guide to Career Strategy.* New York: AMACOM, 1985.

Schmidt, Terry D. *Planning Your Career Success: Nine Self-Guided Steps.* Belmont, Calif.: Lifetime Learning Publications, 1984.

Setting and Achieving Personal Goals (6-hour audiocassette). American Management Association Extension Institute, 135 W. 50th St., New York NY 10020, 1977.

Sredl, Henry J., and William J. Rothwell. *The ASTD Reference Guide to Professional Training Roles and Competencies, Vols. I and II.* Alexandria, VA: ASTD Press, 1987.

Storey, Walter. *Career Dimensions I: Personal Planning Guide.* Rev. ed. San Diego, Calif.: University Associates, 1986.

Stress Reduction (30-minute videocassette). Van Dyck Communications, 832 Folsom St., San Francisco, CA 94107, 1987.

Survival and Advancement (28-minute videocassette). Produced by Sally V. Beaty. Southern California Consortium, 5400 Orange Ave., Suite 215, Cypress, CA 90630, 1983.

Talley, Madelon DeVoe. *Career Hang Gliding: A Personal Guide to Managing Your Career.* New York: Dutton Publishing, 1986.

Tracey, William R. *Critical Skills: The Guide to Top Performance for Human Resources Managers.* New York: AMACOM, 1988.

Where Do I Go from Here? (19-minute videocassette). AMA Film/ Video, Nine Galen St., Watertown, MA 02172, 1986.

15

Leading
Practicing the Ultimate Skill

A prime characteristic of business today is its intensely competitive climate. There is competition within a company for resources, and there is competition with other organizations—both in the United States and abroad—for markets. Add the complexity of modern organizations to this level of competitiveness, and you will immediately see why American organizations demand better leadership at all levels. We need leaders, not merely managers. When people have capable leaders, they feel important. They believe that what they do makes a difference in the organization, that their skills are valuable to the company. Effective leadership also makes them feel part of an extended family. To them, work is exciting and enjoyable. When employees have this outlook, their productivity, creativity, and loyalty are greatly enhanced. Strong leadership, then, provides very tangible benefits.

Benefits to the organization. Effective leaders increase productivity. They improve the quality of products and services and customer relations. They upgrade relationships with unions and reduce the number of formal grievances. They encourage innovation and creativity. And they reduce costs and increase efficiency and profits.

Benefits to managers and supervisors. Effective leadership at the top reduces internal friction and stress. It builds confidence. It promotes good working relationships and improves goal setting. It increases sensitivity to potential people problems and makes possible early identification and solution of operational problems. It reduces the need for close supervision and direction. It improves management.

Benefits to employees. Effective leadership clarifies roles, responsibilities, and relationships, heightens job satisfaction, and improves morale. It reduces misunderstandings and improves the communication of performance standards and feedback. It encourages employee involvement, promotes creativity, and engenders a feeling of accomplishment. It reduces employee grievances, turnover, and substandard performance.

But what is leadership? There are almost as many different definitions as there are writers in the field—and there are plenty of those. Here are two particularly good ones.

Leadership is "the ability to get wholehearted followers. . . . It's not how to be the best person you can be. It's not how to get more productivity out of people. It's not how to be a better supervisor or a better communicator or a more creative thinker. It is how to get from others their genuine 'buy-in'—support, enlistment, owner-ship—for a given course of action."[1]

"Leadership has to do with personal power. It is a process of social influence. One becomes a leader when others allow him (note the verb) to influence their thinking, their attitudes, and their behavior, when others accept him and see him as an effective medium for satisfying some of their more important job-related needs and aspirations."[2]

The role of the manager as a leader is to influence people, both separately and in groups, to act in ways that will help attain the organization's goals and objectives. Thus, the distinguishing charac-teristic of leadership is that it deals with the human aspects of organization, which puts the issue of leadership development squarely within the HR arena.

Is "leadership" simply another way of looking at management, or are they different concepts? I believe leadership is the process of influencing, motivating, and persuading people to take a desired action that is in their own best interests and also the organization's. Leadership is flexible, representative, and empowering. Manage-ment is more rigid, bureaucratic, and controlling; it exercises au-thority and makes decisions. Leaders accept uncertainty with equa-nimity; managers press for order and certainty. Leaders deliberately cause change; managers attempt to adapt or adjust to it. We might say that leaders are people oriented and goal oriented; managers are objectives oriented. Leaders establish and communicate the mission of the organization; managers determine the means of achieving the mission.

However, good management and leadership are not mutually

[1]James C. Georges, "Is It Really Leadership Training?" *Training* (December 1987), p. 120. Reprinted with permission from the December 1987 issue of *Training*, The Magazine of Human Resources Development. Copyright 1987, Lakewood Publica-tions Inc., Minneapolis, MN, 612/333–0471. All rights reserved.
[2]James J. Cribbin, "The Protean Managerial Leader," *Personnel* (March–April 1972), p. 9.

■ ■

PROFILE OF A LEADER

There are many theories on how leadership is developed and practiced, but almost everyone agrees on fundamental attributes that leaders share.

- *Character*. What we are at rock bottom is our character, and it is determined by our values. It includes moral courage, confidence in self and others, self-control, fortitude, patience, and perseverance.
- *Intelligence*. A better-than-average intellect, superior insight, and a reflective mind, with the ability to think big and to resist the temptation to play it safe—these are essential qualities of the successful leader. Leaders know how to introduce needed change, solve problems, innovate, and exercise good judgment.
- *Credibility*. Credibility with subordinates, peers, superiors, and colleagues is achieved by building a record of integrity over time.
- *Energy*. Leaders must have the physical stamina and mental alertness to endure the pressures of their jobs. The ability to hang in there and see a difficult job through to completion regardless of the obstacles is a prime hallmark of leadership.
- *Concern for people*. Outstanding leaders are people centered, and they express their interest and concern in overt actions and tangible terms.
- *Responsibility*. Top leadership rests in a single person, one who alone must assume total responsibility for whatever happens in the organization.
- *Persuasiveness*. With skillful and inspiring communication, competent leaders influence the thinking, values, and behavior of people throughout the organization. The measure of their success is the extent to which people at all levels enthusiastically direct their time, energy, and talents toward accomplishing the organization's goals and objectives.
- *Responsiveness*. Good leaders are alert to everything that happens in the organization. They adjust readily to the great variety of situations and personalities, responding in a timely way and usually right on target.
- *Visibility*. The best leaders put themselves in the trenches—at the point of main effort. By their own example, they embolden, empower, and invigorate people in their organizations.

■ ■

exclusive. Some people have both abilities, and those who do will become more essential to their organizations in the highly competitive, complex world of tomorrow. Unfortunately, today's typical HR manager tends to concentrate on managing, neglecting leadership behaviors.

Challenges for Human Resources

The leadership challenges facing the HR manager today are unprecedented. Unless managers are able to cope with these problems, they will lose more than their credibility—they will forfeit their jobs.

Earning top management respect. Although the HR function has come a long way in many organizations in recent years, there is still a good distance to travel to earn full recognition and respect. HR managers must find ways to get top management to understand the role of the HR department in the organizational scheme of things.

Integrating with strategic plans. HR managers must successfully link their goals, objectives, plans, and programs with corporate strategic plans. An HR department can be justified only by hard evidence that it makes a measurable contribution to overall goals and objectives, such as improving productivity and increasing return on investment. Strategic planning is the right place to start.

Dealing with change. The rate and magnitude of change, and the impact on people, are profound. Consider the challenges of dealing with mergers and takeovers, planning for downsizing, streamlining, and restructuring, and at the same time ensuring the continued viability, efficiency, and profitability of the company. HR managers must deal competently with such changes.

Attracting and retaining good people. A part of the solution to maintaining an advantage in today's highly competitive environment is the ability to get the right people and hold on to them. Adding to the difficulty are the problems of a reduced labor pool, the growing number of functional illiterates, and inadequate communication, reading, and mathematical skills among job applicants.

Training and developing people. Training and development are primary means of improving productivity and quality. Employees must be trained to compensate for deficiencies in their formal education, retrained to keep them employable in the face of advancing technology, and reeducated to help them meet the requirements of their new positions. A related requirement is to create self-directed and effective work teams.

Dealing with people problems. Another facet of the "people" challenge is providing for employee wellness, job satisfaction, and self-realization in an era characterized by monumental problems of substance abuse, increased stress, and employee apathy and lack of commitment. Dealing sensitively, compassionately, and successfully with those problems and their consequences, in on-the-job performance, is an enormous challenge.

Developing managerial potential. From the standpoint of organizational viability, there are other challenges. One is to identify earlier and more reliably those who have the potential to make good managers and executives. Another is to help managers develop an understanding of what leadership means in both domestic and international settings and help them develop strong cross-cultural perspectives. A related challenge involves sensitizing managers to the ethical dimensions of behavior and teaching them to deal with the many ethical challenges that confront them.

Overcoming obstacles to success. Why do so few HR managers seize the opportunity to lead? The organizational culture prevents it. Their timing is off. The organization climate isn't right; the company has a jumble of conflicting goals and policies, and seems unconcerned about the absence of competent leadership. They fear failure. They lack the necessary skills. They don't take the time to figure out what the leadership role involves. They believe that top management "won't let us lead." Or they have a mistaken belief that only CEOs and presidents can be leaders.

Another obstacle is the manager's failure to take the initiative. Seizing the initiative is not easy. It requires considerable thought and a measure of courage. The job of a manager in the leadership role is to persuasively communicate a vision and to influence people to buy into that vision, to get them to do whatever is needed to accomplish the goals and strategies. Managers must remember that a great number of average people must do what is necessary to get things done. The real challenge of leadership is to get things done using those average people.

Leadership Theories and Principles

There are three broad approaches to the practice of leadership; in general terms, they involve adjusting leadership style to fit the situation, changing the situation, and adhering consistently to a set of principles. I will very briefly summarize the main theories, but such a cursory review cannot do justice to the years of work of these researchers; those who are interested should consult their original studies of the leadership process.

Consistency or "one best" leadership. The "one best" leadership approach holds that certain unchanging principles and concepts provide a firm foundation for leadership. Those who support this approach believe that consistency in applying these concepts and principles provides better results than attempts to adjust leadership behavior to fit the situation or change the situation to make it more compatible with leadership precepts and principles.

One research team identified ten "emerging" principles of human behavior they consider critical to the exercise of sound leadership[3]:

1. Participation
2. Candor
3. Trust and respect
4. Involvement and commitment
5. Conflict resolution
6. Consensus
7. Synergy and creativity
8. Goals and objectives
9. Mutual support
10. Changing people

Contingency or situational leadership. Contingency leadership is based on the theory that there is no one best way to manage or lead, but there are likely to be preferred ways of leading under certain circumstances. This theory holds that the best approach to leadership at any particular moment depends on the people being supervised, the task to be accomplished, and the circumstances surrounding those two variables.

Paul Hersey and Kenneth Blanchard developed the situational theory of management, which differentiates leadership styles based on task and relationship behavior.[4] They emphasize that there is no "one best style" appropriate for all situations; each situation requires the manager to analyze it and select the best style.

In Figure 15-1, Blake and Mouton compare the extent to which ten emerging principles of human behavior (which they believe are

---

[3]Robert R. Blake and Jane Srygley Mouton, "How to Choose a Leadership Style," *Training and Development Journal* (February 1982), p. 44.
[4]Paul Hersey and Kenneth H. Blanchard, *Management of Organizational Behavior: Utilization of Human Resources*, 3rd ed. (Englewood Cliffs, N.J.: Prentice-Hall, 1977).

Figure 15-1.   Behavioral science principles in situational and one best leadership approaches.

Concept	Situational leadership theory	One best theory*
Participation	A technique used as socioemotional reward at intermediate maturity levels only.	Skill in the use of inter-dependent interaction process is basic for teamwork at all matur-ity levels.
Candor	Not mentioned.	Prerequisite to effective participation.
Trust and respect	Prerequisite to delega-tion at highest maturity level only.	Essential for shared participation.
Involvement and com-mitment	Boss-controlled and present at highest maturity level only.	Core motivation under-lying learning, problem solving and production at all maturity levels.
Conflict resolution	Not mentioned.	Open confrontation and resolution of differences essential for shared understanding and agreement.
Consensus	Absent.	A shared value which may not always be achievable.
Synergy/creativity	Not mentioned.	Human resources utilization based on teamwork.
Goals and objectives	Set by the boss for subordinates with some subordinate input permitted at higher maturity levels.	Mutually set as the basis for organization and direction of work.
Mutual support	Not dealt with.	A result of team-based interdependence.
Changing people	Use of Skinnerian reinforcement of subor-dinate compliance through giving or with-holding of socioemo-tional rewards. Feed-back disregarded or rarely mentioned.	Use of open critique and feedback for ana-lyzing experience and increasing insight, understanding and effectiveness.

*In the original, this is called "9,9 orientation."

From Robert R. Blake and Jane Srygley Mouton, "How to Choose a Leadership Style," *Training and Development Journal,* February 1982, p. 44. © 1982 by the American Society for Training and Development. Used by permission.

critical to sound leadership) are embedded within situational and one best approaches to leadership.

Context leadership. The most recent theory of leadership holds that human behavior is a natural manifestation of context (beliefs or assumptions) and not a function of content (information and motivation).[5] Therefore, instead of attempting to change undesirable behavior by providing information and motivation, a more fruitful approach is to shift (or create) the context—adjusting how people see themselves in the work environment.

Ten Principles of Leadership

No matter which of the three approaches they use, all manager-leaders must incorporate a solid understanding of these ten principles.

1. *Know yourself, your capabilities, and your limitations.* To be a successful leader, you must understand people, but before you can do that you must know yourself—your strengths and weaknesses, your beliefs and values, and your personality and its impact on people.

2. *Know your job and be proficient in performing it.* Prerequisite to successful performance as a manager and leader is a thorough knowledge of the organization, its mission and goals, and how you as a manager should contribute to the achievement of that mission. That requires a full set of managerial, professional, conceptual, technical, and people skills, and proficiency in their performance.

3. *Look for opportunities to take on responsibilities and be accountable for your actions.* Continuously seek openings to take the initiative to do the things that need to be done to improve your organization, the skills of its people, and the quality of its products and services.

4. *Make sound, balanced, fair, and timely decisions.* Avoid procrastination; that often results in decision by default. Reach decisions and take actions that are equitable, practical, prudent, and credible. To the maximum extent possible, give your people a chance to participate in making the decisions that affect them.

5. *Set a model and standard for others to emulate.* Be an example for your people in all things. Show them how to think and how to act in a professional manner, how to persevere in the pursuit of the

---

[5]"A New Approach to Leadership: Shifting Contexts vs. Managing Content," *Leadership* (vol. 1, no. 1 [undated]), pp. 4–7.

organization's mission and goals, how to be caring about others, how to keep fit mentally, physically, emotionally, and spiritually, and how to be self-disciplined.

6. *Know your people and look out for their welfare.* Learn about the basic needs, values, capabilities, strengths, and weaknesses of your people. Find out what motivates them. Help them meet their physical, social, and self-realization needs and succeed in achieving their aspirations. Assist them with their personal and job-related problems.

7. *Talk with your people.* Keep them abreast of plans, changes, and other upcoming actions. Be very careful about the way you deliver your messages, whether oral or written. Be sure that you use the right tone, the right words, and the right gestures and facial expressions.

8. *Train and develop your people.* Coach them in the skills they need to perform well and to qualify for advancement—problem solving, decision making, and planning, as well as professional and technical skills. Give your people challenging, meaningful, and exciting tasks, and give them authority to command the resources they need to complete them satisfactorily.

9. *Delegate but ensure that all delegated tasks are clearly understood, supervised, and accomplished.* Make clear what is to be accomplished by when, how much authority is delegated, and how accountability will be measured. Check periodically that tasks are being carried out and that results are as expected. Reclarify if needed. Provide frequent feedback.

10. *Train your people as a team.* For success in any complex endeavor, cohesive action is necessary—built on strong bonds of mutual respect, trust, and confidence undergirding a common purpose and objective. In addition, there must be a unity of thought and information among all members at all times. That state of affairs comes about only through team training and effective intra-group communication.

The Question of Style

In recent years researchers and writers have coined literally hundreds of descriptive terms for leadership styles. Here are some of them:

Formal, informal, and nonformal
Directive and nondirective
Person-, task-, and fusion-oriented

Positive and negative
Democratic, delegative, and free-rein
Organizational and personal
Laissez-faire, custodial, and coercive
Authoritarian, autocratic, manipulative, permissive, participative, and emergent
Charismatic, psychologically distant, and supportive

One writer has classified bureaucratic leaders as climbers, conservers, zealots, advocates, and statesmen. Another referred to receptive, exploitive, hoarding, marketing, and productive managers. Another cataloged ineffective managerial types as deserters, missionaries, autocrats, and compromisers and effective managerial types as bureaucrats, developers, benevolent autocrats, and executives. Still another has identified five leadership styles: directive, persuasive, consultative, participative, and delegative. One research team defined managerial styles with a grid, one axis of which depicts concern for people and the other concern for production.[6]

Classification systems like these can be interesting food for thought, but you should realize their limits: they tend to be arbitrary, often overlap, are sometimes contradictory, and are not mutually exclusive. I urge you to be cautious about adopting a single style. As an HR manager, you bring to the job a collection of values, perceptions, aspirations, expectations, and priorities that is uniquely your own. Those ideals and standards will cause you to focus on certain aspects of your position and will lead you to go about achieving organizational and personal goals and objectives in your own way.

Leadership style is probably determined by seven factors:

1. The manager's perception of his or her role
2. The manager's beliefs about the people managed
3. The skills of the manager
4. Employees' beliefs about the nature of their jobs
5. The skills of the employees
6. The mission and culture of the organization

---

[6]Anthony Downes, *Inside Bureaucracy* (Boston: Little, Brown, and Company, 1967), Chapter 9. Ernest Dale, *Management: Theory and Practice*, 2nd ed. (New York: McGraw-Hill Book Company, 1969), pp. 564–565. W. J. Reddin, *Managerial Styles Diagnostic Test* (Frederickton, N.B., Canada: Managerial Effectiveness, Ltd., 1971). Louis E. Tagliaferri, "Tips for Managers and Supervisors," *Catalog of Training, Development and Assessment Material for Training and HRD Professionals* (Fall 1987), p. 13. Robert R. Blake and others, "Managerial Facades," *Advanced Management Journal* (July 1966), p. 31.

7. The feedback the manager receives on his or her management style (success or failure, criticism or commendation)

If the manager believes that people are basically lazy and unmotivated or if the organization discourages cooperation and individual initiative, the result is likely to be an authoritarian atmosphere. If, on the other hand, managers see people as wanting to do the best they can to contribute to the achievement of the company's objectives and if the organization culture promotes and rewards individual initiative and teamwork, the result is likely to be people-centered leadership.

Requirements for Human Resources Leadership

In this section, we will look at leadership as a function and a process. This means examining leadership *behavior,* particularly in connection with leading the HR function.

The functions of a leader, and the skills needed for effectiveness, do not differ radically from one level of HR management to another. Both the HR manager and subordinate supervisors are concerned with people and with analysis and action. But leadership becomes increasingly complex with upward movement in the organization, not simply because the problems are larger, but because a new orientation is necessary.

HR managers as senior leaders have three basic functions:

1. To create and communicate a vision, an image of the organization as it should be in terms of its culture, climate, the quality of work life, and its performance. That means generating a clear and practicable conceptualization, a realistic image of the company, its role and status in its industry, the community, and the world, its reputation, accomplishments, and success. It means transmitting this vision to all members of the organization so successfully that they enthusiastically embrace the conceptualization as their own.

2. To take actions that will result in improved performance of both specific jobs and the overall use of the organization's human resources. Actions include setting worthwhile and achievable goals and measurable objectives, developing forward-looking strategic and tactical plans, establishing workable policies, training subordinates, and evaluating performance. This also includes specific initiatives that will provide people with purpose, direction, and motivation.

3. To take actions that contribute to the improvement of organizational and human relationships. Examples are encouraging risk taking, providing assistance and encouragement, developing and implementing fair and equitable compensation and benefits programs, developing people, rewarding outstanding performance, resolving conflicts and differences, building teams, and improving working conditions and the quality of worklife.

To perform these three functions well, leaders need a particular skill set and a package of behaviors recognized as "leader," bolstered by certain personal characteristics. All leaders need these qualities, but HR managers are probably in a much better position to provide leadership than managers of many other departments simply because their jobs require them to pay special attention to such skills as communicating, listening, coaching, counseling, and negotiation. Their people expect them to lead, and the majority of them enjoy leading because it gives them power, visibility, challenge, satisfaction, and results.

Imperatives

What specific demands does a leadership position make of you in today's organization? There are several—and all are of critical importance to success.

Emotional maturity. You have a healthy view of yourself, accepting your capabilities and limitations. You hold up well under adversity. You can handle lack of appreciation and the censure of superiors, peers, and subordinates. You can live with your failures. Emotional maturity is what makes you dependable and largely predictable.

Independence. You are inner-directed and self-ruled. You don't always agree with stock answers or established policy. You question the status quo. You don't knuckle under to arm twisting or unreasonable demands.

Realism. Your approach is not speculative or sentimental. You are sensible, practical, and reasonable. You tend to think with your head, not with your heart.

Courage. You're willing to take calculated risks—to chance failure, to face trouble, to risk your next bonus or promotion, to put your reputation on the line. You don't fear taking the unpopular position, but you're not impulsive or imprudent.

Integrity. You resolutely adhere to moral principle. You invariably stand up for what's right, even when it costs you. You're honest and upright. You question the very appearance of unethical behavior, whether in peers, superiors, and subordinates.

Idealism. You understand the role of values and put values into action. You examine your own leadership values and those of the organization and learn how others perceive you as a model. You make specific plans for action based on the insights gained by your introspection.

Leader Knowledge

You know yourself—your strengths, weaknesses, prejudices, and biases. You also know people, what motivates and activates them. You understand the criticality of trust among peers and subordinates. You know how to build a cohesive team through example and positive attitude.

You know your organization as a whole, not just your own area of work. You understand and subscribe to the goals, strategic plans, objectives, and priorities of both the organization and your department. You know your role and those of other members of the management team. You know where the power centers are and how to deal with them.

You understand and accept change. You don't fight it; rather, you cause it, manipulate it, and exploit it. You know when to hold firm and when to back off. You have firm and workable concepts of leadership and management.

You know and fully understand the concepts and principles of HR planning and forecasting, budgeting, marketing, training and developing, motivating, appraising and counseling, and negotiating. You know federal and state laws and the provisions of collective bargaining agreements pertaining to recruiting, screening, selecting, assigning, promoting, appraising, disciplining, and terminating employees.

Leader Skills and Abilities

As a leader you must be able to come up with new ideas and to predict how they will affect the organization. You must be able to convince others that your ideas are good and workable and persuade people to do what they may not want to do. You must have the ability to determine what people are thinking, to take the pulse of top management and employees. You must have the ability to retain what is good, to continue the programs of predecessors and not abandon them simply because they were not your ideas.

Other vital skills—listening, speaking, writing, problem sensing, inquiring, problem solving, decision making, hiring, motivating, delegating, appraising, coaching, counseling, negotiating, and team building—are discussed in Tracey, *Critical Skills* (see end of this chapter).

Leader Behaviors

Here are the behaviors required of you for top-notch HR leadership. You must show commitment to a clear set of values and standards. You search for opportunities to improve, innovate, and grow. You develop an image, a mental picture, of the demands that your organization's mission puts on you and on your people, and you use that image to set goals and guide all programs, projects, and services.

You get people to work together rather than compete. You rally groups to a common cause. You develop teamwork by communicating directly with your people and building strong bonds of mutual trust, respect, and caring. You always level with your people, letting them know what you think and why. You are consistent and predictable, and you never misuse your power. You use stress constructively. You continually train your people and emphasize the importance of quality, initiative, responsibility, ethical behavior, and loyalty.

In your relationships with people, you consistently exhibit positive behaviors. You talk *with* rather than *to* your subordinates—and do it often. You tell people how they're doing—the good as well as the bad. You reinforce positively, giving personal accolades and recognition whenever possible. You recognize accomplishments through merit pay increases or bonuses and by day-to-day pats on the back. You never use putdowns, but you tell it like it is, even when the truth may be difficult to hear.

You delegate authority and tie accountability to responsibility. You demonstrate confidence in your people by sharing decision making with them. You encourage your people to exercise initiative. You do not micromanage or oversupervise. You give your people freedom to make mistakes and to benefit from them. You empower people by using "power down" approaches and focusing on teamwork. You consult with those affected by your decisions; and you implement their suggestions whenever possible.

You exercise strong discipline and enforce high standards. Invariably you are a tough critic, but you are always accurate and fair. Although you discipline swiftly when required, you reward instantaneously. You know when and how to criticize, but you criticize performance, not people. On the other hand, you never fail to support subordinates when they need support, and you often run interference for them. You never violate or betray confidences. You cut through red tape. You share hardships with your people.

You focus on products or services, not on organization charts. You plan strategically by assessing strengths and weaknesses of yourself, employees, competitors, and products and services. You establish priorities and communicate them clearly and unequivocally to your people. You stay flexible by making contingency plans. You concentrate on a few key performance indicators, and don't try to do everything. You pace personal and staff effort so that energy and capacity will be there when extraordinary effort is required. You tell your people the standards by which their performance will be measured. You don't retain people who, despite help, are unable to do the job. You question and challenge all constraints. You take risks.

You demonstrate a teaching and caring style of managership. You respect people, treat them courteously, and invest time and funds in their training and development. You help subordinates upgrade their jobs; and you delegate interesting and challenging work. You invariably pass on all the credit to your people when things go right and assume all the blame when things go wrong. You adapt well to change. You are able to change your leadership style when necessary to influence others.

You handle meetings effectively and are composed and comfortable when faced with diverse views. You allow dissent when it is backed by constructive intent. You deal with interpersonal conflict and confrontation objectively and skillfully and are unruffled in tense situations. You convey all the information your subordinates need to perform their duties and tasks, and you listen attentively to their ideas and concerns.

You are consistent in the way you manage. Although you are tough-minded, you are always pleasant. You don't take yourself too seriously. You have the ability to make those around you feel comfortable. In all your activities, you operate in a way that makes people—whether outside customers or persons served within the organization—want to do business with you again.

The Leadership Improvement Process

How can you improve your leadership skills? Basically, there are four alternatives: (1) trial and error, (2) formal education and training, (3) coaching and guided practice, and (4) analysis of feedback from others. I recommend that you use all four; to get you going, here's a systematic approach to self-improvement.

Step 1. Examine your goals and your status. Do you have a vision of what your company and your department should be doing? Do you have clear and realistic long-term goals and midrange objectives, and have you communicated them to your people? Do you have the human, conceptual, analytical, and action skills that your position as HR manager requires? Do you have a plan to shore up your deficiencies?

Step 2. Analyze your leadership style. What style of leadership do you now practice? Has your style changed over the last two or three years? Does your style take into account the mission and culture of your organization? The maturity, skills, and expectations of your people?

Step 3. Get feedback. What kind of feedback have you received from your people, from colleagues, and from superiors? What specifically did the feedback reveal? What specific suggestions has your boss made to improve your leadership? How can you get better and more frequent feedback from all your constituencies (superiors, peers, and subordinates)?

Step 4. Develop an improvement plan. What is your plan to improve your leadership skills? Have you identified specific improvement objectives, a time frame, and a way of accomplishing them?

Summary

Ultimately, the HR manager is responsible for the overall performance of a complex organization—a large number of people functioning in an integrated system of activities.

The effectiveness of HR managers as leaders rests on their ability to create and communicate a vision and to get people at all levels to buy into that vision. They must sense the constantly changing currents in their departments, the organization as a whole, and the external environment, recognize sensitive changes, trends, and developments, and lead their organizations in such a way that the mission is accomplished and serious problems do not arise. That calls for constant awareness of the human factors in day-to-day operations and skill in successfully adapting to a variety of conditions that appear because of those factors.

HR managers are most effective as leaders when they can address the concrete needs of the situations they face. They must be guided by the realities of that situation. There is a confluence of real, existing conditions within which they must operate. Leadership based on reality is not a predetermined set of *best* ways to influence people. Managers need to identify what reality *is* and then take the appropriate action. That requires the ability to make an accurate evaluation of the specific events that are taking place, moving from symptoms to causes, and supply the skillful actions needed to mitigate the causes.

Leadership at the highest levels of HR management is an involved and complex process that requires perceptions and skills of the highest order. The future of human resources development and utilization—that is, the future of American enterprise—hinges on how HR managers develop and use their power and influence and how they apply their leadership in their organizations.

Your personal program of improving your leadership skills should include these steps:

1. Examine your goals and status.
2. Analyze your leadership style.
3. Get feedback from subordinates, peers, and superiors.
4. Develop a plan of action.

For Further Reading, Viewing, and Listening

Achieving Personal Excellence (60-minute videocassette). Produced by Levitz/Sommer Productions, 1986. Distributed by Allesandra & Associates, P.O. Box 2767, La Jolla, CA 92038.

Adair, John. *Effective Leadership: A Self-Development Manual.* Brookfield, Vt.: Gower Publishing Company, 1983.

————. *The Skills of Leadership.* New York: Nichols Publishing Company, 1984.

Argyis, Chris. *Increasing Leadership Effectiveness.* Melbourne, Fla.: Robert E. Krieger Publishing Company, 1983.

Bass, Bernard. *Leadership and Performance Beyond Expectations.* New York: Free Press, 1985.

Bennis, Warren. *Unconscious Conspiracy: Why Leaders Can't Lead.* New York: AMACOM, 1976.

———— and Bert Nanus. *Leaders: The Strategies for Taking Charge.* New York: Harper & Row, 1985.

Blanchard, Kenneth, Patricia Zigarmi, and Drea Zigarmi. *Leadership and the One-Minute Manager: Increasing Effectiveness through Situational Leadership*. New York: William Morrow, 1985.

Bushell, Sylvia. *Paths to Leadership: Power Through Feminine Dignity*. West Sedona, Ariz.: Aldebaran Press, 1987.

Choosing to Lead (18-minute videocassette). Produced by Mystic River Productions, 1986. Distributed by American Management Association, Nine Galen St., Watertown, MA 02172.

Cleveland, Harlan. *The Knowledge Executive: Leadership in an Information Age*. New York: E. P. Dutton, 1985.

Conger, Jay A., Rabindra N. Kanungo, and Associates. *Charismatic Leadership: The Elusive Factor in Organizational Effectiveness*. San Francisco: Jossey-Bass, 1988.

Contracting for Leadership Style (49-minute videocassette). Blanchard Training & Development, 125 State Place, Escondido, CA 92025, 1988.

Determining Your Leadership Style (35-minute videocassette). Blanchard Training & Development, 125 State Place, Escondido, CA 92025, 1988.

Fielder, Fred E., Martin M. Chemers, and Sarah Jobs. *Improving Leadership Effectiveness: The Leader Match Concept*. 2nd ed. New York: John Wiley & Sons, 1984.

Hayes, James L. *Memos for Management: Leadership*. New York: AMACOM, 1983.

Hersey, Paul. *The Situational Leader*. San Diego, Calif.: University Associates, 1987.

Keegan, John. *The Mask of Command*. New York: Viking, 1987.

Kotter, John P. *The Leadership Factor*. New York: Free Press, 1988.

Kouzes, James M., and Barry Z. Posner. *The Leadership Challenge: How to Get Extraordinary Things Done in Organizations*. San Francisco: Jossey-Bass, 1987.

Lawrey, John. *You Can Lead! Essential Skills for the New or Prospective Manager*. New York: AMACOM, 1984.

Leadership Alliance (60-minute videocassette). Produced by Video Publishing House, 1988. Distributed by Excellence in Training Corporation, 8364 Hackman Rd., Des Moines, IA 50322.

The Leadership Edge (18-minute videocassette). Salenger Films, 1635 Twelfth St., Santa Monica, CA 90404-9988, 1988.

Leadership—Maximizing People Potential (60-minute videocassette). Produced by Levitz/Sommers Productions, 1986. Distributed by Alessandra & Associates, P.O. Box 2767, La Jolla, CA 92038.

Levinson, Harry, and Stuart Rosenthal. *Corporate Leadership in Action*. New York: Basic Books, 1986.

Loden, Marilyn. *Feminine Leadership, or How to Succeed in Business Without Being One of the Boys.* New York: Times Books, 1985.

Mears, Larry B. "What Good Leaders Do." *Personnel,* September 1988, pp. 48–52.

Morrison, Ann, Randall P. White, and Ellen Van Velsor. *Breaking the Glass Ceiling: Can Women Reach the Top of America's Largest Corporations?* Reading, Mass.: Addison-Wesley Publishing Company, 1987.

Plachy, Roger. *When I Lead, Why Don't They Follow?* Chicago: Bonus Books, 1986.

Portnoy, Robert A. *Leadership.* Englewood Cliffs, N.J.: Prentice-Hall, 1986.

Shein, Edgar H. *Organizational Culture and Leadership: A Dynamic View.* San Francisco: Jossey-Bass, 1985.

The Situational Leader (three 30-minute videocassettes). Produced by the Center for Leadership Studies, 1985. Distributed by University Associates. 8517 Production Ave., San Diego, CA 92121.

Styles of Leadership (28-minute videocassette). Produced by Sally V. Beaty. Southern California Consortium, 5400 Orange Ave., Suite 215, Cypress, CA 90630, 1983.

Thomas, William J. "Leadership." Chapter 17 in *Human Resources Management and Development Handbook,* edited by William R. Tracey. New York: AMACOM, 1985.

Tichy, Noel M., and Mary Anne Devanna. *The Transformational Leader.* New York: John Wiley & Sons, 1986.

Tracey, William R. *Critical Skills: The Guide to Top Performance for Human Resources Managers.* New York: AMACOM, 1988.

What Followers Expect From Leaders: How to Meet People's Expectations and Build Credibility (two audiocassettes, 120 minutes). Jossey-Bass, 350 Sansome St., San Francisco, CA 94104, 1988.

Where There's a Will: Leadership and Motivation (30-minute videocassette). Produced by Video Arts. Distributed by Films Incorporated, 5547 Ravenswood Ave., Chicago, IL 60640-1199, 1988.

Williamson, John N. *The Leader Manager.* New York: John Wiley & Sons, 1986.

Appendix:
Listings of Organizations
and Conferences

Organizations

Here is a list of associations and societies that provide a host of services to HR managers in the form of catalogs, conventions, conferences, seminars, and the like.

American Association for Adult and Continuing Education (AAACE), 1112 16th St., N.W., Suite 420, Washington, DC 20036; 202/463-6333.

American Association for Counseling and Development, 5999 Stevenson Ave., Alexandria, VA 22304; 703/823-9800.

American Hospital Association, 840 N. Lake Shore Dr., Chicago, IL 60611; 312/280-6111.

American Management Association (AMA), 135 W. 50th St., New York, NY 10020; 212/903-8234.

American Psychological Association, 1200 17th St., N.W., Washington, DC 20036; 202/955-7600.

American Society for Healthcare, Education, and Training (ASHET), 840 N. Lake Shore Drive, Chicago, IL 60611; 312/280-6113.

American Society for Training and Development (ASTD), 1630 Duke St., Alexandria, VA 22313; 703/683-8100.

Association for Educational Communications and Technology (AECT), 1126 16th St., N.W., Washington, DC 20036; 202/466-4780.

Association of Human Resource Systems Professionals (HRSP), P. O. Box 801646, Dallas, TX 75380; 214/661-3727.

Human Resource Planning Society (HRPS), P. O. Box 2553, Grand Central Station, New York, NY 10163; 212/490-6387.

International Personnel Management Association (IPMA), 1617 Duke St., Alexandria, VA 22314; 703/549-7100.

National Management Association (NMA), 2210 Arbor Blvd., Dayton, OH 45439; 513/294-0421.

National Society for Performance and Instruction (NSPI), 1126 16th St., N.W., Suite 214, Washington, DC 20036; 202/861-0777.

Northeast Human Resources Association (NEHRA), 20 William St., Suite 270, Wellesley, MA 02181; 617/235-2900.

The Organization Development Institute (O. D. Institute), 11234 Walnut Ridge Rd., Chesterland, OH 44026-1299; 216/461-4333.

Society for Human Resource Management (formerly the American Society for Personnel Administration), 606 N. Washington St., Alexandria, VA 22314; 703/548-3440.

Society for Intercultural Education, Training and Research (SIETAR International), 1505 22nd St., N.W., Washington, DC 20037; 202/296-4710.

The Society of Nonprofit Organizations, 6314 Odana Rd., Suite 1, Madison, WI 53719.

World Future Society (WFS), 4916 St. Elmo Ave., Bethesda, MD 20814; 301/656-8274.

Trade Shows, Exhibits, and Conferences

Here is a list of various types of shows of interest to marketers of HR products and services. For more information, contact the sponsoring group (addresses for these are found in the organizations section of this Appendix).

American Association for Adult and Continuing Education's annual conference, a six-day meeting that attracts approximately 2,000 teachers and professors of adult education, corporate trainers, and publishers. Topics covered in 200 sessions deal with education and training in human resources, business, industry, and the armed forces, international adult education, and continuing professional education. About 95 exhibitors display their materials.

American Management Association's annual Human Resources Conference and Exposition attracts about 1,200 human resources executives, legal and labor professionals, HR professionals concerned with health and social issues, compensation and benefits specialists, and training and development specialists from all sectors, private and public. More than 90 sessions and 150 exhibits.

American Society for Training and Development's annual Conference and Exposition, a six-day affair, attracts approximately 6,000 business, industrial, and military trainers, organization and career development specialists, consultants, line managers, academicians, and training managers and executives. In more than 250 sessions, seminar leaders and participants address the newest approaches and practices in training and human resources management, development, and utilization. More than

500 exhibitors present their latest product developments and newest services.

American Society for Training and Development's National Conference on Technical and Skills Training is a three-day convocation that draws more than 1,000 professional trainers and managers from business, industry, government, and the military. More than 120 sessions on technical training techniques, tactics, and strategies enable participants to gain new skills and learn new technical training approaches. The conference features approximately 100 booths displaying the latest in technical and skills training hardware, materials, and services.

Association of Human Resource Systems Professionals' annual conference is a three-day conference and exhibit for more than 800 HR and personnel managers, data systems professionals, and functional professionals who use HR information systems data and processes for applications ranging from compensation and benefits administration to productivity analysis and strategic planning. About 35 concurrent sessions in three tracks are offered. Approximately 50 exhibitors display their wares.

Benefits Expo—National Conference and Exposition for Employee Benefits Decisionmakers is a three-day conference and exhibition for benefits managers, HR executives, CEOs, CFOs, consultants, and other employee benefits decision makers. It offers sessions covering benefits planning, nondiscrimination rules, pension reform regulations, problem solving and cost containment, and insights on emerging trends in dependent care, employee financial counseling, flexible benefits, and managed health care. More than 80 exhibitors of employee benefits products and services. Sponsored by *Employee Benefits News*. Write c/o Conference Administrator, 1905 Powers Ferry Rd., #120, Marietta, GA 30067.

Management Training Conference and Exposition is a four-day national conference devoted exclusively to the needs of people who train executives, managers, and supervisors in *Fortune* 1,000 companies, government, and human services. Workshop topics include executive development, management training, supervisory skills, organization development, and the management of change. Exhibitors are limited to about 50 companies that provide consulting services, training materials, management books, training films and videos, management development courses, and public workshops in management development. Sponsored by Warren Business Information, Inc., c/o Conference Administrator, 792 S. Main St., Mansfield, MA 02048.

Meeting World, a three-day, 36-session seminar program, attracts meeting, conference, convention, trade show, and travel planners, and consultants representing business, industry, government, universities, and health care and religious organizations. Exhibits include more than 300 booths, showcasing hotels, convention bureaus, car rental firms, airlines, and audiovisual suppliers. Contact Meeting World, 1515 Broadway, New York, NY 10036.

National Society for Performance and Instruction's annual Conference and Expo, a six-day conference, attracts approximately 1,200 human resources managers, training directors, instructional designers, performance technologists, and organizational development consultants representing industry, business, banks, health services, governmental agencies, universities, and the armed forces. More than 50 providers of training and development products and services exhibit their materials.

Northeast Human Resources Association's Meeting and Exposition is a one-day event open to all organizations that market to the human resources field. It attracts upwards of 400 corporate HR professionals, and gives informational seminars on a variety of HR subjects.

Society for Human Resource Management National Conference and Expositions, a four-day annual conference for human resources and personnel professionals, attracts approximately 2,500 participants. More than 100 sessions are devoted to a broad range of human resources topics and issues and more than 25 companies exhibit their products and services.

Training magazine and *Personnel Journal's* annual Training Conference and Expo, a five-day event, attracts 6,000 personnel and training executives and staffs from business, industry, government, universities, and the armed forces from the United States and abroad. The conference offers 252 skill-building sessions, nine educational and networking special events, and special programs for training directors and personnel executives. More than 425 exhibitors display their products and services. Contact *Training,* Lakewood Publications, Inc., 50 S. Ninth St., Minneapolis, MN 55402.

Index

Human resources professionals are trained to manage. Now they must learn to *lead*. Human resources issues today are especially thorny because of the increasingly complex nature of the business world. The business facts of life—downsizing, mergers, diverse work forces, international competition, and decaying ethics—demand HR professionals with strength and vision.

Human resources managers who want to expand their role from administrator to leader, who want to break through the "HR ceiling" and claim a spot on the executive level, will find *Leadership Skills* a tailor-made guide to becoming a company pacesetter. Author William Tracey, a nationally known expert on human resources management, describes these people as the "redesigned" HR managers.

"These are managers who understand the whole organization and the environment in which it operates; managers who welcome change—accept it, master it, use it, and deliberately cause it; managers who are proactive and innovators; managers who confront all constraints, who take risks, and who continue to develop themselves professionally, technically, and personally."

Leadership Skills presents fifteen crucial skills that are divided into four main areas. Mastery of these skills will create a more dynamic HR manager and will earn the respect of top-level management. The four areas are:

- *The business component*—forecasting, strategic planning, budgeting, marketing
- *The people component*—resolving conflict, disciplining, rewarding, leading
- *The technical component*—innovating, improving productivity, managing change, managing costs
- *The personal component*—managing time, managing ethics, developing oneself